IN DARFUR

Assistant Editor
Lucie Taylor

Letter from the General Editor

The Library of Arabic Literature makes available Arabic editions and English translations of significant works of Arabic literature, with an emphasis on the seventh to nineteenth centuries. The Library of Arabic Literature thus includes texts from the pre-Islamic era to the cusp of the modern period, and encompasses a wide range of genres, including poetry, poetics, fiction, religion, philosophy, law, science, travel writing, history, and historiography.

Books in the series are edited and translated by internationally recognized scholars. They are published in parallel-text and English-only editions in both print and electronic formats. PDFs of Arabic editions are available for free download. The Library of Arabic Literature also publishes distinct scholarly editions with critical apparatus and a separate Arabic-only series aimed at young readers.

The Library encourages scholars to produce authoritative Arabic editions, accompanied by modern, lucid English translations, with the ultimate goal of introducing Arabic's rich literary heritage to a general audience of readers as well as to scholars and students.

The Library of Arabic Literature is supported by a grant from the New York University Abu Dhabi Institute and is published by NYU Press.

Philip F. Kennedy
General Editor, Library of Arabic Literature

About this Paperback

This paperback edition differs in a few respects from its dual-language hardcover predecessor. Because of the compact trim size the pagination has changed. Material that referred to the Arabic edition has been updated to reflect the English-only format, and other material has been corrected and updated where appropriate. For information about the Arabic edition on which this English translation is based and about how the LAL Arabic text was established, readers are referred to the hardcover.

In Darfur

An Account of the Sultanate and Its People

BY

Muḥammad ibn ʿUmar al-Tūnisī

TRANSLATED BY

Humphrey Davies

FOREWORD BY

Kwame Anthony Appiah

HISTORICAL INTRODUCTION BY

R. S. O'Fahey

VOLUME EDITOR

Devin Stewart

NEW YORK UNIVERSITY PRESS
New York

NEW YORK UNIVERSITY PRESS
New York

Library of Congress Cataloging-in-Publication Data
Names: Tūnisī, Muḥammad ibn ʻUmar, author. | Davies, Humphrey T. (Humphrey Taman), translator, editor. | O'Fahey, R. S. (Rex S.), writer of foreword. | Tūnisī, Muḥammad ibn ʻUmar. Tashḥīdh al-adhhān bi-sīrat bilād al-ʻArab wa-al-Sūdān. | Davies, Humphrey T. (Humphrey Taman), translator, editor. | Appiah, Anthony, writer of foreword.
Title: In Darfur : an account of the sultanate and its people / Muḥammad ibn ʻUmar al-Tūnisī; edited and translated by Humphrey Taman Davies ; foreword by Kwame Anthony Appiah ; with a historical foreword by R.S. O'Fahey.
Other titles: Tashḥīdh al-adhhān bi-sīrat bilād al-ʻArab wa-al-Sūdān. English
Description: New York : New York University Press, [2020] | "2020 publication has new foreword by Kwame Anthony Appiah."— Email from publisher. | Includes bibliographical references and index. | Summary: "An Arab merchant's account of his travels through the Sultanate of Darfur in the early nineteenth century."— Provided by publisher.
Identifiers: LCCN 2020012191 (print) | LCCN 2020012192 (ebook) | ISBN 9781479804443 (paperback) | ISBN 9781479804436 (ebook) | ISBN 9781479804450 (ebook)
Subjects: LCSH: Darfur (Sudan)—History—18th century. | Darfur (Sudan)—History—19th century. | Darfur (Sudan)—Description and travel.
Classification: LCC DT159.6.D27 T8613 2020 (print) | LCC DT159.6.D27 (ebook) | DDC 962.7/023—dc23
LC record available at https://lccn.loc.gov/2020012191
LC ebook record available at https://lccn.loc.gov/2020012192

Series design and composition by Nicole Hayward
Typeset in Adobe Text

Manufactured in the United States of America

10 9 8 7 6 5 4 3 2 1

Contents

Foreword

BY KWAME ANTHONY APPIAH

Like anyone born anywhere towards the end of the eighteenth century, Muḥammad ibn ʿUmar al-Tūnisī inhabits a different moral and intellectual universe from ours. He takes slavery entirely for granted. He is not fazed by eunuchs and their castration. He believes in geomancy and accepts that there are men who can turn into lions or transport themselves over fantastic distances in a moment. As for his attitudes to women, well "by and large," he tells us, "women have nothing good in them, with the exception of those whose chastity God has preserved . . ." Indeed, "they are at the root of every disaster that occurs" (§3.2.53). The women of Sudan "are more lustful and libidinous" than other women. And why? First because of the "region's excessive heat"; second, because "they mix so much with men"; third, because of "the lack of surveillance and the fact that they don't keep to their houses"; fourth, because "their husbands don't limit themselves just to them"; and, fifth, "habit" (§3.2.45). Of course, these are not unconventional opinions for a man of his place and time; that doesn't make it easier to read them.

As he travels from his birthplace in Tunis through Egypt and the Hejaz and into Sudan, the Land of the Blacks, he is constantly pursuing adventures and taking notice of the ways in which each new place is different, amusing, or fascinating, and its details worth recording. In Darfur, he tells us, for example, that they put out house fires by waving the loincloth of "an old woman who has never committed adultery" at them (§3.2.46). And it works! But what amuses al-Tūnisī is not just this image of an old lady waving her underwear: it's the fact that when he was staying there a fire broke out in the house of the sultan's grandmother . . . and they couldn't find a chaste woman anywhere in town!

One of only three such accounts before the incorporation of Darfur into Sudan, al-Tūnisī's is the only one by a Muslim Arab observer. His account is important for an understanding of the politics and dynastic history of the region (§§2.2.48–2.3.39), but more remarkable is his ethnographic attention to detail: describing, and providing drawings of, the musical instruments of the Kings of Fur (§§3.1.68–71), for example, or the plants that grow in Darfur (§§4.1–4.39).

In spite of the very different—and sometimes distasteful—moral views he expresses, al-Tūnisī is a keen observer of human nature, and it is hard not to be entertained while voyaging in his company.

Kwame Anthony Appiah
New York University

Historical Introduction

by R. S. O'Fahey

The Darfur Sultanate emerged in about 1650 and flourished until it was first invaded and conquered in 1874 by the Sudanese warlord and slave trader al-Zubayr Pasha Raḥmah (d. 1913).[1] It was restored in 1898 by ʿAlī Dīnār (titular sultan, 1891–98; r. 1898–1916). In 1916, the British invaded the sultanate, killing its last ruler, and annexed it to the then Anglo-Egyptian Sudan (Condominium).[2] Muḥammad al-Tūnisī's 1851 travelogue, *Tashḥīdh al-adhhān,* provides an invaluable glimpse into the Darfur Sultanate at a key period in its history. For readers unfamiliar with the political and social history of the Fur people, this introduction aims to provide a broader context of the society that al-Tūnisī encountered when he lived there from 1803 to 1811.

Geography and Demography

Darfur was one of a series of African Muslim states that emerged in the eastern and central Sahel and savanna belt south of the Sahara in the sixteenth and seventeenth centuries, the major ones being, from east to west, Sinnar (or the Funj kingdom) based on the Blue Nile, Darfur, Wadai, Baqirmi, and Kanem-Borno (by far the oldest state), the latter straddling the modern Chad–Nigeria border. These states had similar structures and cut across from north to south several ecological zones, including desert, Sahel, and savanna—in Darfur's case in the far south, intruding into the Congo–Nile basin. Ethnically, they tended to be the creation of a specific ethnic group, which expanded by conquest and incorporation, mainly in the sixteenth and seventeenth centuries. All were "divine kingship" states, although the ruler's status was increasingly defined by some version of Islam. They were generally administered by elaborate title-holding elites, free and slave, with complex quasi-feudal institutions. They prospered through trans-Saharan trade, selling northward slaves and other commodities, and importing elite consumer goods such as glassware and textiles. During the partition of Africa, significantly for their future fates, they were relatively late victims. Sinnar and Darfur were conquered from the north southward; Wadai and Baqirmi from the south northward by the French. Today the region constitutes one of the poorest and least developed parts of Africa, which explains the constant emigration. While the Khartoum government has sought to dilute Darfur's past and present identity by subdividing the sultanate/province, a sense of identity transcending tribal loyalties remains.

Darfur covers 490,000 square kilometers, approximately the size of Spain. The geographic heart of Darfur is the Marrah Mountains (highest point Jabal Marrah, 3,042 meters), well-watered and fertile on the western slopes, less so on the eastern. North and east of the mountains the land is open savanna that shades northward into Sahel and desert. Rainfall is usually sufficient to sustain the growing of millet, the main staple, and other crops, especially in areas of *qoz*, stabilized sand dunes. Southwest of the mountains, along the seasonal rivers (wadis) of Azum and Barei, is the most fertile region of Darfur, and thus by far the most densely populated. South of the Marrah Massif, rainfall sustains cattle and sheep nomadism. Fundamental to the human geography of Darfur are the great distances between concentrations of fertile land, water, and people; the difficulties of movement; the harshness and precariousness of the environment; and the fluctuation in rainfall.

Earlier ethnographies of Darfur have tended to overemphasize the Arab–African divide, as has much modern reporting on conflict in the region. Ethnically, the central lands are inhabited by African peoples, of whom the Fur are now by far the most numerous. Going from west to east, the major tribes are the Masalit, Tama, and Qimr, while east of the mountains are the Berti, Birged, Daju, and numerous smaller communities.[3] Generally, the peoples west of the mountains still speak their own languages; in the east Arabic is now dominant. In the Sahel zone of the north, both the Zaghāwah and small Arab tribes (ʿIrayqāt, ʿItayfāt, Banī Hilāl, and others) live by camel and sheep nomadism, while in the well-watered southern zone substantial Arab tribes (Rizayqāt, Misīriyyah, Ḥabbāniyyah, Banī Ḥilbah, Taʿāyshah, and others) practice cattle nomadism, hence their collective name, *Baqqārah* "cattle people."

Origins

Darfur has seemingly a long but largely unknown history of state formation before the emergence of the sultanate, associated with the Daju, Tunjūr, and Fur, in that chronological order. This prehistory credits the Daju as the first people to create a state in southeastern Darfur, where they still live. We have a number of references in Arab geographical writings, from al-Idrīsī writing in 1154 to Ibn Saʿīd writing just under a hundred years later (about 1240), to a people called Tajuwa living in what is approximately Darfur. After the mid-thirteenth century, the geographers simply repeat Ibn Saʿīd's report; nothing new has come in.

By the late sixteenth/early seventeenth century we have fragments of contemporary information from disparate sources—a note in an Italian geographical encyclopedia, marginalia from an Arabic manuscript, some comments from a Meccan chronicle. These can be interpreted to indicate that Wadai was newly Islamized, that there was a Tunjūr kingdom in Darfur that was clearly the ancestor of the Keira Sultanate, and that the Tunjūr may or may not have been Muslim, but had endowments in Mecca established in their name. The Tunjūr are a mystery, an ill-defined ethnicity that today survive as sections among a number of different tribes in Darfur. The role of the Tunjūr as the progenitors of the neighboring sultanate to the west, Wadai, is much more clearly remembered than their role in Darfur, where Muslim "Wise Stranger"[4] traditions appear to elide or transform the Tunjūr into Keira and Fur.[5]

How little we know of this Darfur prehistory is underscored by the numerous stone buildings and related sites, especially in and around the Marrah Mountains, that have yet to be investigated, let alone excavated.[6] The Tunjūr were seemingly superseded by the Keira dynasty of the Fur people in about 1650, but the traditions surrounding the transition are contradictory and ambiguous, and the survival of titles in the later sultanate of indeterminate linguistic origin compound the ambiguity.

From a Fur perspective, the foundation story of the Keira–Fur dynasty is associated with its first historical ruler, Sulaymān Solongdungo—Sulaymān "the Arab"—who is credited with introducing Islam as the state religion and conquering the lands previously ruled by the Tunjūr. On seals stamped on documents from later sultans, their pedigree is traced back to Sulaymān and no further. Local traditions, especially from what are now the Fur heartlands in southwestern Darfur, by far the most fertile area of Darfur, strongly suggest that the Fur language and identity spread with the expansion of the state, a change paradigmatically expressed in the ambiguous juxtaposition of "Fur" with "Fartīt," non-Fur pagans who could thus be enslaved, but who were somehow felt to be related to the Fur.

The Eighteenth Century: Conflict and Expansion

Sulaymān (r. ca. 1650–80) was succeeded by his son Mūsā, followed by a powerful ruler, Aḥmad Bukr (r. 1700–20), who seems to have laid the foundations of the administrative system and begun the incorporation of the Zaghāwah nomads of north-central Darfur into the state.

The early eighteenth century saw continuous tension among the Keira dynasts in succession disputes that arose among the sons of Aḥmad Bukr, who are said to have sworn an oath to their father that no son of a son would succeed until the Awlād Bukr were no more.

The last son of Aḥmad Bukr to become sultan was ʿAbd al-Raḥmān, who acceded as late as 1787 or 1788. These disputes were intertwined with a series of wars with the neighboring state to the west, Wadai. Wadai emerged, based on the Maba people but also in origin a Tunjūr state, somewhat later than Darfur. The two states fought a series of inconclusive wars, but with the advantage tending to go to Wadai. Two Darfur sultans were casualties of these wars: ʿUmar Lel and Abū l-Qāsim. ʿUmar Lel (r. ca. 1730–39), who was a grandson of Bukr and who became sultan in succession to his father, Muḥammad Dawra (r. ca. 1720–30), was captured in battle and died a prisoner in Wadai. His uncle and successor, Abū l-Qāsim (r. ca. 1739–52), was a son of Bukr, but sought to strengthen his position at the expense of the Fur titleholders by using slaves and by appointing a Zaghāwī as wazir. He was wounded in battle fighting a Wadaian invasion, but was put to death at the instigation of his chiefs. The wars with Wadai ended in stalemate, although occasionally tension arose between the two states, usually caused by the machinations of the tributary states along the border, Qimr, Tama, or Sila.

An important turning point came with the reign of Muḥammad Tayrāb (1752–53 to 1755–56), who moved his capital east of the Marrah Mountains and consolidated Keira rule. In the early 1780s he led his army into Kordofan, a vast area west of the White Nile under no central rule.

Tayrāb died in Kordofan, in Bara, where his army was encamped, the soldiers having refused to go any farther. As the sultan lay dying, complex negotiations between the various actors led to the emergence of ʿAbd al-Raḥmān al-Rashīd as sultan (vividly described in al-Tunisī), an otherwise unimportant son of Sultan Aḥmad Bukr. ʿAbd al- Raḥmān led the army back to Darfur to confront Isḥāq, who had been nominated (with the title caliph) as the next sultan by his father, Tayrāb. Isḥāq was backed by his mother's people, the Zaghāwah, while ʿAbd al-Raḥmān rallied the Fur. The war lasted nearly three years, with ʿAbd al-Raḥmān finally emerging victorious (1787–88 to 1803). Thereafter, succession to the sultanate was to go from father to son.

Titleholders and the Administrative System

The system through which the sultans ruled their state was complex, made the more so by the multiplicity of titles that were used. Clustered at court around the sultan were a plethora of Fur titleholders, holding titles that were seemingly largely ritual in nature and origin. More powerful in real terms were two royal women: the *iiya kuuri*, or premier wife, responsible for the preparation of food in the *fāshir*, or palace complex, a seriously labor-intensive chore; and the *iiya baasi*, or royal sister, who could play a political role. Zamzam Sendi Suttera, royal sister to Sultan Abū l-Qāsim, was executed alongside her brother. A later Zamzam, *iiya baasi* to her brother Sultan Muḥammad al-Ḥusayn (1838–73), effectively ruled the state after her brother went blind in 1856, riding around with an armed entourage and issuing court rulings under her name.[7] But when her brother died, she starved herself to death.

Some Fur titleholders were in origin very powerful clan (Fur *orre*) chiefs; the *abbo konyunga*, head of the Konyunga clan, which claimed to be Tunjūr in origin, accumulated several major administrative titles and kept their preeminence throughout the sultanate's history.

The basic administrative unit was the *shartāya*, ruled by a *shartāy* (probably from the Daju, *chorti*, meaning "drum/chief"; in Fur, *kiiso*.) *Shartāya*s, which could be large and, outside the Fur areas, were usually ethnically diverse, were divided into sub-chieftainships or *dimlijiyya*s (Fur, *dilmong*). The *shartāya*s were grouped together into larger units, of which the most stable was Dār Diima, southwestern Darfur, which was and is predominantly Fur, divided into twelve *shartāya*s, ruled by a line of chiefs, the *aba diimang*.[8] Southeastern Darfur, Dār Uumo, under the *abbo uumang*, was much smaller and never had much administrative identity. The north was Dār al-Takanāwī, ruled by a line of hereditary governors, the *takanāwī* (written thus, but pronounced *takanyāwī*,[9] which is not Fur and possibly goes back to Tunjūr times). The eastern province was Dār Daali and was geographically the largest, but had very little cohesion, being vaguely under the authority of the *abbo shaykh daali*, the senior slave eunuch of the sultanate.

Around 1800, there emerged a new title/rank, the *maqdūm*, usually a senior titleholder, free or slave, who was commissioned to carry out a specific task or campaign. In northern Darfur Ḥasan Segerre, an Arab who held the Fur title *iringa*, was appointed as *maqdūm*, which position remained in his family until well into the Condominium period. The *takanāwī*s continued to function, but as subordinates to the *maqdūm*s. *Maqdūm*s were appointed in the south, but continual wars with the Baqqārah Arabs, where the advantage lay largely with the nomads, ensured that the *maqdūm*s of the south were short-lived and never became hereditary until the Condominium period, when the *maqdūm*s came from the Konyunga Fur clan. The *maqdūm*s never took hold in Dār Diima.

Privilege and Estate [10]

The administrative system described above was overlaid by the late eighteenth century—and, increasingly, in the nineteenth century—by a quasi-feudal system that may have had its origins in the military-administrative organization that created the Keira state, but that increasingly served to provide the courtiers, holy families, and merchants with tax immunities, land, and income.

We do not know how the system evolved. The oldest documents so far photographed in Darfur are two from about 1700–10, written in a kind of phonetic Arabic, that seemingly grant tax immunity and protection (*jāh*) to members of the Awlād Jābir, a prominent holy family from the riverain Sudan.[11] Whether the granting of landed estates (*iqṭāʿ* or, more colloquially, *ḥakūrah*) grew out of tax immunities is not known. There is a similar ambiguity in Kanem/Borno about the evolution of the *maḥram* system there.[12] By the mid-eighteenth century, we have grants, confirmation of grants, and transcripts of court cases about disputed grants of landed estates, where the boundaries are described in increasing, not to say minute, detail by reference to trees, rocks, and bushes. Within the estates there was often a patchwork of sub-tenancies, where the tenants owed labor and where their status in some instances was similar to serfdom.[13]

Large estates were granted to the major titleholders, who often held several throughout the state. The *Ab shaykh daali*, the premier slave titleholder, held a series of estates along the eastern foothills of Jabal Marrah. Within these estates the *Ab shaykh*s granted smaller estates to holy families.[14] Other estates had their origin when new land was opened up to cultivation (*iḥyāʾ al-mawāt*) and was subsequently confirmed as estates. The larger estates were held by absentee holders, who usually installed a manager or factor. An important aspect of the system is that the sultans did not usually grant judicial or administrative authority to estate-holders; the *shartāy*s continued to be lynchpins of the administrative system, as they were elsewhere in the sultanate. A final comment here is that the language of the charters was culled from the Maliki lawbooks, but had specific meaning in Darfur.

How valuable these estates were to their owners is unclear. It seems that the two main areas geographically so divided were around al-Fāshir and Dār Diima, where almost all of it was divided into estates. Presumably the estates around al-Fāshir were attractive by virtue of their proximity to the sultan, while those in Dār Diima were in well-watered fertile land. One question that cannot yet be answered is whether any system of land management lay behind the granting of estates; the very meticulous demarcation of boundaries and surviving court transcripts of cases over several generations about such boundaries reenforce the suspicion that there is much about the system that we simply do not know.

When in late 1898 ʿAlī Dīnār restored the sultanate after some twenty-five years of misery and chaos, those who had claims to estates beseeched the sultan to restore their lands, which he seems to have invariably done to those who could prove their claims. With the disappearance of the sultanate after 1916, it was the smaller estates held by holy families that kept their documents, while those of the great titleholders simply evaporated. Under the British (1916–56) and during the early years of independence, such documents were treated as legally valid title deeds. In Dār Diima the British simply converted the estate managers or factors into a category of subchief (*dimlij*) under the *shartāy*s.

The estate system or, more accurately, the *ḥakūrah* came back into contention in around 2003, when conflict between Khartoum and a rebel movement broke out in Darfur. The main government proxies were the Arab nomads of northern and central Darfur (*jammāla*; the so-called *Janjawīd*), one of whose justifications for action was that they did not have secure demarcated lands or *ḥakūrah*s of their own. The term had taken on a new and highly politicized meaning.

The Nineteenth Century

When Sultan ʿAbd al-Raḥmān left Kordofan, probably in 1785, to fight the caliph Isḥāq for control of Darfur, he left behind a slave governor, Musallim, to rule the new province. Darfur and Kordofan together covered some 866,000 square kilometers, a huge area that produced animal and other products—above all, in the case of Kordofan and eastern Darfur, gum arabic. These products were the basis of a significant long-distance caravan trade from northern Darfur to Asyut on the Nile in Upper Egypt along a route across the East Libyan Desert known conventionally as the "Forty Days Road," *darb al-arbaʿīn*. The trade was ultimately organized and controlled by the sultans in cooperation with a relatively small group of rich merchants known as *khabīr*s (literally "expert, leader").[15] They were based at Kobbei, living on a string of estates along a wadi or riverbed of the same name a day's journey northeast of al-Fāshir, now established by Sultan ʿAbd al-Raḥmān as the sultanate's permanent capital. The main exports were slaves (nearly 40 percent of the total), gum arabic, alluvial gold, rhinoceros horn, ivory, and other animal products; the main imports included high-value fabrics, glassware, and specialized items like Solingen sword blades.[16]

Foreign trade was primarily of concern to the elites; less well documented, but probably more significant, was interregional trade within the sultanate, animal products for grain, and the like. The Fur of Jabal Marrah traded widely in rock salt.

Darfur rule over Kordofan was to last just under forty years (1785–1821). Muḥammad ʿAlī of Egypt (1811–49) sent an expedition south to conquer the Sudan in 1820, including Darfur. While the main force occupied Sinnar, a subsidiary force under Muḥammad Bey Khusraw set off for Kordofan and Darfur. On August 19, 1821, Musallim was killed and his army crushed by Khusraw at Bāra to the north of al-Ubayyiḍ, Kordofan's capital. Darfur had not simply lost a province; it had acquired an all-too-powerful neighbor that intermittently coveted the sultanate itself—the lucrative trade links between Egypt and Darfur were enough to explain this interest.

Sultan ʿAbd al-Raḥmān died in 1800 and his son, Muḥammad al-Faḍl, was put on the throne by the slave bureaucrat, Muḥammad Kurrā, who for the next few years effectively ran the state. About three years later the young sultan challenged Muḥammad Kurrā, rallying the leading Fur titleholders around him. Muḥammad al-Faḍl and his supporters withdrew northeast of al-Fāshir to Jadīd al-Sayl, returning to the capital with an army. Muḥammad Kurrā was killed in battle.

Two long reigns followed: Muḥammad al-Faḍl (1803–38) and his son, Muḥammad al-Ḥusayn (1838–73), whose accession was smoothly arranged by Ādam Bōsh or Ṭarbūsh, a slave confidant of Muḥammad al-Faḍl, whose grandson, Ibrāhīm Qaraḍ (1873–74), was to be peacefully installed as sultan by Ādam's son, Bakhīt.

For the core sultanate, the first seventy years or more of the nineteenth century were largely peaceful and prosperous. There were occasional clashes with Wadai, and from about the mid-1830s the sultans sent armies southward against the Baqqārah in a series of campaigns that lasted into the mid-1850s. Why the southern frontier leading into the Baḥr al-Ghazāl region should become a contested region is unclear, but there is some evidence of an influx of northern

Sudanese and Darfur traders into the region, which was rich in slaves and elephants. This influx was paralleled by the waterborne penetration of the sudd vegetation barrier on the White Nile by Salīm Qāpūdān in 1839. The opening up of the south by the Egyptian and European traders was followed and increasingly taken over by northern Sudanese traders and slavers turned warlords in the south.[17]

The destruction of the sultanate in 1874 was an early and relatively unknown illustration of the power of the gun. The campaigns against the cattle nomads, particularly the Rizayqāt, were fought by mailed cavalry and infantry levies. Some of the Darfur military leaders sought to create bodies of slave troops using imported guns, but it was too little too late. By contrast, the northern warlords in the south, above all al-Zubayr Pasha Raḥmah (1830–1913), recruited slaves using guns and developed a style of warfare against which knights in chain mail were doomed. By the 1860s al-Zubayr controlled the Baḥr al-Ghazāl and was sending trade goods northward through the sultanate despite attacks by the Baqqārah upon his caravans. Al-Zubayr complained to the sultan, nominal ruler of the nomads, but was powerless to curb them. It is clear from his surviving letters that al-Zubayr had an intimate knowledge of the internal politics of the sultanate.[18] In 1873, al-Zubayr began to move north against the sultanate, now ruled by Sultan Ibrāhīm Qaraḍ. The crucial battle was at Dara, capital of southern Darfur, on October 16, 1874, when the Darfur army was shattered by gunfire. Ibrāhīm escaped from the battlefield with his household troops, and made instinctively for Jabal Marrah. Al-Zubayr caught up with the sultan nine days later at Manawāshī, southeast of the mountains; on October 25 Ibrāhīm was defeated and killed, and was buried in the mosque of Shaykh Ṭāhir Abū Jāmūs, a famous holy man from Borno.

Resistance and Restoration, 1874–1916[19]

The battle of Manawāshī did not mark the end of the Keira dynasty or of a sense of Darfur identity. The Keira put up a resistance in the mountains that lasted until 1891 and seven years later, in 1898, the Keira in the person of Sultan ʿAlī Dīnār (d. 1916) successfully restored the sultanate. Whether this resistance can be characterized as a form of proto-nationalism or nationalism is a matter for discussion, but a line of Keira sultans relentlessly fought in and around the mountains seeking to restore their patrimony. As one contender was hunted down and killed, another took his place.[20] Al-Zubayr, after devastating much of western Darfur, went to Cairo to complain of his treatment by the Egyptian authorities in the Sudan; they had simply hijacked Darfur from him. The Egyptians attempted to set up an administration in the former sultanate, but were frustrated by the unremitting resistance of the Keira and the incompetence of the European officials they employed. Charles Gordon, briefly in Darfur when governor-general of the Sudan (1877–80), thought the only viable policy was to restore the sultanate as a tributary state, in some ways anticipating later British policy (1916–56).

By 1882 Darfur was beginning to be engulfed by the Mahdist revolt and revolution (1881–98) that was to decisively eject the Egyptians from the Sudan, definitively defining the Sudan as not Egypt, despite the latter's attempts in the 1930s to promote the "Unity of the Nile" (*ittiḥād wādī l-Nīl*). The history of the Mahdiyyah (meaning here both the period and the ideology) in Darfur is complex and the Keira and their supporters were only one of the protagonists involved in the endless wars of the period. A climax was reached in 1889 with a messianic movement led by Abū Jummayzah that posed the most serious challenge to Mahdist rule thus far; the threat was averted only by Abū Jummayzah's unexpected death. Finally, in 1891, the then titular Darfur sultan, ʿAlī Dīnār ibn Zakariyyah, a grandson of Sultan Muḥammad al-Faḍl, rode into al-Fāshir and surrendered to the Mahdist governor there. He was sent to Omdurman and spent the next seven years half prisoner, half courtier at the court of the Mahdi's successor, the caliph ʿAbdullāhi (r. 1885–99), himself a Taʿāyshī cattle nomad from the far southwest of Darfur.

ʿAlī Dīnār, although he fought in various Mahdist campaigns, never accepted its ideology, referring to the Mahdiyyah as "the Taʿāyshah revolt" (*al-thawrah al-Taʿāyshiyyah*) in his autobiography. When the British approached Omdurman in August/September 1898, ʿAlī Dīnār seems to have had a clear idea of the likely outcome of the battle to follow; on the eve of the encounter, he and a group of Darfur tribal leaders left and hotfooted it by camel back to Darfur (about 1,200 kilometers). Reaching al-Fāshir in late September, he took the surrender of the Mahdist garrison there and set about reestablishing the sultanate.[21]

Estates were restored to their rightful owners, mosques were rebuilt, a judicial administration was set up, and a palace was built on a ridge overlooking al-Fāshir (perhaps the most beautiful indigenous building in the Sudan,[22] now a well-maintained museum). His problem was the British, who simply regarded him as some kind of colonial subject, a status he never accepted. Although he was successful in reestablishing an administration in the core lands of the sultanate, he was faced with the recurring problem of the Baqqārah, who (especially the Rizayqāt) were very much protégés of the British, who supplied them with firearms. In 1913 Darfur faced a serious famine, while there was always the threat of would-be Mahdists. By 1916, judging from informants, ʿAlī Dīnār's letters and the subsequent actions of the British, the sultan had succeeded in reestablishing order and peace in his kingdom.

Ironically, the British now decided that the French in what is now Chad, despite being allies in the world war then raging, were threatening to move eastward into what the British saw as a potential power vacuum in Darfur, a vacuum here meaning territory not ruled by a European colonial power. After a brief propaganda campaign of vilification alleging that ʿAlī Dīnār was a bad ruler and had allied himself with the Turks, who were Germany's allies, the British invaded Darfur in 1916. The Darfur army of several thousand men was slaughtered in a battle fought just north of al-Fāshir, and ʿAlī Dīnār was hunted down and killed in November.

The British in Darfur, 1916–56[23]

The British had conquered the Sudan in 1896–98 in order to keep the French out; they had added Darfur to the Sudan for the same reason. And they had done so in the middle of a war whose scale and cost was a fearsome novelty. The result was that Darfur was to be ruled on the cheap by a few British army officers seconded first to the Egyptian army and second to serve in the Sudan.[24] This only changed in the late 1920s, when the first civilian officials arrived in the province. But the underlying principle of British administrative practice was clear: to run Darfur in the same way as the sultans. This meant a monopoly on taxation, on the use of the death penalty, and on the appointment and dismissal of chiefs; theories of "indirect rule" introduced in other parts of the Sudan were thus irrelevant in Darfur. A maqdumate held by the family of ʿAlī Dīnār's general Ādam Rijāl, head of the Konyunga Fur, was established in Nyala, and still exists; an emirate was set up under ʿAbd al-Ḥamīd, a son of Ibrāhīm Qaraḍ, to cover Dār Diima, though this did not last; while the attempt to set up a maqdumate in the north was effectively sabotaged by the Zaghāwah. The law administered in the native courts was sultanic law, in which punishments were largely fines. How embedded sultanic precedent was in the British administration can be seen in the *Western Darfur District Handbook*.[25]

Since there was no money, there was no development. Many young Darfur men went to work in the Gezira cotton scheme between the two Niles, or joined the army. It was only in the 1940s that a trickle of bright young Darfurians got to the elite schools in and around Khartoum; even fewer entered Gordon Memorial College (later to become the University of Khartoum). Northern Sudanese traders moved into centers like Nyala, which emerged as the center of the livestock industry in southern Darfur, while Darfur merchants, often from Fulani families, traded into Chad and what became the Central African Republic.[26] Darfur remained part of a central Sudanic world; this was to change in the 1950s and '60s, but in complicated and contradictory ways.

Independence

The Sudan became independent formally on January 1, 1956, under the rule of a small northern Sudanese, Arabic-speaking elite who looked northward to Cairo and vicariously took part in the excitements of Arab nationalism, Nasserism, Baathism, and the issue of Israel. But the first challenge to the northern elite came from the south in 1955–56, with a mutiny in the army there that led to an inchoate Southern political and resistance movement, the Anyanya. Nothing changed in the way Darfur was administered.

Change began to come in the 1960s; many of the rank and file of the northern army fighting in the south were from Darfur, while several Darfurian leaders from the title-holding families were coopted into Khartoum politics. The veterans from the army began to agitate in Darfur, while in 1966 an informal alliance between the chiefs and the Darfur students in Khartoum led to the establishment of the Darfur Development Front as a voice in Khartoum for Darfur concerns. Greater change came after the coup of May 1969 brought Jaʿfar al-Numayrī (1930–2009) to power as president. Al-Numayrī had served in the Darfur garrison, and as president initiated in 1971–72 the abolition of "Native Administration" and the introduction of modern local government. This did not work in Darfur; the chiefs were too powerful and entrenched, and there were insufficient "modern" university-trained governmental workers to replace them. After the fall of al-Numayrī in 1985, the chiefs were reinstated, but now their appointment was in the hands of whoever was in power in Khartoum.

From the mid-1980s, famine became recurrent in Darfur, compounded by other factors such as the breakdown of local government, the influx of firearms from the endless wars in Chad, rapid urbanization especially in and around Nyala, and a general breakdown in law and order. Into this mix was added an ideological ingredient by President ʿUmar al-Bashīr, who seized power in a military coup in 1989. There was now introduced a racial, "Arab" versus "African," dimension into the complex tribal politics of Darfur.[27] The injection of race by Khartoum was disastrous, leading to the emergence of the *Janjawīd* recruited from the northern camel nomads in response to the attack on El Fasher Airport by the Sudan Liberation Army (SLA) in April 2003, which marked the beginning of open warfare.

The United Nations and the African Union became involved in late 2004; peacekeepers from the AU were sent to Darfur, but their effectiveness was limited by the lack of helicopters. The general insecurity has speeded up urbanization, either directly into the towns or into internally displaced people (IDP) camps adjacent to the towns. At one time, Nyala was the second-largest city in the Sudan. The opposition movements in Darfur have inevitably splintered along increasingly tribal lines, with neither Khartoum nor the leaders in Darfur (or outside it) able or willing to negotiate a settlement acceptable to all sides. There are no signs that this situation will change any time soon.

Introduction

In Darfur is the result of a collaboration, undertaken in the rapidly modernizing Egypt of the 1830s and 1840s, between the work's author, the Tunisian–Egyptian Muḥammad ibn ʿUmar al-Tūnisī (1790–1857), and its instigator, copyist, and in some sense editor, the Frenchman Nicolas Perron (1797–1876). The backgrounds of these two men could hardly have been more different in terms of upbringing, language, and culture. They lived, however, in an era of convergence. Under Muḥammad ʿAlī (r. 1805–48), the Egyptian state was recruiting Arab and European professionals and deploying these to its newly created institutions. As Aḥmad Fāris al-Shidyāq, a contemporary who found employment there between 1827 and 1835, put it, Egypt had reached in those days "a peak of splendor, strength, magnificence, munificence, and glory. Those inducted into its service enjoyed a huge salary in the form of money, clothing, and provisions, more than was customary in any other state. Its viceroy awarded high rank and tokens of imperial favor to Muslim and Christian alike . . ."[28]

This was the dynamic that brought al-Tūnisī and Perron together, at the Madrasat al-Ṭibb al-Miṣriyyah (the Egyptian Medical School), the first modern institution of its kind in Egypt, founded in 1827 at Abū Zaʿbal, a military facility north of Cairo that already housed a military hospital. There, Perron worked initially as a teacher of chemistry, probably from 1829, and became director in 1839, while al-Tūnisī participated in the translation into Arabic of European medical texts, some by Perron. As colleagues, the two were part of a wide-ranging translation project based at the school that has been compared, for the importance of its role in the transfer of modern European scientific knowledge to the Arab world and for its impact on the Arabic language, to that housed at the ninth-century Dār al-Ḥikmah, or House of Wisdom, in Baghdad, celebrated as the instrument by which Greek science was translated into Arabic.[29] In addition, their relationship had a side that went beyond the normal limits of professional collaboration, since al-Tūnisī acted as Perron's *shaykh*, or teacher, for a period of half a dozen or so years, during which he gave him lessons in Arabic—lessons that acted as the incubator for the work presented here.

At the time, the Land(s) of the Blacks—as the belt of partially Islamized countries that stretched from the Atlantic south of the Sahara almost to the Red Sea was called by the Arabs—was little known to Arab scholarship and less so to European. Leo Africanus (ca. 1494–1554) had devoted a chapter of his *Description of Africa* (1550)[30] to them, but this was based more on accounts by other travelers than on firsthand experience. During the first half of the nineteenth century, French scholars and travelers began to fill the gap,[31] but the subject of al-Tūnisī's book, Darfur, which today constitutes the westernmost part of the Republic of the Sudan and lies at the center of that belt, remained largely unknown. It had taken shape as a state only in the seventeenth century and, with Wadai (now part of Chad), the other Eastern Sudanic state that al-Tūnisī visited, was less accessible than either the more Islamized states to the west or those closer to the Nile Valley to the east. Before al-Tūnisī's visit, only the Englishman W. G. Browne, who spent from June 1793 to March 1796 there, had left a description of the country; one whose value is diminished by the fact that Browne was not allowed to move freely.[32] Change, however, was afoot. In 1821, the armies of Muḥammad ʿAlī would conquer Kordofan and the Funj sultanate to its east, initiating the process that would lead ultimately to the creation, for the first time, of a country called the Sudan; in 1843, an Egyptian-sponsored army under the command of Muḥammad

Abū l-Madyan, half brother of Sultan Muḥammad Faḍl, attempted to take the country but failed. The sultanate continued to maintain its independence until 1874, when it was finally incorporated into Egyptian Sudan.

Muḥammad ibn ʿUmar al-Tūnisī (1204–74/1790–1857)[33] was born into a family from the city of Tunis that claimed descent from the Prophet Muḥammad and whose male members therefore bore the title *sayyid* ("master") or *sharif* ("of noble pedigree"); al-Tūnisī never fails to use one or other of these titles when referring to his relatives. Descent alone, however, was not the sole criterion by which they judged their lives: scholarship, and recognition for it, were also central. Al-Tūnisī's great-grandfather on his father's mother's side (named Sulaymān, as was his paternal grandfather) bore the sobriquet "al-Azharī," meaning that he had traveled to Cairo to study at the mosque-university of al-Azhar, and wrote several books (topics unspecified), while his son, al-Tūnisī's maternal great-uncle Aḥmad, was "a learned scholar, a trustworthy source, of unimpeachable authority, for the transmission of both hadiths and the law" who taught law in Tunis (§2.1.27). Al-Tūnisī's father, ʿUmar, studied with his uncle Aḥmad (§2.1.27) and later, in Darfur, gave lessons to the local men of religion and wrote scholarly commentaries for the sultan, as his son is at pains to point out (§2.3.23).

A common pattern is discernible in the lives of al-Tūnisī's grandfather and father, lives recounted in some detail in the first two chapters of the work—travel between Tunis, Cairo, the Hejaz, and Sudan; extended and ultimately permanent absences of fathers who left North Africa to settle in "the Land of the Blacks," leaving young families behind them in Tunis or Cairo; sons seeking those same absent fathers; meetings of remarkable coincidence between sons and fathers in the middle of vast, empty spaces—and al-Tūnisī himself would in some ways repeat the pattern. The travel was fueled by trade in commodities such as "mantles and tarbushes" (§2.1.1) and also, when "the Land of the Blacks" was involved, in slaves (§§2.1.28,

2.1.29, etc.). Settlement in the Land of the Blacks was facilitated by their status as learned *sayyids*, for the rulers of the Sudanic nations, from the Funj sultanate in the east to Borno in the west, had a long tradition of encouraging the immigration of such persons, who were seen as lending religious legitimacy to their rule in a region that had been undergoing a slow process of Islamicization for hundreds of years. The coincidental meetings were occasioned by the interconnectedness, however attenuated, of the caravan system that served the trade. Absent from their lives is any but a muted sense of Europe and the non-Muslim world to the north ("French dollars"—a trading currency, and not necessarily French[34]—are one of its rare representatives). For such merchants and *sayyids*, the non-Muslim world consisted primarily of the pagan groups living to the south, who were the source of the slaves.

Against this background, in 1803, fourteen-year-old Muḥammad al-Tūnisī set out from Cairo, to which city the family had moved, in search of his father, ʿUmar, who had left some seven years earlier for Sennar, and subsequently moved, as the boy had by this time discovered, to Darfur. Muḥammad's account of his journey, undertaken under the wing of a fortuitously met friend of his father's, and of his subsequent stay in Darfur (introduced by an overview of political events preceding his arrival), form the bulk of the work. Al-Tūnisī lived in Darfur for almost eight years, most of them without the father he had come so far to find, for the latter, a scant two months after the two were reunited,[35] sought and received the government's permission to return to Tunis, leaving Muḥammad to manage his estates. Eventually, the father would return from Tunis to the Lands of the Blacks, not to Darfur but to the neighboring Sultanate of Wadai, where he would again be welcomed by the sultan and awarded estates as tax farms. After staying on alone in Darfur, Muḥammad also moved to Wadai[36] to join his father, only to find that he had by that time returned yet again to Tunis.

On his departure from Wadai in 1813, the author, still in his twenties, went first to Tunis, then moved to Egypt (exactly when is unclear). There, after a period of unspecified length that he describes as being devoted to study and ending in insolvency (§§1.2–4),[37] he entered government service in Muḥammad ʿAlī's vigorously developing state (§1.5), by which he continued to be employed for the rest of his working life. His first job was as a chaplain (*wāʿiẓ*) in the Egyptian army that fought in Greece's Morea on behalf of the Ottomans from 1823 to 1828 (§1.6).

On his return from Greece, al-Tūnisī joined the staff of the Egyptian Medical School[38] "as a language editor[39] of medical books, specializing in pharmaceutical works" (§1.6). He also edited several canonical texts of Arabic literature[40] for the recently established government press at Būlāq, near Cairo. Toward the end of his life, he gave lessons on Fridays at the important mosque of al-Sayyidah Zaynab.[41]

Nicolas Perron (1797–1876)—at first al-Tūnisī's colleague, later his superior, and for much of the period also his student—trained in Paris initially in languages, but turned later to medicine, becoming a doctor in 1825. His interest in languages continued, however, and he took courses during the same period at the École des langues orientales, where he studied with prominent French orientalists Sylvestre de Sacy and Jean Jacques (the father) and Armand-Pierre (the son) Caussin de Perceval. He became involved with liberal intellectual circles, and in particular those of the Saint-Simonians, followers of utopian socialist Henri de Saint-Simon (1760–1825) who preached the development of a "new harmony" between religion and the scientific spirit, one in which he believed the Islamic world would play a major role. Possibly under the influence of these ideas, though also perhaps in flight from France following the banning of the radical Association Libre to which he had links,[42] Perron went, probably in 1829,[43] to Egypt, a country of special significance for the Saint-Simonians because of the promotion by the movement's founder of a project to join the Mediterranean and Red seas by a canal.[44] There he took up a position at Abū Zaʿbal as a teacher of chemistry and physics. It was while Perron was working in this capacity that he met al-Tūnisī, who would describe him as "the most brilliant man of his day in keenness of mind and understanding, the brightest of his age in industry and knowledge" (§1.6). In 1839, Perron became director of the Medical School,[45] a position he held until his return to France in 1846, having received the honorific title of Qā'immaqām from Muḥammad 'Alī in 1845.[46]

During their time together at the Medical School, al-Tūnisī and Perron were involved, both jointly and separately, in the production of a succession of pioneering translations in the field of contemporary medicine and related sciences.[47] These works were the foundation on which the training of Egypt's new cadre of doctors, pharmacologists, chemists, and other scientists was to be erected. Their importance was not confined to the development of the sciences. Underscoring the importance of these works to the development of a modern formal Arabic language capable of transmitting the influx of new ideas that came with the opening of Egypt to European influence, Khaled Fahmy characterizes the output of the Medical School's translation program as "an impressively lucid Arabic medical prose which was as elegant as it was precise, and which was a far cry from the clumsy and awkward Arabic that was used by the nascent government bureaucracy."[48] Fahmy notes further that this style is "clear, grammatically correct, and precise,"[49] and that the translations avoid transliteration and coin clearly comprehensible new terms.[50] Notable among the works translated with al-Tūnisī's participation were Antoine Fabre's eight-volume dictionary of medicine, *Dictionnaire des dictionnaires de médicine français et étrangers* (*al-Shudhūr al-dhahabiyyah fī l-muṣṭalaḥāt al-ṭibbiyyah*), described by Fahmy as al-Tūnisī's magnum opus,[51] and *Kunūz al-ṣiḥḥah wa-yawāqīt al-minḥah* (*The Treasures of Health and Rubies of Benefaction*), based on the lecture notes of Antoine Barthélemy Clot, better known as Clot Bey, founder and director of the Medical School;[52] the latter, first published in 1844 and intended for both students and the general public, went into seven printings. Al-Shayyāl lists six more scientific works in which al-Tūnisī is credited as a language editor, and O'Fahey adds a further title.[53] A work that must have brought the two together in particularly close collaboration was Perron's *al-Jawāhir al-saniyyah fī l-aʿmāl al-kīmāwiyyah* (*The Sublime Gems Concerning Chemical Operations*), based on his chemistry lecture notes.[54]

At some point during this period of close professional contact, Perron began reading Arabic literary texts with al-Tūnisī, starting with Ibn al-Muqaffaʿ's book of animal fables, *Kalīlah wa-Dimnah* (*Kalīlah and Dimnah*).[55] In this more intimate setting, it would seem that al-Tūnisī was moved to tell Perron of some of the "splendid and amazing things" he had experienced in "the Land of the Blacks," and in response Perron urged him to "adorn the face of [his] copybook with an exposition of the marvels" he had seen and to tell him of the "strange things" that had befallen him (§1.6). These texts then became the subject matter of their lessons, and in 1845 Perron published his French translation of the part of these writings relating to Darfur under the title *Voyage au Darfour* (*Journey to Darfur*).[56] This was followed in 1850 by the publication of a lithographic edition of the Arabic text under the title *Kitāb Tashḥīdh al-adhhān bi-sīrat bilād al-ʿArab wa-l-Sūdān* (*The Book of the Honing of Minds through Consideration of the Condition of the Land of the Arabs and the Blacks*), in Perron's own hand.[57]

Following his return to France in 1846, Perron became involved in the scholarly exploration of Algeria (under French rule since 1830) through his translation of Khalīl ibn Isḥāq al-Jundī's *Epitome* (*al-Mukhtaṣar*), an advanced text on Mālikī law widely used in North and Sudanic Africa to which al-Tūnisī refers in this book (§§2.3.22–23). Perron's translation was part of a wider, unrealized, project to create a new Franco-Muslim legal code; in pursuit of this idea, he also translated the Egyptian ʿAbd al-Wahhāb al-Shaʿrānī's sixteenth-century *The Scales of the Law* (*Mīzān al-sharīʿah*), a Shāfiʿī treatise.

In 1851, Perron published a second work by al-Tūnisī, likewise the outcome of their Arabic lessons, namely, *Voyage au Ouaday*

(*Journey to Wadai*),[58] in which the author describes his experiences during the two years he spent in Wadai after he left Darfur. The Arabic text of this work was never published and has never been found.[59]

Returning to Egypt in 1853, Perron took a position in the public health system in Alexandria.[60] Later, after a period in Algiers, where he directed an experimental Arabic-French school in which both languages were taught by "the direct method,"[61] he returned to France, where he retired in 1872 and died in 1876.[62]

The Darfur that Muḥammad ibn ʿUmar al-Tūnisī knew was an independent sultanate that had been ruled by one dynasty, from the Keira clan of the Fur (the largest ethnic group there), since at least the middle of the seventeenth century. It is not to be equated in any sense with the "Sudan" of the present day, of which no equivalent existed at the time. Rather, it was one of a swathe of "Sudanic" polities that stretched from the Funj sultanate, whose eastern borders reached almost to the Red Sea, followed to the west by Kordofan, then Darfur, then Wadai (now part of present-day Chad), then Borno (now parts of present-day Chad, Niger, Cameroon, and Nigeria), then smaller states stretching almost to the Atlantic (see Map 1). Darfur's links to the world north of this belt were the trading caravans; these, like the one with which the author traveled, took a route from northern Darfur across the desert to Asyut on the Nile in Egypt, following what is sometimes referred to as "the Forty Days Road"; from Asyut boats were taken to Cairo, the entire distance exceeding two thousand miles. Other caravans went east to the Hejaz (2,700 miles) and served pilgrims as well as trade. Contact with the lands to the south of Darfur was through trade and, above all, slave raiding.

Darfur was, as the title of the work signals, a land perceived as being inhabited by two groups, "Arabs" (*al-ʿArab*) and "Blacks" (*al-Sūdān*). However, what these terms meant exactly is difficult to say. O'Fahey points out that "Ethnicity is a very moveable and slippery concept, and nowhere more so than in Darfur,"[63] and goes on to say that "speaking Arabic does not necessarily mean that one is Arab."[64] The primary distinction made among their subjects by the sultans of Darfur was between those who *spoke* Arabic (*al-ʿArab*) and those who did not (*al-ʿAjam*).

The process by which *In Darfur* was created has been the subject of speculation, fueled by the facts that its French translation appeared before the Arabic original, that no original has been found,[65] and that the first, lithographed, edition of the Arabic text is in Perron's hand. Adding to these oddities is the fact that the other product of al-Tūnisī's collaboration with Perron, the *Voyage au Ouaday*, exists only in French translation. As R. S. O'Fahey notes (speaking of the work on Darfur), "The relationship between the Arabic 'original' and the French 'translation' is complicated."[66] Lurking somewhere among these anomalies may be a suspicion on the part of some that the Arabic text originated with Perron rather than al-Tūnisī, a suspicion that we, like earlier editors, reject: it is inconceivable that Perron could have written a work that stands firmly in the Arabic belles lettres tradition, with its particular strategies and conventions, just as it is impossible that he could have composed Arabic riddle poems or praise poems such as those in which the author shows off his erudition, or had the detailed knowledge of Darfur (which he never visited) displayed in the text, to mention only a few of the objections to this notion.

How the relationship between al-Tūnisī and Perron may have found expression in the language, style, and narrative content of the work is discussed in the note on the text below. However, the question of Perron's intellectual influence, if any, on the work also poses itself. That the enterprise itself, namely, the systematic "description of Darfur and its people [and] of their customs" (Book Proper, chapter one), was Perron's idea is a given, stated by al-Tūnisī (§1.6); al-Tūnisī, however, appropriates and validates that idea when he confides to the reader that he believed that "this would be in my own best interest, given the words of the author of *The Poem on*

Words Ending in –ā and ā' . . . that . . . 'Man is but the words that live on after him'" (§1.6). Similarly, Perron states that "I left the form and ordering of his tales . . . as I did his judgments, entirely to"[67] al-Tūnisī. The illustrations, however, which are not intended (whatever their ultimate effect) to be decorative but simply to augment and clarify the text, and which do not occur in the French translation, are surely unique at this period of Arabic literature.[68] Thus, even if we make the large assumption that the somewhat self-consciously encyclopedic presentation of the material owes something to the author's long "embedding" in a European institution and his intense engagement with European scientific literature, we should take note too of the fact that the work as a whole is imbued with the ethos of classical Arabic literature. This is evident in the frequent pious references to the deity, the recounting of tales drawn from life and history to make a moral point, the pleasure taken in conventional verse forms such as praise poetry and puzzle poetry, and the recourse to formal strategies such as the use of poetry to encapsulate a message advanced immediately before in prose and the deployment of technical devices such as rhymed prose.

Al-Tūnisī's description of Darfur, which covers the contemporary and immediately preceding political life of the sultanate as well as its customs, garments, commerce, flora, fauna, diseases, and magical practices, is one of only three to have been made before the country's definitive incorporation into Sudan on the death of its last sultan, 'Ali Dīnār, in 1916.[69] The English traveler W. G. Browne was there from 1793 to 1796 and devotes about 130 pages of his *Travels in Africa, Egypt and Syria from the Year 1792 to 1798* to Darfur.[70] Though he covers some of the same ground as al-Tūnisī, Browne's limited knowledge of Arabic, the suspicion with which he was viewed by the authorities there, and his own dislike of the country and its people limit the reliability and comprehensiveness of his account; compare, for instance, his disdainful comment that "There are several species of trees, but none that produces fruit worth gathering"[71] with al-Tūnisī's lengthy and detailed list of Darfurian trees and fruits and their uses. Some sixty years later, between March and July 1874, on the eve of the invasion of the sultanate by Egyptian forces, a German physician, Gustave Nachtigal, stayed in the capital El-Fasher, and in volume IV of his *Sahara and Sudan* recorded his impressions with greater insight and depth of coverage than had Browne.[72]

The limited nature of these accounts, both by Christian European travelers who stayed for quite short periods, throws into relief the importance of the account of the Muslim and Arab "insider"[73] al-Tūnisī. He was not, of course, a complete insider: he was not a Darfurian, and his understanding of some aspects of the country, as well as the accuracy of his memory after more than thirty years, may be questioned. Nevertheless, as a historian, O'Fahey evaluates al-Tūnisī's works on Darfur and Wadai as "a major source on the history and peoples of the two sultanates,"[74] while another historian, Richard Hill, commends his work as "reliable but unmethodical."[75]

It is not chiefly for these reasons, however, that the work is presented here. It is rather in the belief that its larger-than-life personalities; its accounts of political events and dynastic struggles (as starkly revelatory of the forces behind the rise and fall of states and their rulers as those around which Shakespeare, for example, built his plays); its glimpses of the bewildering practices and hierarchies of an isolated, autonomous, now-vanished world; its narrative of a young person embarking on an adventure with an insatiable appetite just "to see" (§3.1.17); and its bringing back into focus of a lost world through the encyclopedic lens of the early Arab enlightenment, constitute an absorbing and rewarding work of literature.

It remains to acknowledge those who contributed time and expertise to answering my queries or providing references or other valuable support. These include Clifford Cheney, Philippe Chevrant and the staff of the library of the Institut Français d'Archéologie Orientale, Madiha Doss, Khaled Fahmy, Noah Gardiner, Daniel Jacobs, Musa Jargis, Adam Karama, Bariwarig Tooduo Kondo, Raphael

Cormack, Mark Muehlhaeusler, Muhammad Shahpur, Adam Talib, Geert Jan Van Gelder, Christine Waag, Terence Walz, and Nicholas Warner. Above all, my thanks go to Rex Sean O'Fahey, who guided me in the direction of much important material and was unstinting in providing answers to my questions from his unrivaled store of knowledge of Darfur and its history. My heartfelt thanks go also to the administrative and technical team at the Library of Arabic Literature, Chip Rossetti, Gemma Juan-Simó, Amanda Yee, and Stuart Brown, who worked tirelessly, as always, to make the process go smoothly and to whose high standards I have, as always, attempted to rise. Finally, I express my deep appreciation for the efforts of Devin Stewart, my project editor, whose interventions were always for the good.

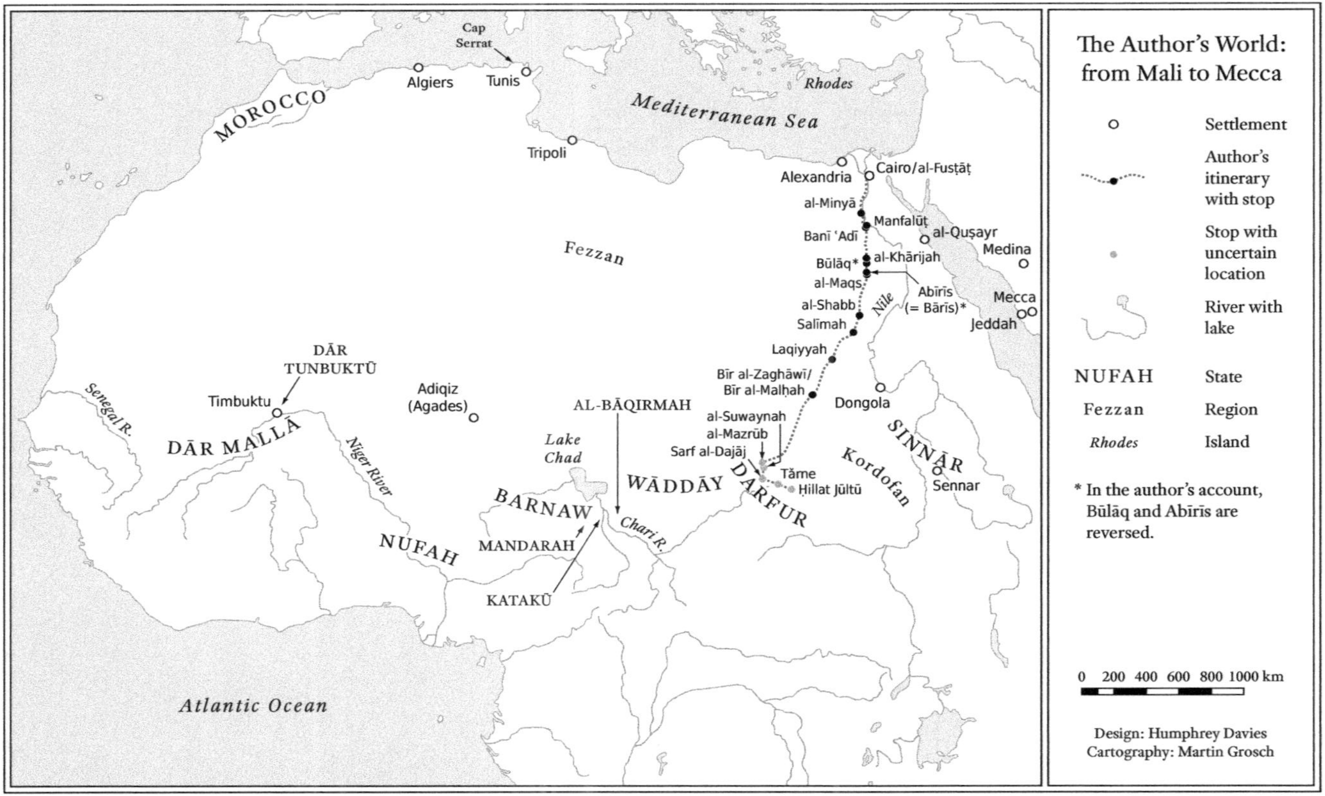
The Author's World: from Mali to Mecca
Settlement
Author's itinerary with stop
Stop with uncertain location
River with lake
NUFAH
State
Fezzan
Region
Rhodes
Island
* In the author's account, Būlāq and Abīrīs are reversed.
0 200 400 600 800 1000 km
Design: Humphrey Davies
Cartography: Martin Grosch
Cap Serrat
Algiers
Tunis
MOROCCO
Mediterranean Sea
Rhodes
Tripoli
Alexandria
Cairo/al-Fusṭāṭ
al-Minyā
Manfalūṭ
Banī ʻAdī
al-Quṣayr
Medina
Fezzan
Būlāq*
al-Khārijah
al-Maqs
Abīrīs (= Bārīs)*
Mecca
Jeddah
al-Shabb
Nile
Salīmah
Laqiyyah
Bīr al-Zaghāwī/
Bīr al-Malḥah
Dongola
DĀR TUNBUKTŪ
Timbuktu
Adiqiz (Agades)
AL-BĀQIRMAH
Senegal R.
DĀR MALLĀ
Niger River
Lake Chad
al-Suwaynah
al-Mazrūb
Sarf al-Dajāj
SINNĀR
Kordofan
Tāme
Ḥillat Jūltū
Sennar
WĀDDĀY
DARFUR
BARNAW
Chari R.
NUFAH
MANDARAH
KATAKŪ
Atlantic Ocean

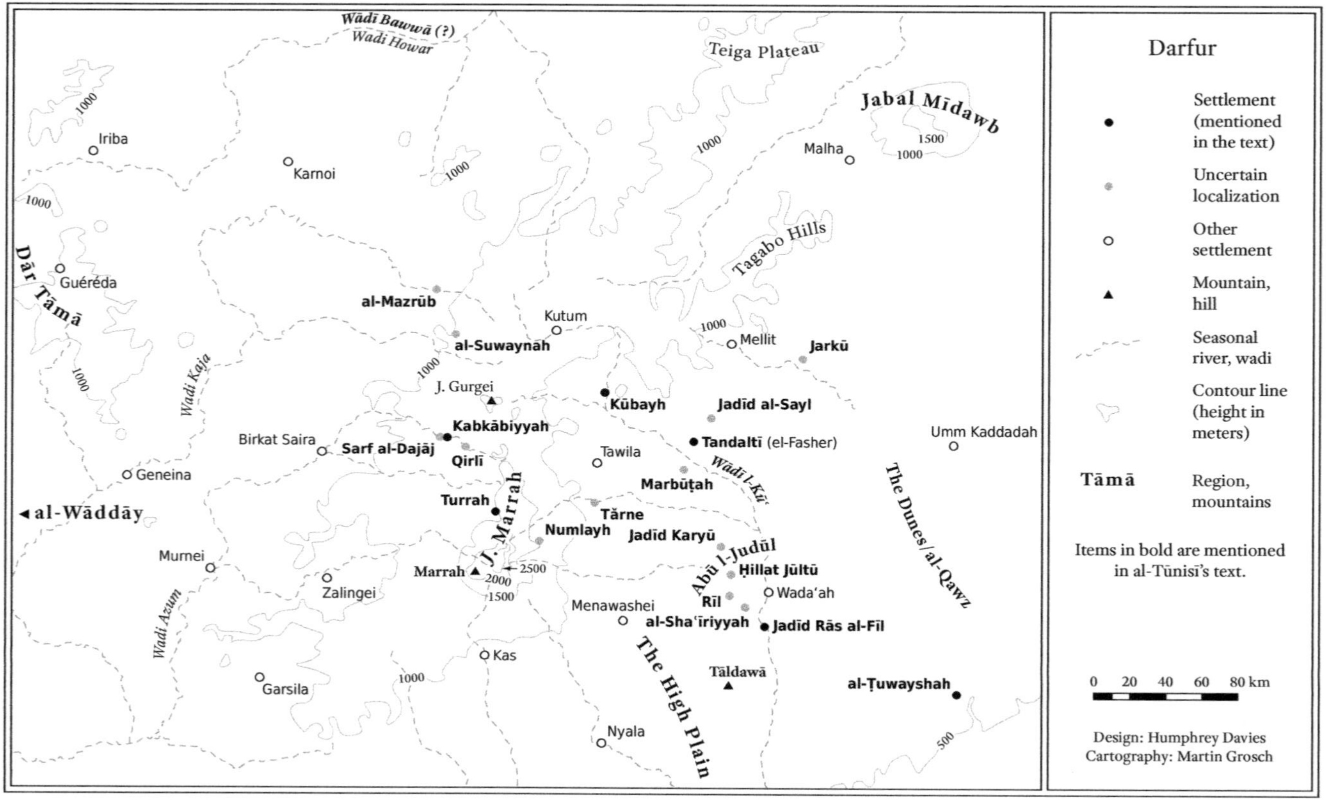
Darfur
Settlement (mentioned in the text)
Uncertain localization
Other settlement
Mountain, hill
Seasonal river, wadi
Contour line (height in meters)
Tāmā
Region, mountains
Items in bold are mentioned in al-Tūnisī's text.
0 20 40 60 80 km
Design: Humphrey Davies
Cartography: Martin Grosch
Wādī Bawwā (?)
Wadi Howar
Teiga Plateau
Jabal Mīdawb
Malha
Iriba
Karnoi
Tagabo Hills
Dār Tāmā
Guéréda
al-Mazrūb
Kutum
al-Suwaynah
Mellit
Jarkū
J. Gurgei
Kūbayh
Jadīd al-Sayl
Kabkābiyyah
Tandaltī (el-Fasher)
Umm Kaddadah
Birkat Saira
Sarf al-Dajāj
Qirlī
Tawila
Wādī l-Kū'
Geneina
Marbūṭah
Wadi Kaja
Turrah
J. Marrah
Tărne
The Dunes/al-Qawz
al-Wādday
Numlayh
Jadīd Karyū
Abū l-Judūl
Ḥillat Jūltū
Murnei
Marrah
Wada'ah
Zalingei
Rīl
Menawashei
al-Sha'īriyyah
Jadīd Rās al-Fīl
Wadi Azum
Kas
The High Plain
Tāldawā
al-Ṭuwayshah
Garsila
Nyala
1000
1500
2000
2500
500

Note on the Text

There are two earlier translations of this work into English. The first, by Bayle St. John, entitled *Travels of an Arab Merchant in Sudan: The Black Kingdoms of Central Africa (Darfur, Wadai)*, appeared in 1854 and is a combined and abridged translation of Nicolas Perron's French translations of both of al-Tūnisī's works, that on Darfur and that on Wadai.[76] The second is an unpublished MA thesis undertaken at Abdullahi Bayero University in 1976 by the late H. S. Umar, entitled "Al-Tūnisī, Travels in Darfur: Translation, Collation and Annotation of *Tashḥīdh al-adhhān bi-sīrat bilād al-ʿArab wa-l-Sūdān*." I have not used St. John's version since it is an abridgment and at two removes from the original. I have reviewed Umar's notes with care and quoted from them on occasion, and have also appealed to his translation for help with occasional problematic passages.[77] I also kept Perron's French translation beside me, making use of his notes and, sparingly, his text; the latter, because of its divergences from the Arabic (see above), has to be treated with care.[78]

Al-Tūnisī's prose style is mostly rather plain, with occasional rhetorical flourishes, and does not, in itself, pose major problems for a translator. Though the text contains a number of colloquialisms and other nonstandard forms, these were not intended, in most cases, to create a special effect, and no attempt has been made, generally speaking, to distinguish them in register from the rest of the text. Verse and the touches of endearingly flat rhymed prose (*sajʿ*) with which the author embellishes certain passages pose a greater challenge. I have rhymed where it came naturally, and where it did not, used assonance, rhythm, and other forms of "musicality" to distinguish these types of language. Some kinds of verse, such as chronograms (see §§2.1.23–25) and puzzle poems (see §§2.2.2–9), usually require, if their secrets are to be decoded, too close a reading to allow for any but a prose-like translation.

Arabic, or Arabized, forms are transcribed in the text according to the Library of Arabic Literature series norms, and no attempt has been made either to render colloquial Sudanese phonetic values (such as *g* for *q*) or, in the case of place and tribal names, to Anglicize (thus Masālīṭ rather than Mesalit and Wāddāy rather than Wadai); however, Anglicized or other recognized forms of names are listed in the glossary in parentheses following the form in which they occur in the text. Likewise, names occurring in both the Arab and non-Arab traditions have been kept in their Arabic forms—Ḥawwā' rather than Eve, Ibrāhīm rather than Abraham—in recognition of the different resonances these may carry in the Arab cultural and religious imagination; their conventional English equivalents are given in the endnotes.

Fur language items have, on the contrary, been transliterated according to a system developed by Fur linguists that avoids nonstandard characters and does not show tone, but does give the language its due as a separate presence within the text.[79] It was decided not to use al-Tūnisī's own transliterations of Fur, though he went to considerable trouble in this regard, even introducing a special character (ی for *ng*), because his transliteration lacks many basic features and is inconsistent. How far the modern versions provided diverge from the language underlying al-Tūnisī's transliterations is for scholars of Fur to decide.

The translation of certain words whose usage is specific to Darfur or even this particular text calls for comment, as follows:

- *Dārfūr* versus *Dār al-Fūr*: both forms occur in the text. *Dārfūr* is a compound term that denotes the state known by that name, with all its lands and ethnic groups; *Dār al-Fūr* should, by analogy with other names of the same structure, such as

Dār Rungā and *Dār Birgid*, denote "the Land of the Fur," i.e., the territories inhabited by the Fur ethnic group. The text is not consistent, however, in maintaining this distinction, and sometimes seems to use *Dār al-Fūr* to denote the country per se (e.g., *sulṭān Dār al-Fūr* ["The sultan of *Dār al-Fūr*"], §3.2.37) or *manṣib al-bāb ghayr mukhṭaṣṣ bi-Dār al-Fūr bal fī Tūnis* ("the Door [i.e., the post of High Chamberlain] is not peculiar to *Dār al-Fūr*; it exists also in Tunis," §3.2.38) or an entity including ethnic groups other than the Fur (e.g., *wa-ajmal al-nisā' fī Dār al-Fūr . . . nisā' al-ʿArab* ["but the most beautiful women in *Dār al-Fūr* . . . are those of the Arabs"], §3.1.13). *Dārfūr* has therefore been translated consistently as Darfur, while *Dār al-Fūr* has been translated according to my reading of the context either as Darfur or as "the Lands of the Fur" (but, to reduce confusion, not as Dār al-Fūr).

- *al-fāshir*: translated as "the sultan's seat" or "the sultan's capital" rather than El-Fasher (name, from the later part of the nineteenth century, of the capital of Darfur and, more recently, of North Darfur); see note 227.
- *māl* (plural *amwāl*): translated variously as "wealth, property, assets, cattle," rather than "money," as coinage had only restricted circulation in Darfur (see §§3.3.41–55) and is never what is intended here by this word.
- *malik*: treated variously, reflecting Darfurian usage:
  (1) translated as "king" when used in its conventional sense as a designation of a monarch (e.g., "the King of Kordofan" [*Malik Kurdufāl*], §2.2.49), including the sultan of Darfur (e.g., "Sultan ʿAbd al-Raḥmān al-Rashīd, king of Darfur" [*al-Sulṭān ʿAbd al-Raḥmān al-Rashīd, malik Dārfūr*], §2.2.15).
  (2) retained in its original form when used as a title of tribal chiefs (e.g., Malik Muḥammad Sanjaq, a Zaghāwah leader, §2.2.19) or leaders with links to the sultanic family (e.g., Malik Ibrāhīm wad Ramād, §2.3.38); however, such persons are called "kings" or "petty kings" when referred to

collectively in order not to lose the connotations of royalty, some of whose Sudanic accoutrements, such as the right to use copper kettledrums among their insignia, still pertained to them.

(3) translated as "master of" when used as a title for an official placed in charge of a significant place or specialized group (e.g., "master of the men's door" [*malik bāb al-rijāl*], §3.1.59), "master of the royal slaves" [*malik al-ʿabīdiyyah*], §3.1.60).

- *al-Sūdān*: never translated as "Sudan," since it refers to people, not a country (and no country of that name existed at that time). Thus *bilād/arāḍī al-Sūdān* are "the Land(s)/Territories of the Blacks" and in the author's usage may refer to either Darfur specifically or the countries of the "Sudanic belt" from western Funj to the Atlantic. When preceded by *ahl* ("the people of"), *al-Sūdān* is translated as "the people of the Land of the Blacks" or simply "the Blacks." As Browne noted, "Soudan in Arabic corresponds to our Nigritia, merely general words for the *country of the blacks*."[80]

Notes to the Frontmatter

Historical Introduction

1 See further my *The Darfur Sultanate* (with an extensive bibliography), *Darfur and the British*, and the earlier *Land in Dar Fur*.

2 After 1916, under the British, Darfur kept approximately the boundaries of the sultanate, but since the 1990s Khartoum has subdivided it into five provinces, namely Central, East, North, South, and West.

3 Ethnographically, Darfur is not well served, but the various studies of the Berti by Ladislav Holy, starting with his *Neighbors and Kinsmen: A Study of the Berti of Darfur*, are a very good introduction.

4 See Holt, *Studies in the History of the Near East*, 76–78.

5 These fragments of information are tentatively analyzed in my *Darfur Sultanate*, 24–39.

6 See further, McGregor, *Darfur (Sudan) in the Age of Stone Architecture c. AD 1000–1750*.

7 Three court transcripts (*sijill*) that I photographed were issued "under the authority of the *iiya baasi* Zamzam Umm al-Nāṣir . . ." *bi-niyaba iiya baasi Umm al-Nasir . . .*

8 Dar Diima was the only region of Darfur for which the British produced a detailed district handbook; this is given in my *Darfur and the British*. A Nyala district handbook was produced, but seemingly never circulated.

9 Similar-sounding titles are used among several peoples in Darfur and Wadai, usually with ritual or religious functions.

10 This section is largely based on the three hundred or so documents I photographed in Darfur between 1970 and 1976. All the material is available in my papers deposited in the University of Bergen Library. My *Land in Dar Fur* gives translations of some fifty documents illustrating the estate system.

11 The texts and putative translations are given in my "Two Early Dar Fur Charters."

12 See my "Endowment, Privilege and Estate on the Central and Eastern Sudan."

13 See my "A Prince and His Neighbours."

14 See my "The Archives of Shoba."

15 In contradistinction to local or petty merchants called *jallaba*.

16 See Walz, *Trade between Egypt and Bilad as-Sudan.*

17 See the early study by Richard Gray, *A History of the Southern Sudan, 1839–1889.*

18 See my "The Conquest of Darfur, 1873–82." This gives translations of the relevant al-Zubayr letters.

19 Many informants used the expression *Umm Kwakiyyah*, meaning "the time of gunfire," to characterize this period.

20 A more detailed account is given in my *Darfur Sultanate*, 275–80.

21 About two hundred letters of ʿAlī Dīnār survive; these include some hundred to be found in the Khartoum Archives and the Sudan Archive at the University of Durham. The other hundred I photographed in Darfur. Copies of all of them are among my papers at the University of Bergen.

22 See the contemporary description quoted in Theobald, *ʿAli Dinar: Last Sultan of Darfur, 1898–1916*, 194.

23 What follows is based on my *Darfur and the British*, a book that has a sad history behind it. In 1970 I spent the summer in al-Fashir going through the five hundred or more British administrative files in the Mudīriyyah or provincial headquarters (then housed in ʿAlī Dīnār's palace). I was given complete access to the files and copied about four hundred pages of notes—there was of course no copy machine nearby. I copied what I thought was relevant to my research. A few years later,

the files were removed and stored in huts, where they were destroyed by the rains. Given the ethnographic interests of the handful of British officials, the destruction of the tribal files (the Zaghāwah file, for example, was in three thick volumes with many Arabic notes) was a catastrophic loss. My original notes are among my papers in Bergen.

24 Few records survive from the early years of the British occupation of Darfur either in the National Records Office in Khartoum, the Public Records Office in London, or the Sudan Archive in Durham.

25 Given in my *Darfur and the British.*

26 During my visits to Darfur in the late 1960s and '70s I found it easier to use French when interacting with the Fulani holy families, but they belonged to networks that stretched as far as west as Senegal.

27 See "The Masalit War" in Flint and de Waal, *Darfur: A Short History of a Long War*, 57–61 for a case study. See also de Waal, ed., *War in Darfur and the Search for Peace.*

Introduction

28 Al-Shidyāq, *Leg over Leg*, 2:119. In material terms, al-Shidyāq may have fared better than Perron, at least before the latter's promotion: in a letter dated August 10, 1838, Perron complains "I am poor, with no fortune but my ink" (Artin, *Lettres du Dr Perron du Caire et d'Alexandrie à M. Jules Mohl, à Paris, 1838–1854*, 46).

29 The scope and importance of this undertaking, and the range and depth of al-Tūnisī's collaboration with Perron both within and without its component translation projects, are only now starting to be recognized. I owe my awareness of these wider dimensions of the relationship to Khaled Fahmy, who has kindly allowed me to draw on his "Translating Bichat and Lavoisier into Arabic," an unpublished paper presented at the Middle East, South Asian, and African Studies Colloquium, Columbia University, February 9, 2015.

30 See Hunwick, "Leo Africanus's Description of the Middle Niger, Hausaland and Bornu," 272–91.

31 For example, Edmé-François Jomard contributed to, edited, and helped to publish the *Journal d'un voyage à Temboctou et à Jenné*

dans l'Afrique Centrale by the explorer René Caillié (Paris, 1830) and P.H.S. Escayrac de Lauture contributed a "Notice sur le Kordofan" (*Bulletin de la Société de géographie de Paris,* Series 4,1 (1851) p. 371) and a "Mémoire sur le Soudan" (Paris, 1855), which includes important interviews, made in Cairo, with pilgrims from Darfur.

32 Browne, W. G. *Travels in Africa, Egypt, and Syria, from the Year 1792 to 1798.* London: T. Caddel Junior and W. Davies, 1799. A second, enlarged, edition was published in 1806; I have not been able to examine a copy.

33 See §2.1.32.

34 See Glossary.

35 See §2.2.35.

36 Al-Tūnisī's two years in Wadai are not covered by *In Darfur.*

37 Al-Tūnisī provides little specific information about his education. He states that he studied at the mosque-university of al-Azhar in Cairo before he left for Darfur at age fourteen (§2.1.34); as he told his father when they were reunited, he had acquired there "a certain amount of scholarship" (§2.2.28). In Darfur, he took lessons with Faqīh Madanī al-Fūtāwī, his father's sponsor's brother (see, e.g., §3.3.18), but gives no information as to what these covered. On his return to Egypt, he studied once more, though he does not specify where, what, or for how long; it is likely, however, that he conducted his studies at al-Azhar and that it was during this period that he acquired the greater part of his education.

38 Heyworth-Dunne, *An Introduction to the History of Education in Modern Egypt,* 125. The earlier editors of this work, Khalīl Maḥmūd ʿAsākir and Muṣṭafā Muḥammad Musʿad, state that al-Tūnisī and Perron worked at the veterinary school associated with the Medical School (*Tashḥīdh,* 1965, 13). This seems to be based on an ambiguous statement by al-Shayyāl ("Duktūr Birrūn (Dr. Perron) wa-l-shaykhān Muḥammad ʿAyyād al-Ṭanṭāwī wa-Muḥammad ʿUmar al-Tūnisī," 193), but neither al-Tūnisī nor Perron mention the veterinary school.

39 Al-Tūnisī describes his role as *taṣḥīḥ,* literally "correction." In this context, this means that he was one of the *muṣaḥḥiḥūn,* or scholars

educated at al-Azhar who corrected the work of the original translators who, being Christians chosen primarily for their knowledge of European languages, often lacked a firm command of Arabic grammar and style (Fahmy, "Translating Bichat," 11). There is no evidence that al-Tūnisī knew French, and, despite the crucial role of the *muṣaḥḥiḥ* in the translation process, the common characterization of him as a translator is potentially misleading. On the title page of the *Voyage au Ouadây*, Perron describes al-Tūnisī as "Réviseur en Chef à l'École de Médicine du Kaire."

40 These included al-Ḥarīrī's *Maqāmāt*, al-Ibshīhī's *al-Mustaṭraf fī kull fann mustaẓraf*, and al-Fīrūzābādī's *al-Qāmūs al-muḥīṭ* (al-Tūnisī, *Tashḥīdh*, 1965, 15). On January 19, 1854, Perron noted in a letter to Jules Mohl that "Cheikh El-Tounsy's *Hariry*, printed at Bulaq, has sold out; there are only four or five copies left. . . . I have just bought the *Moustatraf* of my old teacher El-Tounsy, also printed at Bulaq. It has had a lot of success and sells very well" (Artin, *Lettres*, 107).

41 Artin, *Lettres*, 107.

42 Messaoudi, "Perron," 750.

43 Fahmy, "Translating Bichat," 13.

44 Other Saint-Simonians would follow, most notably the group led by Prosper Enfantin, known to his followers as "Le Père," who arrived in 1833 in search of "La Mère" and left again in 1836 following the failure of the group's engineering project (construction of a barrage on the Nile) and the plague; Perron involved himself in their activities (Messaoudi, "Perron," 750) and helped Enfantin find work when he was penniless (O'Fahey, "Egypt, Saint-Simon and Muḥammad ʿAlī," 21).

45 Perron wrote to Jules Mohl on September 26, 1839: "I have just been appointed director of the School of Medicine. . . . Given the knowledge of the Arabic language that I have acquired, and which corresponds to the needs of the current school set-up, the Pasha [i.e., Muḥammad ʿAlī] approved my promotion immediately" (Artin, *Lettres*, 58). In almost the same breath, however, Perron asks Mohl to find him a position in France, since "I do not want to stay here

for more than a few years, if possible" (Artin, *Lettres*, 59). Perron indicates that his desire to leave Egypt was due to the country's precarious financial situation, which had led to delays in payment of staff salaries and the downsizing of the school.

46 Al-Shayyāl, "Duktūr Birrūn," 184, 184, n. 3, 185. According to al-Shayyāl, Perron resigned in 1846; however, he is described as director of the Medical School on the title page of *Voyage au Ouaday*, published in 1851. He may have regarded himself as merely taking leave in 1846 and been relieved of the post while in France. As early as May 14, 1844, Perron confides in a letter to Jules Mohl that he is thinking of taking six months' leave (Artin, *Lettres*, 83–84), and he repeats his intention to do so in a letter dated January 14, 1845 (Artin, *Lettres*, 89).

47 Fahmy describes in detail the sophisticated methodology used to produce translations, which required the participation of foreign doctors employed by the school, such as Perron, who in some cases had authored the works in question; of Egyptian graduates of the school who had subsequently trained in France as physicians, of whom by 1832 there were twelve and who drafted the translations; and of language editors, such as al-Tūnisī ("Translating Bichat," 12–13). Another member of the team of language editors and correctors with whom Perron worked closely and whom he regarded with as much respect as he did al-Tūnisī was the latter's younger colleague Muḥammad ʿAyyād al-Ṭanṭāwī (1810–61), who would eventually (ca. 1846) leave Egypt for Russia, where he taught at the university in St. Petersburg and wrote, among a number of other works, one of the first teaching grammars of spoken Arabic for foreigners (*Aḥsan al-nukhab fī maʿrifat lisān al-ʿArab*). Perron excepted al-Tūnisī and al-Ṭanṭāwī from his criticism of the Egyptian scholars of his day, which was otherwise excoriating: "These poor *ʿulamāʾ* have nothing of scholarship but the name, are immeasurably lazy and immeasurably ignorant. . . . They do not know the names of the most ordinary Arabic books. . . . None of them writes anything" (Artin, *Lettres*, 90). Apropos of his (unrealized) project to prepare, with the help of

al-Tūnisī, an edition of the renowned fourteenth-century dictionary *al-Qāmūs al-muḥīṭ* (*The Encompassing Ocean*) by Muḥammad al-Fīrūzābādī, he wrote, "there are not more than ten of these scholars who know how to use an Arabic dictionary. They do not even know the word-order system. . . . Let us then give a dictionary to the *ʿulamāʾ*" (Artin, *Lettres*, 92). Perron's negative assessment of contemporary Egyptian scholarship was not necessarily shared by other foreign scholars: Edward Lane had nothing but praise for Ibrahīm al-Disūqī, another member of the Medical School translation team, who assisted him in the preparation of his massive compendium and translation of medieval dictionaries, *An Arabic-English Lexicon* (see Lane, *Lexicon*, 1:5), while Aḥmad Fāris al-Shidyāq, who studied under Egyptian scholars from 1829 to 1832, believed that they were, at least, better than those of his homeland of Lebanon, though their command of grammar was more theoretical than practical and they taught better than they wrote (al-Shidyāq, *Leg over Leg*, 2:383–84).

48 Fahmy, "Translating Bichat," 13.

49 Fahmy, "Translating Bichat," 32.

50 Fahmy, "Translating Bichat," 20.

51 Fabre, ed. *Dictionnaire des dictionnaires de médecine français et étrangers ou traité complet de médecine et de chirurgie pratiques, par une société de médecins.*

52 Clot Bey, *Kunūz al-ṣiḥḥah wa-yawāqīt al-minḥah.*

53 Al-Shayyāl, "Duktūr Birrūn," 221; O'Fahey, *The Writings of Eastern Sudanic Africa to c. 1900*, 67–70. O'Fahey's description of *al-Shudhūr al-dhahabiyyah* as being "based on Clot Bey's lectures" (O'Fahey, *Writings*, 70) should be applied not to this but to *Kunūz al-ṣiḥḥah* (see preceding note).

54 Perron, *al-Jawāhir al-saniyyah fī l-aʿmāl al-kīmāwiyyah.*

55 Though Perron may have known relatively little Arabic on his arrival in France, as the choice for their lessons of these relatively simple animal fables suggests, it is worth noting that he was, according to one historian at least, the only foreign teacher employed by Muḥammad ʿAlī to know any Arabic at all (al-Shayyāl, "Duktūr Birrūn," 181).

56 El-Tounsy, *Voyage au Darfour*. The volume includes material not included in the Arabic text, namely, a twenty-six-page supplement (*appendice*) concerning Muḥammad Abū Madyan, a Keira pretender whom the Egyptian government attempted but failed to place on the throne of Darfur in 1843, plus more than ninety pages of notes, comments, and clarifications, many of them dictated to Perron by al-Tūnisī. Neither al-Tūnisī nor Perron give dates for their work on what would become *The Land of the Blacks* and its sister, French-only, volume, treating al-Tūnisī's briefer stay in Wadai, the *Voyage au Ouadai*. However, Perron's French translation of the first was completed by 1842, as evidenced by Perron's statement in a letter to Jules Mohl dated March 28 of that year that he is sending the manuscript of the translation to the geographer Edmé-François Jomard, "who has allowed me to hope that it will be published" (Artin, *Lettres*, 71). Also, in a note to the translation, Perron (*Voyage au Darfour*, 316, n. 1) states that al-Tūnisī had read the text of the next-to-last chapter of the book four years previously. We may deduce, then, that the two began work no later than 1838. By July 12, 1845, the work on both volumes of translation (that for Wadai as well as that for Darfur) was well underway, Perron telling Mohl that "I have very little left to do. I am drawing the illustrations and a map. The first part of the journey [i.e., the *Voyage au Darfour*] is being printed . . ." (Artin, *Lettres*, 95). By October 5, 1845, the *Voyage au Darfour* was printed (Artin, *Lettres*, 99).

57 Al-Tūnisī ibn Sulaymān [*sic*], Muḥammad ibn al-Sayyid ʿUmar. *Kitāb Tashḥīdh al-adhhān fī sīrat bilād al-ʿArab wa-l-Sūdān* [French title page: *Voyage au Darfour ou l'aiguisement de l'esprit par le voyage au Soudan et parmi les arabes du centre de l'Afrique par le cheykh Mohamed ibn-Omar el-tounsy [*sic*], Autographié et publié par Mr. Perron*]. Paris: Benjamin Duprat, 1850.

58 El-Tounsy, Mohammed ibn-Omar. *Voyage au Ouadây*, traduit de l'arabe par le Dr. Perron, publié par le Dr. Perron et M. Jomard. Paris: Bejamin Duprat, 1851. The end matter includes vocabulary lists for

several languages of the region ("Ouayen, Fôrien, Fertyt," etc.) compiled by Edmé-François Jomard.

59 In addition to his scientific translations and the works produced in collaboration with al-Tūnisī, Perron published the following: an article entitled "Tableau historique des sciences philosophiques" for Bailly de Merlieux's popular encyclopedia (1829); *Abrégé de grammaire . . . de l'arabe vulgaire* (1832); *Précis de jurisprudence* (6 vols., 1848–54), which is the above-mentioned translation of Khalīl ibn Isḥāq's *al-Mukhtaṣar* (3 vols., 1846–51); "Légendes orientales," articles published in *L'Illustration* (1850); "Récits arabes," articles published in (*La Revue orientale et algérienne* (1852); *La Perfection des deux arts, ou, Traité complet d'hippologie et d'hippiatrie* (3 vols., 1852–60), a translation of Abū Bakr ibn Badr's *Kitāb Kāmil al-ṣināʿatayn al-maʿrūf bi-l-Nāṣirī fī l-bayṭarah wa-l-zarṭaqah*; *Les Femmes arabes avant et après l'Islamisme* (1858), which draws on anecdotes from the *Kitāb al-aghānī* (*Book of Songs*); *Glaive-des-couronnes* (1862), a translation of the popular romance *Sayf al-Tījān*; *L'Islamisme, son institution, son influence et son avenir* (written in 1865 for an encyclopedia published in 1877); *Balance de la loi musulmane*, a translation of ʿAbd al-Wahhāb al-Shaʿrānī's *Mīzān al-sharīʿah*, published posthumously in 1898. He also wrote a number of articles for scholarly journals on celebrated figures of Arab lore, of which "Lettre sur les poètes Tarafah et Al-Moutalammis" in *Journal asiatique*, 3rd series, vol. XI, January 1841, pp. 215–47, may be taken as representative (compiled from Messaoudi, "Perron," and al-Shayyāl, "Duktūr Birrūn," 211–15).

60 Artin, *Lettres*, 38: "il était alors attaché comme médicin sanitaire à Alexandrie." Al-Shayyāl, however, says that he worked there as a private physician ("Duktūr Birrūn," 38). Probably he worked in both capacities.

61 Messaoudi, "Perron," 7.

62 The dispiriting coda to this life of intense engagement with the Arab world is that, during the later years of his life, Perron lost his Saint-Simonian enthusiasm for Islam's intellectual heritage. Already in

1850, he could write of Arab scholars that "the Muslims are almost all apers and parroters of the Greeks and the Indians," and by 1865 he had dismissed Islam as a sterile and antipoetic monotheism; his hopes for the future of the Orient were now placed on Bahaism (see Messaoudi, "Perron," 751).

63 O'Fahey, *Darfur Sultanate*, 9.

64 O'Fahey, *Darfur Sultanate*, 12.

65 An Arabic manuscript with the same title housed at the Royal Library in Rabat is a copy of the first, Paris, edition (Umar, "Travels," xviii).

66 O'Fahey, *Writings*, 68.

67 El-Tounsy, *Voyage au Darfour*, lxxi–ii.

68 Though no illustrator is credited, Perron's comment in a letter that he has "only the illustrations to draw, and a map" (Artin, *Lettres*, 95) confirms that he was the artist.

69 Darfur was briefly occupied by Egyptian forces in 1843. It fell again to Egyptian forces in 1874, more than fifty years after Sennar and Kordofan, its neighbors to the east; the seven years that followed are known as the Turkiyyah, referring to the Ottoman affiliations of Egypt's rulers. In 1884, the Egyptians were driven out by the followers of the Mahdi ("the divinely guided leader sent to restore God's kingdom on earth") Muḥammad Hamad ibn ʿAbd Allāh. During the Mahdiyyah that followed, the Keira sultans maintained the resistance they had started during the Turkiyyah and, following the defeat of the Mahdist state by the British in 1898, were able to restore the sultanate, albeit under nominal British suzerainty. Darfur's independence ended with the death in battle of Sultan ʿAli Dīnār in 1916 following his 1915 rebellion against the British and in support of the Ottoman Empire.

70 Browne, *Travels in Africa*, 180–313.

71 Browne, *Travels in Africa*, 255.

72 Nachtigal, *Sahara and Sudan IV: Wadai and Darfur*.

73 O'Fahey, *Darfur Sultanate*, 69.

74 O'Fahey, *Writings*, 68.

75 Hill, *A Biographical Dictionary of the Sudan*, 278.

76 See Introduction, p. xxxiii.

77 I am indebted to R. S. O'Fahey for sharing with me his copy of Umar's translation.

78 I was not able to consult the notes on the work made by Sudanese historian and former official in Darfur Muḥammad ʿAbd al-Raḥīm that are housed in the National Records Office in Khartoum (see O'Fahey, *Writings*, 68).

79 I am indebted to Dr. Christine Waag, Musa Jargis, Adam Karama, and Bariwarig Tooduo Kondo of the Summer Institute for Linguistics for their efforts in this regard, which are all the more appreciated in view of the difficult conditions in which they worked.

80 Browne, *Travels in Africa*, 183.

In Darfur

This Is the Book

of

The Honing of Minds

through

Consideration of the Condition

of

the Land of the Arabs and the Blacks

by Its Author

Muḥammad ibn ʿUmar al-Tūnisī

May God Excuse His Sins

In the Name of God
the Merciful, the Compassionate

1.1 —and may God bless Our Lord Muḥammad and his kin and Companions, and grant them much peace. O You who move the feet of humankind by Your sublime will and have determined the times for «the winter and the summer caravan»[1] by Your radiant wisdom, we praise You as must one who has savored the sweetness of relaxation after suffering the bitterness of travel and privation, and we thank you as must one blessed with settled abode after the toil and turmoil of the road. We beseech You, O Possessor of all that may be possessed, by the course that You have decreed for the stars in their orbits, to cause the showers of Your mercy and Your acceptance to fall, to let the rain of Your blessing and Your peace descend on the best of those who journeyed and settled at journey's end, who traveled from Mecca to Syria[2]—our lord and master Muḥammad, our intercessor on the day when the wrongdoers shall be exposed, who was inspired to recite «Say, "Travel about the land and see what was the end of the deniers"»[3] and on his kin, who left their native lands for love of him, and on his Companions who migrated to Medina out of desire for his proximity, and to grant them all copious tranquility.

1.2 To proceed, the humble petitioner for the mercy of his most gracious Lord, Muḥammad son of al-Sayyid ʿUmar al-Tūnisī son of Sulaymān,[4] declares: after the Almighty had granted me success in the study of the sciences of the Arabic language and filled my cup with, in particular, the literary arts, and I'd come to be counted among the children and kinsmen of polite letters, one of that clan that opens to them their hearts, along came Fate and knelt like a camel upon my fortunes, bearing down with all its weight, leaving only ruin where once had been a solid estate.[5] All my concern at that time was devoted to the acquisition of the sciences, and the gathering of their manifestations in prose and in verse. When, therefore, I observed how Time persisted in its opposition, I quoted, to encapsulate my condition, the words of Eminent Scholar al-Ṣaftī:

Poesy's constellations of gems well known have fallen, one by one, to my attack—
every heaven of knowledge I've scaled.
In the sciences, I've trounced all others and yet,
'twixt me and money, lies a yawning gap.
I marvel then how the banner may go to an ignorant man[6]
while poverty flies o'er the turban of every wise one.

1.3 Given then that I was now emptyhanded and the courtyard bare, my wealth had absconded, my prospects were no longer fair, that the spring had run dry, the meadow turned sere, I recited verses of my own as a commentary on my condition, to wit:

What can I do, when these days are filled with troubles
that harm the noble and protect the lowest sort—
Days that on the pious wage a war
beside which that of al-Basūs must seem as naught?
Any ignorant greenhorn you'll find they raise,
and any man of polish you'll see they hurt and slight.

Likewise, I quoted, to encapsulate my state, the words of the poet that go:[7]

The lions in the forests go to bed hungry
while the flesh of the sheep is thrown to the hound.
Many a pig sleeps on silken sheets
while the learned sleep on dusty ground.

1.4 At this point, an inner voice urged me to seek the assistance of certain people, but I recalled that "not everything red is flesh nor everything white a truffle";[8] likewise that a man may sacrifice his self-respect and not gain his end, and that it's better to sacrifice one's life than one's self-respect, especially if doing so brings with it misery and reversal, the request being made of someone ignoble. The poet says:[9]

Pulling of molars and confinement to prison,
  soul's last gasp and grave vault's frenzy,
Fire's scorch and shame's reproach,
  the selling off of one's house for a quarter penny,
Playing ape leader and enduring biting cold,
  tanning of skin without benefit of sunlight,[10]
Loss of a loved one and narrowness of well-mouth,
  a thousand blows with a thousand rope bights—
All these are easier for a noble man to stand
  than waiting at a rascal's door and taking charity from an
    ignoble hand.

—words confirmed by the discovery, engraved on a stone somewhere by the pen of the power of the Mighty, the Omnipotent, "Eat from the toil of your right hand and the sweat of your brow, and should your confidence falter, call on God and He will come to your aid."

I therefore entered the service of one whose amicable ways each 1.5
new day's page adorn, whose deeds of kindness turn the darkest nights to dawn—God's all-embracing shade that encompasses every land and metropolis, protector of Islam's honor and suppressor of the profligate, who brings men repose under the spreading umbra of his clemency and his charity, and who through his succor and shelter has let them taste the sweetness of security:[11]

Monarch magnificent, clement, beneficent,
  whose beneficence trumps all other munificence,
Sender of justice, injustice's ender,
  standing by God's penalties when pronouncing sentences!
Righteous in deed, veracious in word,
  true in his dealings, he fulfills his promises!

To end wrongdoing is what concerns him,
to set all lands to rights and order their territories.
We in the pastures of his state's protection
live a life free of care under a shade that encompasses.
O ruler whom sublimity protects
from the delimitation of his traits with boundaries,
You, through Our Lord's protection, are forever safe
from the eyes of your enemies and the wiles of the envious.

Yea, he it is who conquered the two noble sanctuaries[12] with his victorious army, he who took possession of the Levantine lands through the agency of that champion, that celebrated lion, his son Ibrāhīm[13]—the Commander of the Faithful, al-Ḥājj Muḥammad ʿAlī Pasha, bestower of benefits, may God raise high the pavilion of his state's honor and cause his rule to last in all its glory and power forever!

1.6 When I began my service, I held the position of preacher in the Eighth Infantry Regiment, traveling with it to the Morea and suffering many hardships.[14] Before that, though, I'd traveled to the Land of the Blacks, where the wonders I saw, if set down in writing, would resemble a flowery bower. Then I was employed at the school at Abū Zaʿbal[15] as a language editor of medical books, specializing in pharmaceutical works. I did this until I met the most brilliant man of his day in keenness of mind and understanding, the brightest of his age in industry and knowledge—the French teacher of chemistry, Dr. Perron.[16] He studied *Kalīlah and Dimnah* with me in Arabic, and I told him some of the splendid and amazing things I'd endured on my travels. He then urged me to "adorn the face of my copybook" with an exposition of the marvels I'd seen and to tell him of the strange things that had befallen me on these journeys. I complied with his command both because of the kindnesses he had shown me and in the belief too that this would be in my own best interest, given the words of the author of *The Poem on Words Ending in –ā and ā' (al-Maqṣūrah)*[17] that go:

Man is but the words that live on after him,
so let those be worthy in the eyes of those who take note.

I then set about extracting those precious pearls from the oyster of the mind and lifting the veil from those beauteous beads to expose them to view, adding anecdotes I'd heard from trusted sources or copied from books, by way of expatiations appropriate to occasions, to make this account of my travels a meadow of blooming flowers to all who upon it turn their gaze, a garden of low-hanging fruit for any who among its topics graze. Likewise, I've spared no effort to make it clear, and not gone diving after arcane words, to make it plain to every ear.

I have organized it in the form of a prolegomenon, the book 1.7
proper, and a conclusion,[18] each made up of chapters, as may be seen from the way in which I have provided it with different headings and named it *The Honing of Minds through Consideration of the Condition of the Land of the Arabs and the Blacks*, and I call on God to envelop it in the mantle of His endorsement, and protect it from attacks by the envious on what it holds by way of content, for

How many have found fault with words that are sound,
their evil thoughts the product of minds that are sick!

I do not, however, claim, even though I have worked it and refined it and poured it into the best of molds, that it is free of flaws or lacking in lapses: I am a mere mortal, liable to error, oversight, and forgetfulness. All the same, I seek refuge with God from the ignoramus who regards it with envious eyes and criticizes it by claiming to all and sundry that it is full of frivolous lies:[19]

Were I to claim this morn was night,
would no one ever again see light?

May God show His mercy to any who sees but discreetly passes 1.8
over a mistake, or finds an error and sets it straight:

Should you find a blemish, pass it by—
  glory be to Him without blemish, Most High.

From God I beg success in finding the straightest way—my best Proxy, the best Trustee, the best Master, the best Ally!

Prolegomenon, in three chapters

CHAPTER 1

The Reasons That Led to My Journey to the Land of the Blacks

My father—may the clouds of God's mercy and approval hover over him!—told me that his grandfather was one of the great men of Tunis, an agent of the Sultan of Morocco, the late Perfect Lord, Just and Victorious, Sharif Muḥammad al-Ḥasanī.[20] As a result, he amassed a great fortune and became one of the richest men of his day. He died leaving three sons. They fought one another over their father's inheritance, sold the common home that had sheltered them in life, and each went to live on his own, with his children and his wife. Now my father's father was, as it happened, a man of learning, with a beautiful hand, who could copy a book and sell it for many times more than anyone else and who also knew how to dye clothes in different colors. Thus he, among all his brothers, with regard to income was the most blessed, as well as the best dressed. Now he conceived a desire to see the Sacred House and visit the tomb of His prophet, upon whom be peace, so he sold some properties he owned and prepared to travel. He bought woolen mantles and tarbushes to take with him, and others gave him large amounts of money to trade with on their behalf, knowing as they did of his honesty and trustworthiness,[21] so that a large part of the ship ended up filled with his goods. 2.1.1

When he set off, his brothers accompanied him to the ship to see him off. He embarked and it sailed off with its passengers under 2.1.2

a good wind. Later, though, the winds turned against the ship and they were blown off course and set on a path for Rhodes. As they sat off that island, safe and at their ease, a great wind suddenly caught them, and the waves battered them and serenity turned to sorrow, as described by the poet when he says:

> You thought well of the days when they were minding their manners
> and feared not the evils Fate might send.
> The nights made up to you and played you for a fool—
> it's when nights are clearest that clouds descend.

Their ship was unsound, and when the waves battered it, forcing it into submission as brutally as did al-Ḥajjāj the people of Iraq, its construction fell apart, its structure was undone, its parts came to bits, its heartstrings were unstrung. Those on board drowned and only a few were saved, among them my aforementioned grandfather, who was delivered, at his last gasp, to the aforementioned land:

> When a man's neck's been saved from perdition,
> wealth means less to him than a fingernail clipping.

2.1.3 My grandfather stayed on Rhodes for a while, making use of a purse in his waistband that contained some gold, which he used for the duration of his stay. Then he bought provisions and sailed to the port city of Alexandria. It was the pilgrimage season, that of departure for the land of "clamor and sacrifice,"[22] so he set off without dereliction or delay and to those celebrated sites made his way, and achieved his goal, having strived as hard as he could strive, his actions expressive of the words (even before he could arrive):

> The most blest of days was when I was told,
> "This is Ṭaybah! This is al-Kuthub!
> This is the garden of Ṭāhā the Chosen!
> This, before you, is al-Zarqāʾ, so drink!"

(In the word *hādhī*, the *yāʾ* is in place of the *hāʾ*).[23]

Once he had completed his duties and diligently made his visit to the Beloved and his two companions,[24] he recovered from his dazed state, regained his equanimity, and thought of his wealth that had been lost, deciding that to reenter Tunis in hardship and poverty, after having left it in affluence and vitality, would be to expose himself to disgrace, wondering too how he could endure hard labor after a life of ease and what the people of the city would think when they saw him so debased. Then, remembering all that had passed, he recited, in earnest, not in jest:[25] 2.1.4

I shall roam the horizons from east to west
and grow rich, or die in a foreign land.
Should I lose my life, God will give me back my soul
and should I survive, return is ever close at hand.

Everyone knows that it is not easy for a man to live through trouble, sickness, and toil in a land where he knows no one, especially these days, when the Jew is honored for his money, and the sharif despised for his indigence and poverty. God have mercy on the soul of the poet who said:[26] 2.1.5

The poor man begins his day with everything against him
and the earth shuts its doors in his face.
Observe how he's hated though he's done nothing wrong
and meets with an enmity whose cause he cannot trace.
Even the dogs, seeing a rich man,
fawn on him and wag their tails
But when they see a pauper, half-naked,
bark at him and bare their teeth.

It is this that caused Imam ʿAlī, may God honor him, to say, "Poverty is a disease that knows no cure: if I make it known, it brings me shame, and if I keep it hidden, it kills me." It is said too that "If a man becomes poor, those whom he used to trust will betray him, those who used to think well of him will think badly of him, those who used to keep him by their side will keep him at 2.1.6

a distance, and those who used to love him will no longer find him to their taste":

If my wealth diminishes, no friend will help me,
    but if I grow rich, everyone's my friend.

Would that a man, when he loses his money, be left alone and not despised—and not just that, I swear, but be called a liar when he opens his mouth, even if he speaks the truth, and be despised even if what he says is blameless:

The lips of one with two pennies to rub together
    will learn all kinds of things to say and speak out loud
And stand before his brethren while they give him ear
    and seem to you as one of those who steps out proud—
Yet were it not for the coins in his purse
    you'd see him as the worst of the crowd.
When the rich man speaks wrong,
    they say, "You speak true and have uttered no fantasy,"
But when the poor man gets it right, as one they exclaim,
    "You've got it wrong, you there. You've uttered a travesty."
In every country, silver pieces
    cloak a man in gravitas and make of him a pleasing sight.
They are the tongue of all who seek to persuade,
    the weapon of all who wish to fight.

Things being so, those of noble line are better off dead than dirtying their hands:

Better death for the generous man
    than a life of privation!
Better death for the nobly born
    than pleading and supplication!

2.1.7 Likewise the Prophet, God bless him and grant him peace, when he learned that the poor were despised when once they had been honored, and brought low when once they had enjoyed high standing and respect, said, “Honor the great man among you who has been brought low and the rich man among you who has become poor!”—all of which, however, simply reflects what the Mighty, the Bountiful, has written in the Original Book and has decreed in His foreknowledge; otherwise, how could it be that so many poor men have been rescued by the fates and so many rich ones ended up without a quarter dinar to their name? By way of example, the vizier al-Muhallabī was, in his early days, a poor man who owned less than nothing. It happened that he traveled on foot from Baghdad to Mecca with a caravan. Wracked by hunger and unable to sleep, he recited the following lines:

Is there no death for sale that I might buy it?
This is a life that holds no charms!
May the Lord of All have mercy on the soul of a mortal
who grants death to his brother as alms!

One of the merchants heard him and gave him a loaf and a silver piece. Then things changed and al-Muhallabī rose to the vizierate, whereas the merchant became so poor that he could no longer lay his hands on his daily bread. When he heard that al-Muhallabī had risen to the vizierate, he went to his residence and wrote him the following on a scrap of paper:

Do give the vizier—may my soul be his ransom—
a word to remind him of what he may have forgotten:
“Remember how you said when you wanted to die,
‘Is there no death for sale that I might buy?’”

This he dispatched via a servant. When al-Muhallabī read it he wept copiously and, recalling what had gone before, ordered that the man be given work and seven hundred silver pieces, and wrote to him on a scrap of paper: «Those who spend their wealth for God’s cause may be compared to a grain of corn which sprouts into seven ears, with a hundred grains in each ear.»[27] From this, one should draw the lesson that one must honor any who have become poor after being rich and been brought low after reaching the highest standing, and if need should weigh on a person's mind and he wishes to ask others for help, he will, if he has any sense, ask only those persons who are generous and chivalrous and not those who have become wealthy after being poor or reached high standing after being lowly. Says the poet:

Ask a boon of those who of old enjoyed excess,
but not of a rich man, raised in poverty, who has acquired wealth!

2.1.8 It is also true that money endears its owner to others' hearts and makes its owners' pockets its counterparts. Through it, wishes are realized and every need fulfilled. Al-Ḥarīrī puts it well when, praising a gold piece, he says:[28]

How noble something yellow—a yellow pellucid—
A rover of horizons on journeys far-flung!
Its repute and its fame to us have come down,
In the lines on its brow wealth's secret is hung.
Success in endeavor keeps pace with its gait,
While men fall in love with its forehead's blaze
As though from their very hearts it was minted—
Those with a purse of it will have their ways,
Be their tribes extinct or enfeebled.
How excellent its purity and its beauty!
How excellent its sufficiency and its support!
How many commanders' commands with its help run featly!
How many coddled rich men without it would live in constant sorrow!
How many mighty armies by its attack have been tamed!
How many full moons[29] ten thousand of it have brought to heel!
How many raging furiosos, their embers aflame,
Have held secret parley with it and found their ire curtailed!
How many captives of whose release families despaired

Has it rescued and their happiness restored!
By a Lord due to whose creative genius it appeared,
I'd declare, but for the impiety, "May its power be revered!"

It has been observed that when a stutterer becomes rich he acquires fluency and when a man with an eye disease acquires wealth his sight is restored. Proof of this is that while on this journey of mine I saw a man called Muḥammad al-Muknī, a client of Yūsuf Pasha, overlord of Libyan Tripoli. His eyes were diseased, his lids ulcerated, his tears never stopped, and he barely slept. He remained like this until he became governor of the province of Fezzan. At that moment, the disease disappeared, his eyelashes grew back, the pain left him, and his tears stopped. He became the handsomest man of his day and the most distinguished in the region where he lived. I would add that it may be that the diseases that afflict the poor are a result of the humiliation, poverty, nakedness, and hunger they experience, for they worry over the constraints within which they live and their lack of affluence, and as a result their minds become disordered and their bodies sick. The rich man is not so. True, he may have worries, but they arise from other causes: 2.1.9

Who praises the world for something that pleases
will reproach it, I swear, for a trifle.
Back turned, it brings a man grief.
Smiling, it brings no relief.

The rich man, however, can always realize his desires by spending money.

This is shown by the tale of how ʿAlī Pasha I, Lord of Tunis, before his rule began, fled to Algiers to ask its ruler to lend him soldiers for support in taking Tunis from his cousin, Ḥusayn Pasha,[30] which the Lord of Algiers did. News of this reached Ḥusayn Pasha, and every time he heard anything about the matter he'd become distressed, knowing the decline in status and loss of command and authority this would mean for him. On one occasion, he received 2.1.10

news that worried and disquieted him. Preoccupied, he rode out with his entourage through the middle of Tunis. One of his viziers, who was by his side, was speaking to him and, noticing his condition, asked him what had upset him. Ḥusayn Pasha told him of the news he had received. "God make our lord triumphant and grant him victory!" the vizier said. "Why worry over nothing? On the contrary, so long as you are still here he cannot, I assure you, do a thing." Then he turned to his right—they were in the area known as the Tile Market—and saw a dry branch lying on the ground, and said to him, "The day this branch turns green again, ʿAlī Pasha will take Tunis and become its ruler," intending by this to reassure his master.

2.1.11 Only a few days were to pass before ʿAlī Pasha arrived with a massive army from Algiers, killed Ḥusayn Pasha,[31] and temporarily confirmed this same vizier in his position until things sorted themselves out. One day, ʿAlī Pasha happened to ride out in the midst of his entourage and entered Tunis, the said vizier at his side, as he had been at Ḥusayn Pasha's, and they proceeded till they came to the Tile Market. ʿAlī Pasha turned and saw the branch lying where it had been and said to the vizier, "If this branch turns back into a green tree, will ʿAlī Pasha come back as ruler of Tunis?"—for enemies of the vizier had told him the story, though he'd said nothing of it till that moment. After that, ʿAlī Pasha turned away from the vizier and stopped speaking to him. From this, the vizier knew he was a dead man, no doubt about it, given what he knew of ʿAlī Pasha's evil nature—for he was a bloodthirsty murderer who would kill for a trifle, let alone something of this sort. They continued on their way until ʿAlī Pasha came to his place of power and portico of pomp, and there the vizier presented himself to ʿAlī Pasha before he had time to issue any orders concerning him, saying, "God aid our master! When he heard of your approach, your cousin Ḥusayn Pasha deposited large amounts of money with me, which I hid in a place known only to me. I know well that you intend to kill me and I am afraid that, should I die while it is still in its hiding place, my master will not have the benefit of it. If it pleases my lord to release me so that I may bring it to him, let him do so."

ʿAlī Pasha was overjoyed and believed him, and ordered him to set off with ten *ḥawnab*s to accompany him, a *ḥawnab* being in the language of Tunis what is called a *qawwāṣ* in the language of Egypt.[32] Before they set off he told the *ḥawnab*s, "If he escapes, I shall kill you all." They went with him till they reached his house, where he made them wait below while he went upstairs to get the women out of the way. The *ḥawnab*s waited, and as soon as the vizier was upstairs he made a beeline for the safe where he kept his money and filled his pockets with gold; he also took with him a small casket of the sort that in Tunis they call a *fnīq*, which likewise was filled with gold. Then he went out onto the roof, crossed over to another house, climbed down the wall to the street, and made for the house of the British consul, informing him as soon as he was in his presence that he was seeking refuge with him, and he told him his story. Then he gave him the casket and all its contents and said, "I want you to order one of your ships to take me to England immediately." The consul promptly wrote an order to one of his commanders, which said, "Set sail for England the moment this letter reaches you. Do not delay for even one minute," and he gave the vizier the letter and sent his dragoman with him. They traveled on the water until they reached the ship. When the ship's captain read the consul's letter, he left the harborage and fired a gun as a signal to the consul that he had set off. Now, it occurred to the *ḥawnab*s that he was taking a long time so they called out, "You! Come down!" but the women told them he had left immediately after going upstairs. They thought the women were lying and stormed the house but found no one. When ʿAlī Pasha learned of his escape he was furious and realized that it had been a ruse and he'd fallen for it. 2.1.12

Ponder this case, God bless you. Do you imagine that if this vizier had not used those gold pieces, he would have made it to safety? I swear not! ʿAlī Pasha would certainly have killed him and taken his money and it would have availed him nothing, for if a gold or silver piece isn't spent, it's of no use and will provide its owner with nothing of his needs. On the contrary, if he were a governor, he'd be dismissed, and if a merchant, despised.

2.1.13 In the same vein, when Khūrshīd Pasha, the former viceroy of Egypt, was dismissed for failing to give the troops their pay and His Excellency[33] became the country's ruler, our shaykh of shaykhs, Erudite Scholar Muḥammad al-Amīr al-Kabīr,[34] said to the same effect:

> They fired you when you said, "I shall not
> give," and appointed another, who knew how to spend.
> Did no one ever tell you: *mā*'s
> a particle that brings regency to an end?[35]

Al-Ḥarīrī puts it well when he denounces the gold piece for being of no use to its owner until it has escaped his grasp. He says:

> The worst thing about it?
> It can't help in a fix,
> Unless it first flees you like a slave on the run.
> Woe both to the one who throws it off a high cliff
> And the one to whom, as it whispers sweet nothings,
> It tells it straight and says,
> "Our love has no future, so up sticks!"

And there is a Tunisian proverb that goes, "A gold piece placed over the mouth of tribulation silences it," and an Egyptian proverb that goes, "Love your money, lose your friends," meaning that one who loves his money and hoards it has no friends.

2.1.14 There is a similar story that took place in Tunis, to wit that Abū Muḥammad Ḥammūdah Pasha of glorious memory—may God cool the earth in which he lies—had a vizier called Yūsuf the Seal Bearer (i.e., "the *Muhurdār*," meaning the official who carries the seal with which the pasha seals his orders). This Yūsuf had previously been the slave of a head of the garrison at Sfax, a man named Muḥammad al-Jallūlī,[36] and was possessed of great beauty, mannerliness, and modesty. Word of him reached the pasha, who sent to al-Jallūlī, telling him, "I hear you have a slave of such and such a description called Yūsuf. When this letter reaches you, send him to me with its bearer. Farewell." When al-Jallūlī read the letter, he could see no alternative but to send the man, and when the pasha had him in his possession, he delighted in his good looks, intelligence, quick-wittedness, honesty, and trustworthiness.

Now it happened that some slaves, having agreed among themselves to kill the pasha, entered his room while he was sleeping and put the blade to his throat.[37] He called out for help and it was this Yūsuf's good fortune to be the one who saved the pasha. The latter raised him to high estate and treated him as he did his own children, bestowing upon him posts of great importance, so that banners now fluttered above his head[38] and men took to pointing at him with the tips of their fingers.[39] This Yūsuf was so charming, so deft in his dealings, so victorious in war, so blessed in all he did, so openhanded, that his polished ways appealed to all men's hearts. The pasha made him commander of land forces at the Battle of Serrat, between the ruler of Tunis and the master of Algiers.[40] To Yūsuf's good fortune, the Algerians suffered a calamitous defeat. The Tunisian forces captured their tents, horses, camels, and weapons, and a huge number of Algerian soldiers were taken prisoner. After this, he became the commander of land and sea forces at Ḥalq al-Wād, at a time when the Algerian fleet was advancing, once again, to do battle with Tunis. He lived in the fortress of Ḥalq al-Wād, and organized the army, ships, stores, and nightly patrols along the coast. The notables of Tunis used to seek him out there and have their affairs attended to, as he controlled everything. 2.1.15

One man who used to come to his court was Muḥammad al-Jallūlī, the son of his former master, but he would arrive with an arrogant air, with guards, and without following the code of etiquette appropriate to an official of Yūsuf's importance. The seal bearer noticed this in him but paid no attention until the leading members of his court spoke to him about it, citing many instances. 2.1.16

They even said, "He still looks upon you as his father's slave and has said so openly many times." This annoyed Yūsuf, and he schemed to have his revenge. He was told al-Jallūlī would enter his house mounted, not dismounting outside like the other emirs, and that al-Jallūlī's groom would take his mule and tether it alongside Yūsuf's own mounts. Yūsuf therefore summoned the chief groom and said, "They tell me that al-Jallūlī's groom tethers his mule with my mounts. If after today I hear that he has tethered it with my horses, you will have only yourself to blame for the consequences." "I hear and obey," said the man. One day, al-Jallūlī came and dismounted as was his wont, and his groom took his mule and tethered it as was his wont (Yūsuf's groom being absent), and al-Jallūlī went upstairs to the seal bearer's meeting chamber and sat down. While he was thus seated he heard a ruckus and cries, so he looked out of a window and saw that his mule was running loose and that his groom had been beaten, blood welling from his head. He went downstairs in a fury, and his groom told him that the chief groom had come and found his mule tethered, and that he had set it loose and struck it, causing it to run off. "When I heard this," the man said, "I asked him, 'Why did you set my master's mule loose?' and he swore at me, so I swore back at him. Then he beat me and left me in the condition you find me in."

2.1.17 Al-Jallūlī went back in a rage to the seal bearer and said to him, "How could my mule be set loose and my servant be beaten before your eyes?" Yūsuf, however, did not look at him and gave no reply. Al-Jallūlī became even angrier, realizing that the servant would never have done what he did without his master's permission. He went down, mounted forthwith, and set off for an audience with the pasha. He went in to see the late Ḥammūdah Pasha and complained of all he had suffered at the seal bearer's hands. The pasha, however, paid no attention to his complaints and would not even look at him. At this point, al-Jallūlī was bursting with rage. He left the pasha's presence and went home depressed and distressed, at a loss as to what to do. One of his friends came to see him, and finding him thus asked him why he was upset. He told him what had happened, and the man chided him for what he had done, and especially for complaining to the pasha. "Are you not aware," he said, "that the seal bearer is his favorite and it's his word that is heard? Do you want to make him your enemy? Do you think you can complain about him to the pasha and have your petition against him heeded? How wretchedly you have acted, and what foolish delusions you have harbored! Bethink yourself and put things right, or you will suffer the harm that is coming to you and will have only yourself to blame. Have you not heard the words of the poet that go:

> Should God's favor fall on the purchased slave,
> his commands will govern his masters?"

"So how do I get out of this situation?" asked al-Jallūlī. "What strategy should I use to escape my predicament?" "Know this," his friend told him. "If a man doesn't spend his money when it comes to a critical business such as this, it's of no more use to him than the stones of his house. Your strategy should be to put together a dazzling gift, present it to the seal bearer, and beg his forgiveness through his dearest friends, such as His Excellency Ibn Abī al-Ḍiyāf,[41] Qāsim the Doorman, Ṣāliḥ Abū Ghudayr, and their like, spending enough money on them to make them contented and active intercessors on your behalf: what is money for, if not critical situations like this?" Al-Jallūlī accepted his advice and prepared a costly gift, including a sword that was beyond price by virtue of the beauty of its gems, a huge seal ring made with diamonds that was likewise beyond price, a dagger inlaid with diamonds and rubies, a snuffbox and a watch, both inlaid, and ten thousand gold sequins. Taking a large sum of money, he wheedled away until he obtained a meeting with the seal bearer's friends and informed them he wanted to use them to gain access to the seal bearer so that they could entreat him to forgive him. He gave them presents to win their good will and handed over to them the gift, which they took to their friend, informing him that al-Jallūlī had come to apologize and seek His Excellency's 2.1.18

forgiveness. They showed him the gift and outlined the advantages of calling a truce with the man and of excusing him and not seeking vengeance, so long as he didn't do it again.

2.1.19 The gift excited Yūsuf's greed, so he accepted it and forgave the man. He ordered them to have him brought before them and to counsel him forcefully that he must follow the rules of etiquette, abandon his former arrogance, and cease to regard himself as better than everyone else; rather, he should adopt a servile manner, since "to us, he's no different from any other commander in the army, and if he reverts to his old ways he will have only himself to blame for the consequences." They obeyed his command, fetched him, and counseled him. Then they brought him into the presence of the seal bearer who, when he saw him, gave him a friendly smile, ordered him to be seated, made much of his having come, paid him every attention, and made no reference to what had happened. Then the seal bearer wrote to his master the pasha and told him what had taken place with al-Jallūlī—that al-Jallūlī had sought his favor with a gift and that he had granted him his favor—and he sent the gift with the bearer of the letter. When the letter reached the pasha, he read it and he had the gift brought and inspected it; then he returned it to Yūsuf, writing to him as follows: "Your letter has reached us, and we have understood what it contains and found the gift to be excellent. However, we think its contents better suited to you than to us, so we have returned it to you and give you permission to enjoy it, for you are a young man and love adornment, while we have nothing to do with such things. As for the ten thousand, spend them on the needs of the army. We grant al-Jallūlī our favor because you have granted him yours. Farewell." The following morning, al-Jallūlī went in to see the pasha, who made much of seeing him and welcomed him and gave him a further district to administer in addition to those he already had, and the man found himself very well off.

Observe this case and give it due consideration. Do you think that if al-Jallūlī hadn't spent his money he'd have been restored to his former station? I swear he wouldn't! On the contrary, he would have been stripped of his estates and might well have been killed on the spot.

Since our discussion has led us to the life of the late Ḥammūdah Pasha and his vizier Yūsuf the Seal Bearer, let us record a small portion of their history, for we are determined that this travel narrative of ours not be without attractive and informative parables, and there is nothing more enjoyable than talk of just kings whose conduct was good and whose subjects led comfortable lives because of them. We begin with mention of the pasha, as follows: 2.1.20

The Resolute, Sagacious, Just, Virtuous, Sublime Master Abū Muḥammad Ḥammūdah Pasha, son of ʿAlī Pasha, son of Ḥusayn Pasha, son of ʿAlī, was born on the eve of Saturday, Rabiʿ al-Thani 18, 1173 [December 8, 1759]. Allegiance was paid to him the day his father died in 1191 [1777–78].[42] He himself died on the eve of the Feast of the Fast-Breaking in 1229 [September 15, 1814]. He was possessed of a high degree of resolve, discrimination, and justice, and was courageous, inspiring of respect, chaste, and bold. He constructed the Manūbah Garden that is now so famous and that has eclipsed the Garden of Abū Fihr, of which Abū ʿAbd Allāh Muḥammad al-Wirghī said:

Stand here, at lovely Abū Fihr—
  no stranger to the days of prideful beaux!
Observe the curves and those they grace—like a line of palms,
    each touching
  another as, weighed down by clusters, they're brought low,
Or like well-bred virgins who, rising to dance, have placed their
    arms around each other's necks
  lest they fall to dancing out of step.

It was he too who built the great wall around Tunis, fortified it with towers and cannons, and manned the towers with soldiery. He removed the mounds of refuse that lay between Tunis and the lake, which had been like mighty mountains, blocking the good air and putting the city at risk, since the days of the Hafsids. For seven 2.1.21

years, he went to great lengths to have them removed and replaced with a huge plantation, thus relieving the people of Tunis of a great nuisance. He also built a place for the construction of large guns and fortified Ḥalq al-Wād and its wondrous towers and buildings, with the result that now not even a small sailing ship can enter without two gates first being opened to let it through. He also built the citadel at al-Kāf and released Tunis and its possessions from the slaver's noose imposed by the Algerians[43] so that they could enjoy absolute freedom. He was victorious, favored by fortune, and dashed the hopes of any who attacked him—so the Algerians could do nothing against him. Among his felicitous acts was the appointment of the previously mentioned Yūsuf the Seal Bearer as a vizier, whom he granted freedom to act in all things, as we have already mentioned. Yūsuf was very judicious, an excellent planner, zealous, a lover of scholars and learned men, predisposed by nature to acts of charity, generous, and inspiring of respect.

2.1.22 Yūsuf built the mosque in Tunis's al -Ḥalfāwīn market that now bears his name[44] and a large school for the acquisition of knowledge next to it, providing lavish salaries for its administrators and those of the mosque. For example, he awarded the directorship of the school to the man of his day most outstanding in both learning and piety, the Most Sublime Master and Skilled Man of Letters, My Master Shaykh Ibrāhīm al-Riyāḥī, our teacher and currently the shaykh of shaykhs of Tunis. The latter made it a condition at the school that two classes be given each day, one in law, the other in Qur'anic commentary. The shaykh himself contributed two further classes, one in Hadith, the other in grammar. The seal bearer spent vast sums to build the aforementioned mosque and school, with the result that the mosque is now the greatest in all of Tunis in terms of beauty and perfection of construction. Indeed, there may be nothing more perfectly constructed or wonderful, despite its small size, unless it is one I haven't yet seen, and I have seen many mosques, in Cairo, Libyan Tripoli, the Morea, and the Hejaz. Despite this, I have never seen any more perfectly constructed, though it is said that the Umayyad mosque in Damascus, the Qarawiyyīn mosque in Fez, and the mosque of Hagia Sophia in Constantinople are more impressive. In front of the mosque he built a great market for merchants, and above it a mighty palace for himself to sit in. He also built several schools for young children and placed drinking fountains everywhere.

I saw one of the fountains he constructed. It bore a chronogram[45] written by our teacher, Erudite Scholar Ibrāhīm al-Riyāḥī, which went as follows: 2.1.23

This is a fountain generously donated
by one who hopes for his Lord's reward:
Yūsuf, Counselor of Him Who Is Most Content with God's Favors[46]
and seal bearer of the magnificent,
Nobility's boast, Ḥammūdah
Pasha, and is of his largesse.
O you who drink, pray and speak
its date *on drinking of it.*

The individual words yield the date 1209 [1794–95] and are composed using the *ayqash* system, i.e., that used by westerners for calculation.[47] I declare: this chronogram (i.e., the words *bi-shurbihī*) is ineloquent, i.e., contains no pleasing sense. It is nothing compared to that written by the outstanding man of letters, Master Shaykh Muḥammad Shihāb al-Dīn al-Miṣrī, on the public drinking fountain constructed by Maḥmūd Effendi in Cairo the Protected between al-Azhar and the Shrine of al-Ḥusayn,[48] which goes as follows:

O you who drink from a spring whose source is pure,
quaff and good health to you, for this sweet water has been brought especially,
And see how excellent it is and how dated
His well inclines to good, is worthy of praise with felicity.[49]

The individual words yield the values 107, 160, 870, and 98, i.e., 1235 [1819–20].[50]

2.1.24 A chronogram by the Great Writer of His Day, Shaykh ʿAlī al-Darwīsh, on the covering of the Sacred House goes:

Ah, how brightens the eye that beholds a covering
 that fine stuffs are proud to adorn!
Glad tidings from al-Khalīl[51] to any who looks upon it,
 for by so doing he acquires good fortune—
And Fortune declared, to date it,
 A seemly covering for the House of God, may He be glorified.

The individual words yield the values 660, 442, 66, and 77, i.e., 1245 [1829–30].

And even that is nothing compared to the two chronograms I composed for the late Sayyid Muḥammad al-Maḥrūqī when he constructed the Sufi hospice opposite that of Shaykh al-ʿAfīfī in the Lesser Cemetery[52] and the water source at al-Raṭlī Pond in Cairo the Protected. The first goes:

Behold a Sufi hospice whose beauty's complete
 and to which all yearning hearts aspire!
It emerged so perfect as to beggar description
 by any who speaks by sign or word
And it is illumined by the grace of a *sayyid*. Date it:
 It has become filled with the light of Sayyid al-Maḥrūqī!

The individual words yield the values 480, 258, 105, and 395, i.e., 1238 [1822–23].

The second goes:

Observe what the hand of might and pride has built
 and you will see a water source made magnificent by grace
  and beauty,
Its builder, of the line of the noblest messenger,
 a gallant man whose glory tops al-Suhā's zenith.[53]
Muḥammad al-Maḥrūqī erected it, in hope of
 reward from a god whose limits know no end.

When it was finished, Fortune said to those who drank, "Date it:
Sweet water, curative, excellent, to be desired."

The individual words yield the values 68, 381, 17, 17, and 755, i.e., 1238 [1822–23].

The late Yūsuf Khōjah the Seal Bearer died in the month Safar 1230 [January 1813].[54] A man to whom men once feared to raise their eyes, he was murdered and his body dragged through the markets, so glory to Him who raises and brings low! Our teacher, Erudite Scholar Ibrāhīm al-Riyāḥī, elegized him in lines that were written on his tomb, as follows: 2.1.25

God alone may last forever;
others are death's booty.
Equal are they in their discomfiture,
whether their station be high or low.
Where are the kings; where those
whose rights were honored?
They took naught with them save what
they did of good, which therefore lasted.
This is what this great soul hoped to obtain
by his good deeds
—and rarely can man dispense with generosity!—
And by mosques and schools for the young
and water sources to quench the thirst.
May God have mercy on Yūsuf,
Seal of the Noble,[55] which no one can deny.
Small wonder that I have expressed the date as:
With his death, the noble have ceased to exist.

The individual words yield the values 488, 450, and 292, i.e., 1230 [1814–15].

Let us now return to the matter at hand. My grandfather then traveled from Mecca the Ennobled to the *bandar*—meaning port[56]—of Jeddah, and stayed there copying books for money; as 2.1.26

we have mentioned, he had a beautiful hand. During this period, chance threw him together with people from the Island of Sinnār,[57] one of whom became fond of him, and a bond of friendship was formed. This man asked him, "What country are you from?" and he answered, "Tunis." The man asked him why he'd settled in Jeddah, so my grandfather told him all that had befallen him, and the man from Sinnār asked him, "Why don't you go with us to the city of Sinnār? There you will find respect and esteem, for our *makk*—meaning 'our king'—is an openhanded man who cares nothing for the glitter of gold or silver's gleam. He loves, on the contrary, learning and its fraternity, assigning to each his rightful place and giving what aid he can to the Prophet's posterity. I guarantee that if you go with us he will console you and compensate you for your lost chattels, and you will find yourself possessed of wealth and gifts, slaves, and camels." Coveting the largesse of the aforementioned *makk*, my grandfather set off with them, hoping for joy and pleasure, and when they reached the Island of Sinnār, they took him to meet the *makk* and informed him that he was a man of learning and a stranger in their country, one whose ship had foundered on the main, leaving not a penny to his name. The *makk* welcomed him, made much of meeting him, assured him of a life of ease to come, congratulated him, put him up in his guesthouse, and ordered that the best of his favors be bestowed upon him. Among the things so bestowed was a gorgeous, superb, extremely valuable Abyssinian slave girl called Ḥalīmah. She was so beautiful my grandfather took her as his concubine and she bore him a boy and a girl as beautiful as she. The *makk* also allocated him an income. So my grandfather settled down in Sinnār, oblivious of his family and young sons in Tunis, now so far.

2.1.27 On his departure from Tunis, he had left behind three sons, as well as their mother. The oldest of them was my uncle, the late Sayyid Muḥammad, who was nine at the time; in the middle was my late lamented father, who was six; and the youngest was the late Sayyid Muḥammad Ṭāhir, who was three. This is what I heard from my father and my grandmother—may the clouds of God's mercy rain upon them—and I report this on their authority. Their maternal uncle, the exemplary, perfect, outstanding master, the expert in law, Hadith scholar, and adept of both the religious sciences and the literary arts, Sayyid Aḥmad, son of the scholar, traveler, and reliable source of hadiths, Sayyid Sulaymān al-Azharī, author of numerous works and informative compositions, then took care of them. Sayyid Aḥmad was a learned scholar, a trustworthy source, of unimpeachable authority, for the transmission of both hadiths and the law, who was offered a post as a judge in Tunis. This, though, he refused, being more concerned with teaching. Instead, he assumed a position at the college of law established by ʿAlī Pasha I, and this he stuck to. At the end of his life, he was afflicted by a chronic sickness, so he gave his lessons at home, and these were attended by the most advanced students and learned men. This uncle continued to look after my grandfather's sons until my father became an adolescent and attained manhood. My father had memorized the Qur'an and attended some classes in the religious sciences with his maternal uncle and others. While thus occupied, he was seized by a desire to make the pilgrimage, so he consulted his uncle about the journey, and his uncle was seized by the same desire. They therefore prepared themselves for the journey and sailed on the boat from Tunis to Alexandria, then to Cairo, and from Cairo they set off for al-Quṣayr.[58] This was before the pilgrimage months had begun.

While on the road with their caravan, another, coming from Sinnār, crossed their path, and someone called out to them, "You westerners, is there anyone with you from Tunis?" so my father said, "Yes. We're from there." The man said, "Do you know Sayyid Aḥmad ibn Sulaymān?" "Yes," said my father, "we know him. And who are you?" The man replied, "I am Aḥmad's kinsman by marriage. I left Tunis thus-and-so-many years ago, leaving behind my sons and my parents, and I have no idea whether they are alive or dead." My father's uncle was in a camel litter, lying down and out of sight, and he overheard all this and told my father, "ʿUmar, say 2.1.28

hello to your father!" and my father threw himself at his father's feet and greeted him, kissing his hand and informing him that his uncle was in the litter. Then my grandfather went and greeted his in-law. When the greetings were over, my father said to his father, "Is it nothing to you that you left us all this time without support, when we were still young, and that, if God in his generosity hadn't sent us our uncle, we would have been destitute?" "What was I to do," said his father, "when fate and destiny follow the courses set for them by the Divine Will?

What is decreed is a created fact that cannot be erased.
One is safe, though, from what has not been decreed."

Then my father asked his father, "Isn't it about time you returned to your country and gave us the joy of laying our eyes on you?" "So be it," said his father, "God willing." "When?" asked my father. "Right now," said the other, "I'm on my way to Cairo to sell the slaves I have with me. After that, I'll return to Sinnār, gather my belongings and my children, and come to Cairo. You are on your way to make the pilgrimage and will be returning to Cairo, so we'll meet there, and let the first to arrive wait for the other." Then he bade them farewell and each party went its way, as the words of the poet describe:[59]

Barely had I finished greeting him on his arrival
than I began bidding him farewell on his departure.

2.1.29 My father and his uncle then set off for the pilgrimage, while my grandfather set off for Cairo the Protected. There he sold his slaves, bought what he needed, and went back to Sinnār, while my father and his uncle made their way to the Hejaz and stayed in al-Ṭā'if until the time of the pilgrimage, when they proceeded to Mecca and performed the rites. After they'd done so, my uncle died in Ennobled Mecca and was buried at Bāb al-Muʿallā. My father returned to Cairo, only to find that his father wasn't there. He waited for him for a time, but the man never came. During this period, my father was attending lessons at the mosque of al-Azhar. When he grew tired of waiting, however, he set off for Sinnār with a caravan that had come from there. On his arrival, he found his father settled in his house, reveling in his children and dependents, giving no thought to anyone else and with no intention of leaving. My father asked him why he'd broken his promise—why for earnestness he'd substituted jest, and the man let fall an excuse too feeble for any to stoop to address, saying, "My son, some people owe me money and have been dilatory in paying it back. I cannot travel, whatever might befall, until I have received what I am owed, in total and in full, that my needs be provided for, even at the lowest level, and my backbone stiffened, at least enough to travel." My father stayed with him for about six months. Then a caravan prepared to depart for the land of Egypt, so he gave his father two options, saying, "A caravan is preparing to leave. Either you and I both go with it or you grant me permission to go alone." His father refused him on both counts, however, saying, "It is impossible for me to go myself because of the monies that I owe in Tunis, and all the more because word has reached me that your mother has married again. As to your going, so be it, but with another caravan, the Almighty willing, to give me time to assemble slaves, camels, gold, and merchandise, so that you don't return empty-handed." My father, though, refused to prolong his stay, saying, "I long to study, and by staying here I am wasting time with nothing to show for it." Their views differed, and a coolness arose between them.

My father left in a temper and set off with the caravan with nothing to his name, but three days later his father sent after him three camels along with four female slaves and two male, the camels bearing all the provisions and water he would need for the journey. One of the camels was loaded with gum arabic. My father took these things and continued with the caravan. On their way, they got lost[60] and were overtaken by thirst. They were late in reaching their destination, the slaves and the camels had died, and my father reached Cairo as poor as he had left it: 2.1.30

When the world looks with favor upon you, it can be led by a thread.
When it turns against you, it breaks chains.

Now, through the grace of God, Mighty and Sublime, the leader of the caravan happened to fall ill: he had a headache that prevented him from sleeping and no one could cure him. When news of this reached my father, he wrote something on a slip of paper[61] and the leader took it with faith in his heart, placed it on the place that hurt, and was immediately cured. He then became convinced that my father was one of the righteous, ordered that he be given a mount, and had a sack of gum arabic loaded onto his camel.

2.1.31 After all these tribulations, my father returned to Cairo, sold the sack of gum for seventy-five sequins, and enrolled at the mosque of al-Azhar to continue his studies. At that time too, he married my mother, with whom he lived for about two years, during which she bore him a boy whom he named Aḥmad, who lived for one year and three months and then died. Mourning for him, my father summed up the situation by quoting the words of the poet that go:

The days betrayed you and closed the gap
between the day of death and the night of nativity

and the words of another that go:

Marvel at a babe who died ere
he could see the days of childhood to an end—
As though, so selfless and good was he,
he gave his life back to his begetters, and died

and also the words of al-Tuhāmī on his son:

Ah star! How short its life—
but so it is with stars that rise at dawn.

2.1.32 My father then set off for Tunis, taking with him my mother and her mother, my mother being then pregnant. When he got there, he stayed in the house of his brother, the late Sayyid Muḥammad, who was a well-known shopkeeper in the market of the *shāshiyyah*—meaning the tarbush—makers. I was born five months later at the third hour of a Friday in mid-Dhū l-Qaʿdah of the year 1204.[62] My father stayed there three more years. Then a coolness developed between him and his two brothers, so in 1207 [1792–93] he took us by caravan to Cairo and studied at al-Azhar, where he attended the lessons of the late Erudite Shaykh ʿArafah al-Dusūqī al-Mālikī, and of our shaykh of shaykhs, the late Unique Scholar Shaykh Muḥammad al-Amīr al-Kabīr.[63] Then he assumed the deanship of the hall[64] of the Maghrebi *sayyid*s and became moderately well off. He continued like this until the beginning of 1211 [1796–97], when he received a letter from his half brother brought by the caravan from Sinnār, which read as follows: "Greetings. Know that our father has died and passed into the mercy of the Almighty. He left a quantity of books, but these were stolen from us by a man named Aḥmad al-Banzartī, in whose trust we had placed our house because he claimed to be related to our father. We now find ourselves in a position to bring pleasure to our enemies and disquiet to our friends. If this letter reaches you, hasten to us so that you can take us back with you and we can live the life you live. Farewell." When my father read the letter, he wept and shed tears and was overcome with pity for his brothers, so he hastened to them. I was seven years old at the time—I had been through the Qur'an once to learn it by heart and had gotten as far as the end of Āl ʿImrān[65] on the second time round; and I had a brother aged four. My father left us enough money to last six months, but we survived on it for a year, during which my mother sold much of her copperware and jewelry.

Then my youngest paternal uncle, the one called al-Ṭāhir, came and devoted himself to our upbringing. He had come for the pilgrimage[66] and to trade, and brought with him a son like a blazing sun in a clear sky, whose name was Muḥammad. He was about a year and a half older than me and used to go to Qur'an school with me, until his father took him to perform the pilgrimage at the end of 1212.[67] Then the French entered Cairo, taking it at the beginning 2.1.33

of 1213,[68] when my uncle was still with the pilgrims. The Turkish soldiery fled and were ripped to shreds, and the pilgrims returned to find the French in Egypt and its provinces. There they remained until the beginning of 1216 [May 1801], when the vizier came accompanied by his soldiers, and they left.[69] My aforementioned cousin had memorized the whole of the Qur'an and had begun to attend lectures in the higher sciences; he was extremely modest and polite. In the same year, epidemics broke out and they seized this cousin of mine, taking him from palace to grave; nay, to that place where he could sport forever with many a sloe-eyed maid.[70] When he died, his father grieved greatly; indeed, he almost perished of sorrow and was in such pain and anguish that he was on the verge of going to his own tomb—and may God extend His mercy to the poet who said:[71]

> People are to death as horses to a race—
> the first to arrive is in quality the first.
> Death's an assayer with gems in his hand
> from which he picks those of greatest worth.

He could not abide the thought of remaining in Egypt because it no longer contained his son, the apple of his eye—on which topic I myself have said:

> Should the beloved depart the homeland,
> For his absence, I should hate that homeland.

Consequently, he decided to seek relief from his pain and to dampen his anguish by making pilgrimage to God's Holy House and by looking on the tomb of His prophet, upon whom be blessings and peace—and how excellently he put it who said:[72]

> Shift your affections as you will,
> the only true love's the first.

And the Prophet, peace and blessings be upon him, said to the same effect, "If any of you is stricken by a catastrophe, let him remember the catastrophe with which he is stricken by loss of me, for that is the greatest of them all."

Bear patiently each mishap and endure
  and know that no man lives forever.
If stricken by the loss of a beloved
  remember what you have lost in the Prophet Muḥammad.

My uncle therefore went to the Hejaz, leaving me in Cairo to continue my studies at al-Azhar with enough money to last four months, but he stayed there longer than that. I ran out of money and could accomplish nothing—I was in the prime of my youth at the time—and found myself at a loss, not knowing what to do and scorning the idea of abandoning my studies and learning a craft. While thus at a loss and surviving in straitened circumstances due to my lack of wherewithal, I heard that a caravan had arrived from the Land of the Blacks, from Darfur—for which, we had heard earlier, my father had left Sinnār, accompanied by his brother. When the caravan had settled itself at the Caravanserai of the Jallābah,[73] I went there to ask after my father, to find out if he was still alive and might yet arrive, or had been placed in the bare-walled vault on his demise. By coincidence, I came across a man—elderly, imposing, and dignified—called Sayyid Aḥmad Badawī, who was with the caravan. I kissed his hand and stood before him for a while, until he asked me gently, "What do you want?" I replied, "I'm looking for a man I know who has disappeared into your country. Perhaps one of you knows him and can guide me to him." "Who is he?" he asked, "and what is his name?" "His name is Sayyid ʿUmar al-Tūnisī, and he is a man of learning," I replied. "It so happens that you've come upon one who knows him well!" he said. "He is my friend and no one knows him better than I. I see a resemblance in you to him. I think you must be his son." "I am," I answered, "though my outward appearance is changed, my inner self deranged." "Then what prevents you, dear boy," he next asked, "from setting off to seek your father and finding, when you meet him, joy?" "Lack of means," I 2.1.34

replied, "and of provisions and the necessary gear." "Your father," said the man, "is regarded by the sultan as a very great man and is among those to whom he is most generous, more than any other at his court. Should you wish to go to him, I'll take care of your provisions, your mount, and your comfort till you reach him and stand before him." "Do you really mean that?" I asked him. "By the life of the Messenger, I do!" he replied. "Your father once did me a favor I could never repay were I to spend all that I own, every penny I possess." "I am your obedient servant," I said, "and will follow you in everything." I therefore made a pact with him to that effect, and gave him my word then and there, and took to visiting him often until he was ready and told me, "Tomorrow we leave. Spend the night with us, if you like, so we can make an early start!" to which I replied, "That will I do, with all my heart!"

2.1.35 I spent the night at his lodgings in the most luxurious and comfortable of circumstances and best and happiest of states till morning came and the air was suffused with light. We rose for the prescribed prayer and performed it, and uncovered the camel litters and brought them out. Then the camels were brought and the loads put on them so that before the sun's disk could peep above the horizon, the loading was done and the golden-white camels had set off at an easy stride, which they kept up until they were kneeled at al-Fusṭāṭ,[74] on the banks of the Nile, and the men set about loading them onto the boat, till all were on board. Then we waited till we'd performed our Friday prayers behind the imam, and went on board, having bade Cairo salaam.

CHAPTER 2

The Journey from al-Fusṭāṭ to Darfur

On mounting our ash-gray she-camel[75] for this great journey, we declared, «In God's Name shall be its course and its berthing; surely my Lord is Merciful and Forgiving.»[76] Yet, as we set sail from the shore of al-Fusṭāṭ, heading for faraway places and distant lands, I thought of travel's travails and of the dangers that it brings, especially to those in a state of grinding poverty and harrowing hardship such as myself, and my heart filled with misgivings and distress, and I found myself overwhelmed by oppressive feelings and stress, all the more so because I found myself without any of my own race—among, indeed, nations of whose speech I understood but little and among whom I saw no cheerful, comely face. Tears welling, I recited: 2.2.1

> Your body, your clothes, and your countenance
> are black upon black upon black

and I regretted that I'd exposed myself to danger with the sons of Ḥām, recalling the antagonism that existed between them and the sons of Sām,[77] and was overcome by such panic as I cannot describe—so much so that I came close to asking if I might return to where I normally reside.

Then God's hidden graces caught me by surprise, and I remembered how eloquent literary tongues have spoken of journeying 2.2.2

with praise, and in particular the saying found among those attributed to the Creator of Humankind which goes, "Travel, and I will create a new source of livelihood for you." I recalled too that the Best of Humankind journeyed from Mecca to Syria,[78] and that scholars have said that "travel reveals a man's morals and divides the males from their ankleted sisters." Furthermore, it has been said that "were pearls never taken from their beds, they would ne'er adorn crowns" and "if the full moon didn't move, it would be forever on the wane." As says the poet:

> Travel, for pearls have moved and found themselves in crowns,
> and you too may reach the ranks of the noble and high.
> Likewise, the full moon, if it ne'er moved in its course,
> would be forever waning in the sky.

And another[79] says:

> Leave your lands and seek high station!
> Journey—for five good things come from travel:
> Escape from care, a way to earn your living,
> knowledge, savoir faire, and the friendship of the noble.
> Though some say travel means abjection in exile,
> and loss of friends and a life of trouble;
> Still, better a young man die than live
> in a land of ignominy, midst jealousy and tittle-tattle.

And how well al-Ṭughrāʾī[80] put it when he said:

> High Standing addressed me and spoke true:
> "Glory," said she, "lies in change of location.
> If hopes could be attained through nobility of domicile,
> the sun would never leave its ovine station."[81]

2.2.3 The point being that, had I stayed in Cairo in the state I was in, I would have met with nothing but evil. At this, I encapsulated my feelings in the words of that most excellent poet al-Ṭughrāʾī when he says:

Wherefore should I reside in Baghdad of the Concave Gates? I have no house there,
neither is my she-camel there, nor yet my he-camel![82]

And in the words of another, who says:[83]

Take yourself off from a land where you're despised
and on parting from your people do not mourn.
See you not that gold, in the mother lode, is but dust,
yet, when it travels, on men's necks is borne?

Thus did I reconcile myself to journeying to distant lands, though I be scorched in the doing by fiery brands.

We set off with a good wind that stayed with us through the day, our ship surging majestically to it in a wondrous way, moving, so fine it was, with a joyful sway, while it filled its sail, causing the ship to lengthen its stride as it pursued its way—and apropos of ships and how to describe their progress I'm reminded of my riddling poem that I addressed to Erudite Shaykh Muṣṭafā Kassāb,[84] the shaykh at the school of veterinary medicine established by His Excellency next door to the Medical School at Abū Zaʿbal, to wit:[85] 2.2.4

O Master, "Acquirer"[86] of knowledge and godliness,
O sea of wisdom that men find sweet to drink,
What's something three letters long
with which my rascally heart's enamored, tormented?[87]
It comes in the Revelation[88] and the matter's clear,
and such as you constantly recite it, and write it too.
It has another name, of letters five, that comes
in the feminine, men to delight.[89]
The one who pines goes into raptures at its sound, and his tears run down
and from its radicals the swiftly moving draws its name.[90]
Likewise, it has a name, well-known among humankind,
of four letters,[91] from which it's composed.

The thing of which I speak, erudite scholar, is but one[92]
and you are wise, so this can't from you be hidden.
The mount of my resolve,[93] an ash-gray she-camel, has reached you now,
you who are unique in your age, and the answer I ask.
The characteristics of that of which I speak have become renowned
as those of a pretty maid, a stealer of hearts:[94]
It struts when decked out and runs with great speed,[95]
but when stripped it fears to run and is dismayed.[96]
It bears what others find impossible to bear
and a cargo, O people, at which you wonder.[97]
When it runs, it moves on the flat of its back[98]
while its legs, for walloping, stick out on each side.[99]
It obeys the wind[100] while fearing the rising of the storm
while in the winds of love she revels, makes merry, and plays.
Enough then of my clues. Out with the answer,
for Your Eminence is still requested to provide the solution.

2.2.5 He, God preserve him, replied with the following:

O scholar who for his knowledge, wits,
and learning is by all other scholars loved,
Whose intelligence has been bruited both east and west,
and who puzzles the mind with verse refined—
And how could it not be so when he has mastered poesy in its entirety
and when all that is errant and ungraspable obeys his command?
Where in the works of Quss and Imru' al-Qays is one to find their like,
words like these, fit to excite lovers and send them into ecstasy?—
You have offered verses like the breeze in delicacy
(and any who claims them as his own is without doubt a liar)

And made your riddle on the name of a thing whose benefits to
the sea are everywhere,
that carries loads that exhaust and tire,
And that Noah took in hand and excelled at fashioning[101]—
Noah who was saved from the Flood while the waves played
And said, "Embark on it, for in God's name shall be its course
and likewise its berthing, so it will not sink!"[102]
Muḥammad al-Tūnisī's riddle now is solved—
a beacon of scholarship he, to whom great deeds are attributed and ascribed
And who forever produces from the fruits of his thinking
precious gems, unlike the grammarians' wrangles.

I also made up a riddle on the word *baḥr* ("sea"), saying: 2.2.6

To one proficient in the sciences and to whom
riddles are become obedient and have dropped their veil,
Say, God save you, what is three letters long
that names something by whose billows people are buffeted
And that, if you reverse it, means room[103] for any who come
and, if you wish, may be a past-tense verb,[104] not to be feared,
And if you omit the first of its letters,
then name it the antonym of "cold," that is, its opposite.[105]
If you scramble it, three meanings appear
—observe them, for this is a wondrous thing:
A leader in the sciences, and ink, and the third
of its meanings is something unpleasing to any afflicted by it[106]
And if you drop its second letter, then the opposite of its name
is what it becomes[107]—so the answer cannot be hard for you.

I also composed a riddle on the word *miṣbāḥ* ("lamp"), saying: 2.2.7

Do say, to one who has achieved good style and understanding
and to whom out of all humankind the Lord of the Throne
has granted knowledge,

"I'd give my father for you—what has five letters
whose benefits, Eminent Scholar, have extended to all mankind,
Small as a fingertip, if you measure its body,
yet which, despite its size, can fill a house most definitely?
When a breeze arises, it bends in ardent love,
and however much it is strengthened, it must die of its passion inevitably.
It is unique in excellent qualities with which it is raised to the heavens,
and the best of these is that it guides a person to his destination.
The longer its nose[108] gets, my friend, the sicker it becomes,
yet if it is trimmed, it revives and has no memory of its distress.
It shines brightly when deepest darkness descends, and when it sees
the sun risen in splendor, it becomes weak from shame.
Two letters, taken from its name, yield something much liked
from one whose lips are pretty, that is, a cool-saliva'ed lover.[109]
The remaining part is a past-tense verb (now exercise your wits!)
whose subject, if a person, merits censure.[110]
Throw out its first letter and you'll find that what
remains is a synonym of 'morrow,'[111] so be astute.
Enough clues have I given now, so out with the answer!
It comes also in the Revelation,[112] so look for it there! Now I'm done."

2.2.8 And I also made up a riddle on *al-samāʾ* ("the sky"), saying:

You who have risen to the heavens of knowledge and wisdom
and whose bounty has come to pour down like steady rains,
Reveal to us the name of a thing the sight of which brings pleasure
and whose beauty is clear to both Arabs and others,

Though it is of such a height that none alight there
save those who have been rewarded by the creator of life.
Out of it lamps[113] appear and brightly burn,
providing guidance for us in gloomy darkness.
We delight in its shining dazzling beauty
because it is mentioned in the Revelation,[114] with its wise words.
It is composed of four letters when written out
one after the other. Take note of the ordering and the wording!
Now I'm done—please provide an answer nice and clear,
may you ever continue, great scholar, to aspire to greatness!

Remembering these riddles made me think of one by that ne plus ultra of critics, the Shāfiʿī imam Ibn Ḥajar, God have mercy on him, on the word *mudām* ("wine"), which goes as follows: 2.2.9

What is a thing whose insides are a disease[115]
And whose first and last are the same.
If its last is taken away, it's a plural[116]
which would have an edge, and likewise sharpness![117]
And if you ignore its first, it's a verb,[118]
capable of being either imperfect or subjunctive.

But let us here rein in our pen, halt its gallop across this maidan—for were I to follow the track of everything I've composed by way of poems and riddles, it would take forever and be conducive to torpor—and return to our topic.

We therefore declare: in the evening the breeze died down, it ceased to gust, and neither northerly nor southerly remained. We were opposite al-Minyā, where there was a gang of Turkish soldiers whom God had relieved of the garments of glory.[119] They seized us by naked force and compelled our ship to pull in to shore. Their camp was pitched in the open space between the town and the Nile, and there they resided so that they could plunder passing voyagers. They made our friend pay a large sum of money. When we were released, we set sail again immediately. 2.2.10

2.2.11 On the third day, we alighted at Manfalūṭ,[120] from which we took what we needed, then sailed until we came to Banī ʿAdī, where we stayed while the caravan equipped itself, the men sewing the water-skins and putting together their provisions. Then the camels were brought, their loads loaded, and we set off across an arid waste. On the evening of the fifth day, we reached al-Khārijah, which we found to be surrounded by palm groves—as a leg by an anklet is encased, or the beloved's cloak by the hands of a lover seeking an embrace. It is full of the most delicious and beautiful dates; their price is low, and their quality excellent. We stayed there for five days, departed on the morning of the sixth, and proceeded for about two days, alighting on the third at a town called Abīrīs[121]—a settlement overtaken by ruin due to rulers' tyranny, its people scattered when once they lived a life of harmony; its palm groves therefore are now in disrepair, the splendor gone from what was once so fair.

2.2.12 We stayed there for two days, until our mounts had recovered and cast off their fatigue, then traveled two days and on the third set up camp at a town called Būlāq, whose inhabitants have been reduced to poverty.[122] Most of its landmarks have disappeared and most of its finest and most celebrated buildings are full of cracks. An odd thing is that its palm trees are extremely short: when they bear dates the gatherer doesn't have to go to the trouble of climbing—he can simply pick them by hand, even lying on his back. Its name made me think of the Būlāq of Cairo the Protected, may God secure her from every infestation and disaster, and my tears poured out, my passion, love, and yearning were excited, and I declaimed:

I thought of Būlāq and of Cairo and its people,
moved by this other Būlāq to recollection.
I beg you, O my eye, come to my aid with tears
that haply my heart may cool once more, after its incineration!

Then we traveled some more, pressing on hard without hesitation till we made camp on the evening of the same day in a town called al-Maqs: 2.2.13

> And many a town there is that holds no friendly presence,
> only the antelope, only the white-gold camel.

It's said that this was once a most flourishing town. Then it went the way of Lubad,[123] its people were scattered, and no one remained. It has few trees, mainly kinds of tamarisk. We stayed there two days, filled our waterskins, and set off again, entering now into the true desert, and we continued for five days in arid wastes and a dust-blown wilderness in which the only plants were a little camel-thorn, and where no trees suitable as resting places were to be found. During this period, our cooking was done using whatever dry camel dung the servants could glean, there being so little by way of vegetal matter on which to depend for help. On the evening of the fifth day, we reached a place called al-Shabb[124] (set among sandy dunes o'er which the lonesome zephyr croons). We rested there two days, then departed, and our entry into the next desert started.

This we crossed, moving now fast, now slow, over a space of four 2.2.14
days, setting up camp on the forenoon of the fifth at a well called Salīmah. At this well are ancient buildings. It lies opposite a mountain of the same name. We stayed there two days till we had rested, for it is one of the peculiarities of the place that anyone who alights there settles down comfortably and feels no unease. A wonder to be noted is that the young men of the caravan climb to the top of the mountain there and strike the stones with small sticks, as one would a drum, and the stones make drumlike sounds. No one knows why this is so—because of cavities in the stones, or because they are set over empty spaces; glory to Him who knows the truth of the matter! The people with the caravan told me that on certain nights—I think they said on the night preceding each Friday—the sounds of drums would be heard coming from the mountain, as though a wedding were taking place, and no one knows the explanation.[125]

2.2.15 Early on the morning of the third day, after filling the waterskins, we set off again and entered a desert through which we traveled for five days, arriving in the late morning of the sixth at a place called Laqiyyah, where we found wells with sweet clear water amid the sands. Before we reached it, a caravan coming from the natron well called al-Zaghāwī crossed our path,[126] the people of the caravan being Arabs of the tribe known as al-ʿAmāyim. They received us with greetings, then left us in peace. We stayed two days in Laqiyyah, and set off early on the morning of the third, making for al-Zaghāwī, crossing paths on the way with a rider on a swift camel coming from Darfur, who informed us of the death of the late just and glorious monarch, Sultan ʿAbd al-Raḥmān al-Rashīd, king of Darfur and its dependencies, sultan of its farthest and nearest reaches. The rider said he was on his way to Cairo to have a new seal ring made for the sultan's son, Sultan Muḥammad Faḍl, as there was no one in Darfur with the skills to do so. It was of the sort with which the sultan's commands are stamped.[127] The sultan had died early in the month of Rajab the Separate, 1218 [October 17–November 16, 1803]. The people of the caravan mourned the death of their sultan and feared the outbreak of conflict in their lands, as he had been a just and generous sultan who loved scholarship and those who practice it and hated ignorance and those who pursue it.[128] We shall speak later, God Almighty willing, of his justice and his rule, and in the most expansive terms.[129]

2.2.16 We traveled on from there for five days, kneeling our camels on the sixth at Bīr al-Zaghāwī, also called Bīr al-Malḥah,[130] which is a full ten days' travel from Darfur. We stayed there eleven days putting ourselves to rights and resting, while our animals grazed so as to be strong enough for the crossing of that forbidding waste. During our stay, many meat camels were slaughtered and their flesh distributed among the people of the caravan, and we met with desert Arabs from Darfur, who brought us camel's milk and clarified butter, and from whom we bought what we needed. They come to this well to get salt and natron for Darfur, since all the natron and most of the salt is brought from there and there alone. Before alighting at al-Zaghāwī, our caravan had sent a rider on a fast camel ahead to Darfur with papers addressed to the state and its inhabitants informing them of our coming and of the caravan's safe return. I too sent a letter, addressed to my father, of which the following is the text:

> To my honored father and the dearest person to me, ʿUmar al-Tūnisī, may God preserve his life, amen. I first kiss your noble hands, then inform you that I have come with the caravan led by Khabīr Faraj Allāh in the company of your dear friend Sayyid Aḥmad Badawī, who for your sake has shown me such kindnesses as are too numerous to describe to Your Excellency. Farewell. Signed, your son, Muḥammad ʿUmar ibn Sulaymān.

The camel rider took the papers and set off right away. And here I have to say that in all my travels, I never had an easier journey, or one on which I enjoyed greater comfort. This was because, on our departure from Banī ʿAdī, Sayyid Aḥmad Badawī ordered his slaves to put my tent on the calmest camel and make it kneel nicely for mounting. They did so, and he took my hand and placed in it the camel's reins. He also ordered them to bring a canteen full of water, which they did, and it was hung on the camel. "This is your camel," he said, "Ride it whenever you want and dismount whenever you want. Drink from this canteen whenever you need to, and whenever it becomes empty tell one of the slaves to fill it for you." And he ordered all the slaves and servants to obey me in this. 2.2.17

He had with him seven adult male slaves and one young one, plus eight servants. He also had sixty-eight camels, of which eight were equipped to carry water, four to carry provisions;[131] on moving into the desert, two skins of water would be hung on each camel. He also had five concubines with him and a sixth woman, his niece, Mistress Jamāl, a most beautiful woman. He also had a black stallion from Dongola,[132] of a beauty beyond price, which wore a saddle with a 2.2.18

green velvet saddlecloth and was led by its own special slave. Sayyid Aḥmad treated me as kindly as a father would his son: when the caravan set up camp I would sometimes fall asleep, exhausted by the riding, the rocking of the camel, and the heat of the sun, and he would cover me with a blanket. Then, when dinner was brought, he would wake me gently and call for water and wash my face and hands and tell me to rinse out my mouth to wake myself up, and he would take my hands and place them on the dish and on occasion take food and place it in my mouth. He treated me like this all the while until we had safely arrived.

2.2.19 Then we left Bīr al-Zaghāwī. We pressed on hard for ten days, spending the first part of the night in travel and marching likewise in the last part, until, in the late morning of the eleventh day, we reached al-Mazrūb, which is a well in the first district of Darfur. Some three or four hours before we got there we were met by Bedouin with skins of water and milk who were filled with joy at our safe arrival. We alighted at the aforementioned well and stayed there the rest of the day. Early on the following morning, we proceeded for about four hours and arrived at a well called al-Suwaynah,[133] where we were met by its governor, "Malik" Muḥammad Sanjaq by name; he is the leader of the Zaghāwah, who are a mighty tribe among the blacks, in whose lands the people refer to a tribal leader as Malik, meaning "king." He had with him a massive army, of around five hundred horsemen, I think. The governor greeted the people of the caravan and congratulated them on their safe arrival. We stayed there two days,[134] then left, and everyone dispersed, each party taking the road that led to its own country, for not all the people of the caravan were from the same place. Most of them were from a town well-known there called Kūbayh, some from Kabkābiyyah, some, like my friend Sayyid Aḥmad, from Sarf al-Dajāj, some from al-Shaʿīriyyah, some from Jadīd Karyū, and some from Jadīd al-Sayl.[135]

2.2.20 Everyone went his own way, and we took the road to Sarf al-Dajāj, making easy going for about three days and alighting around noon on the fourth in the shadow of a mountain close to a well, where we took a siesta. Many came to congratulate us on our arrival. Badawī, Sayyid Aḥmad's son, appeared too, accompanied by slaves and servants with large quantities of food. He greeted his father and congratulated him on his safe arrival, and we lunched—staying till day had begun to wane and yellow to o'ertake the setting sun, turning all to flame. Then the loads were loaded, the burdens hoisted, and by the time sunset had arrived, we were atop the backs of our trusty steeds and moving down the track. Thus we entered Sarf al-Dajāj after the evening prayer:

> Then she threw down her stick, her destination thereby settling,
> just as the traveler's eye finds settled comfort on his return.

We spent an uncomfortable night, what with so many well-wishers and others coming in and out, despite which Sayyid Aḥmad didn't forget me or allow himself to be distracted from me. On the contrary, he gave me my own room and filled it with all the bedding and vessels I could need. I was unaware of this, and when I felt I had stayed up long enough, I went to him and asked, "Where am I to sleep?" He called one of his slaves, told him, "Show your master his room," and the man took me and led me into a room where I found a bed, bedding, and vessels—everything indeed that I might need. I spent a very comfortable night, and when morning came I got dressed and went to see him. I found him sitting in great splendor among his servants, slave women, and children, as settled and happy as though he'd never left.

He welcomed me warmly and I kissed his hand and sat with him. 2.2.21
"My nephew," he said, "young Sayyid Aḥmad, is putting on a welcome banquet today and has asked me to invite you to honor his gathering hall with your presence. If you have the energy, and would like to oblige him, it's up to you. I don't want you to put yourself to any trouble." "I hear and obey," I said, "but I don't know his house," so he ordered one of his young male slaves to show me the house. I attended his party and he welcomed me and made a great fuss over

me—it was a great day. Then everyone who had been in the caravan started putting on banquets one after another, and they'd invite me to every banquet and I'd go. This went on until my uncle arrived and I set off with him to see my father.

2.2.22 This came about as follows: I'd been at a party given by some friends. I came home close to evening and entered the room that had been prepared for me to find two men and two slaves. One of the men was short and dark-complexioned, his color about that of an Ethiopian, well-dressed and in handsome clothes. The other was black and shabbily dressed. I greeted them, they returned my greeting, and I sat down, wondering how they could enter my room without my permission. Then I noticed them winking at one another and one said to the other, "Is that him?" "Yes," the other replied, "that's him," though I didn't know why they said this. Then the first man asked me, "Are you from here?" "No," I answered, "I'm from Cairo and have come to look for my father." "And who is your father?" he asked. "My father is Sayyid ʿUmar al-Tūnisī," I replied.

2.2.23 The black-skinned man said, "Salute your uncle, Sayyid Aḥmad Zarrūq,"[136] so I saluted him and he showed me a letter that said:

> Greetings. We have received a letter from our son, Sayyid Muḥammad, informing me that he has come here in your company and that you have done him the kindnesses we would expect of you—may God reward you with good fortune for what you have done for us! This is an act of generosity for which I can scarcely find words to thank you, one I shall never be able to repay. It is well known that the exchange of gifts is a custom practiced from the beginning of time, and that the Lord of ʿAdnān's Offspring[137] accepted presents. This is why he said, may he enjoy the blessings of our Ever-Generous Lord, "Give each other presents and you will love each other, and the rancor will leave your hearts." I have sent your honored person, in the company of my brother Sayyid Aḥmad Zarrūq, two *sudāsī* slaves[138]

and a red foal. I hope Your Excellency will accept them, though they are more in keeping with my station than with yours—and how well the poet put it when he said:

The lark on parade day to Sulaymān came[139]
and gave him a locust it had in its beak.
Then with nature's tongue[140] it spoke these words:
"Gifts are proportionate to the giver, be he mighty or meek.
If each according to his worth were given,
your gift would be the World and all you therein seek!"

Greetings from us to you, to your children, to the people of your household, and to all who fill your happy assembly.

Sayyid Aḥmad Zarrūq then said to me, "Take this letter and read it to your uncle Sayyid Aḥmad,"[141] so I did, taking along the gift, which he saw and expressed thanks for. Then he said, "I accept it and give it to this son of mine," meaning me. My uncle and I insisted that he should take the gift but he refused any such thing, saying, "Were I to spend every penny I own on making him happy, it would not repay his father for the kindnesses he has shown me." At this, I was so bold as to say to him, "For the Almighty's sake, do please tell me about this kindness that my father did for you!" "You should know, dear boy," he replied, "that my enemies spread false rumors about me to His Highness the Sultan, to the effect that I was selling free men as slaves, and they painted such a picture of me that it became fixed in his mind that it was true. He was furious and said, 'That a merchant as rich as he should do such a thing! Poverty is more fitting for him.' They brought me from my house in disarray and when I entered his presence, he upbraided me and chided me harshly. I asked for an investigation into what had been said about me but was unable to secure this, and he wouldn't listen to a word I said. On the contrary, he ordered that I be seized, that chains be placed around my neck, and that I be confined to jail. 2.2.24

2.2.25 "It was a blessing from the Almighty that your father was present at the gathering, as the sultan was so furious with me that no one had the courage to intercede on my behalf. When your father saw this, he came forward, cleared his throat, quoted hadiths concerning pardon for offenders, and recited: «Believers, if an evildoer brings you news, ascertain the correctness of the report fully.»[142] Then he interceded for me, and the sultan accepted his intercession and ordered that I be released. Later, he realized I was innocent, but if God hadn't at that moment used your father as His instrument, I would have lost my life and all my money. What favor could be greater than that, or what action of greater import? Yet, despite all this, your father's true reward for what he did for me will come from God. For a long time now I have been waiting for some need of his to come to my attention so that I might satisfy it for him, and the only thing to have been vouchsafed me is this service. Perhaps, by fulfilling it, I have discharged some of the duty that I owe, though I do not believe so."

2.2.26 My uncle wanted to set out the morning of the next day, but Sayyid Aḥmad refused to allow this, so we stayed three more days. Early on the morning of the fourth I went to see him and say goodbye. He gave me a large supply of the beads that the women of the Blacks put around their waists as a kind of adornment and which they call *ruqād al-fāqah*, meaning "restful sleep." He also gave me another costly kind of bead that they place around their necks, which is of various types. One type is called *rīsh*; these are elongated white beads with brown stripes; they are known by the same name in Egypt. Another kind is called *manṣūṣ*; these are round, flattened, yellow beads made of amber. A further kind is a matte-red bead of rounded shape called *ʿaqīq*; he gave me enough of these for more than two necklaces, with a value of around three hundred slaves. He also gave me a new turban of green muslin, as well as some spikenard and mahaleb and a great quantity of sandalwood, which are three aromatic substances the women of the Blacks use to perfume themselves. "Divide these things up among your father's womenfolk," he told me, "and slaughter a ewe on our behalf and roast it on hot stones" (in their language[143] this is called *naṣīṣ*). He added even more things of the same sort to our supplies and bade us farewell and we mounted.

My uncle had another slave with him, so I rode the horse, my uncle rode a camel, the other man rode a tall donkey, and the slave ran in front of us. We proceeded thus, heading for where my father was, a place called Abū l-Judūl, six days' journey from Sarf al-Dajāj. We exited Sarf al-Dajāj and passed by the town called Kabkābiyyah, which resembles a town of the Egyptian Delta, though more prosperous and fertile, its streets thronged with inhabitants, its people rich merchants with slaves too many to count.[144] They have palm groves and extensive lands, with wells whose water is close to the surface. On these lands, they grow vegetables and pulses such as okra, Jew's mallow, squash, eggplant, long cucumber, pumpkin, onions, fenugreek, cumin, pepper, and cress, all of them in the varieties with which we are familiar, except for the pepper, which has a small berry slightly fatter than barley. They also have some lemon trees. Next to them is a mountain range called Jabal Marrah, which runs a straight course through the middle of the Fur region from beginning to end and through which run several roads people use to climb it. Each part of the range has its own name, different from the overall name. The Fur live at the top and know nothing of the lowlands; indeed, they believe that doing so is safer for them and their properties. We shall explain this point in greater detail below.[145] 2.2.27

When passing through Kabkābiyyah, we found its market in full swing, so we bought everything we needed there. Then we set off again and traveled for three days across Jabal Marrah, spending the night in the towns of wild peoples who hate guests, especially if they're Arabs. We had to put up with a great deal of aggravation from them; so much so that in the end we were staying overnight in their towns against their will, even though we had our own provisions and needed nothing from them—it was just in their natures to hate us. After this, we descended to the plain, where we spent 2.2.28

one night in a place called Tărne, where they treated us well, putting on a huge party for us. Late in the morning of the sixth day, we entered the town my father was in, called Ḥillat Jūltū, one of the villages of Abū l-Judūl. At the gate of my father's house, we found the horses, donkeys, and servants of some guests who were visiting him. We entered the house, passing by male and female slaves, who greeted us and congratulated us on our safe arrival. After his guests had mounted, my father came out to greet me. I rose, kissed his hand, and stood before him at his service. He ordered me to sit and I did. He asked me what professional skills I had acquired and I said, "The Qur'an and a certain amount of scholarship." This pleased him, and the second day after my arrival he put on a banquet for which he slaughtered several ewes and cows. He invited everyone, so large numbers came and ate, and it was a happy day.

2.2.29 Three days later, my father provisioned my uncle and me for the journey to the Sultanic Portals,[146] bearing gifts for the Sultan's noble person, for the Grand Vizier (who at that time was Shaykh-Father Muḥammad Kurrā[147]), and for Faqīh Mālik al-Fūtāwī,[148] who was my father's agent and in charge of all my father's business with the state.[149] He belonged to a tribe called the Fullān, whom the Darfurians call the Fallātah (though Fallātā, ending in a long *ā*, is more correct). This Faqīh Mālik was the greatest of the viziers of Arab descent.[150] In those days, Sultan Muḥammad Faḍl, son of the late Sultan ʿAbd al-Raḥmān, was young and the management of affairs was entirely in the hands of Shaykh-Father Muḥammad Kurrā, whose last name means "the Tall" in the language of the Fur; it was he who supported the claim of Sultan Muḥammad Faḍl after his father's death, placed him on his throne, and, in view of his young age, acted as his regent in making rulings and managing the realm. A rumor has spread on the tongues of the Darfurians that he had once been a slave of the sultan, but that is not the case. The truth is he was a freeborn man who served the sultan, grew rich in his service, dealt with the burden of affairs, and eventually rose to the grand vizierate through his good management, one who controlled the

Darfurian realm to the point that no word, after that of the sultan, carried greater weight than his.[151] He possessed, God have mercy on his soul, a shrewdness, cunning, courage, boldness, and vigor in the execution of affairs that ensured that his intentions were seen through. His history, along with those of Sultan ʿAbd al-Raḥmān, his son Sultan Muḥammad Faḍl, and the former's brother Sultan Muḥammad Tayrāb, will be told in detail, God Almighty willing.[152]

On the first of Shaʿbān, 1218 [November 16, 1803], we rode from Abū l-Judūl to Tandaltī, the seat of the sultanate. Such a seat is known in their language as a *fāshir*: any place where the sultan resides is called a *fāshir*.[153] We traveled at an easy pace for two days and entered the place on the morning of the third to find a town teeming with people—some mounted, some on foot, some seated, some coming, some going, with drums thundering and horses galloping. We entered the house of Faqīh Mālik and found him sitting among his servants and entourage, surrounded by those who had business to conduct with him. We approached, my uncle saluted him, and he welcomed us with much ceremony. My uncle told him who I was, and he greeted me, smiled at me, and welcomed me. Then my uncle gave him the letter addressed to him and the letters addressed to the government. He read his letter, welcomed us, and had a private room assigned to us in which to put our things. Then he took us right away to the house of the Shaykh-Father Muḥammad Kurrā, which had at its gate horses and other riding animals too many to count. We went in and found him sitting in a crowded gathering hall surrounded by the chief officers of the state. He greeted us but didn't know who I was, so he asked, "Who is that?" and Faqīh Mālik answered. "This is the son of Sharif ʿUmar al-Tūnisī, the scholar who lives at Abū l-Judūl. He's sent him with his uncle to salute Your Excellency; this is a letter from his father." The shaykh-father took the letter and opened it, and once he'd read it, talked to us indulgently and spoke kind words to us, out of respect for my father. I presented him with the gift, and he accepted it, ordered that it be put away in his treasure house, and 2.2.30

went on conversing indulgently and kindly to us out of respect for my father. Then he ordered Faqīh Mālik to keep us at his house until he gave us leave to go, so we remained at Faqīh Mālik's three days, during which we enjoyed the most generous hospitality and delightful company.

2.2.31 On the fourth day, Shaykh-Father Muḥammad Kurrā summoned us through Faqīh Mālik and presented me with a green cashmere shawl,[154] a green open-fronted gown, and a caftan of Indian cotton, and commanded that I be given two girl slaves and a male. He also wrote a letter to my father that I read to him later, and which went as follows:

> From one to whom the Generous Lord has been generous and who is never without His blessings and favors, Grand Vizier Shaykh-Father Muḥammad Kurrā, who places his trust in Him who hears and sees all, to the Grand Teacher and Most Eminent Refuge, the Erudite Scholar of the Age, the Flower of the Progeny of the Lord of 'Adnān's Offspring,[155] Sharif 'Umar al-Tūnisī, may his glory last forever, amen. Your most noble son has come to us, accompanied by your respected and venerated brother, bringing the gifts you have sent us as set out in your letter. We have thus experienced the utmost joy, for two reasons: first, that you have been reunited with the apple of your eye, and second (and this is the burden of what we intend to convey) because we place high hopes on your presence in our land, that we may experience grace through you, O People of the House.[156] He bears with him what we have presented to him and we hope you find it acceptable. Were we not so busy, more would have been done to show our esteem. Our excuses, then, to you, and we hope that you will not deprive us of the benefit of your prayers. And may peace be upon you and the mercy of God and His blessings.

Then Faqīh Mālik presented me with a perky-breasted slave girl and a letter, which I also read later and which went as follows: 2.2.32

> Greetings. Your letter has reached us, accompanied by your son and your brother, and we have presented them to the honored Shaykh-Father Muḥammad Kurrā. He experienced such joy at the coming of your son as only God can understand, as his letter will make clear to you, we being even more overjoyed than he in view of the affection that exists between us. What Shaykh-Father Muḥammad Kurrā presented to him will be handed over to you and will be yours to dispose of. I myself have presented him with a slave called Ḥumaydah,[157] a distressed damsel, *kawʿabah matrabah*, for a slave—

He should have said *kāʿibah* for the first word, while *matrabah*, as used here, has no meaning. This was due to the Faqīh's ignorance. These words, i.e., *kāʿibah* and *matrabah*, occur in the Qurʾan in descriptions of the houris of Paradise.[158] The Faqīh wanted to be reckoned a scholar, but committed an error and produced nonsense.

> Perhaps she will be regarded with approval, which is our hope. Farewell.

We then took all these things and set off in high spirits to return to my father, who rejoiced at our arrival. Thereafter, we stayed together for the whole of Ramadan. When the month was over, my father set off for the seat of the sultan, to make his salutations. He met the Shaykh-Father Muḥammad Kurrā and requested permission to leave for Tunis to see his mother and brothers and be together with them before his mother died. He informed him that he would leave me in his house and on his lands, because the town he was in was one of the fiefs[159] granted to him by the late Sultan ʿAbd al-Raḥmān before his death. Before that he'd granted him villages in the area called Qirlī, but my father had refused to live 2.2.33

there because its inhabitants spoke a different language and had no knowledge of Arabic,[160] so the sultan transferred him to this place. The fief embraced three villages—Ḥillat Jūltū, where our house was, al-Dibbah, and Umm Baʿūḍah. He agreed with Shaykh-Father Muḥammad Kurrā that he would leave me on these lands, to collect their tax and reap the benefits of farming them. Then my father gave the shaykh-father pledges that he would return, and the shaykh-father gave him permission to leave, writing for him a number of orders addressed to the tax collectors along his route that instructed them to give him everything he needed and send mounted soldiers with him to escort him to the next safe place. My father bade him farewell and returned to us, his mind preoccupied with travel.

2.2.34 My father equipped himself in the shortest possible time, achieving this by selling his cotton; he had a lot of it, around a hundredweight, because he'd sown a piece of land, of more than twenty feddans by the Egyptian measure, from which he would gather fourteen *rééka*s every day at the height of the cotton season, the *rééka* being in Darfurian parlance what they call a *quffah* in Egypt; if one were to fill it with grain, it would perhaps take around five *rubʿ*s as these are measured in Egypt.[161] All of this he sold, and he also sold a sheep pasture and likewise the cattle and the donkeys. He took all his female and male slaves and everything I'd been given by Sayyid Aḥmad Badawī and Shaykh-Father Muḥammad Kurrā and left me only a female slave with cataracts in both eyes called Farḥānah, plus two male slaves and their wives, a donkey, and a weak riding camel. He also left with me one of his wives, called Zuhrah, and his brother's wife, each of whom had a daughter. And he sold the granaries, leaving me only one, and gave me the deed to the fief that had been written for him by the late Sultan ʿAbd al-Rahmān when he'd granted him the land.[162] It went as follows:

> From the Grand Sultan and Most Eminent Refuge, sultan of the Arabs and the non-Arabs, in whose grasp are the necks of the nations, sultan of the two lands and the two

> seas, servitor of the two noble sanctuaries, who places his trust in the solicitude of the King who creates and recreates, Sultan ʿAbd al-Raḥmān al-Rashīd, to the petty kings, governors, *shartays*, *dimlijs*, sons of sultans, tax collectors, and people of the sultan's realm, be they Arabs or Blacks. Now, the above-named sultan—by God blessed, aided, made victorious, and supported—has deigned to extend his assistance to Erudite Scholar Sharif ʿUmar al-Tūnisī and grant him a parcel of land located at Abū l-Judūl and embracing the three villages of Ḥillat Jūltū, al-Dibbah, and Umm Baʿūḍah, according to their recognized boundaries and frontiers as demarcated by Malik Jawhar for Malik Khamīs ʿArmān,[163] no subject of the realm being permitted to stand against him or challenge his right to these places, and specifically not those who collect the tax on the staple grains.[164] This is his to administer in any way he wills, as a gift for the sake of Almighty God and in the hope of reward in the Hereafter. Beware and beware again of any disagreement or objection, from noble or commoner!

Then my father loaded up his belongings, took his slaves, his troop of soldiers, and his brother, and set off, leaving me on my own in the village.[165]

In the month of Rajab 1219 [October–November 1804], Shaykh-Father Muḥammad Kurrā was killed in a great battle that broke out between him and Sultan Muḥammad Faḍl. Shaykh-Father Muḥammad Kurrā's enemies had driven a wedge between him and the sultan, using intrigue and slander and telling the latter that the shaykh-father wanted to wrest the kingdom from his hands and place over it his own brother, Báási ʿAwaḍ Allāh.[166] The atmosphere between them was fraught and the sultan and his men schemed to arrest him.[167] This was not easily done, however, as the shaykh-father had secluded himself and his men in another compound that belonged to him in Tandaltī, far from that of the sultan. The sultan 2.2.35

sent someone to bring him in but he refused to go. When the sultan and his men could find no way to arrest him and he refused to obey their demands, they cut off his water supply and for three days he drank from Jadīd al-Sayl. When his men could stand the thirst no longer, they told him, "We're thirsty and don't have the animals or waterskins to bring us enough water—either take us to some other place, where there's water for us to drink, or come up with some other plan."

2.2.36 So he and his soldiery mounted and set off for al-Rahad, which is the pool at Tandaltī.[168] There he found a guard sent by the sultan's government with a mass of soldiery, barring their way. This was Malik Muḥammad Daldan, son of Sultan Muḥammad Faḍl's aunt. The shaykh-father killed him and his men in a dreadful slaughter. When the sultan's men heard about this, they set out against him and a battle broke out. The sultan's men were exposed—this was at noon on the Thursday—and the sultan, fearing for his safety, fled to Jadīd al-Sayl: it was a day that went against, not for, the sultan and his men. The fighting continued until evening, at which point Shaykh-Father Muḥammad Kurrā pitched camp with his men along the stream and the sultan's men pitched camp on the other side, opposite them, waiting for morning. During the night, the shaykh-father inspected his men and discovered that his brother, Báási ʿAwaḍ Allāh, had been killed in the battle. He was grief-stricken and said, "For whom shall I fight when my brother, the person dearest to me, is dead?" Among those who had taken up arms with him was Báási Ṭāhir, son of Sultan Aḥmad Bukur, uncle of Sultan Muḥammad Faḍl, to whom he had pledged allegiance as sultan. This was a ruse by the shaykh-father to ensure that the Darfurians wouldn't regard him with aversion, for it was their custom that only someone who was the offspring of a royal personage from their sultanate's ruling family should rule over them.

2.2.37 When the shaykh-father learned of the death of his brother, he said to those around him, "I have come to hate this life. Tomorrow I forbid you to fight! Let me enter the battle and you save yourselves."

When word of this got out, all his despicable soldiers fled and the only ones left were his relatives, who made up a small band not exceeding a thousand in number, or a little more. When morning came, the war drums sounded and the sultan's men mounted. The shaykh-father mounted too, in the midst of his men. They went into battle with him and the fighting began. The shaykh-father plunged into the midst of the sultan's men, breaking through the ranks till no one stood between him and the sultan—had he wanted to kill him he could have. However, he remembered the sultan's kindnesses toward him and stayed his hand, standing before him for a little while and addressing him as follows, "You son of a whore, would you listen to the lies people tell about me? Is this how you reward me?" At that moment, the sultan, fearing for his life at his hands and seeking to flee, called out, "He has come to kill me!" and people closed in on him from all sides and formed a circle around him, tight as a ring on a finger. Finding none to come to his aid, the shaykh-father fought them with all his might, killing several champions and sustaining only light wounds, to which he paid no heed. For their part, they were afraid that one of his own men would reach him and that he would escape them, even though all his men had been cut off from him and he was alone among the enemy. He therefore set to and fought them for about an hour. When they failed to reach him, they hamstrung his horse, which fell to the ground. He could not get up because of the weight—he was wearing two suits of chain mail—and they fell upon him in great numbers with spears and with swords until they had killed him, may God have mercy on his soul.[169] After his death, they stripped him and found on his body around a hundred wounds, sword blows, and lance thrusts. His wife's son, Muḥammad Shīlfūt,[170] returned, thinking he would find him alive and be able to save him, but he found he'd been killed, so he unsheathed his sword and plunged into their midst, killing a number of champions and calling out, "Revenge for Shaykh-Father Muḥammad Kurrā!" In the end, they fell upon him, and he too perished, but only after he'd killed more than twenty of those present.

2.2.38 Now that we've spoken of how Shaykh-Father Muḥammad Kurrā was killed, let us speak of his beginnings and of his rise to power. Let me also pass in review the sultans of Darfur according to the information we received from trustworthy informants among the people there and what I was told by most of their old people. Sultan Muḥammad Faḍl was the son of Sultan ʿAbd al-Raḥmān, son of Aḥmad Bukur. It is said that Sultan Aḥmad Bukur had seven sons—ʿUmar,[171] Abū l-Qāsim, Rīz, Rīfā, Tayrāb, Ṭāhir, and ʿAbd al-Raḥmān, known as the Orphan because his father died and left him while he was still in the womb. When death was close, Sultan Aḥmad Bukur gathered the high officers of the state and bestowed the succession on all his sons, who were each to rule the country, one after the other in order of age, and made it a condition that none of their children should take over until all the fathers were dead. Thus, when Aḥmad Bukur died, the oldest of them, ʿUmar, became the ruler. He reigned for seven years. He was killed in a battle between him and Sultan Jawdah,[172] sultan of Dār Ṣulayḥ, also known as Dār Wāddāy and Dār Barqū.[173] Then his brother al-Qāsim succeeded him and he too was killed in a war with the sultan of Barqū.

2.2.39 Al-Qāsim was succeeded by Sultan Muḥammad Tayrāb, who hated war and exercised absolute power in his country for thirty-three years. He was known as "Seed of Syria's Soil" because the Fur had heard that the earth in Syria was fertile, and was taken from the soil of Paradise, especially because it is there that the dead will be marshaled for judgment on the Last Day. It is also "the nest of the prophets." They gave the sultan this title because beautiful deeds issued from him, just as all the plants produced by the soil of Syria are beautiful.[174] The meaning of *tayrāb* in their language is "the seed that grows in the dirt (*turāb*)," or what Egyptians call *taqāwī* and western Arabs *zarrīʿah*.[175] They also gave him this title because he was a clement, generous man, forbearing, an excellent manager of affairs, and solicitous of the lowly. He was full of kindliness and enjoyed ribaldry, loving adornment and all kinds of sport. His rule was all abundance, peacefulness, and low prices—though toward the end of his days people hated him because of the injustices meted out by his offspring—he had around thirty male children, not to mention the females. These took to riding out and poking around in the country. Whenever they heard of something beautiful, they'd take it from its owner, and they imposed on their subjects more than the latter could bear. There was even one son, called Musāʿid, who in his arrogance and tyranny refused to ride horses, riding instead on the backs of men: whenever he found a young man, he would have him seized and ride him till he had worn him out. Sometimes he would cover great distances without mounting either horse or donkey but instead moving around on people, until his journey's end. If he couldn't find a stranger, he'd ride one of his own men. The subjects took their complaints to the father,[176] who refused to listen and would accept nothing they said; indeed, sometimes he'd grow impatient and say, "Now here's a wonder! A territory this big, and it can't support my sons? Whenever they commit some petty offense, the people come complaining to me?" When people saw this, they stopped complaining and referred their affairs to God, Great and Glorious.

Sultan Muḥammad Tayrāb used to appoint his wives' relations to high positions; all his viziers were relatives of his wives. His oldest son was Isḥāq, known as "the Successor." This Isḥāq was brave, inspired deference, and was a man of insight and resolve, but there was something of the tyrant and the despot in him. He was called the Successor because his father had appointed him to succeed him, given him that title, and created a government for him just like his own, with viziers like his, the sultan commanding every senior vizier who had a son to bring him to the Successor so that the boy could play the same role for him as the boy's father did for the sultan. This went on for a while, until Sultan Tayrāb traveled to Kordofan and left Isḥāq behind to rule Darfur, as we shall describe later, the Almighty willing. Sultan Tayrāb loved licentiousness and fun, to the point that boys would sport with girls in front of him, meaning that the girls and boys would dance together while he watched. Once it 2.2.40

happened that a group of Birqid, a tribe of the Blacks who have a well-known dance called the *tindinga*, came before him. Now, it is a custom of theirs for each couple to go and sit together on their own when they tire of dancing, and so they did on this occasion. One of the boys said to his girl, "Would you like to have a husband?" and she said, "Yes. What will you give me as a dowry?" "I'm a poor man," he answered, "and see nothing more valuable to give you than the man sitting opposite us," and he pointed to the sultan, who was seated on a chair opposite them, and the girl said, "I accept." The sultan noticed that they were pointing at him and summoned them. When they stood before him, he asked them about it, and the boy said, "I asked my sweetheart here to marry me, and she agreed and asked me what the dowry would be, so I said I own nothing more valuable than this man sitting opposite me and I pointed to you." The sultan was pleased with his words and said, "Do you agree that I be her dowry?" and the boy said, "Yes." Then the sultan said, "Will you agree to a swap, and that I buy myself back?" and she said, "Yes, I agree." Then he summoned her father, asked him for her hand, concluded the contract for her, paid her a dowry of two female slaves, gave the groom a male slave, and commanded the couple be given an income on which to live. This is the height of noble manners, for there is nothing greater than to bring two lovers together in sanctioned matrimony.

2.2.41 A similar example is to be found in the story told of Abū Bakr al-Ṣiddīq, may God be pleased with him, to the effect that when he was caliph, he would roam Medina the Illumined by night to find out how people were living and to discover which were oppressed and which oppressors. While on his rounds, he suddenly heard a young woman singing the following verses:

> I loved him before the cutting of my amulet[177]—
> whippy as a peeled wand,
> A boy of Hāshim's best,[178] the moon's effulgence mimicking, it seemed to me, his face
> as it waxed and waned.

He then, may God be pleased with him, knocked on her door and asked her, "With whom did you fall in love?" to which she replied, "Leave me alone!" "You must tell me," he said. "By the dweller in the grave,"[179] she said, "leave me alone!" "I will not stir from where I stand till you tell me!" he said, so she heaved a sigh and said:

I am she whose heart by passion has been galled—
she who's in love with Muḥammad ibn al-Qāsim.[180]

"Are you a free woman?" he asked her. "No," she answered, "a bought slave." "Belonging to whom?" he asked, and she gave him the man's name. He left, may God be pleased with him, and the next morning asked after Muḥammad ibn al-Qāsim and found that he was raiding the infidels in Iraq, so he sent to her master, bought her from him, and sent her to Muḥammad ibn al-Qāsim in Iraq with a letter telling him the story. Then he recited, "Know, dear boy, that it's a matter of 'How many a one has died for them when sick and how many a one has perished at their hands though sound!'"[181]

Likewise, the story is told that Sulaymān ibn ʿAbd al-Malik ibn 2.2.42
Marwān was extremely jealous where women were concerned—so much so that he was capable of shedding the blood of anyone he suspected of looking amorously at one of his concubines. Once he had a musician brought (this was during the day), had him seated below his couch, and ordered him to sing, while he lay back on the couch. He had a slave girl fanning him because it was so hot, and he fell asleep. The musician raised his head without warning and, seeing that the caliph was asleep while the slave girl fanned him, took a good look at her and found her to be as radiant as the sun at its prime. Enchanted, yet unable to talk to her for fear of the caliph, his tears gushed and his desire surged, so he took a sheet of paper and wrote on it:

In my dreams I saw you in my bed
while I drank up the cool saliva of your mouth—
As if . . . as if . . . as if . . .
we'd spent the night as one, upon a single couch.

Then he tossed the piece of paper to her. She took it, read it, and wrote on it:

> How well you saw, and all that you desire
> of me you'll get, in spite of any who may envy.
> You'll spend the night between my anklets and my bracelets
> and melt between my lips and you'll embrace me,
> And we shall be the first two lovers to meet,
> despite the times, without fear of any jealousy.

She tossed the paper to him but the caliph caught it before it got to him. When he read it, his eyes turned red, he almost exploded with fury, and he said, "What drove you to do this? Is this a long-standing love between you or a passion that has just taken hold?" "Not at all," they said. "It took us, we swear, at this very moment, and we knew nothing of it before," and their tears gushed. When he saw their state, he felt pity for them and told the singer, "Take her, and let us never see you again."

2.2.43 Sultan Tayrāb lived long, as we have mentioned, and took many wives and concubines, such that he had more than thirty male children old enough to ride horses, not to mention females and younger ones. It was during this period that Shaykh-Father Muḥammad Kurrā entered his service, though he was still only an adolescent. The sultan ordered him to join the *kóór kwa*, or warriors, meaning he should be one of the company who carry spears behind the sultan when he rides out and when he sits in judgment. This is not something peculiar to the sultan: every one of the petty kings of the Fur as well as every one of their commanders has men called *kóór kwa* who carry spears behind him when he rides out or sits in judgment. In their eyes, it is an essential part of the apparatus of royal rule, required to preserve the natural order and inspire dread of the overlord in his subjects' hearts. Shaykh-Father Muḥammad Kurrā served in this role for a period, and showed signs of promise. Sultan Tayrāb therefore loved him and transferred him to the *soom'íng dogólá*. *Soom* means "house," *–íng* is the marker of the genitive, and *dogólá* means "children," and it means, as they would say, "the *durā* of the children," *durā* being a word for "place" or "house" in their dialect of Arabic.[182] The people of the *soom'íng dogólá* are the agents who oversee their master's business; he sends them on his confidential missions and their chief is of higher standing than the chief of the *kóór kwa*.

Shaykh-Father Muḥammad Kurrā grew rich in the sultan's service, and eventually the sultan would call on no one else for most of his needs. As a result, a member of the household became jealous of him and told tales against him to the sultan, saying, "Muḥammad Kurrā is a traitor and an ingrate, and I see him meeting every night with so-and-so, the concubine, who brings him delicious food." This infuriated the sultan, who decided to take ruthless action against him. Word of it reached Kurrā, who took a knife, went into a room on his own, and cut off his genitals with his own hand. Then he took them to the sultan, who was nearby, and threw them down in front of him, saying, "The only reason rumors have spread about me is that I am equipped with these. See, now I have cut them off so that the heart of my master the sultan can harbor no further suspicion of me." Then he fainted. As a result, the sultan had mercy on him and ordered that he be cared for until he was better. Subsequently, the sultan commanded that he be attached to Counselor[183] ʿAlī wad Jāmiʿ, one of the grand viziers, recommending him to him with the words, "Take this youth into your household. Look after him, treat him well, and woe betide you should you treat him with disrespect, for I expect him to succeed you in your office." The counselor therefore took him, against his will, into the *soom'íng dogólá*, with the same rank he had held with the sultan. As we just explained, the people of the *soom'íng dogólá* are the agents of the sultan who oversee important business and whom the master of the household sends on confidential missions. 2.2.44

Muḥammad Kurrā remained there for a while. He would never leave his master's door, and whenever the counselor called for someone from the *soom'íng dogólá*, Muḥammad Kurrā would answer; 2.2.45

often, indeed, he would find no one else. He would therefore send him to see to his affairs. It was Muḥammad Kurrā's custom never to set out to take care of some business without ensuring that he did so successfully and made himself useful. Thus, despite himself, the counselor came to love him for the competence he saw in him and he put him in charge of the people who worked in the *soom'íng dogólá*, giving him a special status. All the servants thus ended up under his command. On assuming this position, Muḥammad Kurrā made even greater efforts to serve than he had before and never left his master's door.

2.2.46 Now, the counselor was a bit lax. For example, at lunch and at dinner, about a thousand dishes of food would be sent to him. He gave no thought to this. On the contrary, he'd be sent enough for him and anyone with him, and the rest the servants would distribute haphazardly. Often the dishes would return to the women's quarters full. Muḥammad Kurrā noticed this and organized things very well: he'd send the servants in among his master's followers and see which of them had a guest; the servants would then let him know and say, "So-and-so has a guest, and also so-and-so," and so on. Then, when the food came, he'd select enough of the best of it to satisfy his master and those with him, give that amount to the servants to give to them, then distribute the rest among the guests, each according to his condition in terms of rank, wealth, standing, and learning, instructing the bearers to tell them, "The counselor has sent you this hospitality," though the counselor was quite unaware of what was going on. Then everyone would thank the counselor and sing his praises, and when they came to see him they'd say, "God reward you with good fortune! You sent us wonderful hospitality. There's no one else like you among the sultan's agents," and they'd praise him, in his presence and out of it.

2.2.47 Since he didn't know why, the counselor was astonished and said, "These people thank me and say I sent them food when I did nothing of the sort!" For a while he was at a loss as to the reason. When he happened to be in the women's quarters one evening, he came out into the public offices and saw Muḥammad Kurrā distributing the different dishes. As he became aware of what was going on, he concealed himself in a chamber and waited. Then he heard Shaykh-Father Muḥammad ask the servants, "How many guests are there in the house of such and such a high official?" and heard them answer with this or that figure, at which the shaykh-father would say, "Take them such and such vessels and tell them, 'The counselor sends you this dinner.'" In this way he distributed all the food. "So this is where it all comes from!" said the counselor, and after that he clung to him as to a precious object, treating him magnanimously, raising his rank, and putting him in charge of the *kūrāyāt*, who, in their parlance, are the persons who manage the horses and all the servants. It is a position held in great esteem among them, though in the practice of other nations he would simply be head groom. Muḥammad Kurrā stayed with Counselor ʿAlī in this capacity until the latter traveled to Kordofan in the entourage of Sultan Tayrāb, at which point Shaykh-Father Muḥammad Kurrā went with him.

Why Sultan Muḥammad Tayrāb Went to Kordofan

A trusted authority on pedigrees told me that Sultan Solóng, known as Sulaymān, the original ancestor of the sultans of Darfur, had a brother called al-Musabbaʿ, and that he and his brother divided up the two territories: Sultan Sulaymān took Darfur and al-Musabbaʿ took Kordofan,[184] and they made a pact that neither would betray the other, and the two territories remained thus until the reign of Sultan Muḥammad Tayrāb. The ruler of Kordofan then was Sultan Hāshim al-Musabbaʿāwī, a descendant of al-Musabbaʿ. Possessed of great manliness, courage, and enterprise in the execution of demanding affairs, he carried out numerous raids against the lands of the Turūj and the Bedouin of the desert and became very wealthy. He had some ten thousand armed slaves, and a rabble made 2.2.48

up of people from Dongola, and the Shāyijiyyah,[185] Kabābīsh, and Rizayqāt Arab tribes rallied to him. Together they formed a massive army.[186] His greed then urged him to take over Darfur. He consulted the chief officers of his government and they advised him to first dispatch squadrons of troops to harry the borders and thus weaken the Darfurians, and then go there himself. He accepted their advice and the squadrons he sent to the Darfurian borders murdered, took captives, and made off with large herds of animals. Sultan Tayrāb then sent Sultan Hāshim a letter in which he wrote:

> Greetings, Cousin. You have dispatched your squadrons to the borders of my country though you know of the love between us and that we have done nothing to violate that love. At the same time, you know that those whose animals have been taken are Muslims and those who have been murdered acknowledged the oneness of God. These are deeds that no man regards as lawful and that no man in his right mind would undertake. Desist, therefore, when this letter of mine reaches you, or the wrongdoer shall meet his end. Farewell.

2.2.49 When the letter reached him, Sultan Hāshim's insolence and arrogance only increased and he dispatched his squadrons a second time. Sultan Tayrāb realized that if he didn't take steps to prevent him and remove him root and branch, his evil deeds would only increase and would lead to the ruination of the country. He therefore made his preparations and set off against him. This was Sultan Tayrāb's overt motive. His covert motive was that he knew his people were unhappy with him and wouldn't agree to be ruled by any of his sons, especially since the signatories to the pact of Aḥmad Bukur, namely, his uncles, were still alive,[187] and especially when they thought of the injustices he and his sons had committed. The sultan himself wanted the succession to pass to his eldest son, known as Isḥāq the Successor, as previously noted.[188] So, when Hāshim, King of Kordofan, did what he did, he seized the opportunity and put on a show of anger, proclaiming that only he could take care of the matter, though had he sent Counselor ʿAlī, or one of his viziers, he could have saved himself the supplies for the journey and its hardships. He was, however, determined to make the journey and take with him all the sultan's sons, young and old,[189] and to plunge them into battle and thus destroy them, and with them the viziers. The latter did not want the succession to go to his son, as it would mean that Isḥāq would take control of the country, its wealth and its men, and be the only one to go down in history.[190]

Having decided on this, he gathered all the sons of Sultan Aḥmad Bukur and the grand viziers, and set off with them, leaving the viziers' children with the Successor, each in the office held by his father[191]—yet even though he hid his intentions, they still become apparent in the end, in keeping with the words of the poet who said: 2.2.50

Any qualities a man may have,
though he think them hidden from others, will become well known.[192]

In reality, however, the treatment he received from God was the opposite of what he intended: the Almighty punished him with the death of his son, and all his planning went for nothing. God bless the poet who said:

Verily, the kindnesses of my God
have left not a strait in the world for me to suffer.
Whenever I wish to pull off some gambit
they tell me, "Have done!
Leave things to us—
we've a better right to you than you yourself, or any other."

In this world, things always work out the opposite of what one wishes. As al-Mutanabbī says:[193]

Not all a man hopes for does he attain—
the winds may blow in ways the ships do not desire.

2.2.51 When the King of Kordofan heard that Sultan Tayrāb was coming, he fled with his men and sought refuge with the King of Sinnār, in whose country he took up residence. The sultan thus entered the land without a fight and set about sending out squadrons and cavalry troopers to all corners of the country, until he had subjugated it and collected taxes, and things were quiet. He remained there a full year, by the end of which his forces had become fed up with inactivity and asked if they could go back to their own country. This angered him, as he hadn't achieved his goal, but he hid this and asked, "How can we go back when I'm told Hāshim has taken refuge with the Makk of Sinnār, who has raised him an army and is planning to attack us? If we go back and he comes after we've left, he'll think we fled before him and that he has gotten what he wanted from the country. Then he'll raid us and force us to go back again. I am presently mulling over whether I should set off against him before he comes—but let us wait till the news is confirmed."

2.2.52 They went on like this for a while, but nothing the sultan told them materialized, so their hearts became estranged and their morale worsened. Homesick for their wives and children, they conspired in secret. The vizier, Counselor ʿAlī wad Barqū, the sultan's in-law (the sultan being married to his daughter), said to them, "What will you do for me if I kill him and rid you of him, leaving you free to appoint whomever you like to rule over you?" and they gave him guarantees of great wealth and made a pact with him to that effect. They agreed that the sign for them to act should be the sound of the drums, and that they would be ready and listening out for them. Counselor ʿAli waited until night fell, then dressed in two coats of strong, body-length chain mail, over which he put his clothes. He buckled on his sword, entered the sultan's house, and made his way to his daughter's chamber, knowing full well how the sultan loved her, for the sultan was extremely solicitous of her, and he had often found him there. When he entered, she saw the evil in his face, and his luck let him down too: the sultan wasn't with her that night. He asked her about the sultan and she said, "I don't know where he is, but if you like I'll look for him and tell him you've come." "That would be a good thing for you to do," he replied, "as I need to see him urgently tonight." While they were talking, she noticed the collar of the coat of mail underneath the collar of his top clothes and became convinced that evil was afoot. She went to the sultan and informed him that her father had come looking for him and that she had noticed things that made her suspicious, among them that he was wearing chain mail under his clothes, had his sword strapped on—even though it was their custom that no one ever went to see the sultan wearing a sword—and that she had seen signs of anger in his face. The sultan now realized that evil was afoot, for it was Counselor ʿAlī who had been urging him to go back, speaking to him in the strongest terms. The sultan ordered her not to go back to him and went out and summoned the chief officers of the watch, ordering them to arrest anyone who tried to leave the house, saying that if any escaped they would have only themselves to blame for the consequences. He himself took several of them, fully armed, as guards, plunged into the depths of his house, entered the bedchamber of one of his wives, and placed a guard around it.

Counselor ʿAlī sat waiting for his daughter to come back, but she 2.2.53
did not, and neither did the sultan, that ʿAlī might have his way with him. Indeed, no one came and he was like the sheep that digs its grave with its own hoof,[194] or the man who cuts off his nose with his own hand. As the poet[195] says:

> To my demise my foot has led me—
> meseems my foot has shed my blood.

When he grew tired of waiting, he rose to go home, afraid that daylight would come and he'd be discovered. He walked a little way until he found himself confronted by the watch, who told him, "Go back where you came from!" He refused and told them who he was, expecting that they'd let him through, but he couldn't persuade them. In fact, they said, "We have orders to arrest you if you don't go back to where you came from." He cursed at them and tried to force them to let him leave, so they set upon him, meaning to tie him up till morning came, but he fought them, wounding a number. At that they fell upon him and killed him. Thus, all he gained from his evil action was his preordained annihilation. Because of such things he upon whom be God's peace and blessings has said, "Every evildoer will meet with a violent death," or as Sayyid ʿAlī al-Ghurāb, God bless him, says:

To sow evil deeds is to reap regret,
so seek peace if you hope for salvation.
Trust not in fate, for not all who do evil
get what they wish for and their dreams' consummation.
Many a wish is a mount that brings us
to our fates, and a wellspring for contrition.
Many a time the attainment they picture to the wisher
is no more than a dreamer's vision.
Many a one strives to garner life's perfume
while, all unknowing, what he harvests is his perdition.

2.2.54 When the sultan was informed of the counselor's death, he said, "Wrap him in a cloak and put him in a room until morning." When dawn came, the sultan ordered that all his slaves be brought, fully armed. They came, and he set them at the doors. Then he ordered the doorkeepers to open the doors, leave them open till no one was left inside, then close them upon him and his men. He also forbade them to allow any of the army commanders' bodyguards to enter and told them to allow only the emirs in. And he ordered a group of slaves to go to him, once the doors had been closed, and stand in front of him and surround any who might be in the assembly hall. Then he ordered that the drums be beaten in a mournful and distressing rhythm—for they have a recognized beat for glad times, as they have another for sad—and the drums were beaten as he commanded, and the viziers and the kings came, all according to their various ranks, thinking that ʿAlī wad Barqū had done what he'd agreed with them. They came armed, but when they arrived at the door of the sultan's house, they found that things weren't as they'd expected. They could see, however, that they had no choice but to enter; their followers tried to enter with them, but they were stopped and separated from their commanders. The slaves the sultan had ordered to surround them now came and did so, bristling with arms, their faces showing their fury; and the sultan came out to them swathed in black garments and with a red cashmere shawl draped over his head and shoulders—a mark of extreme anger. The sultan took his seat in the place prepared for him and ordered them to bring the murdered man. He was brought, wrapped in the cloak, and the sultan ordered them to place him in the middle of the circle. "I want you to identify this person," he said, so they went up to him and uncovered his face, and they recognized him. None of them dared speak, so furious was the sultan. When the sultan asked them, "Do you know him?" all remained silent.

Then one of them, a man of unusual shrewdness, stood up and said, "We know him. He is Counselor ʿAlī wad Barqū, and he entered your house with the knowledge of us all. If you want to kill us, here we stand before you. If you decide to pardon us, the decision is yours." "What drove you to do this?" asked the sultan. "You brought us here," the other replied, "knowing full well that we have wives and children in our country, and have been deprived of the sight of them and of the enjoyment of their company. We have nothing to excuse you in our eyes for keeping us here and we can see no intention on your part to return, even though life has no sweetness for us anywhere but in our homeland. The best thing you can do is to send us back to our own country—our hearts are sick for it and will have no more truck with exile. As the poet says: 2.2.55

> My hankering and my longing are for the first dirt
> and for the first land whose dust made contact with my body.

"This is especially true, given that the Lord of ʿAdnān's Offspring[196] is reported to have said, 'Love of homeland is intrinsic to faith.'" When the sultan heard the man's words, he perceived the truth of them and feared that, if he were to deal violently with any of them, all hell would break loose, for in their own eyes they were in the right. He only got out of the predicament they posed for him by saying, "Don't be in a hurry to kill me for I'm a dead man in any case. I have a sickness whose nature I cannot reveal to you. It is that which prevents me from traveling, but if God saves me in the coming days, I will take you back. Please do nothing more of this sort. Farewell."

2.2.56 A few days later, he pretended to be sick, even though his body was in good health, and stopped going to the court or dealing with people's business, unaware that those who fake sickness may find that their joke has turned serious, become truly sick, and even die. He upon whom be the most perfect peace and the best of blessings has said, "Do not feign sickness, for then you will indeed become sick and die." Now the tables were turned, sickness and aversion became his lot, and he felt sure that he was doomed to perish. At that point he wrote a letter to the Successor saying, "Greetings. Know, my son, that the first signs of that from which there is neither escape nor sanctuary have descended upon me, so when this letter reaches you, leave your son Khalīl in your place as ruler of Darfur and come quickly. You may reach me before I breathe my last and I shall perhaps be able to arrange something for you that will be to your advantage. Farewell." He sealed the letter and sent it by swift camel rider. News that the sickness had taken the sultan hard and that he was on the point of death got out, and it was the only thing anyone could talk about.

2.2.57 Now, Muḥammad Kurrā often used to visit the sultan's house and meet with his womenfolk. Among them was Iyā Kurī Kinānah, the greatest of the sultan's women and the highest in rank—for every sultan who ever ruled has surely loved one of his women, and the one whom he loves and to whom he entrusts the management of his household is called "the true *Iyā kurī*." *Iyā kurī* means "royal lady,"[197] and if any other of the sultan's women is called *Iyā kurī* it is simply as a courtesy. This Kinānah was gifted with insight and good management. Sultan Tayrāb was only passingly intimate with the other women, which is why he bestowed this office on her, for this is an office that comes with fiefs, customary dues, and assets from which taxes could be levied on her behalf, and she issued orders and had officers to keep her wealth and affairs in order. When Iyā Kurī Kinānah saw that the sultan was bound to die, she feared for her life; she had a son called Ḥabīb for whom she also feared. She therefore met with Muḥammad Kurrā and said, "Muḥammad, have you thought of a plan to save me and my son from what's going on?" "I have," he replied. "You should call on your relationship with the Orphan, because he will be master of the state after Sultan Tayrāb, seeing that everyone accepts him." "Can you," she asked, "make a pact between him and me that when he becomes ruler, he will make me *Iyā kurī* and my son Ḥabīb his successor?" and Muḥammad Kurrā said, "That I shall do. God willing, you will be pleased."

Kinānah feared what Isḥāq the Successor might do to her son **2.2.58** Ḥabīb because the former was the son of her co-wife. Knowing that the Orphan had no children, she thought, "He can raise my son as his own." Muḥammad Kurrā therefore went to him, passed on to him her greetings, and informed him that Kinānah wanted to help him accede to the throne, but with one condition—that he marry her and make her son his successor. He made a pact with her to that effect, and Muḥammad Kurrā then said, "And what will you do for me if I keep this secret of yours, use my good offices to help you gain the throne, and devote my energies to devising schemes to that end?

> Do not belittle the cunning of the weak—
> many a viper has died from a scorpion's venom!"

The Orphan said, "If you do this and are of help, I shall bestow on you the office of shaykh-father," and he made a pact with him to that effect. Then Muḥammad Kurrā returned and informed her that he had gotten from him what she wanted. This put her mind at ease, and as events unfolded she began sending the Orphan news of the sultan through him.

2.2.59 When Sultan Tayrāb's illness grew worse and he despaired of the arrival of his son Isḥāq the Successor, he had Counselor ʿAlī wad Jāmiʿ,[198] Muḥammad Kurrā, Counselor Ḥasab Allāh Jirān,[199] Counselor Ibrāhīm wad Ramād, Shaykh-Father ʿAbd Allāh Juthā,[200] and another counselor whose name I've forgotten brought to him and said, "I have done each of you favors, and I hope that you will repay me for this by carrying out my last wishes, which I am about to entrust to you." "We hear and obey," they said. To Counselor ʿAlī he said, "I ask that when I die you gather all my soldiers under your command and deliver them to my son Isḥāq in Darfur." "I hear and obey," he said. To Counselor Ḥasab Allāh he said, "I hereby place in your charge the coffers of my wealth. When I die, deliver them to my son." "I hear and obey," he said. To Counselor Ibrāhīm wad Ramād he said, "I hereby place in your charge my animals and my horses. When I die, deliver them to my son in Darfur." To the shaykh-father he said, "I hereby bestow on you guardianship of the harem, the young children, and the servants. When I die, deliver them to my son." To the remaining counselor he said, "I hereby place in your charge my weapons, my clothes, and my sons. When I die, deliver them to my son." They acceded obediently to his request, prayed that God grant him good health, and wept for his illness, for they were all his in-laws, except for the shaykh-father, who was a eunuch. Then they returned to their quarters, and the sultan expired in their absence. When he died, Kinānah sent the sultan's prayer beads, kerchief, seal ring, and amulet to the Orphan, by hand of Muḥammad Kurrā, to let him know.

2.2.60 The viziers to whom he had revealed his last wishes returned and found that he'd passed away. Regretting they'd left him, they devised a stratagem, agreeing to place his corpse in a litter after first opening it, removing the innards, and embalming it; after that, it was to be covered, and a cordon of soldiers placed around it, with no one allowed to get to it. Any who asked would be told he was sick, until they reached Darfur and had handed everything over to his son, Isḥāq the Successor.

Shaykh-Father Muḥammad Kurrā took the things that were mentioned above, went to see the Orphan, and told him, "God compensate you with good for the loss of your brother!" and he gave him the ring, the prayer beads, and the kerchief. The Orphan was thus apprised of his brother's death and he took the things and went to his older brother, whose name was Rīz. When he told him, Rīz arose and took Rīfā and Ṭāhir, and they went to the sultan's quarters. No one could stand in their way. They went on through the house until they got to where the sultan's men were, as well as Sultan Tayrāb himself, who was laid out in front of them while they wept over him. They entered the room without speaking. In fact, they sat down around their brother and wept till they regained their composure. Then they turned to his men, and Rīz asked them, "Isn't it enough that you profited from our brother's benevolence throughout his life? Yet now you want to take his cadaver too so that he can be yours in death as well? We have seen with our own eyes that he's dead, so do what you like. We leave him to you." Then they exited, leaving them. 2.2.61

When they'd gone, his men changed their minds, saying, "Our plan has gone awry and they've seen that the sultan is dead. We can't carry out his last wishes now." But Counselor ʿAlī wad Jāmiʿ said, "I shall carry out his wishes, or perish in the attempt," and called out, "Muḥammad Kurrā, go to my son Muḥammad and tell him to assemble my soldiers and have them put on their chain mail and their swords and come to the sultan's door." "I hear and obey," replied Muḥammad Kurrā, and he went to Muḥammad, the counselor's son, and told him, "The honorable counselor orders you to ready the soldiers and ride with them to the sons of the sultan and assist them till you receive further orders from him." "I hear and obey," said Counselor Muḥammad,[201] and he called for his soldiers and they readied themselves, mounted, and went to join the sons of the sultan. Muḥammad Kurrā, meanwhile, returned to the counselor and told him, "I went and I found that my young master had already taken the soldiers and gone to the sons of the sultan." The 2.2.62

counselor was enraged and realized that he would be unable to carry out Sultan Tayrāb's wishes. He was also struck by dread because of the oaths and pacts he'd made. Pulling out a little box that he had on his person, he opened it and swallowed some of its contents. Then he fell down dead. With the counselor dead, the others were left in the lurch and couldn't agree. This was a great trick that Muḥammad Kurrā played on the counselor and his son, and because of it he and Counselor Muḥammad, son of the aforementioned counselor, became enemies.

2.2.63 After this, the sultan's men split up, and each went to his own army, while the people simmered and seethed, everyone knowing that the state had to have a sultan to take care of their affairs and to speak for the people with one voice. The sons of Sultan Aḥmad Bukur, the brothers of the deceased, were assembled with their followers in one place, the sons of their brothers with their followers in another, and the commoners in a third. A group of those who manage the affairs of state then arose and called for the judge and religious scholars and sent them to the sons of Sultan Aḥmad Bukur because they were the elders and parties to the pact made by their father. These high officials told the judge and the scholars, "Say to the sons of Sultan Aḥmad Bukur, 'Greetings. Know that this matter requires a sultan, to speak for the people with one voice and to see to their affairs. You hold supreme authority, and you are those who dispose of it. Appoint us, therefore, a sultan whom both you and we can accept.'" The scholars and the judge then went and gave them this message, and the sons of Sultan Aḥmad Bukur said, "We appoint our brother Rīz because he is the oldest among us and our lord, and we are at his command."

2.2.64 Next, the scholars went to the young sons of the sultans[202] and informed them that Báási Rīz would be sultan over them, but they refused, saying, "Báási Rīz is our uncle and like a father to us, but we don't want him to rule us because he is intractable and impetuous, and the havoc he may cause is to be feared, especially because we're young. We want a mild-natured sultan to raise us, one who will treat us with clemency should any of us step out of line." The commoners said, "Báási Rīz is one of our royal princes and the son of our king, but he is impetuous, and it would be better if he himself were to choose someone else, because he is a sultan whether he rules or not." The scholars then returned and informed the sons of Sultan Aḥmad Bukur of all this. Báási Rīz said, "We accept their reservations and appoint Báási Ṭāhir to rule over them." They informed the sons of the sultans of this, but these said, "We do not accept our uncle Ṭāhir because he has many sons and he will be too busy with them to pay attention to our upbringing." The commoners said, "We hated Sultan Muḥammad Tayrāb precisely because he had so many sons. They may appoint Ṭāhir to be our sultan, but we would prefer the Successor as sultan because he has fewer sons." So the scholars went back and informed the sons of Sultan Aḥmad Bukur, and Rīz said, "We appoint the Orphan to rule over you," so they informed the others of this, and everyone, commoners and royalty, was satisfied and the matter was made official. They took him, conveyed him to the sultan's house, placed the ring on his finger, and sat him on the throne of the kingdom, and no two disputed his right.[203]

CHAPTER 3

A Brief Excerpt from the History of Sultan ʿAbd al-Raḥmān, Called the Rightly Guided: His Early Days, His Rule, and His Death

2.3.1 We have mentioned above that Sultan Aḥmad Bukur left seven sons,[204] among them the aforementioned Sultan ʿAbd al-Raḥmān, who was the youngest of them because his father died while he was in his mother's belly, which is why he was called the Orphan. He grew up to be a fine young man, learned the Qur'an by heart, studied religious law, and knew what religion allowed and what it forbade. He had no interest in the things that interested royal sons in Darfur. When any of these grows up, he launches himself on the country, imposing himself as a guest and plundering people's wealth. Every time he sees something that he likes, he takes it without paying, with the words, "Everyone in Darfur is my father's slave." In contrast, ʿAbd al-Raḥmān was, from his earliest days, righteous, God-fearing, purehearted, and virtuous. He lived in greatly straitened circumstances. If he was on a journey and evening found him in a village, he would say to the person in whose house he was to stay, "I am God's guest." Then, if the man accepted him, he'd stay, and if the man did not, he'd go elsewhere. He was never heard to have treated anyone unjustly and he never forgot to return a favor. On the contrary, he'd remember it and reward the doer.[205]

2.3.2 Once, for example, he was on a journey and put up at the house of a man from a tribe called the Bartī. The man recognized him, slaughtered a fat ram for him, and treated him kindly. When dinnertime came and the food was brought, Sultan ʿAbd al-Raḥmān saw that the man had put himself to great expense for him and said, "Friend, wouldn't less have been enough? If you'd slaughtered us a chicken, it would have fed us just as well and you would still have performed your duty." "No, my lord," the man said. "I swear, if I owned a meat camel, I would slaughter her for you! Are you not ʿAbd al-Raḥmān the Orphan, son of our sultan?" "By what did you recognize me?" asked the Orphan. "I recognized you by your virtuous nature and your godliness. One day you will be a man of consequence." The Orphan said, "If I ever come to power, I will feed you with something fatter than what you slaughtered for us," and that is exactly what happened. When he assumed power, he summoned the man (whose name was Muḥammad Dardūk), appointed him to high office, and sent him out to collect the taxes from the Majānīn Arabs, a great tribe whose members have many camels. The man collected from them cattle and both cow and bull camels in numbers too large to count.

Similarly, he was once passing through Dār al-Rīḥ and put up at the house of a poor man called Jiddū.[206] The man provided him with the best hospitality he could. Now, the man was from a great house, and his father had been a great lord, holding the office of Tikináwi. When the Orphan assumed power, he appointed the man to his father's office. I saw him and met with him. Likewise, Faqīh Mālik al-Fūtāwī, whom we have mentioned above, once had a dream, as follows: he saw a moon in the sky and everyone was looking at it and saying, "It's the orphan,"[207] which he interpreted to mean that ʿAbd al-Raḥmān would assume power. When he went and gave him the good news, ʿAbd al-Raḥmān averred, "If your vision turns out to be true, we shall certainly raise your standing," and it was as he promised. He also fasted every Thursday and Monday and during the months of Rajab, Shaʿbān, and Ramaḍān, and he loved and was generous to men of religion. 2.3.3

A few days before he assumed power, word went around among astrologers and geomancers that the Orphan was the one who 2.3.4

would assume the sultanate after Sultan Muḥammad Tayrāb. The latter heard this and hated him for it and tried to kill him several times, but God prevented him from doing so. He'd invite him to take food and poison it, but the Orphan would say, "I'm fasting,"[208] and eat none of it. I was told by a witness that at the time of his assumption of the sultanate, when they took him into the palace, he was wearing a shirt so tattered that his shoulders showed and that he was carrying wooden prayer beads worth but half a piaster in Egypt. He remained a bachelor until gray hairs began to appear in his beard, by reason of poverty and lack of money to take a concubine or marry. He didn't know a woman until he went to Kordofan in the company of his brother Sultan Muḥammad Tayrāb. When he passed through a land called al-Bīqū, its lord gave him an uncouth slave girl called Anbūsah.[209] He slept with her and she bore him Sultan Muḥammad Faḍl.

2.3.5 When he was recognized, they sat him on the royal throne, as previously mentioned, and pledged their allegiance to him. The first to do so was his eldest brother, Rīz, followed by Rīfā, then Ṭāhir, then the sons of the sultans. After these had pledged allegiance, so too did the judge and the scholars, followed by the commanders of the army. The mourning drums were beaten to announce the death of Sultan Tayrāb. Then they stopped and the drums of good tiding were beaten to announce the succession to the throne of Sultan ʿAbd al-Raḥmān. It had been a custom of Fur royalty that when the sultan assumed power, he would stay seven days in his house, giving no thought to government or to the issuance of commands or prohibitions. Instead, he'd simply sit to receive congratulations and expressions of joy, and the scholars, viziers, and officers of state would come in to visit him. When Sultan ʿAbd al-Raḥmān came to the throne, he abolished this custom. He went out early on the morning of his accession, and when the viziers came, they found him sitting in his court, dealing with cases. They chided him, saying, "This is not the custom," but he replied, "That was a bad custom, not to be found in God's Book or the practice of His Prophet." Then he gathered together all the officers of state and told them, "If you want me to be your sultan, in authority over you, abandon injustice and don't let your appetites seduce you into it, but repent to God of it and give it up. Injustice is the ruin of states and brings untimely ends to kings." "We hear and obey," they said.

Early in the morning of the third day, he ordered all Sultan 2.3.6
Tayrāb's coffers brought out and this was done. Everything in them by way of gold, silver, and clothes he distributed to religious scholars, descendants of the prophet, and the poor. He found a great quantity of moth-eaten cashmere and broadcloth, which he ordered thrown down in front of the houses for anyone who found anything of use to take. They took it out and there was so much it looked like a mighty mountain. The poor gathered around and plundered it, stretching out their hands in blessing for Sultan ʿAbd al-Raḥmān. On the seventh day, he brought out Sultan Tayrāb's slave girls and distributed them too; no one was left but the free women and the mothers of children whom his brother had contractually married. Next he distributed the offices, making Muḥammad Dukkumī a counselor with the same responsibilities as his father, Counselor ʿAlī wad Jāmiʿ. Then he ordered the office holders to prepare to leave for Darfur, and they readied the army for travel.

When they left Kordofan, they went by way of Jabal al-Turūj, 2.3.7
falling upon it, taking every young man and girl there, and leaving only the old. Sultan ʿAbd al-Raḥmān met with the shaykhs of the Rizayqāt and the Misīriyyah Bedouin tribes and requested they march with him to do battle with the Successor, on the basis that whatever property, weapons, and horses they might take would become theirs. Thousands of them rallied to his banner and he set off for Darfur. However, instead of coming to it from the east, he came to it from the south, and before arriving, he wrote the Successor a letter saying:

> From ʿAbd al-Raḥmān, Sultan of Darfur, to his nephew Isḥāq. I offer you my condolences on the death of your

> father, even though he was my brother, because you are closer kin to him than I, and I commend to you the virtue of filial respect. If you understand this, you will understand too that I am your uncle and as inviolate to you as your own father and that it is shameful for a son to stand in the way of his father or his uncle, to say nothing of drawing his sword in his face. I forbid you therefore to fight, and beware lest the rashness of youth provoke you into listening to the words of any evildoers who may strive to come between us. You have my word before God and His covenant that I will designate you successor to the throne as you were in the time of your father and that I will make you my crown prince just as you were your father's. Listen to my words and spare the blood of the Muslims. If, however, you oppose me, you will regret it «and the wrongdoers will soon know how evil a turn their affairs will take.»[210]

2.3.8 When the letter reached the Successor and he was apprised of its contents, he wrote to Sultan ʿAbd al-Raḥmān, saying:

> Greetings. I gave my word before the Almighty that I would tread no carpet but my father's.[211] I am his appointed successor, and you have no rights over me. If you fight me, I shall be the injured party. Farewell.

Then he mustered a massive army under al-Ḥājj Muftāḥ,[212] who had been his governor as a child and was the most senior of his slaves, and this army and that of Sultan ʿAbd al-Raḥmān came face to face at a place called Tabaldiyyah.[213] Each man in Sultan ʿAbd al-Raḥmān's army had a *safrūk*, a *safrūk* being a piece of stick that looks like this, and when «the two hosts met,»[214] the sultan's men threw their *safrūk*s at the Successor's men, crying, "God

is greater!"[215] and the others fled and the sultan's men chased them, taking captives, spoils, and horses. The Bedouin chased them too, and seized large quantities of plunder. Al-Ḥājj Muftāḥ survived and fled headlong from his companions on his fleet steed. When al-Ḥājj Muftāḥ went in to see the Successor, the latter asked him, "What do you leave behind you?" and the former replied, "My lord, take my advice. Make peace with your uncle, and if he asks you for compensation, give it to him. Make me the first thing given to him. Let me be your ransom." When the Successor heard these words, he rebuked him, saying, "You have reverted to your origins, evil slave! But it is my fault for having put you in charge of the troops." Then the Successor marshaled great numbers, opened his coffers, distributed wealth, and gave out fiefs. Thus, he gathered an army so immense it had neither beginning nor end, and he marched out, expecting victory over the sultan.

He reached a place called Tāldawā, where the sultan caught up with him, and when each had looked the other over, they set their armies in order and drew up their ranks. Among the Successor's men was a *malik* called Baḥr the Tax Collector;[216] he was the person responsible for collecting the grain tax for the sultanate. With him were his followers, numbering some ten thousand horsemen, not to mention foot soldiers. When the two hosts met, he took his men and marched against Sultan ʿAbd al-Raḥmān's army as if intending to engage them, but instead joined them and added his ranks to theirs and started fighting the Successor. This took a great swathe out of the Successor's army and made a breach that they couldn't fill, and the courage of the Successor's soldiery deserted them in the face of what Malik Baḥr had done. Battle was joined, but the Successor's army retreated in a flash. When the Successor saw this, he went out to fight them himself, and everyone who recognized him turned aside from him out of respect for him and his father. He continued to fight till he saw that his army had been defeated and he was left surrounded by a small company. He followed after his army but found that most had been killed. The sultan's soldiers pursued 2.3.9

them, taking captives and plunder, till evening came. Someone who was present told me that, at the moment when the two armies joined battle, he saw stars in the sky though it was late in the morning. I saw the battlefield and found it bare of vegetation, though it was spring; I asked why and was told no plants could grow there because there was too much blood.

2.3.10 The Successor then set off for the north with his companions, leaving the sultan in possession of the south. Once the Successor had disengaged from the sultan and put distance between them, he acted like a tyrant, transgressor, and oppressor. He began forcing people to join him, and whenever he came across a fine horse he would take it, and any assets he found he would carry off. Thus, he accumulated great wealth and many followers. As his evil grew ever greater, the people appealed to the sultan for help against him. The sultan wanted to go after him himself, but the high officers of the state prevented him, so instead he wrote him a letter, saying,

> After whatever greeting may be appropriate: you have tyrannized, oppressed, mistreated, and transgressed. I advised you the first time to spare the people's blood, but you refused and you suffered at our hands what you suffered. Now you have decided to mistreat the people and loot their possessions instead of fighting us. I hereby advise you, a second time, to abandon the rashness, the use of force, and the arrogance in which you are embroiled. If you return to us again, we shall accept you and reward you as we promised to do the first time. If you refuse, the sin is yours, and you will be the one to blame, and if you insist on fighting, the common people will be guiltless.[217] Cleanse yourself then of the wealth of others! I hereby place my wealth before you. Take of it whatever you want, until such time as God delivers his verdict.[218] Farewell.

2.3.11 When the letter reached the Successor and he had apprised himself of its contents, he tore it up and sent no answer. His evil deeds grew in number and those who complained about him multiplied. The sultan therefore sent the *malik* of the northern region, who was known in the army as the Tikináwi, against him. The Tikináwi went after him and caught up with him at a place called Bawwā. When the Successor saw the army had come, he drew up his ranks and stood his ground till it reached him. Then the two hosts joined battle. The Successor's army had been cowed by the battle of Tāldawā and was on the verge of defeat, but the Successor steadied them and waded into the battle himself, along with the men his age, but whenever he appeared, the enemy would run away from him, out of embarrassment, not fear. In the end, he plunged into the middle of the army and reached the Tikináwi, to whom he said, "Evil slave! Didn't you belong to my father? Would you turn traitor and fight me?" And he drew his sword and struck him dead. When the Tikináwi fell, his battle formation was disrupted and his troops defeated. The Successor's soldiers pursued them, either killing them, taking them captive, or robbing them for plunder. Only a small number of the vanquished survived, and these the Successor despoiled of their horses, weapons, and everything they had with them. This consoled him and he looked forward to victory over his uncle, reinforcing himself with the spoils he'd taken.

News of this reached Sultan ʿAbd al-Raḥmān and he became furious. He sent his brother Rīfā with another army. Rīfā caught up with the Successor at Bawwā again, and when the Successor saw him he drew up his ranks and put his army into a state of readiness, having previously prepared an ambush in a depression; he told them, "I shall withdraw with my soldiers and they, being eager to seize me, will come after me. When you see that they've done so, wait till they are in front of you. You'll be behind them and you can fall on them and harass them, and we shall wheel around and attack them. We shall be in front of them, and you behind, and no one will escape." And that is what happened. When the two hosts met, the Successor's men retreated, and the sultan's men, thinking them defeated, pressed on among them till they found themselves, all 2.3.12

unawares, before the ambush. At this, the troops who were lying in wait emerged and put them to the slaughter. Wheeling around, the Successor returned to the charge, and the sultan's army was thrown off balance. It became disordered, and its ranks fell into disarray. Báási Rīfā, the sultan's brother, was killed, as were most of the army, leaving only a few survivors. At this, the Successor's energy was revived, and he became eager to go once more against the sultan and fight him, giving no thought to the fact that the affairs of men are decided by powers beyond their control. When the sultan heard of his brother's death, he grieved greatly and blamed himself for staying at home and not going to war. He said, "If I'd refused to listen and gone myself, this would not have happened—«and the command of God is a decree determined.»"[219] That same day he departed for the Successor's territory, with an army so immense it filled mountain and plain. When the Successor's spies came, they saw the sultan's army and all the soldiers in it, who were too many for any describer to describe or counter to count, and they hurried to take him the news.

2.3.13 He then feared for his life and his men's lives, and he set off the next morning, striking camp and making for Zaghāwah territory: its overlord was his maternal uncle and he wanted to stay with him, hoping his uncle would provide him with some of his own troops. Through the land he rode, by day and by night, the sultan following in his tracks as his spies had told him of the Successor's intended destination. The sultan was afraid that, if he reached Zaghāwah, the Successor's uncle would indeed provide him with an army. Then he'd find himself in a difficult position, and the conflict between them would be prolonged. The sultan therefore pressed on, hard in his pursuit, and eventually caught up with him at a place called Jarkū. In the vanguard of the sultan's army was Counselor Muḥammad Dukkumī, son of Counselor 'Alī wad Jāmi' who had poisoned himself in Kordofan, as mentioned earlier. When the two sides met, the Successor thought that was all there was to the army, so he wheeled round, attacked them, and skirmished with them, joining in the fighting himself. Everyone fled before him until he reached Counselor Muḥammad Dukkumī, where he halted and began striking at him with his sword, saying, "Slave! Betrayer! Traitor! Have you the gall to covet my wealth and that of my father?" But the counselor remained silent, uttering not a single word, bitter or sweet. He was, however, wearing two coats of mail so the Successor's sword had no effect on him. When the Successor got fed up with this, he decided to leave him be and was about to go. Counselor Muḥammad Dukkumī waited until he turned and then struck him on his right shoulder with his sword and broke his collarbone (he was a strong man), the sword breaking at the hilt and flying off into the field. The Successor's hand went numb and his arm went slack. Counselor Muḥammad noticed this and was eager to take him, but the Successor's men freed him just as the counselor was about to seize him. The Successor's army was now defeated, and Counselor Muḥammad sent his own after it, dispatching the broken sword to Sultan ʿAbd al-Raḥmān to inform him of what had happened. Immediately, the sultan sent to Counselor Muḥammad two mighty swords set with gems, ordered him to march after the Successor, and told him he was following their tracks.

There was at that time a man among the native Egyptian soldiery[220] called Zabādī who was said to be an Egyptian fellah. He hunted using a musket[221] and always hit his mark. He went boldly up to the sultan and said to him, "My Lord, if I rid you of your enemy right now, what will you give me?" The sultan answered, "If you rid me of him, I'll give you a hundred slaves." "Send me to the counselor's army," said the man, "so that I can be among his soldiers, and you shall see what will happen this day." The sultan sent him right away to the counselor with a letter in which he stated, "Zabādī has undertaken to rid us of our enemy, and we have undertaken to reward him for doing so. He asked to be with your soldiers, and now has reached you. If he requests anything of you, help him, and treat him well. I am coming along behind you." So Zabādī mounted a swift camel and caught up with the counselor's army and 2.3.14

gave him the sultan's order. The counselor read it and welcomed him, and he joined his forces. Now, the Divine Will had ordained that the Successor's arm should hurt him, making him want to dismount and take a rest, but the high officers of the state forbade him to do so. "Why do you prevent me?" he asked them. "Counselor Muḥammad is pursuing us with his army," they replied, "and the fighting between us continues." The Successor grew angry and said, "He still has not turned back and left us alone?" They said, "No." So he wheeled around to attack the counselor's soldiers. His high officials opposed him in this too, but he said, "It must be so."

2.3.15 While he was arguing with them that they should turn back, and they were trying to persuade him with gentle words to abandon the idea, Zabādī arrived, recognized and picked out the Successor, took aim, fired, and hit the target, some say in the chest, others in the head.[222] The Successor fell, but they propped him up. He walked a little way and started to expire. When the officials saw he was dying, they set up a large tent for him and set him down in it. The army halted and warded off their attackers, but the fighting between the two sides went on. Eventually the counselor arrived and saw that the soldiery had halted and that the battle was ongoing. He asked what was happening and was told that the Successor had been hit by a bullet, was expiring, and was unable to move. That was why they'd erected this tent for him and the army had halted to defend him. "Stop fighting, then," he said, "and encircle them and let us wait and see what happens," and he sent word to the sultan that the Successor had been injured by a bullet fired by Zabādī and was dying and that "if it is possible for our lord to go to him before he gives up the ghost, he should do so." Shortly after the messenger was sent to the sultan, the Successor died, loud weeping was heard, and the soldiers who had been fighting dismounted from their horses, as did the counselor's soldiers. As the poet says:

> No evildoer escapes Fate, though he be a king
>   whose troops fill plain and mountain!

And the writer of these words has said:

No army, though mighty, can fend off destruction
nor well-built tower Fate!

Soon after, the sultan and his army arrived and broke through the opposing ranks: when the Successor's army saw him, they surrendered. With Counselor Muḥammad and a group of high officers of the state, the sultan entered the tent, lifted the covering from the face of the Successor, and wept bitterly, saying, "My son, you did this to yourself. We gave you advice but you refused it, «and the command of God is a decree determined.»"[223] Then he turned to the high officers of the Successor's court and told them, "You made fighting seem so attractive to my son that you killed him. Wasn't there even one among you with the good sense to deter him and advise him more wisely?" They all swore that they were innocent of what he'd done and that they'd advised him against it, but that he'd refused to accept their advice. They told him, "Our Lord, we accepted his favor and we fought for him until God brought about his death, and we did not betray him. If you accept us, we will fight for you in the same way. If we'd betrayed him and then entered your service, we would have ended up betraying you too." The sultan saw the truth of their words and said, "I pardon you. Any of you who wants to be with me retains his rank and standing and any who does not, let him meet with nothing but good." Then he ordered that the Successor be buried in that same place and refused to let him be buried in the tombs of the kings, saying, "He was a rebel, and is not to be buried in our tombs."[224] So he was buried there. 2.3.16

The sultan stayed there the rest of the day and the following night, and in the morning set off to return to his seat, trailing clouds of victory, happy that the time of hardship was over—as though it were he whom Abū l-Ṭayyib al-Mutanabbī had in mind when he said:[225] 2.3.17

Go where you will—there shall light alight
and the fates ensure your hopes come true,

And when you depart, may safety be your companion
where'er you go, and a steady, quiet rain that never flags.
From any source you plunder you will emerge the richest,
all eyes raised to watch your coming.
You are he with talk of whom time is besotted,
with talk of whom men's evenings are adorned.
Should you remove your favor, death's the penalty you mete out,
should you be forgiving, longevity's your gift—
And kings may give gifts, but to the favored you give gifts
beside which the best of what kings may give is dust.
God save your heart! It fears not ruin,
only that shame come near you.
You have turned aside from all that marks man's mortal nature,
while before you mighty armies with all their panoply swerve aside.
O you, whose protégé lords it o'er the powerful
while the tyrant before his assaults is brought low,
Where'er you be, no desert shall come between us,
and our meeting, and the place where we shall visit you, are not far off.

2.3.18 At the time, the sultan's seat was at a place called Qirlī, while Sultan Tayrāb's seat had been at Rīl,[226] and that of the Successor at Jadīd Rās al-Fīl. Later, Sultan ʿAbd al-Raḥmān moved and made his seat at a place called Tandaltī, which is now the seat of his son. It was never before the custom of the Fur to remain in one capital as they have in the place called Tandaltī.[227]

2.3.19 After the sultan had rested and recovered from fighting the Successor, and his agitation had abated, he turned his attention to the condition of his subjects. He abolished local tolls, removed illegal imposts, filled offices, and attended to the country's prosperity and affluence. He prohibited the consumption of alcohol[228] in public, and fornication, and reestablished security on the highways, which had been terrifying places but which now became so safe a woman could walk from one end of the country to the other loaded with jewelry and carrying goods and fear none but God. Trading activities increased, the land produced crops without interruption, and the sultan displayed perfect justice, neither honoring nor aiding oppressors, even when they were his relatives.

A trusted source told me that one day two Bedouin crossed the sultan's path, as he was returning from the hunt. One of them told him, "I have suffered an injustice, Rashīd! God keep you, Rashīd, I have suffered an injustice!" It is their custom, if one of them finds himself in the presence of the sultan, to place two fingers of his right hand, namely, the index finger and the thumb, against the corners of his mouth and to flick them, producing a loud sound that contains a *k* and lots of *r*s followed by *u*.[229] This sound that emerges from the mouth they call *karawrāk*, and it is made only by one who has been afflicted by some disaster. The Bedouin made this sound and every time he did so he would say, "God keep you, Rashīd! I have suffered an injustice!" The sultan, however, paid him no attention, either because he was busy or because he couldn't hear him above all the drumming and singing and the clamor of the troops. The Bedouin performed the *karawrāk* several times, and when the sultan did not respond, his friend said to him, "Leave him be. He's 'rightly guided' when it comes to his own interests, not yours."[230] The sultan heard him, halted, and asked the other Bedouin why he'd said that. "My brother here," replied the man, "has performed the *karawrāk* several times and complained to you, crying out, 'Rashīd, I have suffered an injustice.' When you failed to respond to him, I told him, 'Leave him be: he's "rightly guided" when it comes to his own interests, not when it comes to yours.'" The sultan laughed and said, "Not at all. I'm rightly guided when it comes to yours too. Tell me who has done you this injustice." "Báási Khabīr has done me an injustice," said the man (Báási Khabīr was a relative of the sultan's). "What did he take from you?" he asked. "He took five she-camels from me," the man said. The sultan stayed where he was, summoned Báási Khabīr, and questioned him. He confessed, and 2.3.20

the sultan ordered him to pay ten she-camels, five as the man's right and five as a punishment. He paid, and the Bedouin left in transports of joy.

2.3.21 It was now that he appointed Muḥammad Kurrā to the office of shaykh-father, the highest office in Darfur. Its occupant exercises rights over life and death, has a government apparatus like that of the sultan, and insignia like those of the sultan. It is customary for this office to be occupied by a eunuch and only a eunuch, since it's feared that if any other occupies it and his sense of his own importance grows, he may set himself up against the sultan and seek to take the realm for himself.[231] Once Shaykh-Father Muḥammad Kurrā had been appointed, the sultan sent him out into the country,[232] and he stopped at Abū l-Judūl, where he established justice among the people and set things to rights, to the extent of having many men executed for injustices they'd committed.

2.3.22 When the sultan's justice became plain for all to see, and scholars, the learned, and the sharifs all began to love him, sharifs and scholars came from many parts of the country to pay him their respects. The first to go was my father, may clouds of mercy and acceptance hover over him. When he first arrived in Darfur, my father stayed at Kūbayh with Faqīh Ḥasan wad ʿAwūḍah, who informed the people of the town that a man of learning from Tunis had arrived.[233] Their great men, such as Faqīh Muḥammad Kuraytīm, Sharif Surūr ibn Abī l-Jūd, ʿAbd al-Karīm (Faqīh Ḥasan wad ʿAwūḍah's son), and their like, came to see him and asked him to give lessons in Shaykh Khalīl's *Epitome*, so he took them through the section on acts of worship. Word of my father reached Faqīh Mālik al-Fūtāwī, who told the sultan about him, and the latter summoned my father. My father went to him and the sultan did him honor, gave him several female slaves, and ordered him to stay with Faqīh Nūr al-Anṣārī, the husband of his daughter, Mééram Ḥawwāʾ. He was descended from the Anṣār—a lover of the learned and a knowledgeable man. He studied under my father a portion of al-Bukhārī's collection of hadiths of the Prophet titled *The Reliable Compendium*.

The holy man told the sultan of my father's qualifications as a scholar and that he was skilled in both the rational and the transmitted sciences.[234] So he had him brought before him and, during the month of Ramadan, studied under him some of the hadiths of the Prophet. Faqīh Mālik pinned his hopes on him and ordered his sons to attend his classes. Of Faqīh Mālik's brothers, Faqīh Ibrāhīm, Faqīh Madanī, and Faqīh Yaʿqūb attended his classes, and of his sons, al-Zākī, al-Sanūsī, and Muḥammad Jalāl al-Dīn, as well as his nephew Faqīh Muḥammad al-Barkāwī. Faqīh Ḥusayn wad Tūris also attended. In addition, the sultan ordered him to write a commentary on Mughulṭāy al-Turkī's *Qualities,* so he wrote an enormous commentary on it in some sixteen fascicules that he called *The Perfect Pearl Regarding the Qualities of Muḥammad.* He also asked him for a commentary on the *Epitome* of Shaykh Khalīl al-Mālikī concerning jurisprudence, so he wrote a two-volume commentary on it that he entitled *The Perfectly Matched Pearls on the Text of the Erudite Khalīl ibn Isḥāq.* He also wrote a large commentary on *Ibn Ājurrūm's Text* within which he included about two hundred lines from *The One-Thousand-Line Poem* of Ibn Mālik, which made up a huge volume that he subsequently abridged in several fascicules. And he wrote a graceful commentary on *The Glittering Ladder*, in fascicules, and he authored an epistle on palmistry.[235] 2.3.23

Sultan ʿAbd al-Raḥmān was also visited by that ascetic and reclusive man of religion Shaykh Tamurrū al-Fullānī, and likewise by the distinguished man of religion Shaykh Ḥusayn ʿAmmārī al-Azharī. Another who came to pay his respects was the Meccan sharif Musāʿid, who I was told was a son of Sharif Surūr.[236] Sultan ʿAbd al-Raḥmān's judge was that irreproachable man of religion Shaykh ʿIzz al-Dīn al-Jāmiʿī, who is currently chief judge of Darfur and its territories.[237] Sultan ʿAbd al-Raḥmān was generous, noble, just, and unassuming. He was of medium height, extremely black, with gray hair; he was fierce in his anger, quick to be reconciled, a good manager of affairs. One example of that last trait is that when the French entered Egypt and the Turkish soldiery fled, a certain *kāshif* 2.3.24

named Zawānah Kāshif,[238] who was said to be one of Murād Bayk's Mamluks or one of al-Alfī's *kāshifs*, came to Darfur, bringing with him more than ten Mamluks and a large quantity of baggage, as well as camels, servants, a cook, a housekeeper, and grooms. He also brought a cannon and a mortar. When he stopped in Darfur, Sultan ʿAbd al-Raḥmān treated him as an honored guest and gave him a warm welcome, putting him up in a good hostelry and providing for him so well that the man ended up with so many slaves he couldn't tell one from the other. Then he asked the sultan if he might build a house like those in Egypt, and the sultan gave him permission to do so. He cast bricks, used the slaves to cut stones, and made a beautiful house, which he surrounded with a wall, which he made thick, with two loopholes in it, opposite the sultan's house. In one of these loopholes he placed the cannon and in the other the mortar.

2.3.25 This house was on higher ground than the sultan's, allowing him to observe the sultan's comings and goings. He then let himself be seduced by the idea that he could kill the sultan and rule the country by watching him as he went in and out, firing the cannon at him, and killing him. At the same time, he was afraid that if he killed the sultan, the people and the high officers of the realm would refuse to obey him, so he arranged to meet privately with Faqīh al-Ṭayyib wad Muṣṭafā, who had been a vizier of Sultan Tayrāb's and was his in-law, by which I mean that Sultan Tayrāb was married to his sister, who had borne him children. When Zawānah Kāshif met with him, he confessed his secret, after making him promise to tell no one, and said, "I'm told your sister's son is a son of the sultan. I want you to join forces with me in killing the latter so your nephew can assume power and the realm can be ours." Faqīh al-Ṭayyib agreed to this. Then they said, "This will not work unless we involve people who have soldiers." "That's up to you to arrange," said Zawānah, "for you know the people better." So Faqīh al-Ṭayyib set about cozening people and bringing them to the Kāshif, and the Kāshif would award them goods and make them swear to be with him. Eventually, they involved a number of men in the matter.

Now, it happened that Faqīh al-Ṭayyib cozened one of the army commanders and brought him to the Kāshif, who gave him a handsome gift, let him in on what was planned, and swore him to secrecy. The man swore, took the gift, and took it to the sultan, and revealed the full extent and truth of the matter. The sultan told him, "Take your gift, go, and be with them just as you are now, and be sure not to tell anyone that you came to see me." The following morning, Zawānah Kāshif came to the sultan's house and the latter did him even more honor than before, giving him, on this occasion, one hundred male slaves and one hundred female, one hundred she-camels, one hundred jars of clarified butter, one hundred of molasses, and one hundred loads of millet, and he clothed him in a red cashmere shawl and a coat of red broadcloth and presented him with a sword and gave him a fine steed with a saddle of gold. The Kāshif left for his house overjoyed at what the sultan had given him, saying, "These are assets God has put in my way to use for this business." That evening, after the prayer, the sultan ordered that one of the petty kings, along with his soldiery, be brought to stand and wait until he saw the Kāshif entering the sultan's house, and then, while he was away, go in and seize everything of value that was in the Kāshif's house, warning him to let nothing escape him. After that, he sent a boy to the Kāshif to tell him, "My master has taken his seat for his evening gathering with his friends and has expressed the desire that you attend his assembly, now." And the sultan placed slaves in position to arrest him whenever he should give the order. 2.3.26

The boy went and told the Kāshif what the sultan had said, and the man went back with him. When he entered the sultan's presence, the latter treated him with honor. With him were some servants, who passed through two doors with him but were prevented from going through the third.[239] They were told, "Wait here till your master comes back," so they huddled there together. The sultan sat conversing with the Kāshif until a part of the night had passed, and then the sultan said, "I'm hungry," and requested something to eat, so some roast meat of the sort called *naṣīs*, meaning the kind that's 2.3.27

roasted on hot stones, was brought, uncut. They called for a knife but no one could find one, so the Kāshif pulled out a knife he had on him and was about to cut up the meat when one of those present swore that he mustn't do so and that he'd see to it, and he took the knife from him and started cutting up the meat. Then the Kāshif took out his dagger and another took that from him and at that point the sultan gave the order to arrest him. Once he'd been seized, the sultan asked him, "What wrong did I do you that you should want to kill me and mislead and cozen my soldiers?" "Pardon me!" said the man. "May God not pardon me if I pardon you!" said the sultan, and he ordered that he be slaughtered on the spot, and he was, like a sheep. Right away, his possessions were brought too, along with his slaves and other things he possessed, so that in the end there was nothing left in the house. The sultan ordered that the house be torn down, so it was torn down and all vestige of it erased, as though it had never been, and his followers were seized the same evening and spent the night as prisoners. Next morning, the sultan summoned them, and when they were before him, pardoned them and released them, placing the Kāshif's treasurer, whose name was Yūsuf, in command of them. Then he pursued all those who had made a pact with the Kāshif and seized them one by one till none were left. The last to be arrested was Faqīh al-Ṭayyib. He arrested him and made him suffer the worst of deaths, and he imprisoned the man's nephew for life, till he should die.

2.3.28 The arrest of the aforementioned Faqīh took place in the following manner. The sultan gave him complete freedom to do what he wanted, bestowing wealth on him and showing him the utmost affection, so that it never occurred to Faqīh al-Ṭayyib that the sultan had any awareness that he'd been involved with Zawānah Kāshif. Things went on like this till a day came when Faqīh al-Ṭayyib was present in the sultan's house. The sultan was seated in his court and some camels loaded down with honey were brought him, so he gave them to Faqīh al-Ṭayyib and ordered that he be given a set of clothes, and they brought him a fine set of clothes and a red cashmere shawl.

He put these on and called down blessings on the sultan, calling for the preservation of his rule, and then sat; it is a custom of the petty kings of the Fur that if one of them dresses someone in red clothes, it means he's angry with him and has decided to kill him. At the end of the gathering, the sultan recalled what the Faqīh had done and his duplicitous behavior with the Kāshif and he turned to those present and said, "I ask you, in God's name, to bear witness: was this Faqīh more comfortably off or wealthier in the days of my brother than he is now?" They all responded, "No, by God. He's more comfortably off, wealthier, and more influential now!" "Ask him, then," said the sultan, "why he betrayed me and plotted with the Kāshif to kill me and bring ruin to my house." They asked him, and the man adjured the sultan by Mighty God to kill him rather than force him to answer that question, since to die, he thought, would be easier. The sultan honored his wish and gave the order, and he was slaughtered like a sheep. The sultan took all his property and estates; nothing escaped him. I heard that he'd dispatched the soldiers to take his property from his estates some time previously and gave the order to seize them on that precise day, for he was afraid that otherwise word would get out and something escape him. This was an example of the good fortune that accompanied him always. Another example of this good fortune was that everyone who sought to do him ill failed and God delivered them into his hands.

Another example of that same good fortune was the incident with Iyā Kurī Kinānah, mother of Ḥabīb, who was mentioned earlier.[240] What happened was that the sultan ignored her and failed to fulfill his promise to her, either because he was too busy or because he was afraid that either she or her son would try to kill him. When she saw how he ignored her (she was living at that time in the sultan's house while her son Ḥabīb had been provided with his own), she made a contract with some of the members of the royal family that they would support her son and agree to let them help Ḥabīb rule when he was sultan—her hopes had been dashed on her discovery that the sultan had had more sons, making her fear for her own. 2.3.29

The sultan, though he ignored her, had left her in office—she had power to command and forbid, and the reins of household affairs were still entirely in her hands.

2.3.30 When she made up her mind to betray the sultan, she asked his permission to allow her son Ḥabīb to fulfil his wish to hold a banquet, saying, "I'd like to provide him with food from here." The sultan agreed, so she started to bring in huge bowls, placing chain mail coats in them and putting food on top in such a way that anyone who looked at a bowl would think that there was nothing in it but food;[241] in one she would put coats of chain mail, in the next swords. She was able to send out more than a hundred bowls in this way. She waited and, after a few days, asked his permission for another banquet, which he gave without giving the matter a second thought, for he was openhearted and harbored no suspicions of evil. And she did as she had the first time. A few days later she asked for permission again, but before the third banquet was announced it happened that the sultan unexpectedly set eyes on a daughter of one of the notables, a pretty girl she was raising, and he fell in love with her and made up his mind to speak to the Iyā Kūrī about her and become engaged to her. Umm Ḥabīb[242] must have sensed this in the sultan and she started mistreating the girl whom she'd been grooming to marry her son Ḥabīb. The girl couldn't stand the mistreatment, especially since she'd discovered the Iyā Kūrī's betrayal of the sultan and what she wanted to do to him. She therefore slipped away, met with the sultan in private, and told him that Umm Ḥabīb had broken into the weapons and supplies storehouses, that the vessels for the banquet had all been filled with chain mail and swords, and that she'd engaged with Malik So-and-so and Malik So-and-so "to help her kill you and make Ḥabīb sovereign, and if you doubt what I say, overturn any of the bowls that are sent out for the banquet tomorrow and you'll see my words are true." "Go back to your place," said the sultan, "and be careful not to let anyone know that you've told me anything." She went back, and the sultan, angry at what he had heard, said to one of his servants, "Inform me tomorrow before the food for the banquet is sent over to Ḥabīb's," telling him to keep it to himself, which he did.

This was how things stood when morning came, when the banquet was laid out and Umm Ḥabīb summoned the men and women slaves to carry the bowls. The servant told the Sultan then that the banquet was ready, so he went in and saw her organizing the food for delivery. "Not so fast!" said the sultan, and then, "Lift the covers and show me my son Ḥabīb's banquet." They lifted the covers and he saw fine food. Going over to a bowl that contained a kind of food that he liked, he said, "Set this aside for me and put the contents into small dishes so that I and some of my guests may partake of it." "We hear and obey!" they replied. When word of this reached Umm Ḥabīb, she came and said, "I swear on my father and mother, we have lots of that dish! May my lord leave that bowl, and we'll bring him a great quantity of it." "No doubt," he replied, "but I've taken a fancy to this: perhaps what you send me may not be as good, and, even if it's the very same dish, may not appeal to me." At this, she could think of no alternative but to do as he asked, and said, "Allow the servants to remove these other bowls while you keep this one aside." "No," said he. "This bowl must be emptied and filled just as it was and then all the food loaded up at one time." 2.3.31

When the small dishes were brought and the food was being ladled out of the bowl, the chain mail came into view from beneath the food, and he called out, "Umm Ḥabīb, what is this?" Abashed, she said nothing. He ordered, therefore, that she be seized and all the bowls turned upside down, and discovered all the chain mail coats, swords, French dollars, and so on. "What wrong did I do you that you should plot my destruction?" he asked her. She didn't answer, so he ordered her to be killed there and then, and she was. Then he immediately sent one of his chiefs to Ḥabīb's house, having first invited Ḥabīb to come to him. Ḥabīb came, thinking nothing was amiss. When he appeared before him, the sultan ordered that he be seized, and he was placed in the lock-up. Then he sent him under cover of night to Jabal Marrah,[243] stripped him of all his 2.3.32

wealth, and had the chain mail and weapons returned to their place. Subsequently, he seized all those who had conspired with Ḥabīb and left not a single one alive.

2.3.33 Now that order was restored, Sultan ʿAbd al-Raḥmān appointed Faqīh Mālik al-Fūtāwī as vizier, because he believed him to be a scholar and a righteous man; al-Fūtāwī also claimed to know the "secret of the letter" and the science of talismans,[244] even though he was in fact a man of mediocre literary culture and would often make a show of being God-fearing and righteous while concealing the opposite in his heart. This was something I suspected of him, and then God proved the truth of my suspicions at a single gathering. The way this came about was that when he was promoted to the viziership, the entire Fullān tribe in Darfur fell under his command, and he started taking their side with the sultan whenever there was some incident between them and their enemies among the other tribes. He also released them from their obligations to the state to the point that no taxes were collected from them and everything they took as plunder from other tribes stuck with them. As a result, they became one of the most powerful and richest tribes.

2.3.34 Now it happened that the Fullān raided the Masālīṭ, killing many of them and taking a large portion of their wealth in the form of cattle, horses, and slaves. The head of the Fullān, whose name was Jidd al-ʿAyyāl,[245] came, bringing as a gift for Faqīh Mālik some of the horses, cattle, and slaves that had been plundered, so that he would defend the tribe's interests. It was the month of Ramadan and late afternoon, and at that moment Faqīh Mālik was reading from al-Qurṭubī's *Memorandum*, where it describes the people of hellfire. He came to the place where the author says, "And the fire keeps saying, 'O Lord, add to me,' until the Merciful puts His *rijl* in it, a *rijl* being a company of people, as evidenced by the verse:

> And a company of the clan passed by us (*fa-marra binā rijlun*)
> and retired."[246]

The Faqīh read out "And the fire keeps saying, 'O Lord, add to me'" and—it being his habit to repeat after every word or two "Yes, indeed! Thus sayeth the book!"—he said, "And the fire keeps saying, 'O Lord, add to me.' (Yes, indeed! Thus sayeth the book!) And the fire keeps saying, 'O Lord, add to me.' (Yes, indeed! Thus sayeth the book!) until the Merciful puts his *rijl* in it (Yes, indeed! Thus sayeth the book!), a *rijl* being a company of people (Yes, indeed! Thus sayeth the book!) as in the verse (Yes, indeed! Thus sayeth the book!), 'And a man ran off with us' (*farra binā rajulun*) (Yes, indeed! Thus sayeth the book!)." He repeated this numerous times until his son, al-Sanūsī, said to him, "*Abbo! Fir! Binā rajulun!* ('Sir! Flee! There's a man upon us!')" and the Faqīh repeated "Yes, indeed!—*Fir! Binā rajulun*" and said it several times. I was sitting there and couldn't keep silent, so I took a copy from a man who was next to me and saw written, "*fa-marra binā rijlun min al-ḥayy*," etc., so I said, "*Abbo*, it's *fa-marra binā rijlun,*" but he said to me, "Shut up. You're still too young to understand these things; plus, he's the one who has the qualification to be a witness." So I shut up.[247]

Another example of the mediocrity of his literary culture is contained in the story told to me by my father, may clouds of mercy and acceptance hover above him, to the effect that the sultan asked the same Faqīh to preach on the day of the Feast, so he went to my father and asked him to write him a sermon. This my father did, putting at the end, "Composed by the one in need of his Bountiful Lord, ʿUmar al-Tūnisī ibn Sulaymān, on such and such a day and year," and gave it to him. On the day of the Feast, the Faqīh prayed with the sultan, then mounted the pulpit and gave the sermon, saying at the end, "Composed by . . . ," etc., without realizing that these words weren't part of the sermon. He was one of the richest high officers of state and held about five hundred villages as fiefs, not counting those held by his brothers. 2.3.35

The sultan granted Shaykh-Father Muḥammad Kurrā exalted status, giving his word authority greater than any other's. He received news that Hāshim al-Musabbaʿāwī, King of Kordofan, had returned 2.3.36

and taken it back from the sultan's governor. He therefore equipped a massive army under the command of Shaykh-Father Muḥammad Kurrā, and the latter went to Kordofan, where he scored a great success, wresting it from Sultan Hāshim's control, killing his soldiers, and chasing him into the desert. Shaykh-Father Muḥammad Kurrā made Kordofan his home for seven years,[248] during which time he sent the sultan vast wealth in the form of slaves, gold, and other things. Some of his enemies told tales against him to the sultan,[249] so the sultan dispatched Counselor Muḥammad,[250] the son of Counselor 'Alī wad Jāmi', and his army against him. He gave him a pair of shackles and told him, "Take these shackles and put them on him." Then he sent him off with his army. This was a test on the part of the sultan. When Counselor Muḥammad reached Kordofan, he expected Shaykh-Father Muḥammad would oppose or resist him, but he did nothing of the sort. On the contrary, when the counselor reached him, he said, "What did the sultan order you to do?" "To shackle you," he said, "and send you to him." "I hear and obey," he responded. "Give me the shackles." Counselor Muḥammad gave them to him and the shaykh-father took them and put them on with own hands and then summoned the blacksmith and ordered him to close them with a pin and file it down, in compliance with the sultan's order. The man did so, and the next day Shaykh-Father Muḥammad left on his journey, wearing the shackles on his feet all the way to Darfur. When the sultan was informed of his coming, he sent him someone to strike the shackles from his feet and said, "Didn't I say Muḥammad Kurrā would never disobey me?" Then he ordered him to come, with his entourage, to where the sultan was holding court. He arrived in great state, and the sultan went out to meet him and made much of him, in front of the viziers and those present, giving him gold bracelets to wear, going to the greatest lengths to honor him, and restoring him to his previous status; indeed, he now became greater than ever before. This act of the sultan's was the luckiest thing that could have happened to his son Muḥammad Faḍl, because when the sultan died, Shaykh-Father

Muḥammad Kurrā took up his cause. If he had not, no one would have spared him a glance or cared about him one way or the other.[251]

This came about as follows. When the sultan's last illness grew serious, Faqīh Mālik al-Fūtāwī went in to see him and found Shaykh-Father Muḥammad Kurrā with him. He told the sultan, "My master, there is much to be gained by stating one's last wishes. Your kindnesses to the people are beyond description and all your viziers and all the inhabitants of your realm think well of you. If, therefore, you express a wish, I believe—in fact, I am certain—that it will be put into effect without demur. So tell us your wishes; your children may well benefit from your doing so." The sultan replied, saying, "And who would want to play the role of God? He alone is equal to it." Faqīh Mālik repeated what he had said, and the sultan responded as before. Then he said it a third time, and the sultan responded as before. After the third time, Faqīh Mālik left him. Then the sultan, may clouds of mercy hover above him, died. When he died, the shaykh-father and Faqīh Mālik wept. When they had done, Faqīh Mālik said to the shaykh-father, "What are you going to do now?" and the shaykh-father said, "I will show you what I shall do," and that second he entered the sultan's house and called for Muḥammad Faḍl, who was the elder of the dead sultan's two sons, for the sultan had left behind him only two male offspring (Muḥammad Faḍl and Bukhārī[252]) and three female (Ḥawwā, Sitt al-Nisā', and Umm Salmā). He sat Muḥammad Faḍl[253] down, placed the seal ring on his finger and the turban on his head, girded him with the sword, and made him sit on the sultan's throne. Then he took Muḥammad Faḍl into a chamber, covered the doorway with a curtain, and immediately sent for his men. These came, wearing their swords, bristling with weapons, and he stood them at the doors,[254] detailing a group to act as his personal guard. He was helped in this by a secret door between his house and that of the sultan by which the soldiers entered undetected. 2.3.37

Then he sent someone to Malik Ibrāhīm wad Ramād, the most powerful of the viziers in terms of the number of men he 2.3.38

commanded and the one with the fiercest fighting spirit, and said, "The sultan commands your presence." So Malik Ibrāhīm went, and when he passed through the door, he found the soldiers standing there. Their presence took him by surprise, so he could see no alternative but to go on in. When he reached where the sultan was, he found Shaykh-Father Muḥammad Kurrā and Faqīh Mālik sitting, the dead sultan wrapped in a shroud between them. Seeing him thus, he wept. When he'd recovered, the shaykh-father said to him, "The sultan is dead. What do you think we should do?" "I think we should do whatever you think."[255] "Will you give me your word on that?" asked the shaykh-father. "Yes," he said. So he made him swear and accepted his assurances that he wouldn't oppose his opinion, and then raised the curtain and said, "This is the sultan," meaning Muḥammad Faḍl. "So be it," said Malik Ibrāhīm. Then the shaykh-father said, "Arise and give him your oath of allegiance," so he gave him his oath of allegiance then and there and sat down again.[256] Then the shaykh-father sent for the viziers and petty kings, one after another, and did with each as he had done with Malik Ibrāhīm until all the great men of the state had given their assurances, and the only ones left were those who had no power.

2.3.39 He now announced the death of the sultan, and the mourning drums were beaten. On hearing these, the sons of the sultans[257] mounted and rode, bristling with weapons, to launch an attack on the sultan's house. They found things in a state that caused them dread, with troops surrounding it and guarding it, against them and any others besides. When they couldn't find a way to get in, they attacked the town and started looting property, and the mob rallied to them, turning them into a massive army—terrible was the damage they did, and great the harm. The shaykh-father equipped an army against them under the command of Malik Daldan, whom we have mentioned above,[258] the son of Sultan Muḥammad Faḍl's aunt, and he went out against them and attacked them, and the mob that had gathered around them was defeated. Many were killed, and the sons of the sultans were overwhelmed and brought to the shaykh-father in irons. The shaykh-father sent them to prison in Jabal Marrah,[259] the uprising died down, and order was restored. Then the shaykh-father ordered the sultan, in view of his youth and lack of experience, to devote himself to study and the pursuit of learning. The boy found this tedious but had no choice but to obey, and he put up with the drudgery of education for about two years. During this period, Shaykh-Father Muḥammad Kurrā killed some maliks who staged an uprising, threw others into prison—all of them of the sultan's family and lineage—and appointed his own men to their positions. The high officers of state found this intolerable and feared what he might do to them, so they urged the sultan to kill or imprison him. Eventually, war broke out between them and he was killed, all of which we have already described,[260] though God knows best the truth of the matter.

The Book Proper, in three chapters

CHAPTER 1

A Description of Darfur and Its People, of Their Customs and the Customs of Their Kings, and of the Names of the Positions and Ranks Held by the Latter, in Five Sections[261]

Section 1: A Description of Darfur

Darfur is the third of the territories regarded as belonging to the kingdoms of the Blacks. This is so because, when approaching from the east, the first kingdom and territory one comes to is the Kingdom of Sinnār, after which is Kordofan, then the Land of the Fūr. Thus, Darfur is clearly the third. According to this reckoning, the territory of Wadadāy[262] is the fourth, al-Bāqirmah the fifth, Barnaw the sixth, Adiqiz the seventh, Nufah the eighth, Dār Tunbuktū the ninth, and Dār Mullā or Mallā (which is the base of the king of the Fullān, who, as we have mentioned earlier, are the same as the Fallātā) the tenth. Coming from the west, however, one would consider Mallā to be the first, Tunbuktū the second, Nufah the third, and so on. 3.1.1

The ancients gave the name Takrūr[263] to certain of the inhabitants of the Land of the Blacks, meaning by it the people of the kingdom of Barnaw. Now, however, this name has come to include several kingdoms, the first[264] being the territory of Waddāy or Wadadāy, also known as Dār Ṣulayḥ, and the last Barnaw; as such, it embraces Bāqirmah, Katakū, and Mandarah, and the people of all these lands are now referred to as "Takrūr," and this has become their custom. A few days ago, I met a man from these lands and 3.1.2

asked him, "Where are you from?" "From Takrūr," he said, or perhaps, if I remember rightly, "I'm a Takrūrī." I then asked him, "From where among all the Takrūrs?" and he said "Bāqirmah," but he only told me this after a tussle, as he thought I wouldn't know the place. When he told me, and I asked him about some places there, he was quite amazed and spoke more freely with me.

3.1.3 The limits of the Fur on the east are the farthest reaches of al-Ṭuwayshah, and on the west Dār Masālīṭ, meaning the kingdom of the Masālīṭ, and the last parts of Dār Qimir and the first of Dār Tāmah, which is the empty area located between Dār Ṣulayḥ and Darfur. On the south, the limit is the empty area between Dār Tāmah and Dār Fartīt and, on the north, al-Mazrūb, which is the first well one encounters when entering Darfur from Egyptian territory. Several small kingdoms belong to Darfur. On the north is the kingdom of the Zaghāwah, which is large, with countless inhabitants who have their own sultan, though in terms of his relationship with the sultan of the Fur he is more like one of his army commanders. Also to the north are the kingdoms of the Mīdawb and the Bartī, which are both large: the inhabitants of the second are more numerous than those of the first, but despite their large numbers are more submissive to the Fur sultan than are the Mīdawb.

3.1.4 Scattered around Darfur are the kingdoms of the Birqid, Barqū, Tunjūr, and Mīmah. The kingdoms of the Birqid and the Tunjūr are in the center, those of the Barqū and the Mīmah to the east, and those of the Dājū and the Bīqū, as well as the kingdom of Farāwujayh, to the south. Each has a ruler called a sultan, but he is appointed by the sultan of the Fur. These all follow the same pattern in terms of outward appearance and dress, except for the king of the Tunjūr, who wears a black turban. I asked him why, and he told me that at the beginning the kingdom of Darfur had belonged to his forefathers, so he wore the black turban as a sign of mourning for its loss.[265]

3.1.5 On its eastern and southern sides, Darfur is surrounded by large numbers of savannah Arabs, such as the Brown Misīriyyah, the Rizayqāt, and the Fullān,[266] all of them too numerous to count.

They own many cattle and horses and much equipage, and most of them are wealthy. They do not mix with the settled population; on the contrary, they follow the grazing, wherever it may be. To their number should be added the tribe called the Banū Ḥalbah, who are also cattle herders; they penetrate deep into Darfur and practice agriculture there. Among the camel herders there are the Fazārah (comprising the Maḥāmīd and the Majānīn), the Banū ʿUmrān, the Banū Jarrār, the Black Misīriyyah, and others. Each of these tribes pays a tax, which the sultan takes annually in animals.

There are differences, however. The Brown Misīriyyah and the Rizayqāt, because they are strong and go far out into the desert, give the sultan only the worst of their animals, and the tax official can only acquire the good ones by paying them off. If he sets his heart on getting more, he is expelled, or even killed, and the sultan can do nothing about it. I've been told that the Rizayqāt once refused to accept the rule of Sultan Tayrāb, who sent an army against them, which they defeated. He then took the field against them himself. They fled and took their herds into the Barajūb. He followed them and they killed large numbers of his men and he could lay his hands on nothing. The Barajūb is a place that takes the traveler ten days to cross. It consists of soft mud covered with water that reaches to around the groin: the mud is so soft that the legs of riding animals sink into it. What's more, it is full of thorny trees. It stops raining there for only two months a year, during the winter. 3.1.6

It takes about sixty days to traverse Darfur from end to end, beginning at Dār al-Zaghāwah and ending at Dār Rungah. In fact, if one were to take its dependencies, such as Dār Rungah, Fanqarū, Dār Bandalah, Bīngah, and Shālā, into account as well, it would take more than seventy days—this according to information provided by the people of the country. I, however, don't believe that it extends so far, and think that at its greatest extent it may take fifty days or fewer, and then only if one counts the five kingdoms of the Fartīt referred to above, which at that time were dependencies under treaties with the sultan of Darfur and paid him an annual land tax. To 3.1.7

be specific, if you enter Dār al-Zaghāwah from al-Mazrūb and make straight for Kūbayh, the journey takes about six days. From Kūbayh to Tandaltī, which is the sultan's seat, takes two days. From the sultan's seat to Jadīd Karyū is two days and from there to Rīl is two days. This makes twelve days. From Rīl to Jadīd Rās al-Fīl is four days and from there to Taldawā three or four days, while from there to Tabaldiyyah takes eight days—Tabaldiyyah is at the eastern limits of the Fur. Then you enter the territories of the Dāju and the Bīqū, and proceed for another eight days. This makes thirty-four days in all.[267]

3.1.8 If you leave these territories going east, you find a savannah pullulating with desert nomads too many for any but their Creator to count, such as the Brown Misīriyyah, the Ḥabbāniyyah, and the Rizayqāt, and if you turn west, you enter Dār Ába Dima'ng, which will take you around ten days to cross. Then you enter a savannah that you must cross for two days before entering Dār Rungah, which takes about three days to cross. Dār Fanqarū takes the same, or slightly less. Beyond these is a savannah that takes around two days to cross, after which you enter Dār Bīngah and Shālā, which take two days to cross. In sum, you can see from what I've told you that the whole length of Darfur, from north to south, along with its dependencies, takes not more than around fifty days to cross.

3.1.9 These dependencies are the southern lands beyond Dār al-Farāwujayh, the far border of Farāwujayh being the border of the Fur kingdoms proper. The area that the Fur call the High Plain[268] stretches from Rīl to the southern limit of the Lands of the Fūr. Dār Ába Dima'ng takes as much as ten days to cross—the ába dima'ng rules over twelve petty kings, each of whom rules over an independent vassal state. Dār Ába Dima'ng is Dār Tomorókkóngá: the name, as we shall describe later, is that of an office and means "the sultan's right arm," and the governor who bears this title rules over the land of the Tomorókkóngá; Dār Tomorókkóngá is thus known as Dār Ába Dima'ng. The name is on a par with tikináwi, which is likewise the name of an office, and means "the sultan's left arm."[269] The tikináwi also rules over twelve petty kings, and is the ruler of the Zaghāwah and the lands beyond them to the east; for the same reason, then, Dār al-Zaghāwah is also known as Dār al-Tikináwi. If you were to ask, "Given that the ába dima'ng and the tikináwi are on a par, why is Dār Ába Dima'ng twelve days' riding in length, whereas Dār Tikináwi is only five?" I would respond that Dār Tikináwi is wider than Dār Ába Dima'ng: it takes a little over five days to cross Dār Ába Dima'ng from side to side, whereas Dār Tikináwi takes around seven, so what it lacks in length it makes up for in extra width.

Darfur is arranged in a very precise way. We have stated earlier that it is divided down the middle by Jabal Marrah, that the half that's east of Jabal Marrah is a plain, and that the width of Jabal Marrah is equal to about two days' travel as the crow flies. Behind the mountains, to the west, lies another plain. To the north, however, are the Zaghāwah and the Bartī, two mighty tribes: the Bartī to the east, the Zaghāwah to the west. In the middle of the mountains, to the south, is Jadīd Karyū, which is inhabited by two mighty tribes, the Tunjūr and the Birqid. Moving farther south, one comes to Jadīd Rās al-Fīl and beyond; indeed, one will eventually come to Tabaldiyyah, though there are small towns and tribes between them. From there on live the Dājū and Bīqū, all the way to the savannah in the south and east and to Dār Ába Dima'ng. The Dājū are to the west, the Bīqū to the east. To the east of Jadīd Karyū live two mighty tribes, the Barqū and the Mīmah. 3.1.10

Jabal Marrah is inhabited exclusively by non-Arabic-speaking Fur. These consist of three tribes: the Kunjáara, who live from Qirlī to beyond the little mountain itself called Marrah, which is the true Marrah; coming soon after this and extending all the way to the border with Dār Ába Dima'ng are the Fur called the Karakiriit; the Fur who live in Dār Ába Dima'ng are called the Tomorókkóngá. After Dār Ába Dima'ng come Dār Rūngah and Dār Farūjayh, Dār Rūngah on the west and Dār Farūjayh on the east. Dār Fanqarū follows Dār Farūjayh, and Dār Rūngah follows Dār Silā, though this 3.1.11

slopes more toward the west, which is why it's ruled by the people of Wāddāy.

3.1.12 Jabal Marrah is not one mountain, but several, both large and small. Before one enters Dār Ába Dima'ng, the mountains come to an end, and what remains is a flat land inhabited by the Fullān, up to the point where they approach the Masālīṭ on the west. Then come the Banū Ḥalbah and the Black Misīriyyah. Except for the Bedouin, all those whom we've mentioned live on Darfur's northern, eastern, and southern edges. People born neither into the tribes nor the Fur they call "territorials," meaning they are people whose origins may be traced to some territory.[270] They are in the middle and are not deemed a tribe. If you want to get from me a clear exposition of Darfur and of how the home territories of these tribes and of the Bedouin who surround it are arranged, take a look at what I've drawn—more or less in the form of a chart—to make it easy to grasp (suppose this end to be south). Let me add that if I have not been able to give an absolutely clear exposition, owing to my ignorance of drawing and the small paper size, it is in essence as shown. Someone with the necessary skills will be able to turn it into a better likeness.[271]

3.1.13 The most prosperous lands to the north are those of the Bartī and the Zaghāwah, because of the great number of people. Observe now God's wisdom, for the two tribes are on the same line of travel, but the Bartī are more kindhearted and have handsomer faces, and their women are more beautiful, while the Zaghāwah are the opposite. Likewise, the Dājū and the Bīqū are on the same line of travel and the daughters of the Bīqū are more beautiful than those of the Dājū. As for the Birqid and the Tunjūr, both comely and ugly are to be found among them, but the Birqid are treacherous, being thieves by night and fearing neither God nor His messenger by day, whereas the Tunjūr have a modicum of religion and a modicum of reason, which prevent them from such behavior. The people of the mountain are all the same in terms of both ugliness and uncouthness, but when one gets to Dār Ába Dima'ng, one finds that the men and the

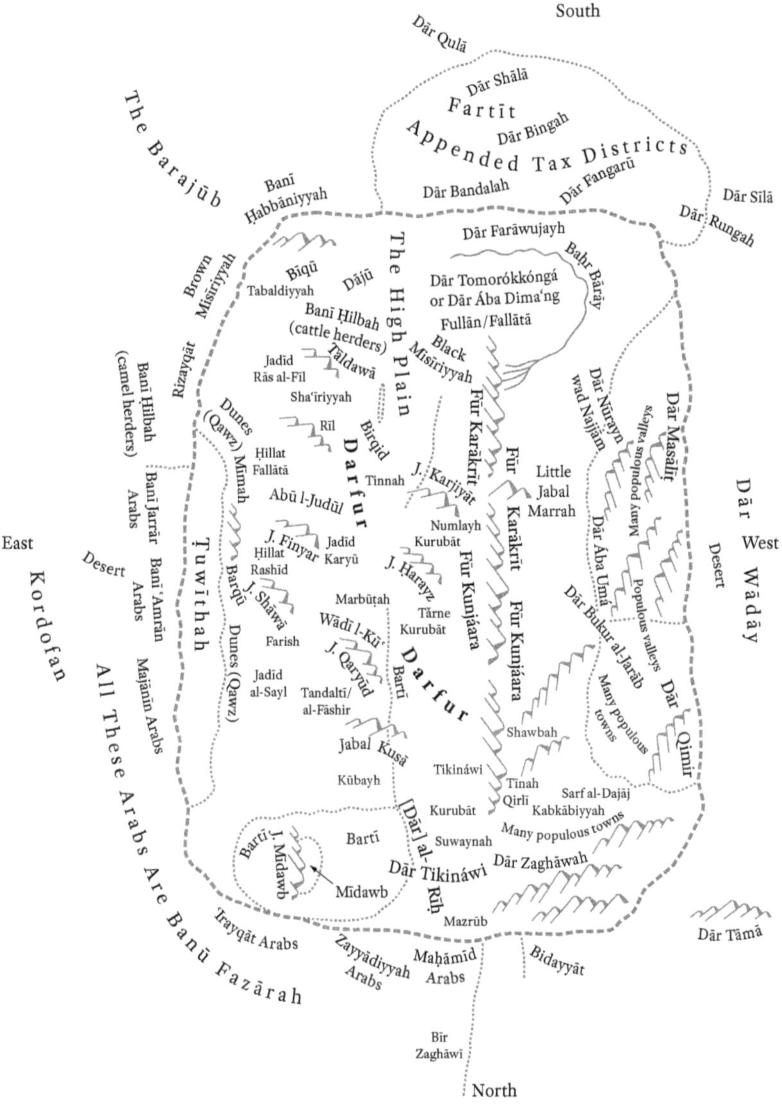

women are both beautiful; glory then to Him whose work this is! The women of the Masālīṭ captivate the mind and bewitch the heart, but the most beautiful women in Darfur, without a doubt, are those of the Arabs; indeed, even their men are beautiful. Not a living soul is to be found between Wāddāy and Darfur other than the people of Jabal Tāmah; we shall recount later how Sultan Ṣābūn, sultan of Wāddāy, raided the latter and assumed power over its people.[272]

3.1.14 Know too that the territories in Darfur are all divided up among the high officers of the state, each of whom holds a portion of them according to his office and condition.[273] The largest territories are Dār Ába Dima'ng and Dār Tikináwi: each of the two office-holders in question has twelve petty kings under him, and each king an independent tax district; such petty kings are called *shartāy*s. Thus, the ába dima'ng rules over the Tomorókkóngá, and the tikináwi over Dār Zaghāwah, the Bartī, and what lies beyond them. The ába umá,[274] who is the counterpart of the kaamíne, rules over four petty kings of the Masālīṭ, and the poora'ng ába rules over four kings of the Karakiriit. The orondolong, who is the sultan's face,[275] rules over four kings of Dār Birqid, and the shaykh-father rules over four kings too. The órré'ng ába rules over two kings. These lands do not include those of the counselors, sharifs, leading men of religion, and judges. The sultan has no lands of his own except for the houses of his fathers and his forefathers, such as Qirlī, Rīl, Tandaltī, and so on.[276]

3.1.15 The writ of the shaykh-father runs south from Abū l-Judūl and even includes a large part of Dār Birqid. The counselors rule over the area of Marrah, while each petty sultan rules over the lands of his own people, such as the Birqid, Mīmah, Tunjūr, Dājū, Bīqū, and Zaghāwah. Each of these sultans has a fief off which he lives, even though the territory may have another governor.[277] For example, the sultan of the Zaghāwah is the ruler of his people even though he's within Dār Tikináwi; he holds a fief that has come down to him from his forefathers, and the tikináwi doesn't oppose him in that. The yield of the rest of the lands is taken by the tikináwi, and it's the same with the rest of the petty sultans. All territories other than the six I have mentioned are ruled by petty kings.

3.1.16 In width, Darfur runs from the savannah that lies between it and Dār Ṣulayḥ (also known as Dār Wāddāy) to the outer edge of al-Ṭuwayshah, that is, to the beginning of the savannah between it and Kordofan, or around eighteen days' travel. Half of this territory consists of a plain of slightly sandy soil. The exceptions are its far eastern reaches, where there is a great deal of sand, which is why they are called the Dunes.[278] The soil of Jabal Marrah, on the other hand, is a black mud. Jabal Marrah is a mountain range that splits the Land of the Fūr in half from end to end. Some people even say it's connected to the Muqaṭṭam Hills that overlook Cairo but it isn't continuous; it's scattered over a number of places, and many roads lead to it. In these mountains are nations and people too numerous to count. There is a tribe there known as the Kunjáara to which the sultan of Darfur traces his origins. And in these mountains are many caves in which royal princes are imprisoned, and others for the imprisonment of viziers. Jabal Marrah produces great yields because there are more cattle and flocks of sheep and goats there than anywhere else. The amazing thing is that all their animals graze on their own, without anyone to mind them, and the people have no fear of thieves, lions, or wolves.

In 1220 [1805–6], I asked Sultan Muḥammad Faḍl for permission to go to Jabal Marrah, to see. At first he withheld his permission because he feared I might suffer at the hands of its inhabitants. He subsequently gave it, appointed servants to go with me, and wrote a royal order to all the district chiefs, in which he stated: 3.1.17

> From the presence of the Most Mighty Sultan and Ennobled Khāqān, Sultan Muḥammad Faḍl the Victorious, Sultan of the Arabs and the Non-Arabs, who trusts in the solicitude of the Just and Patient King, to all the petty kings of Jabal Marrah—The sayyid and sharif Muḥammad al-Tūnisī, son of the sharif Learned Scholar ʿUmar al-Tūnisī, has requested our permission to see Jabal Marrah and what it contains and to enquire as to all that is manifest and all that is hidden, and we have granted him permission to do so. He must not, therefore, be barred from any place that he wishes to see. I also command every king with whom he stays to treat him hospitably and give him a warm welcome. I have provided him with two of my own royal messengers

to act as intermediaries, so that they may pass on to you what he says and achieve the desired end. Farewell.

3.1.18 I set off in the company of the two messengers plus two slaves of my own and a man from the town where I was living. We traveled for two days, and on the third we came to the foothills. We put up in a village called Numlayh, which had a headman called Faqīh Namr, who had one son called Faqīh Muḥammad and another called Sulaymān. When we alighted at the house of the town's headman, he and his sons came and received us with open arms. We told them of our intentions and showed them the sultan's order. When they saw this, they paid me many attentions and treated me most hospitably, and so we spent the night. In the morning, they took me to the Numlayh market, which is held every Monday and attended by all the inhabitants of the mountain, men and women, who buy what they need there. I saw many extremely black people, with red eyes and teeth.

3.1.19 When the people saw me, they gathered around me, wondering at my ruddy color. Troop after troop came to see me because they had never seen an Arab before, and wanted to kill me out of contempt. At the time, I knew not a word of the Fur language and I only became scared when I noticed that the men who were with me had seized their weapons and bared them in the others' faces, placing themselves between me and them. I asked them why, and they told me that they'd wanted to murder me. "What for?" I asked, and they replied, "Because they're so stupid. Some were saying, 'This one didn't ripen properly in his mother's belly,' others, 'If a fly settled on him, it would draw blood!' and one of them said, 'Hang on a moment and I'll prick him with a spear to see how much blood comes out!' When we heard this, we feared for your life and made a circle around you." Then my men got me out of the market, pursued by a throng of people, whom they chased off only with great difficulty. After this, they took me to a wadi where I saw palm trees, banana trees, and some lemon trees, and I saw that onions, garlic, and red peppers with pods smaller and narrower than a grain of barley had been planted in the same wadi, along with great quantities of cumin, coriander, fenugreek, cucumber, and squash. It was fall, and the dates had turned red, so they cut me down two clusters, one red, the other yellow, and gave me a gourd full of honey the like of which I had never come across before, it was of such a beautiful color and so delicious. Then we spent the night in the lap of luxury, enjoying the most generous hospitality.

In the morning, I asked if we could see more things, so they took 3.1.20
me into the wadis, and we crossed one after another, each less than a mile from the next. In each were amazing crops and water that gushed over the sand like silver, the trees encircling each wadi like a fence on all sides so that the beholder could only hope that he would never have to leave. We sat on edge of one wadi in the shade of a tree, and a fat ram was slaughtered for us and cooked under hot stones. After we had eaten our fill, we went on to a village beneath the mountain where we spent the night coddled in the most generous hospitality. The next morning, we went up the mountain, climbing for about three hours without stopping until we reached the top, where we found numerous peoples and widely dispersed villages. People there took us to see the Shaykh of the Mountain, who at that time was named Abū Bakr and whom we found seated inside his place of retreat. Entering, we found him to be an old man, close to sixty and showing signs of age. We greeted him, and he welcomed us and invited us to sit down.

A curiosity: the skies clear over this mountain for only a few 3.1.21
days a year, and because there's so much rain, they can plant wheat. The wheat that grows in their land is of exceedingly good quality, without peer except in the countries of the Arab west and those of Europe. Wheat doesn't grow in the rest of Darfur because the soil is unsuited to it and because of the lack of rain, though there is a little good soil at Kūbayh and Kabkābiyyah, where they grow wheat that they irrigate from wells till it ripens.

There is a certain day, known to all, when people come from all 3.1.22
over the area to visit this shaykh, and he tells them what will happen

during the coming year regarding drought and rain, war and peace, ease and hardship, sickness and health, and the people believe what he says. The Darfurians differ over this. Some say that it is due to mystical illumination, that anyone who holds the rank of shaykh is a saint,[279] and that whatever he tells people is the result of such illumination; this is what people who know the religious sciences say. Others say that the jinn tell him everything that will happen and he passes this on to the people. I have no idea which of the two is correct. In fact, many claims have been made on his authority only for the opposite to happen. We pulled out the royal order, and Faqīh Muḥammad read it out to him, so he welcomed us, honored us, and invited us to eat. Then he beat a drum of the kind called *tómbol*,[280] and crowds of people arrived. He chose about a hundred young men, put one of his relatives—Faqīh Zayd, who was known for his courage—in charge of them, and ordered him and his men to escort me and to look lively and be on guard against the wild mountain people.

3.1.23 We now mounted and set off for a place where there is a small mountain called Marrah, from which the whole range takes its name. On it we found what seemed to be a temple for all the mountain people, who believe they must honor it and hold it as sacred as any mosque. We entered. It is shaded by a tree so large that the sun never sees it. We sat inside for a little and found there servants responsible for cleaning it and for receiving votive offerings from those who bring them. Then we moved on from there, the soldiers walking ahead of us, and many people, women and men, followed us. They took me for a marvel, falling upon me and crowding around me, and the soldiers were unable to disperse them. Eventually one of them said that the sultan had sent the people of the mountain a treat in the form of a man who'd failed to ripen in his mother's belly, to which some responded, "But he's a man," while others said, "He isn't a man, he's an edible animal in the form of a man"—for they refuse to accept that a man can be white or ruddy-complexioned. The only Arabic these people know is the two phrases of the profession of faith, which they pronounce in broken fashion and with an ugly accent. When the men with me could no longer hold them back, Faqīh Zayd came and told me to cover my face with a veil through which only my eyes were visible. I put it on and the soldiers formed a circle around me. When the Blacks couldn't see me, because I'd veiled myself, they were puzzled and asked, "Where did the red man go?" The soldiers said, "He went to the sultan," so the crowd thinned out a bit.

Next, we set off for the place of incarceration, meaning the caves where imprisoned royal princes and viziers are kept, but the guards barred us from reaching them. They and our men almost came to blows, but Faqīh Zayd sorted things out, took the royal order from me, and went to the commander of the guard and read it out to him. At this, the man submitted, but said, "If it must be so, then let the subject of the order come on his own and look. The rest can sit at a distance till he's done and returns to them." The faqīh came back and informed me of this, but I refused, overwhelmed by fear. I disclaimed any desire to enter the caves and asked to go back, so we went back. 3.1.24

One of their strange customs is that a man only gets married to a woman after he's spent some time with her as a friend and she's borne him one or two children. When they reach this point, they decide that she's fertile, and he makes a contract with her and lives with her. Another custom is that the women do not keep themselves out of sight of men. Indeed, if a man enters his house and finds his wife on her own with another man, he shows no concern and doesn't get upset, unless he finds him on top of her. By nature, they are coarse-grained and bad-tempered, especially when drunk. They are also extremely miserly and won't entertain a guest unless he's a relative, or there's some relationship between them, or he's someone they fear. Another custom of theirs is that the young boys and girls wear nothing to make themselves decent until after puberty, when the boy puts on a shift and the female ties a loincloth around her waist, leaving everything from her navel to her face exposed. 3.1.25

Another custom is the lack of expensive ingredients and variety in their food. In fact, they eat whatever they can find and don't turn up their noses at bitter or rotten food; they may actually like bitter food and rotten meat and prefer it to anything else.

3.1.26 Another custom is that the young men in every village have a chief, as do the women. The men's chief is called the ŏrnang and the women's the mééram. At weddings, religious feasts, and holidays, the men's chief gathers his followers and seats them in a certain place, and the women's chief and her followers come and sit down in front of them separately. Then the ŏrnang goes on his own, approaches the mééram, and addresses her using words that both he and she know. Then the mééram orders her women to distribute themselves among the ŏrnang's group, each young man takes a young woman, and they go somewhere and sleep until morning. No shame attaches to any of the young women for this.

3.1.27 The men of Darfur have no independent decision-making power whatsoever, except over whether to go to war, which the women have nothing to do with. In all other matters, men and women are equal. Indeed, most kinds of labor, and the most demanding forms of it, are women's to do, and the men mix with them to an amazing degree, by night and by day, in all types of work.

3.1.28 A strange thing about the people of Jabal Marrah is that they don't eat the wheat they grow. Instead, they sell it and trade it for millet. Stranger still are their crude sensibilities and their rough-hewnness, even though they mix with their women without restriction. This contradicts the belief held by all Franks[281] that when men mix with women, their crudeness vanishes and they acquire refinement and good dispositions. An example of their crudeness is that a man will travel several leagues on foot, with a donkey, and will drive it ahead of him instead of riding it, and if you ask him why, he'll tell you, "It would slow me down!"

3.1.29 Their language is full of enthusiasm.[282] Its words resemble Turkish, because, when they call to someone, they say *kéla*[283] while the Turks say *gel* ("come!"). When I say they're alike, I don't mean they're close in meaning. Rather, the resemblance is just in the sounds, even when the meaning is different. Thus, the Fur call a mare *yáa murtá'ng*, which to the Turks is a word for eggs (*yumurta*).[284] To the Fur, something ugly is *jitti*, which to the Turks is a past tense verb meaning "he went."[285] I have never heard a more deficient language than theirs, because the numbers in their language end at six, after which they continue in Arabic. Thus, they say *díg* for one, *aw* for two, *iis* for three, *ongngal* for four, *oos* for five, and *oosandíg* for six. After that they continue in Arabic: *sabʿah*, *tamanyah*, *tisʿah* ("seven, eight, nine").[286] Then they say *wayye*, which is a term they use for the tens.[287]

A Curiosity: One of the strangest things I heard when I was on Jabal Marrah was that the jinn there look after their livestock—the ones grazing in the pastures—and these do not have shepherds. Several men whose word one would normally trust told me that if anyone were to pass by their livestock and see there was no shepherd and perhaps give in to the temptation to take a ewe or a cow or anything else and then try to slaughter it, his hand would stick to the knife at the creature's throat, and he'd be unable to let go of it until its owners came. They would seize him and force him to pay the highest price for it, after reviling him and giving him a painful beating. I heard this so often it achieved the number of independent transmitters it would need, were it a prophetic hadith, to be accepted as authentic—but I still didn't believe it. 3.1.30

When I was on Jabal Marrah, I went to the house of a local man in Numlayh to ask about this but found no one at home. However, I did hear, coming from inside the house, a terrifying, coarse voice that made my skin crawl, telling me, "*Á keeba!*" meaning "He's not here!" At that very moment, I tried to advance and ask, "Where is he?" but a passerby dragged me away, saying, "Get back! The one you're talking to isn't human." "What is he then?" I asked. "He's his guardian jinni," he said, "for every one of us has a guardian among the jinn, and in the language of the Fur he's called a *damsuga*." That scared me, and I retraced my steps. 3.1.31

3.1.32 When I got back from this journey and went to the sultan's seat, I met with Sharif Aḥmad Badawī, the man who had brought me from Egypt to Darfur, and I told him the story. "Believe it!" he said, and told me stranger things still: "My boy," he said to me, "when I was young I used to hear that *damsuga*s could be bought and sold and that anyone who wanted a *damsuga* would go to someone he knew had them and buy one at whatever price the other would accept. Then he'd bring a gourd of milk and hand it over to the master of the house, who'd take it and go into the room where the *damsugas* were, greet them, and hang the gourd containing the milk on a hanger in the house. After that, he'd tell them, 'My friend so-and-so has great wealth, which he's afraid will be stolen from him, and he's asked for a guardian. Will any of you go to his house? He has much milk there and lots of good things, and has brought this gourd, full of milk.' At first, the *damsuga*s would refuse and say, 'None of us will go with him,' so he'd talk to them gently and flatter them until they agreed. Then he'd say, 'Whichever of you wants to go should get into the gourd,' and he'd remove himself from them a little. Once he'd heard the *damsuga* fall into the milk, he'd stop the gourd with palm leaves, take it, covered, from its hanger, and hand it over to his friend who'd bought it. Then the latter would take it home and hang it up in his house, where he'd put a slave girl or a woman in charge of going every morning and taking the gourd, emptying it of whatever milk it might contain, and washing it well, after which she'd put new milk in it, fresh from the cow, and hang it up. If he did so, that person could be sure that his property would be safe from theft and loss.

3.1.33 "I thought these were lies. But then my wealth increased and the slaves and servants began stealing from it. I tried everything I could to put a stop to that but couldn't, so I complained to a friend of mine and he advised me to buy a *damsuga*, saying that I'd then be protected from the evil of theft. My love of wealth prompted me to go to a man I'd heard had *damsuga*s. 'Give me a *damsuga* to guard my property for me,' I said, and gave him what he asked. Then he said, 'Go and fill a gourd with fresh milk and bring it here.' I did that and took him the gourd, filled with milk. He took it and went off and after an hour returned with the gourd, covered. 'Hang it where your wealth is stored,' he said to me, and taught me what I had to do every day by way of washing the vessel and filling it with fresh milk. I did this and put a slave girl in charge of it and became so convinced my wealth was safe that I'd leave my treasury open, and no one would be able to get to it. It contained large quantities of goods and belongings, and anyone who tried to take something without my permission would end up with a broken neck. I lost several slaves that way. I lived for a while without worrying about my wealth until a son of mine called Muḥammad became a young man and, having reached puberty, started setting his sights on girls. He wanted to give them beads and trinkets, so one day he waited until I wasn't paying attention, took the keys, opened the storeroom where my property was kept, and was about to enter when the *damsuga* broke his neck, and he died on the spot. I loved him dearly. When I was informed of his death, I mourned for him greatly and asked how he had died. I was told that he'd tried to take some of my belongings, so the *damsuga* had killed him. I swore then that the *damsuga* would not stay another moment in my house and tried to expel it, but I couldn't. I complained to a friend of mine, and he advised me to hold a banquet and gather lots of men together, each with a musket and gunpowder, and have them all come at once, firing their muskets and yelling with one voice in the language of the Fur, '*Damsuga ây yé?*' meaning 'Where is the devil?' and have them keep on firing and shouting those words all the way till they entered the place where my belongings were kept. Then it might become scared and run away. I did this, and it did flee, praise be to God, and I stopped keeping company with *damsugas*, or, to put it bluntly, with devils."

Several men told me that among the kettledrums in the sultan's house there is one called the Victorious that belongs to the jinn. Sometimes it sounds when there is no one there to strike it, and when that happens some great event occurs in Darfur, either 3.1.34

war with one of their enemies or among themselves. This will be discussed again in more detail when we speak of the customs of their kings.

3.1.35 The customs of the other tribes, such as the Bartī, the Dājū, the Bīqū, the Zaghāwah, the Barqū, the Mīmah, and others are in some cases close to those of the people of the mountain but in others different. Insofar as they differ, it's because some of these tribes possess nobility, courage, and refined dispositions, having mixed with the Arabs of the desert and the merchants who come from Egypt and elsewhere. You find that when such tribes see guests, they adjure them not to leave and treat them very hospitably, and when they see a stranger, they honor him. This is the contrary of the non-Arabic-speaking Fur, such as those of Jabal Marrah and Tomorókkóngá. These will neither so honor him nor behave toward him in a friendly manner, and they will not put a guest up in their houses unless forced to.

Section 2: Customs of the Kings of the Fur

3.1.36 God, glorified and exalted, has created all people through His power, distinguished them, in His wisdom, one from another, and caused the differences among their customs and conditions to be a lesson for those who have eyes to see and a reminder for those who have minds to ponder. He has done this so that the rational person must inevitably become aware—on contemplating the conditions of different states, their varied endowments and constitutions, their virtues, and their advantages—of the fact that the Greatest and Most Powerful Creator, of power stupendous and will tremendous, has made the circumstances prevailing in this world to be of many kinds, bestowing on this or that people some particular advantage not to be found in others, in order that the magnitude of His power and His wisdom may be known. Likewise, if the rational person observes the differences among their tongues, colors, costumes, and means of sustenance, he or she will realize that these things are a major sign of God's power: as the Almighty has said, «Among His signs are your sleep, at night or in daytime» «and the diversity of your languages and colors.»[288] In addition, God has given a particular nature to every clime. Thus, some are hot, others cold, and yet others, depending on the nearness or distance of the clime to or from the equator, occupy a midpoint. Glory then to Him who effects what He desires; "should He have wished it, He could have made them all one nation."[289] Through difference, however, virtues are made manifest, and the soul yearns to know what it did not. Were it not so, the restless would not roam and lives not be given over, in search of knowledge and wealth, to journeying far from home. With this established, we declare:

The customary practice of the monarchs of the Fur is at odds 3.1.37 with those of other countries. Their king has absolute authority over them. Should he kill thousands, no one will ask why, and should he strip an officeholder of his office, again no one will ask why. He has total freedom of action to do everything he wishes, and if he gives a command, he may not be questioned, even if it be an abomination, other than through intercession,[290] and he may never be contradicted. If, however, he acts with an unbefitting degree of tyranny and oppression, they will come to hate him in their hearts, though they can do nothing against him.

The first custom is that the monarch must be from their royal 3.1.38 house, meaning of their own line: no outsider may assume power, even a sharif whose line of descent they have verified. The second is that when the monarch takes power, he stays in his house for seven days and issues no commands or prohibitions, and no case may be tried before him. All of them have followed this practice, with the exception of Sultan ʿAbd al-Raḥmān: he broke with tradition, as mentioned when we spoke of his assumption of power.[291] The third is that there are among them old women called the Grandmothers,[292] who form a powerful faction. They have a chief who's called the Mistress of the Grandmothers, and when the sultan leaves his house on the eighth day, they assemble and go to him, each holding four pieces of iron, called "scourges." They look either

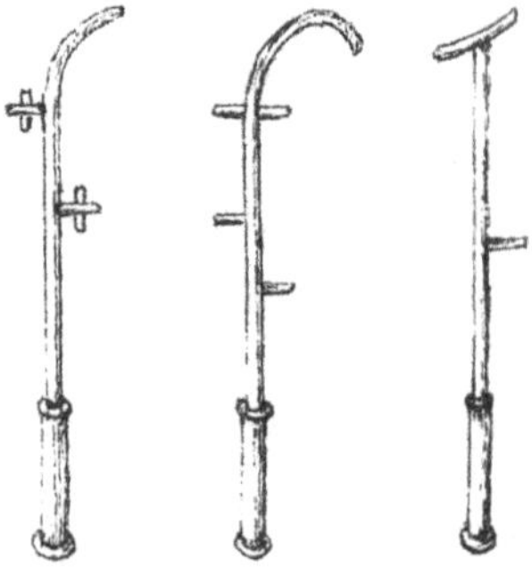

like this like this or like this. In each hand, they hold two scourges, which they strike against each other.[293] One of them has a handful of white palm leaves in her hand and carries a liquid—the people of Darfur differ on the nature of its composition.[294] The old woman wets the palm leaves with this liquid and sprinkles it over the sultan while uttering words of which only the Grandmothers know the meaning. They take the sultan into their midst, circumambulate the house, and then go to the Drum House,[295] which is where the kettledrums—the sultan's drums—are kept.[296] They enter, go to the drum called the Victorious, and stand in a circle with the drum in the middle. The sultan is alone with them, and they strike the scourges against each other and speak words in that language of theirs. Then they conduct the sultan back to the throne of his kingdom, and as soon as he's seated on it cases are brought to him and he starts pronouncing judgments.

3.1.39 Another custom of theirs is that the sultan only salutes people via an interpreter, whether the one saluted is young or old, mighty or mean. This is done as follows: when people come in to see him, they kneel; then the interpreter advances and says their names, one after another, until he's named them all. He says, "*Ínni tawrá falān dóngá kee nágí dárí*," which means "Here, outside, so-and-so, greetings, he gives obedience."[297] When he's finished listing the names of those in attendance at the assembly, he says, "*Kí kíeng dogóla kerker*," meaning "They have children behind them, even their followers and their servants."[298] Then the slaves who stand behind the sultan and are called *kóór kwa*, whom we've mentioned earlier,[299] say, "*Dóngá rǎy dóngá! Dóngá rǎy dóngá!*" meaning "Greetings! Greetings! Greetings! Greetings!" If the sultan is holding formal audience, a drum called *dinqār* is then beaten; this is a huge drum made of wood and covered with hide on one side. It has the shape of an inverted pyramid, like this: 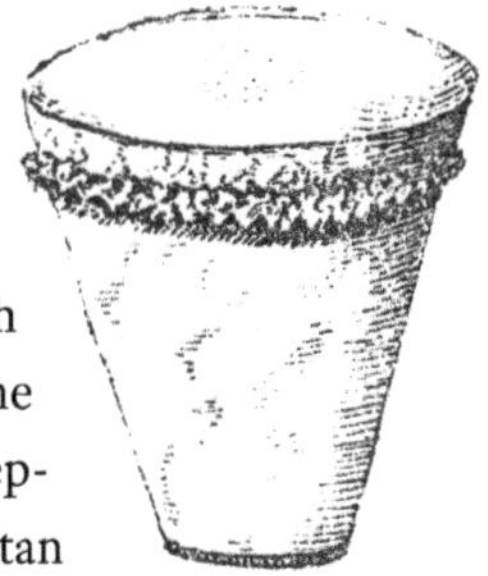 and makes a loud noise. If the audience is not that sort, then this isn't done.

Furthermore, they exalt the sultan to such a degree that when he spits on the ground, one of the servants sitting in front of him or keeping their eyes permanently trained on the sultan and his actions and movements wipes it up with his hand. When he clears his throat, they all say, "*Ts ts*," the *t* being contracted into the *s* with no vowel, the tongue striking the edge of the gums above the teeth. When he sneezes, they spit out letters that only a gecko or someone driving a donkey could pronounce. When he sits down and remains seated for a while, they fan him with ostrich-feather fans. And when he goes hunting, they shade him with an umbrella and four large ostrich-feather fans encased in red broadcloth; these fans are called "the feathers" and look like this: 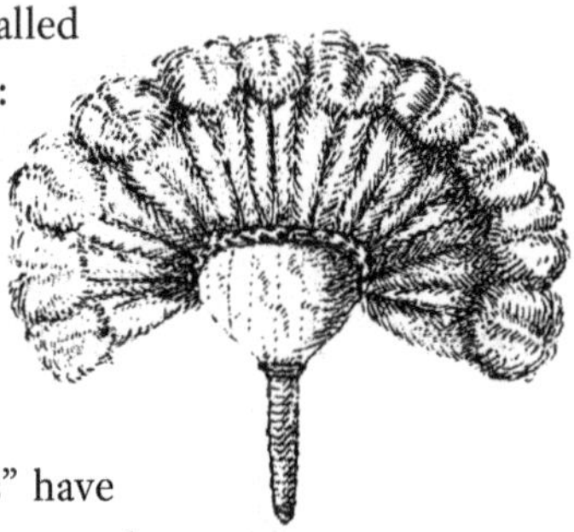 They hold the umbrella over the sultan's head and place two fans on the right and two on the left, ensuring that a large area of shade embraces him. The aforementioned umbrella and "feathers" have their own exclusive master and helpers, who take turns handling them, as they proceed on foot. Another custom relating to the sultan is that when he rides out, they roll a carpet out in front of him and this too has a master and helpers who manage it. Another example of their exaltation of the sultan is that if his horse gallops and stumbles and throws him, or the violence of the gallop 3.1.40

makes him fall off, they all throw themselves off their horses' backs; it is unthinkable that any of them remain firmly mounted once the sultan has fallen. In fact, if the servants see that any of them is still firmly seated on his horse's back and hasn't thrown himself off, they throw him off themselves and beat him severely, even if he's someone important, because they think that to remain well seated is to show contempt for the sultan.

3.1.41 When the sultan sits in judgment in his place of audience, he doesn't address the people directly but does so through an interpreter, so long as the audience isn't public. If it's a public audience, they're seven—these interpreters—the first of them standing next to the sultan, the last next to the petitioners. The interpreters are in the middle, the soldiers around the sultan, and the *kóór kwa* behind him, while the scholars of religion and sharifs are seated. The audience space looks like this:

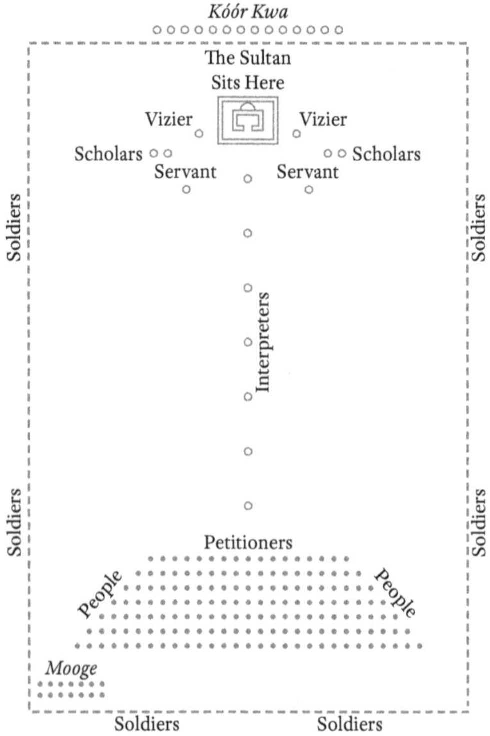

The people are on their knees in front of him with their hands on the ground, and the *mooge*, of whom we shall give an account,[300] remain standing. When the sultan greets them, they rub their hands in the dust, and when anyone speaks in his court, if he is Arab he must first say, "*Sallim ʿalā sayyidnā*" ("Give greetings to my lord"), while if he is Fur, he must say, "*Ába kuri dóngá janí*," which means the same thing. When the sultan speaks, he says, "*Sallim ʿalayh*" ("Give greetings to him"), when speaking Arabic, and the interpreter says, "*Dónga dáíng sīdī*."[301] If the sultan is speaking Fur, he says, "*Dóngá janí*" ("Greetings") if his addressee is not an Arabic speaker; if he's an Arab, he says, "*Sallim ʿalayh*."[302] This is not peculiar to the sultan's court. The same is said at every gathering where cases are heard, even those of the judges and the village shaykhs, and no case may be heard without *Dóngá janí*! It follows that discussion is long even when substance is short, because they repeat the phrase after every one or two words. If anyone opens a case without them, they find fault with him and call him uncivilized. Indeed, if he's at the gathering of a ruler, he will be disciplined with a rebuke, unless he be a stranger, in which case he will be forgiven.

It is a custom of the Fur kings to "cover the drums," a custom found only in Darfur. "Covering the drums" means changing the skins on the sort of drums that in Egypt are called *naqāqīr* ("kettledrums"). They make much of this covering and each year set a special seven-day holiday aside for it.[303] This is done in the following fashion: the sultan commands that all the skins be stripped off the drums on the same day, and this is done. Then brown bulls are brought, they slaughter them, take a portion of their hides, and cover those same drums with them. The people of Darfur have a story about this that no rational, well-read person can accept, despite which they all agree on it. They claim that these bulls are of a breed of cattle well known to them and that at the moment of slaughter they lie down of their own accord with nobody holding them and without anyone pronouncing the name of God when their throats are cut. They say it is the jinn who hold them and lay them on their sides. 3.1.42

3.1.43 They then take the meat, place it in pits, and leave it in salt for six days. On the seventh day, they bring large numbers of cattle and goats, slaughter them all, and cook the flesh.[304] While it is cooking, they take the meat that was in the pits and cut it up into small pieces, a few of which they put into each cauldron, mixed in with the new meat. Then tables are allotted to the petty kings, the sons of the kings, and the viziers, according to rank, and over each stands a guard sent by the sultan, who watches to see who eats the meat and who does not. If the guard informs the sultan that so-and-so did not eat, he immediately orders him seized, and if anyone makes the excuse that he is sick, or cannot attend, vessels containing some of the meat are sent to him with a trusted guard, who watches to see whether the man eats or not. If he refuses, he's seized, unless he is excused because of the severity of his illness. Some Darfurians say that a boy and a girl who have not yet reached puberty are brought and secretly slaughtered and that their flesh is cut up and put into the pots with the meat of the slaughtered animals. Some say that the boy's name has to be Muḥammad and the girl's Fāṭimah. If this were true it would be an extreme example of misbelief in God and His messenger. I did not witness it myself or attend such a ceremony, for I was a stranger, and strangers are not allowed to observe such things under any circumstances. All the same, I heard it from numerous people who swore mighty oaths that it was true, down to the last detail.[305]

3.1.44 Before the food is brought out, the soldiers all come and stand in a wide, open space in front of the sultan's house. Then the sultan appears in all his finery and pomp, and each petty king, together with his followers, presents his army to him, one after another. The review takes place in the following fashion: each king takes his followers and runs until he reaches the sultan. If he is one of the notables, the sultan moves forward two or three paces from his company to meet him, and if he is not the sultan remains where he is. Then the king and his followers fall back. This is done three times, and on the third they parade before the sultan, after which they go back to where they were standing, and another king comes forward with his army and does the same, and so it continues.

When the review is over, the sultan comes out at a run and follows after the petty kings, going first to the greatest of them, then to one who is like him in rank, then to one who is less than he, and so on till he has visited them all, so that none take offense. Each time he approaches a company they shout at him words extolling his might, crying out, "Mantle![306] Nobly born among sultans! Fetter of kings! Chastiser of the rebellious! Breaker and scatterer of the unlevied mountains!"[307] and so on. When the review is finished, the sultan enters his house, all the officers of state—viziers, petty kings, and sons of sultans—entering behind him, and he goes to the Drum House and takes a rod and strikes the drum called the Victorious three times. The old women, which is to say the Grandmothers, surround him, holding their scourges and striking them against each other as previously described.[308] Then they walk two by two, as shown here the sultan between the last pair, until they've escorted the sultan to the place where he sits. I witnessed this. 3.1.45

Next, the different dishes are distributed as we've described. If any vizier or army commander is absent from the sultan's seat of government at the time of the covering of the drums, and comes afterward and is accused of treachery or treason, he is given *kilí* water to drink.[309] This is water in which fruits of a tree called *kilí* have been steeped; the fruit resembles walnuts. The people of Darfur say that if the accused drinks and he is innocent, he will immediately vomit it back; if not, he will drink till his belly is full and not vomit even if he drink a caskful. I 3.1.46

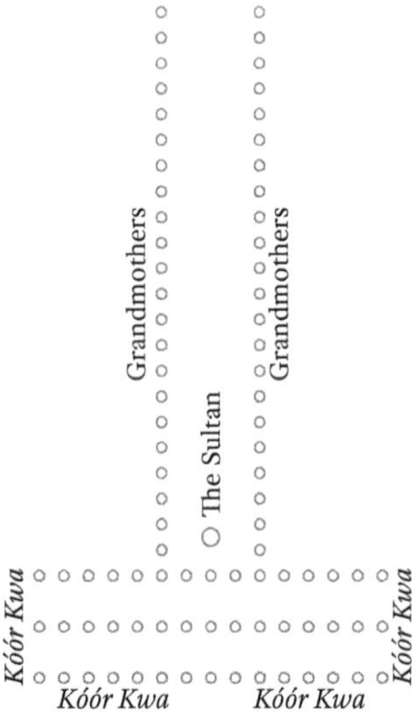

witnessed this, but the accusation was theft. This may be a property of plants, for the plants of Darfur have amazing properties, which we shall discuss later, the Almighty willing.[310]

3.1.47 Another custom of the Fur is that the sultan has a farm in a particular place that he plants each year for himself.[311] On the day after the rains, when the seed is sown, he goes out in a mighty procession accompanied by beautiful girls adorned with trinkets and trappings—about a hundred maidens chosen from among his personal concubines, each carrying on her head a vessel full of costly foods, these vessels being called *ʿumār* (singular *ʿumrah*). These girls walk behind the sultan's horse, accompanied by the young spear-carrying slave boys called *kóór kwa* and by others with pipes. The girls sing while the others blow their pipes, and the spear-carrying *kóór kwa* sing along with them. In other words, when the girls go out with the sultan, they sing along with these others too, and their companies make a most beautiful sound.

3.1.48 When the sultan arrives at the farm, he dismounts from his horse and takes the seed grain, while one of his slaves comes and makes a hole in the ground with a mattock he has brought with him. The sultan then throws in the grain, this being the first seed to fall on the ground in the part of the country where the sultan is. At this, the chieftains, viziers, and army commanders follow suit and sow grain, getting the farm sown in the shortest possible time. Once the whole farm has been sown, the food that was carried on the heads of the girls is brought and placed before the sultan, and he and his ministers eat. Then he rides in procession as before, until he reaches his royal seat. This is one of Darfur's most celebrated holidays.

Section 3: On the Offices Held by the Kings of the Fur[312]

3.1.49 He of Necessary Existence, whose essence, unique in the absoluteness of its power and the untrammeled nature of its perfect will, is sanctified beyond dependence on any helper, has caused kings to have need of viziers, officials, and aides, so that their powerlessness to act independently in the disposal of their kingdoms and interests may be known. Were it not for that need, they would behave even more tyrannically and oppressively than they already do. Indeed, they might lay claim to the divinity that sorts ill with any but His sublime essence. To each land, however, He has given its own particular regulation and organization, which is why one finds that the names of the offices of the viziers of caliphs differ from those of the viziers of present-day kings, and likewise that the names of the offices of the viziers of present-day kings differ one from the other. Thus, in the Ottoman state, the names of the officers are chief vizier, minister of home affairs, keeper of the treasury, keeper of the arms, keeper of the seal, keeper of the pen case, keeper of the wardrobe, and chief doorman, as well as head doorkeeper and others of the same style such as head tobacconist, head sherbet maker, head coffee maker, supervisor of the caftans, and supervisor of the towels, not to mention the pashas, brigade commanders, and regimental commanders.

The people of Darfur, however, so revere their sultan that their sole point of reference is his body, and they consequently name their offices after its parts.[313] The first of their offices is the orondolong, an office of great power whose holder is known as the sultan's head.[314] Attached to this office are vast fiefs and villages. The fief holder is always greeted with "*Dóngá rǎy dóngá!*" and a carpet is taken up and carried before him just as it is for the sultan. If the sultan is on the move or hunting, it is the task of the holder of this office to march in front of the army, and no one may precede him. 3.1.50

The second office is that of the kaamíne, which is higher in might and majesty than the orondolong. He is known as the sultan's neck. If the sultan is killed in war and the kaamíne escapes to a place of safety, it is the Fur custom to kill him; they strangle him in secret, then appoint someone else for the incoming sultan. If the sultan dies in his bed, the kaamíne is not killed. The kaamíne is called by Fur speakers ába poor-ii, meaning "Father of the Fur."[315] The holder of the office has magnificent fiefs and many soldiers and acts 3.1.51

just like the sultan. His task is to march behind the troops of the orondolong.[316]

3.1.52 The third is the ába ăw mang, who is the kaamíne's opposite number in everything. The term means the sultan's spine, and it is his task to march at the armies' rear accompanied by an army behind which no one else may march. If an enemy is pursuing the main army, this army of his is sufficient to repel it and keep it at bay until it can be relieved and rendered assistance by the main armies.

3.1.53 The fourth is the ába dima'ng,[317] who is greater than all the preceding in majesty, pomp, and number of soldiers. He commands twelve of the petty kings of the Fur, has an extensive territory known as Tomorókkóngá, and all the insignia and pomp of the sultan except for the copper drums, for his drum is the *dinqār*.[318] He is known as the sultan's right arm, and his task is to march with his soldiers on the sultan's right.

3.1.54 The fifth is the tikináwi,[319] who is the ába dima'ng's opposite number in everything and is known as the sultan's left arm. He commands twelve of the northern petty kings and has an extensive territory.

3.1.55 The sixth is the office of shaykh-father. He is higher than all of the abovementioned—there is effectively no difference between him and the sultan—and his commands are obeyed by all the preceding officeholders and others. He has magnificent estates and an extensive territory. The holder of this office carries a naked sword and may kill without permission. All the natives of the kingdom are his to dispose of. He corresponds to the sultan's buttocks. I mentioned some of this earlier when speaking of Shaykh-Father Muḥammad Kurrā.[320]

3.1.56 The seventh is the office of counselor. There are four, each of whom bears this title. The holders of this office have estates and soldiers but none of the insignia of the king. The four of them are attached to the sultan's assembly.[321]

3.1.57 Eighth is the office of the groom, which is a position of great power but one rank lower than that of counselor. There are likewise four holders of this office.

The ninth is the office of the overseer of the pages' place.[322] Its holder has great power and is possessed of great pomp, estates, and abundant wealth. After him comes the office of the chief of[323] the *kóór kwa*. 3.1.58

Higher than either of the immediately preceding offices is that of órré bayyâ.[324] This is a great and powerful office. It is the custom of the Fur kings that its holder be a eunuch, because he will assume the office of the shaykh-father following the death of the holder of that title, and, as we have seen earlier, the office of shaykh-father may only be held by a eunuch. The holder of this post commands all the eunuchs in charge of the sultan's women and is also, as "keeper of the sultan's anger," in charge of the prison. In other words, when the sultan is angry with someone, he gives him to the órré bayyâ, and the latter puts him in his prison. He has many soldiers at his command. The meaning of órré bayyâ in Fur is "the women's door," and the holder of the office is under the command of the shaykh-father. He is followed by the office of "master of the órré dee," meaning master of the men's door, for every house belonging to a petty king or vizier has two doors, one for men and one for women: the men's door is called órré dee, the women's órré bayyâ. 3.1.59

Next comes the office of master of the royal slaves. This is an office of high power whose holder commands all those of the sultan's slaves who are outside his house in the villages, along with their women and children.[325] He also has at his disposal the sultan's livestock and travel equipment, such as tents and waterskins. 3.1.60

After him comes the master of the *qawwārīn*, meaning the market-toll collectors. This is a high office whose holder commands all market-toll collectors and all traders. He has large estates and numerous soldiers. 3.1.61

Higher than this is the office of master of the tax ollectors, whose holder has great pomp and is an important *malik*. He is master of the tax collectors, i.e., those who collect the grain from the villages, "tax" meaning here that they take one-tenth of the grain that is produced and place it in silos for the sultan's use. 3.1.62

3.1.63 There are many more petty kings besides. They call the rulers of the different territories *sharātī* (singular: *shartāy*) and the rulers of the tribes *damālij* (singular: *dimlij*). Each *shartāy* has many soldiers and each *dimlij*[326] has his helpers. This is not to mention the petty sultans of whom we spoke earlier.[327]

3.1.64 The sultan gives none of the abovementioned officeholders a salary, and none of them is inscribed on his payroll. Instead, every officeholder has an estate, the revenue from which he uses to buy horses, weapons, coats of mail, and clothes to distribute to his soldiers.

3.1.65 Under their tax collection system, the zakat tax on grain goes in its entirety to the sultan, as does the zakat on cattle[328]—the petty kings have no share in it. Each of them does, however, have many feddans that he sows with millet, sorghum, sesame, fava beans, and cotton, which his subjects cultivate, harvest, and thresh under threat of force.

3.1.66 The master of the tax collectors also gets "the strays," which is anything that has gone astray, whether slaves, cattle, sheep and goats, or donkeys. These are sold for him and he takes the proceeds. And he receives "the gifts," which is what they give him on his appointment and on his arrival in the villages, and "the offense," which in their custom is property forfeited to the ruler by a criminal; they also call it "the sentence." If one man gives another a sword blow to the head, money is taken from the offender and given to the ruler, and if a man gets a woman pregnant out of wedlock, money is taken from both, each according to his or her circumstances. He also gets "the bloodwite," which in their custom is when a man is killed unlawfully and blood money paid; the ruler then shares in the blood money with the relatives, whether the killing was deliberate or accidental. And this is not to mention the illegal imposts that they take without justification or the hard labor they impose on the people, who build their houses for them and whom they use as forced labor in all their works.

3.1.67 Another office of state among the Fur is master of the *mooge*, which we've kept till last because it requires such a long discussion and because of the strangeness of the *mooge*—both the office and the behavior of those who hold it. It is, in their view, the lowest office and least in rank. Before speaking of it, however, we must provide some background. The Lord of Eternal Wisdom and Everlasting Power, who has given us minds and granted us His benevolence, has provided each human being with a mind with which to distinguish good, that he or she may follow it, from evil, that he or she may be on guard against it. Likewise, He has placed in each human being a love of the opinion adopted by his or her own soul and mind, with the result that every person believes his or her mind to be more perfect and his or her opinion to be better than anyone else's—exception being made for those to whom God has granted insight into their faults and taught the powerlessness of their appetites to secure what is good for them and fend off what is bad.

In view of this, we can state that a tendency to sport and levity, to 3.1.68
playfulness and ecstasy, is in the nature of the Fur. The least stimulus to enjoyment provokes them. You find that their every moment, whether they be kings or commoners, is lived to the accompaniment of a singer. They have therefore assembled every musical instrument possible, and you find that every petty king has young boys with beautiful voices, these being what are called *kóór kwa*. They have pipes on which they make a whistling sound that is at the same time a kind of singing. The beauty of the pipes combines with that of the boys' voices to produce lovely music.

This is done in the following fashion: if a king has, 3.1.69
for example, ten of these boys, two or three will have pipes while a fourth will have in his hand a dry, hollow gourd, oblong in shape, wide at one end and narrow at the other, so that the hand can grasp it. It looks like this: Into this they put some pebbles and the boy holds it and shakes it, the mouth having first been necessarily plugged with pitch. The stones inside produce a sound that accompanies that of the pipes, and the six remaining boys sing. Sometimes the sultan sends out some of his

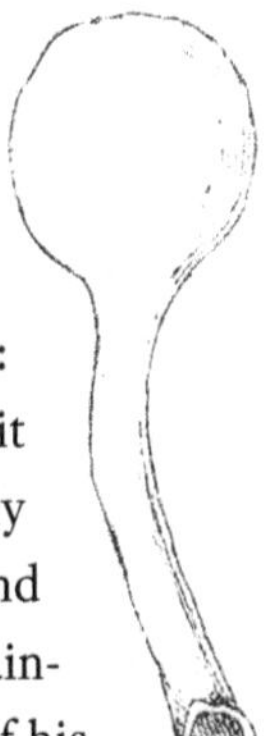

slave girls dressed in their finery, carrying vessels of food for the sultan. They walk behind the troupe of boys and sing along with them and the pipes. To these instruments they sometimes add elongated wooden drums like the one called in the common parlance of Egypt *darabukkah* and which they call *togjêl.* It looks like this and has a strap attached, as in the illustration. The player puts his hand through the strap and places it over his shoulder so that the drum is under his arm and, using both hands, he strikes it with sharp blows that are closely matched to the sound of the pipes. They sing in the language of the Fur and have teachers who teach them how to play the pipes, sing, and beat the drum.

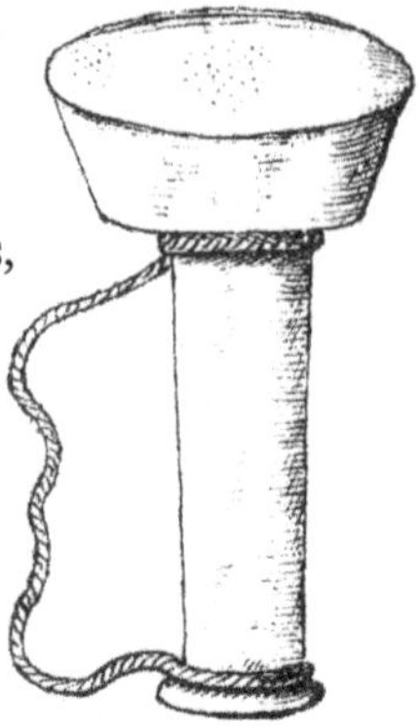

3.1.70 The foot soldiers who walk before and around the sultan sing on their own, forming small groups, each of which has one particular singer to whom the rest respond in a loud voice. Thus, when the sultan rides out and the drums beat and everyone, mounted and on foot, sings, a mighty clamor is heard, and this, together with the sound of the pipes and the songs of the boys, strikes fear into all who hear it because it is so loud. The pipes are called "birds of the High Plain" because in that region there are birds with beautiful voices which they call by that name, and they invented these pipes to imitate the sounds these birds make.

3.1.71 To these voices are added those of the *mooge*, a Fur word that is used for both singular and plural. The *mooge* are a mighty company, with their own master, the word corresponding in the common language of the Fur to *khalbūṣ* ("jester"), or in that of the Egyptians to *maskharah* ("buffoon"), or in that of the Turks to *soytarı* ("clown"). The *mooge*, however, is different from these because he is responsible for executing anyone the sultan orders killed. The *mooge* wears a band on his head that incorporates a round, concave sheet of metal. Inside this headband is another piece of metal like a nail, hung from a thread adjusted to fit the depression in the metal sheet. Thus, when he shakes his head, it strikes against the depression and makes a ringing sound. Placed above both of these in the headband are one or two ostrich feathers. The headband looks like this:

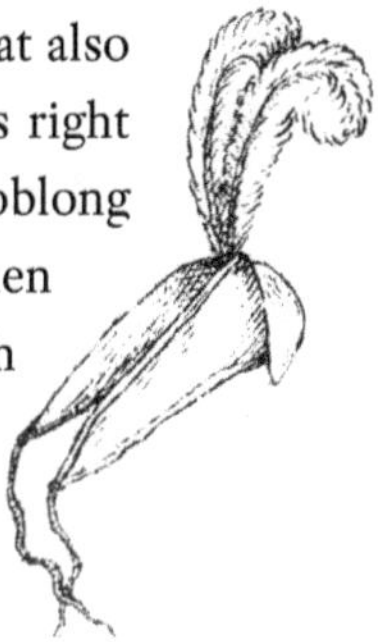

On the tall cap he wears are shells and beads that also hang down. There are two metal anklets on his right foot and one on his left. Under his arm is a small oblong bag into which he puts his headband and cap when he's not wearing them, and he carries a stick with a crook at the top like this to which jingles are

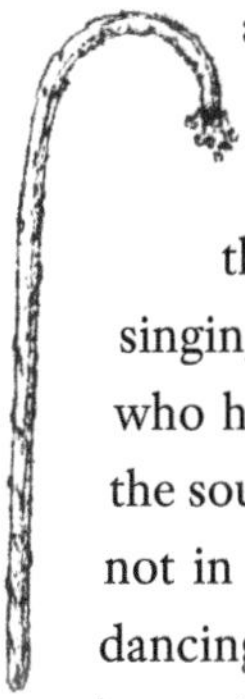

attached. Two or three such *mooge* stand before the sultan when he holds audience. When he is on the move or hunting, four or five go ahead of him, each singing and dancing and saying funny things to make those who hear them laugh, and imitating the barking of dogs or the sounds of cats. Their songs are in the language of the Fur, not in Arabic, and there is no bending of the body in their dancing; they shake their heads right and left and strike one leg against the other, making the metal piece in the bands on their heads ring, and the anklets on their feet too. If the sultan is on the move or hunting, instead of singing they all give one great shout together at the top of their lungs, going, "*Yaa! Yaa!*" and they keep this up as long as the sultan is mounted.

This is not peculiar to the sultan: each of the more important 3.1.72
petty kings of the Fur has his *mooge* who stand before him in his court and walk in front of him when he's traveling. The *mooge* do not fear the sultan's evil or fury and are extremely daring with him and with those below him. They hide nothing from the sultan—when they hear something scandalous, they announce it in his assembly, naming the one who said it, be he lowly or mighty, without fear of censure. If the sultan wishes to spread some item of news far and wide, or announce some judgment, he orders the *mooge* to cry it. They do so between the sunset and evening prayers with a cry that reaches elite and commoner alike.

3.1.73 Sultan ʿAbd al-Raḥmān happened to love the company of scholars of religion and spent much time sitting with them by day and by night. Rarely would he sit in his assembly without a couple of them. This angered the viziers, who complained and said, "How can he shun us and spend his time with them? Once this sultan dies, however, we shall never again allow to rule over us any man who can read!" One of the *mooge* heard this and left them to their own devices until the sultan was seated in his court and these same viziers were in attendance. Then the *mooge* came and said something in Fur to the effect that "No one who knows how to read or write is ever again going to rule over us." The sultan turned to him and asked, "How so?" and the man replied, "Because you shun your viziers and spend your time with scholars." This made the sultan furious and he looked at him angrily. The *mooge* feared he'd assault him and said, "What's it got to do with me?" and he pointed to the viziers. "I heard those men saying that, so I repeated it." The sultan turned to them, rebuked them, and wanted to have them arrested, and they were only saved from his anger after great effort and trouble. Truly, I observed, "The ignorant are ever the enemy of those with knowledge!"[329]

3.1.74 A reliable source in Darfur told me a similar story to the effect that Sultan Tayrāb, mentioned earlier, held a banquet for some reason I've forgotten, and when the food came he inspected it closely to see which dishes were best. When he came to one made by Iyā Kūrī Kinānah and took off the cover, he found it to his liking, so he ordered it be taken to the scholars. However, she objected, saying, "Is my standing with you so low that you would give my food to shaykhs and the food made by others to viziers and kings?" "I only ordered it taken to the shaykhs," he replied, "because it's so good, and so that you can benefit from their grace." "Let my food be eaten by the viziers and kings," she said. "I have no need of their grace!" "None but the shaykhs shall taste it!" he said, but she said, "I beg you, don't let the shaykhs eat it!" In the end, she had her way, and he sent it to the petty kings and chose food made by someone else for the scholars.

The *mooge* are numbered among the poorest people in Darfur because their only profession is begging. This is why they always target princes and leave ordinary people alone. The princes fear them and treat them generously because they disclose everything they hear. If someone treats them well, they praise him and put it about how generous he is, but if someone is stingy with them, they hold him up to scorn and make it known to all. In this they are like poets: they write eulogies to those who give them gifts and ridicule those who rebuff them.[330] 3.1.75

Among the other offices of the Fur are that of iyā kurī, to which we have alluded earlier,[331] and that of the Grandmothers, which we have also mentioned.[332] Also, if the reigning sultan has a mother, she holds an office, and if he has a grandmother, she holds one too. These offices, however, are not permanent: they come into being when these two persons exist. I saw Sultan Muḥammad Faḍl's mother, and she was an uncouth slave woman. If put on sale in Darfur, she wouldn't have fetched ten francs. I saw his grandmother too, and she was an uncouth old crone, one of the ugliest women I ever saw among the Blacks, and a half-wit to boot—witness the fact that when she went on a long journey, she'd sit on a chair borne on men's necks, with a great crowd of soldiers around her. Someone whispered to her that the people of Darfur were saying, "This serving woman (*khādim*) has gone too far in her whoring."[333] When she heard this, she sat in her court, summoned all her followers, and said, "I am the *ḥādim*. The *ḥādim* brought silver and the silver brought gold"[334] (saying *ḥādim* instead of *khādim* because, not being an Arabic speaker, she couldn't pronounce the *kh*). There are other offices that we've opted not to mention because they aren't important enough. 3.1.76

Section 4: The Functioning of the Sultan's Court[335]

Regarding the sultan's court, his house is in his town, which is called the *fāshir*.[336] The people live around it, which is why it is built with two doors. The greater door is called the *órré dee*, meaning 3.1.77

"the men's door," the other the *órré bayyâ*, meaning "the women's door"; the sultan has a court in both.[337] The court of the *órré dee* is the Greater Audience Chamber and is located immediately after you pass through the first door. This court is spacious, and the sultan holds court there only on great holidays and special occasions.

3.1.78 We should mention that all Fur construction is done with stalks of millet or of *marhabayb*,[338] and the place where the court is held is called a *liqdābah* or *rākūbah*.[339] It is made by fetching long, smooth poles of wood, each with a fork at the end, like this:

Then they dig holes of equal depth and cut the poles to equal length. The holes are in lines opposite each other, each lined up precisely with the next so that they look like this:

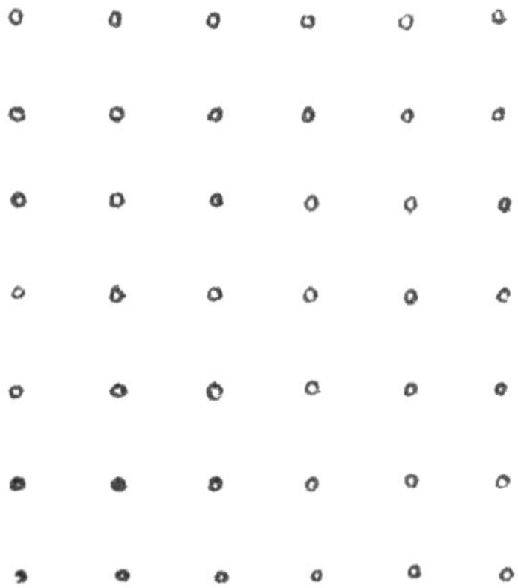

The holes must, however, all be of the same size and in straight rows. They put a pole in each hole, turning the forks in each row so that they face the same direction, and place on top a piece of wood called the *baldāyā* (i.e., they place it so that it runs between the forks in that row). When it is complete, they take thin branches called *maṭāriq*,[340] gather four or five of them, and tie them with tree bark, making them into sheaves, which they attach to one another till they reach the length of the aforementioned *liqdābah*. Then they make an assemblage from the branches in the same way and arrange them into a single elongated square [*sic*] with squares in the middle so that it looks like this: They place these frames on top of the aforementioned *baldāyā*s and on top of them they place bundled reeds, which they tie to the branches with the bark. All of it together makes an excellent roof, by their building standards.

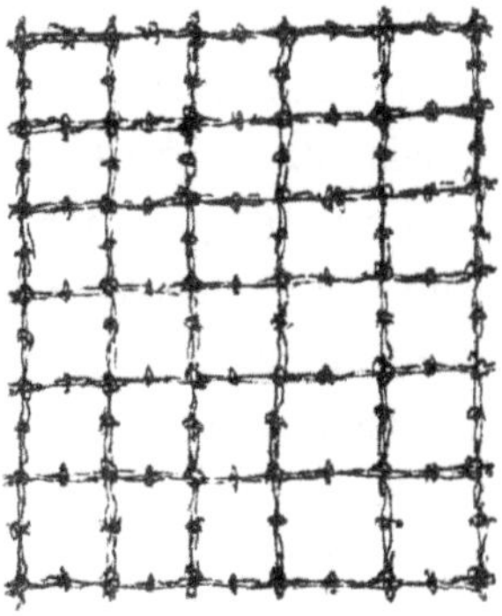

In the *órré dee*, this *liqdābah*, or open-sided pavilion, is spacious. Made as described here, the roof is so high that a man riding a camel can pass beneath it without his head touching it. In the past, however, the roof was lower, so that only a man riding a horse could pass beneath it, but it once happened that two men who were skilled camel riders attended the sultan, each claiming to be more skilled than his companion, and they quarreled. They agreed to make bets on mounting and passing under the roof of the pavilion with their animals. The sultan and the people left the pavilion and the men mounted and came at a gallop. When they reached the pavilion, one of them leaped up and landed on the top, leaving his camel, and ran fast and caught up with his camel as it emerged from beneath the roof; then he mounted and charged ahead at high speed with nothing to impede him. When the second rider reached the pavilion, he leaned down to the camel's side, holding on with his hands until he emerged from the other end. Each of them did something extraordinary, so the sultan rewarded them well and people acknowledged that they were both excellent riders, two bright stars in a single sky. Some, however, held a minority opinion and claimed that the one who had left his camel and run over the pavilion's roof was cleverer, while others held that the one who had leaned to the side of the camel was cleverer. The sultan judged in favor of the latter, and from that time on the pavilion was made higher. 3.1.79

3.1.80 When the sultan sits in this audience chamber, he sits in the middle. They have therefore built a raised place for him within it, the center higher than the sides, like this:

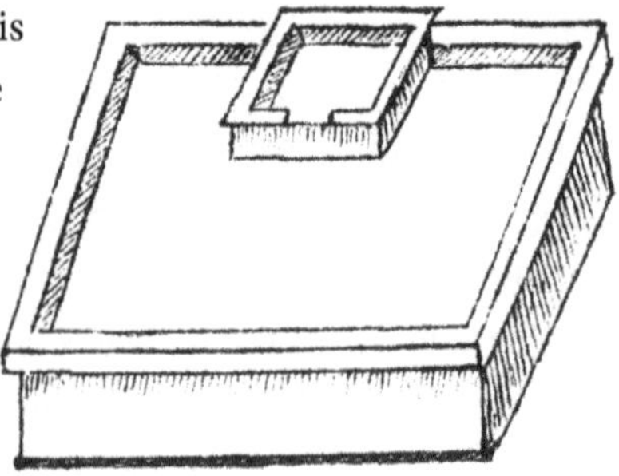

The high place in the center is where the sultan sits, the part that is slightly lower on the right is where the scholars of religion sit, and the part on the left is where the sharifs, the faqīhs, and the great men of the people sit, with a wide space in front of them. If the sultan wishes to sit for a general audience, receive the messenger of a petty king, or celebrate a day of festivity and happiness, his sitting place is decorated with weapons and brocades, and he is given a chair with a silk cushion. The sultan takes his seat in all his finery; the scholars, faqīhs, and sharifs take their seats around him; and his two viziers stand before him, these being the "counselors." His chief interpreter stands close by in front of him, and the six other interpreters in front of the first, with a distance between them short enough to allow each to hear the one next to him well. The *kóór kwa*, along with the player of the *dinqār*, stand with their pipes behind the sultan, while the sultan's slaves, jailers, and executioners stand behind the people. Each of the remaining persons sits in the place appropriate to him, and the master of the *mooge* stands close to the first interpreter. The arrangement of the court is thus complete. We have made a drawing of how it functions in the section on the customs of the Fur, which you may consult if you wish.[341] When the sultan takes his seat in the *órré bayyâ*, however, the court is reduced and is closer to a private court, since the pavilion in which he sits is small. On such occasions, only one interpreter and one, two, or at most three *mooge* stand in front of the sultan.

3.1.81 The sultan may be seated, mostly at night, or he may be mounted,[342] mostly by day. If he is seated, then it will be in a high place, but not one that is decorated. On such occasions, the place has no furnishings except for a single carpet with a cushion next to it. We have already mentioned that custom dictates that the sultan be greeted exclusively with the words "*Dóngá rǎy dóngá!*" and that if he spits, the place where he spat is wiped immediately, and if he clears his throat, they make a sound like a gecko. We have explained all this above, so there is no point in doing so again.[343]

This, then, is how the court of the Fur sultan functions. The court of the sultan of Wāddāy functions differently. The people of Wāddāy always screen the sultan from people's eyes, going to great lengths to do so. No one is allowed to see him clearly and the petty kings do not come and meet with him as they do with the sultan of the Fur: the Wāddāy think it more awe-inspiring and more likely to ensure that his orders are carried out if people do not meet him. This being so, and out of fear lest any injustice or injury come about, it is ordained that the sultan shall sit to hear complaints on Mondays and Thursdays. They have a special procedure for these occasions, on which the monarch's laws are applied, oppressors rebuked, and the oppressed given fair treatment. They have devised a form of assembly that allows for this without any mixing with the common people. 3.1.82

We shall describe elsewhere[344] how the building methods of the people of Wāddāy differ from those of the Fur, the difference lying in the fact that the Fur only rarely build with mud brick, whereas the people of Wāddāy use mud brick more than anything else. This has allowed them to construct an elevated room for the sultan to hold such audiences,[345] and there the sultan sits with some of his retainers every Monday and Thursday, though the people cannot see him. The only way to tell that he is holding court is that a flag is stuck through an aperture in the wall where he is seated, and the sound of the *baradiyyah* is heard. As soon as the flag appears and the *baradiyyah* (which is a drum like the goblet drum that in Egypt they call *darabukkah*) sounds, the *kabartū* hear it and they blow their trumpets and beat the *togjêl*, and the people hear. Those with 3.1.83

petitions have, after all, all been sitting in the sultan's compound waiting for that day, as have the *kamkūlaks*, who are present on a permanent basis at the compound to hear petitions. The officeholders and persons of rank also wait on that same day for the sultan to seat himself in the audience chamber. When he does so, the interpreters known as "the language mouths," the provincial and tribal governors general,[346] and the petty kings of all ranks come, as do the judge, the sharifs, and the scholars of religion, and they sit in the shade of a *sayāl* tree inside the royal compound. When the flag appears through the aperture and the *baradiyyah* sounds, a "language-mouth" enters and climbs a ladder inside the house and emerges from an aperture onto a balcony that has been prepared for him to sit on in such a way that he can position himself to hear the sultan easily. He stands there, the soldiers form rows, and the judge and the scholars seat themselves by rank, as do the sharifs and the merchants. Anyone with a petition then comes and presents it to the sultan, though only after the "language-mouth" has said, "The sultan salutes you, O people of the capital! The sultan salutes you, O judge of the sultan! The sultan salutes you, O scholars!" and so on, just as is done on Fridays.[347]

3.1.84 Let us now return to our primary concern, the description of the Fur. We shall give a brief notice of the characteristics of Tandaltī, the seat of the sultan, and of his house, and a description of each, to the best of our ability.

3.1.85 Tandaltī is now the base of the Fur kingdom. The first monarch to settle there and the one who laid it out was Sultan ʿAbd al-Raḥmān, in 1206 [1791–12]. Its soil is as sandy as any of the sand dunes to the east, and it is bisected laterally by a seasonal watercourse that is a spur of the larger watercourse named Wādī l-Kūʿ. In the rainy season, the wadi fills with water, and no one can cross it except at a point far to the east. When the water dries up, which is generally at the end of the winter, though sometimes at the beginning of the summer, they dig wells in it—everyone in the sultan's capital drinks from these. The sultan, because of his fear of magic, sometimes drinks from the wadi, but sometimes they bring him water from Jadīd al-Sayl, which is close to Tandaltī, about three miles to the east.

The Fur build exclusively with millet stalks,[348] and the outer fence 3.1.86
around their houses consists entirely of thorns. This outer fence they call the *zarībah*, while the inner they call the *ṣarīf*. The houses, by which I mean the dwelling places, are all dome-shaped, like tents, the inner fences thus serving as a dust-break.[349] They employ various types of construction for their houses. There are the houses of the poor, which they call *buyūt*,[350] made of millet stalks; and there are the houses of the commanders and kings, built of the thin canes called *marhabayb*, as we shall mention below. There is also a type called *suktāyah*, another called a *tukultī*, and another called a *kurnug*. The *suktāyah* looks like this:

It resembles a tent but is tall and narrow at the top. They bring ostrich eggs and make two holes in each, one at either end, and insert a stick. They put three or four eggs onto each stick and, between each, a ball of red earthenware (either the body of a *dullong* or of a large pot such as those made at Kīrī), and they set the stick on top of the dome. The *tukultī* looks like this:

On top, it is a semicircle standing on two wooden pillars. The *kurnug* resembles it but its roof stands on four wooden pillars. The sultan puts ostrich eggs on his *suktāyah*s, *tukultī*s, and *kurnug*s, but he also dresses their topknots with red and white lengths of cloth, of the sort shown here:

to distinguish himself from others. The lower part of the circular wall that forms the *suktāyah*s of the sultan, the iyā kūrī, the concubines, and the high officers of the state is built of mud, while the upper part is made of the thin canes called *marhabayb*, which are hard to find. This circular wall is called the *durdur* and its diameter is that of an ordinary tent.

3.1.87 The inhabitants of the sultan's capital are divided into two halves, one of which consists of the people of the *órré dee*, the other of the people of the *órré bayyâ*. The sultan's dwelling lies between them.[351] The people of the *órré dee* live on the side of the men's door that is called *órré dee* and the people of the *órré bayyâ* live on the side of the door that is called *órré bayyâ*. The sultan's *zarībah*, or outer fence, is placed on the edge of the wadi, on the rise there, which is north of the wadi, and there are only a few paces between the two. It extends for a long way to the north. The men's door opens to the north, and on the other side of it is the enclosure known as the *fāshir*, which is a huge expanse forming approximately two-thirds of a circle.

3.1.88 We shall now describe the sultan's outer fence and houses. The fence is made of black thorn or gum arabic branches—three rows, with tree trunks on which some branches have been left between each row. Deep holes are dug in the ground for these and there are thorns in front of them and thorns behind them, put down in layers. The fence is taller than a man and the tree trunks rise above it. Each year, any gaps that may appear are repaired. Between the thorns and the dwellings is a space of about four paces.

3.1.89 *Órré dee* has four doors, each of which has doorkeepers who watch over it in turns. The doors, however, are not like ordinary doors, by which I mean that they are not made of planks of wood: rather, they are made of logs lashed together with straps of rawhide, by which I mean untanned hide, and they are put together in the form of a grating, like this:

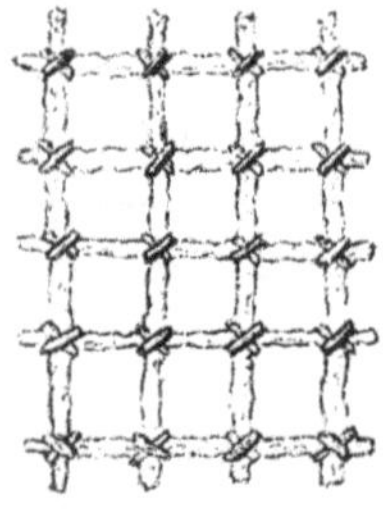

An iron chain is attached to each door and each door opening has, attached to its edge, numerous pieces of wood. The chain is attached to one of these. A lock like those used for chests is inserted through the doorpost and the door. The doorkeepers' dwelling is close to the door.

3.1.90 If one enters *órré dee* by the first door, one first comes to a wide space at the end of which is the Great Pavilion, which is the sultan's audience chamber. This is on the left as one enters. We have mentioned this above and drawn a picture of it, so there is no need to go over it again. On one's right as one enters is the place of the *kūrāyāt*, who are what we would call grooms. The stables are close by and consist of a long, not very wide, pavilion where the monarch's horses are tethered. After the stables is the Drum House, and close by are the houses of the servitors of the drums. The second door leads to the Pages' Place, the third to the *kóór kwa*, and the fourth to the eunuchs. Between each door and the next there is a space and an inner fence, into which a door has been let. Beyond the second door is another pavilion in which the sultan sits with his intimates, and beyond the third is a third, small, pavilion where the sultan sits with those with whom he is most intimate. Beyond the fourth door are the women of the household, the slave women, and the sultan's private apartments, as we shall show in a drawing, God willing.

The *órré bayyâ* is a door through which one enters a courtyard 3.1.91
longer than it is wide and at the end of which is a large pavilion, about one-third the size of the great pavilion of the *órré dee*. This pavilion is on the left as one enters. On one's right, at a distance, are buildings for the heralds and the doorkeepers. Beyond the second door is another pavilion, smaller than the last, where the sultan spends the evening in the company of whichever of his intimates he wishes, and on the left of this pavilion is the third door, which is, as it were, in a corner[352] of the inner fence. Slave guards are posted there, as at the other doors. This last door leads directly to the women's quarters, which consist of a considerable number of houses, where the concubines live. Each has her own house, for herself and the slaves assigned to serve her. Beyond are the living quarters of the iyā kūrī and, to the right, those of the sultan. The iyā kūrī's are composed of seven or eight *suktāyah*s within her inner fence, which are occupied by the iyā kūrī herself and the women attached to her service. The living quarters of the sultan are formed, as I have said, of two very tall *suktāyah*s within a separate inner fence that has two doors. In front of the sultan's inner fence are two buildings of

mud brick, called *dinjāyah*s, which are the furniture depositories or, more accurately, the sultan's magazines. These are made of mud brick to avoid the incineration, should an accidental fire break out in the *suktāyah*, of the jewels, costumes, silver, and precious objects held in them. Finally, on the left is a very long pavilion where slave women spend the day grinding millet and wheat using hand mills. These women, whose houses are in front of their pavilion, are called *marāhīk* (singular *marhākah*), meaning "millers." Here, as you will see on the following page, we have drawn a picture of the sultan's outer fence and the houses, so that you may become as conversant with its features as if you'd seen it with your own eyes; it constitutes an overview of the sultan's abode.

3.1.92 Every inhabitant of the capital, whether of the people of the *órré dee* or of the *órré bayyâ*, maintains the same place of residence from one generation to the next, because everyone who assumes an office builds his home in the same place as the first holder of that office, or close to it. Thus, a person from the *órré dee* will never reside in the *órré bayyâ*, and vice versa. Nor is this something peculiar to the long-term settlements, for they maintain their places even on the march: if the sultan moves with his soldiers, as soon as his tent is pitched, the soldiers pitch theirs, each, in accordance with this system, in its accustomed place. Thus, there is no difference between the city and the site where they halt when traveling, except for the size of the plots and the dimensions of the houses. As far as finding one's way around is concerned, everyone knows where everyone else is, so it's just as though they were in the city. For example, when the sultan comes to the campsite at night, he knows where his accommodation is without having to ask, and it is the same with his entourage: each vizier and emir knows the location of his campsite simply because they keep to the same positions. This has certain advantages. For example, if the sultan sends for someone at night, the messenger does not have to ask; he knows that so-and-so's campsite is in such and such a direction, so he goes there without asking anyone. Similarly, if one vizier or petty king

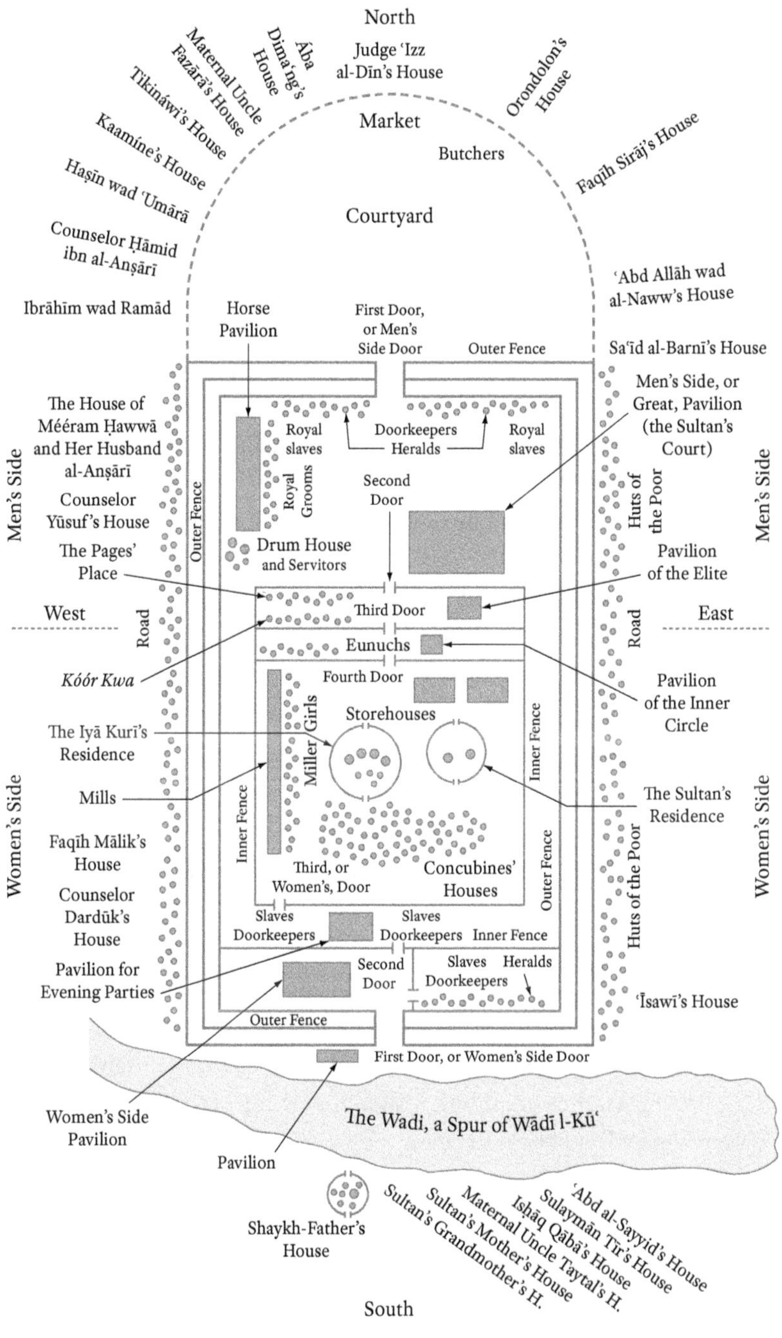

North
Judge ʿIzz al-Dīn's House
Âba Dima'ng's House
Maternal Uncle Fazārā's House
Tikináwi's House
Kaamíne's House
Ḥaṣīn wad ʿUmārā
Counselor Ḥāmid ibn al-Anṣārī
Ibrāhīm wad Ramād
Orondolon's House
Faqīh Sirāj's House
ʿAbd Allāh wad al-Naww's House
Saʿīd al-Barnī's House
Market
Butchers
Courtyard
Horse Pavilion
First Door, or Men's Side Door
Outer Fence
Men's Side, or Great, Pavilion (the Sultan's Court)
Royal slaves
Doorkeepers
Heralds
Royal slaves
Royal Grooms
Second Door
Huts of the Poor
The House of Mééram Ḥawwā and Her Husband al-Anṣārī
Counselor Yūsuf's House
Men's Side
Men's Side
Outer Fence
Drum House and Servitors
The Pages' Place
Pavilion of the Elite
Third Door
West
East
Road
Road
Eunuchs
Kóór Kwa
Fourth Door
Pavilion of the Inner Circle
Storehouses
Miller Girls
The Iyā Kurī's Residence
Inner Fence
Mills
The Sultan's Residence
Inner Fence
Faqīh Mālik's House
Women's Side
Women's Side
Concubines' Houses
Third, or Women's, Door
Outer Fence
Huts of the Poor
Counselor Dardūk's House
Slaves Doorkeepers
Slaves Doorkeepers
Inner Fence
Pavilion for Evening Parties
Second Door
Slaves Doorkeepers
Heralds
ʿĪsawī's House
Outer Fence
First Door, or Women's Side Door
The Wadi, a Spur of Wādī l-Kūʿ
Women's Side Pavilion
Pavilion
Shaykh-Father's House
Sultan's Grandmother's H.
Sultan's Mother's House
Maternal Uncle Taytal's H.
Isḥāq Qābā's House
Sulaymān Tīr's House
ʿAbd al-Sayyid's House
South

sends a message to another, the messengers face no difficulties, as the same sites are maintained: each one knows where his friend's dwelling is. This is quite remarkable.

Section 5: Garments of the Kings of the Fur[353]

3.1.93 Regarding their garments and how they wear them, their countries are extremely hot, and they accordingly can wear only lightweight clothes. All the same, there are differences among them. The rich wear very fine clothes, of white or black cloth. The poor, on the other hand, wear clothes of coarsely woven fabric. The sultan, viziers, and petty kings all wear two garments of very fine quality resembling shifts, either imported for them from Egypt or made in Darfur. The white ones are extremely white and clean, the black likewise.

3.1.94 The sultan is indistinguishable from others except that he wears garments in addition to the two shifts. He wears his cashmere shawl over his head, which others aren't allowed to; he also veils his face with white muslin, which he arranges over his head in folds so that it covers his mouth and nose as well as his forehead, leaving only his eyes visible. The orondolong and the kaamíne also cover their mouths, veiling themselves in the same way as the sultan, and the petty sultans do the same. The sultan is distinguished, however, by his gilded sword and gilded amulet,[354] and if he is mounted, by the umbrella, as well as by "the feathers," the gilded saddle and stirrups, and the caparison of his steed, which is of a kind no one else is allowed to use for his horse. If he is in his court, only he may be veiled. Others mentioned are only allowed to veil themselves in his presence if they are riding with him or if any of them is in his own realm and audience chamber.

3.1.95 The various imported garments worn by the rich of Darfur are made of muslin, English cotton baft, and, on festive occasions such as the Feast and the day of the covering of the drums, silk stuffs. They also swathe themselves in wraps resembling the *milāʾah* which people wrap around themselves in Egypt.[355] This is made either of a glossy, striped material of cotton mixed with silk or of muslin, but with a long fringe. This wrap is thrown loosely over the person or placed over the chest and shoulders. If someone wearing a wrap of this sort finds himself in the sultan's presence, he ties it around his waist, it being considered the acme of good manners to do so.

If the garment isn't imported, it will be of *kalkaf*, which is a stuff made of cotton of a very fine yarn that comes in bolts of twenty cubits in length and a cubit in width. The middling people wear, among the imported stuffs, *shawtar*, which is a kind of blue-dyed camlet. Certain kinds of cloth are also imported from the west, i.e., from the countries of Wāddāy, Barnaw, and Bāqirmah. These are called *tīkaw* and *qudānī*, but aren't wide, the width of a piece being no more than a couple of inches.[356] This makes them difficult to sew. The *tīkaw* and the *qudānī* mentioned here are black, but some red may be detected in the *qudānī*, despite its dark color, so that it looks like the neck of a black pigeon. I observed a remarkable thing about this: if its wearer hawks, the sputum comes up black from his chest. This is because the indigo enters his pores and permeates his body till it affects his chest. In general, the rich man, be he sultan, vizier, or petty king, wears two layers of dress plus baggy drawers, with a tarbush on his head, while the rest wear a single layer of dress with baggy drawers, plus, on occasion, a wrap, with a white or black skullcap on their heads, though most go bareheaded. 3.1.96

The women wear an apron around their waists that they call in their parlance *fardah*. In addition, virgins wear a small piece of cloth called a *durrāʿah* over their chests;[357] for the daughters of the rich, this is made of silk, cotton mixed with silk, or coarse cotton baft; for the daughters of the poor, of lengths of raw calico. Around their waists, they tie bands to which they attach a *kanfūs*, which in their dialect is a kind of woven fabric four inches wide and about thirty cubits long. A woman takes one and passes the front end of it through the band at her waist; she passes the other end between her thighs and knots it onto the band at the back. It acts like the 3.1.97

breechclout the city women use when they have their periods. The Fur women don't, however, wear the *kanfūs* only for the menses; they wear it all the time. When a virgin marries, she wears a large length of cloth that is called a *thawb* in their parlance, which is a sort of wrap with which the woman envelops herself. This also varies according to people's standing in terms of rich or poor: the *thawb*s of poor women are of raw calico, whereas those of the rich are of blue camlet, *kalkaf, tīkaw, qudānī,* or baft. They don't use silk or cotton mixed with silk.

3.1.98 Regarding jewelry, the women wear the nose ring, which is made of gold for the rich, silver for the middling, and copper for the poor. There are two types, "ring" and "thorn." The "ring" is a ring with a gap in which a piece of coral is fixed. It looks like this:

The "thorn" is a ring, half of which is thick and half thin, like a thorn. They attach four pieces of coral to it with a gold bead between each piece, or three beads, one of which is gold with a thick knob resembling a four-sided bead at the end. It looks like this:

3.1.99 In their ears, they wear large hoop earrings of silver, each weighing half a pound. So that these don't injure their ears, they tie them with a strap to their heads, thus relieving their ears of the weight. An earring of this type consists of a large ring, one of whose ends is in the form of a thorn and the other like the four-sided bead on the nose ring. The woman who can't afford a nose ring or hoop earrings stops the hole in her nose with a piece of coral or a single oblong bead and the holes in her ears with a bit of millet-cane pith, a grain of sorghum, or a bit of wood.

3.1.100 Around their necks, they wear necklaces made from beads such as the *manṣūṣ*, which in their usage is a kind of yellow bead made from amber and comes in two forms, spherical and flattened, individual specimens of both kinds varying in size. There are also "feathers," which are white elongated beads, some marked with white circular stripes, others with dark stripes. They come in various forms, of which the best is what they call *soomiit*. In all forms, it is as unyielding and hard as marble. It is imported from India—a slender elongated bead with many darkish striations. There is also the *ʿaqīq*, which is a spherical red bead no two of which are the same size and which is made of agate;[358] there is coral, which comes in two types, one of which is called "cut," which is a slightly elongated cylindrical bead, and the other "ground," which is a spherical bead; there is the *dam-l-raʿāf*,[359] which is a dark-red bead, some cylindrical and some spherical, and which is made of glass and imported from Europe; and there is the *păw*, which is an artificial coral, spherical and long in all cases. From all of these kinds they make necklaces, each woman according to her degree of affluence or lack thereof. Some you'll see wearing one string, others two, like this  and some three. The richest women never wear more than four, like this:  They arrange the abovementioned beads prettily, in such a way as to catch the eye and draw the heart to the one wearing them.

3.1.101 On their heads, the women place amulets made from the seeds of a plant called *shūsh*[360]—the seeds are small and red, like those of the pomegranate flower; each has a black spot on its side and they are very pleasing to the eye—as well as amulets made of shells and of beans. In their country,[361] these beans are colored, some being bright red, some straw-colored, some black, some honey-colored. They bore a hole in the *shūsh*, the shells, or the beans. They also make the *shūsh* into amulets on their own, though they attach to the bottom of each amulet either a little bell or a shell, and make them into clusters, like this:  However, they separate each pedicel from the next with a blue bead.

3.1.102 The women wear various kinds of beads around their waists.[362] The women of the rich wear beads as large as walnuts that they call *ruqād al-fāqah*,[363] the women of the middle class wear *manjūr*,[364] and the women of the poor either *ḥarish*[365] or *khaddūr*. All the kinds mentioned here are made in Hebron, in the hinterland of Damascus.[366] The *ruqād al-fāqah*, however, are very glossy and the color is something between green, blue, and yellow. There is also the *mishāhrah*, which is a black bead with white spots. The *manjūr* are the same in color but smaller and somewhat rough and crudely made. The *ḥarish* are of the same color as the last two but small, the size of prayer beads, and rough all over, with corrugations. The *khaddūr* is a cylindrical bead and is either red or white.[367]

3.1.103 On their arms, at the wrist, the women wear a string of beads called a *madraʿah*. This is composed of cylindrical beads, each about two inches long and either white or black. It is also called a *shuwūr*. They string a white bead and then a black and separate each pair with one of another kind—either of genuine or "cooked" (meaning artificial)—coral, or of *raʿāf*,[368] depending on how well off they are. Another form of finery they wear is the *laddāy*, which is a thick, semicircular silver wire with a curved-over bit like a fishhook at either end. Thin copper wire is taken, *manṣūṣ*, coral, and *ʿaqīq* are threaded onto it, and the two ends are secured at the curved-over bit that is like a fishhook, one at each end, so that the thin wire and everything that's threaded onto it are like the string of a bow. It looks like this:[369] They place the string close to their foreheads

and fix the thick wire in their hair. On their hands, they wear bracelets of ivory, horn (the latter called *kīm*), or copper. The bracelets worn by the daughters of the rich, however, are of silver and ivory together. On their legs are anklets, which are copper for everyone, but those of the daughters of the poor are of red copper, those of the daughters of the rich of copper mixed with zinc, as a way of reducing the everyday red of the copper in favor of a yellow close to gold. They also make bands from the various kinds of small colored beads, to be worn on their foreheads and wrists.

3.1.104 The perfumes worn by the women are spikenard; mahaleb; *kaʿb al-ṭīb* (called "white root" in the parlance of the Fur because of its color, which is white with a touch of brown and yellow, and in Egypt "root of violet" because of its smell); sandalwood; something like a small mollusk, called *ẓufr*, which ranges from brown to black; artemisia;[370] and myrtle. Some great men perfume themselves with *jalād*, which is the skin of musk glands.[371] They also use the fruit of a sweet-smelling tree called *dāyūq*;[372] this is a yellowish-red berry that the women crush and mix with their perfume. It is a custom of the women to use a kohl made of antimony. However, they do not put the kohl on their eyes but on the lower and upper outer surfaces of their eyelids, and the antimony is made to adhere with fat. The women anoint their lovers' eyes this way, and one sees all the young men and women made up like this. It's also a custom of theirs for a lover to take some piece of finery from his beloved and wear it out of pride and as a memento; if any trouble befalls him, or he suffers some setback, he'll say, "I'm brother to" this or that woman, and women do the same.[373]

Most of the men aren't jealous of their honor. A man will enter his 3.1.105
house to find his wife alone with another man and not be angry, so long as he doesn't find the man on top of her. If he enters and finds his daughter or his sister with someone from outside the family, he sees nothing wrong with that. Indeed, he may rejoice and think it will lead to her getting married. Another custom of theirs is to give a girl a room of her own to sleep in when her breasts start to grow, where anyone who loves her may come to her and spend the night. Most of their daughters become pregnant as a result, but there's no shame on them for this, and a boy born out of wedlock is regarded by them as the offspring of his maternal uncle. A girl in the same situation will be found a groom by her maternal uncle, who benefits materially from the bride-price, especially if she's pretty. Generally speaking, in the lands of the Fur the women can't be kept from the men, nor the men from the women. In fact, no man, even if he's powerful, can keep his daughter under his wing, and if he's poor, he's regarded with contempt and may be harmed, or even killed, if he tries to do so.

For example, it happened that a man had a daughter of whom he 3.1.106
was very protective and to whom he allowed no outsider to speak.

So frightened was he for her that he used to force her to spend the night in the same room as he. She was extremely beautiful and young men used to come, as is their custom, to her father's house. When he heard them, he'd berate them, curse them, and throw them out. Fed up with this, they decided to play a trick on him and took a slightly elongated gourd, egg-shaped but ending with a neck, cut it open at the top, extracted its flesh, filled it with feces and urine, shook it so that everything was well mixed, and went at night to his house. There, they called out to him, "Hey Dad, tell so-and-so to come out and talk to us!" As usual, he got up and cursed and swore and scolded, but it did no good; in fact, they told him, "We aren't leaving till you bring her out to us." He became very angry with them and came out himself, intending to drive them away, as they usually fled in fear when they heard him coming out. That night, however, they stood their ground, and one of them took the gourd by its neck and hid out of sight until the man poked his head out of the door of the house. Then he raised his hand and brought it down hard and struck the man on his head with the gourd, which broke, and the filth inside it poured over his head, clothes, and face. When he smelled the horrible smell, he shouted curses but they told him, "Hold your tongue! Tonight we've done this to you. Tomorrow night, if you stand in our way, we'll kill you." So the man woke his family and they came and washed him with water. He bathed and put on perfume and slept, and he was afraid of them. In the morning, having no other choice, he gave his daughter a room of her own to sleep in, and things went with her as they usually do.

3.1.107 If the father is rich and a man of respectable ways and outward show, with slaves and servants, they'll try any trick to get into the harem at night, even if they have to dress as women. For example, it happened that a great man had seven sons and one daughter. She was of a unique beauty, and many had asked for her hand, but he'd refused them all. When things had gone on like this too long for the girl's liking, she played a trick and brought in a nice young man known for his courage, who spent with her what time God was pleased to allow him. His family noticed his absence and could find no trace of him. Now it happened that he'd brought with him something to drink. He drank, and when the intoxication took hold, he wanted to leave. "Wait till night," said the girl, but he refused, saying, "I have to leave right now!" and forced her to let him go. Her father and brothers were sitting at the door of their house and caught sight of the youth as he was leaving. The father shouted to the doorkeeper, "Close the door!" and when he'd done so, ordered the slaves to seize the boy. The slaves gathered to do so, but he wounded some of them and kept out of their reach. Then the seven sons came out, unsheathing their weapons and bent on killing him. He beseeched them in God's name to stay away from him and let him go his way, but they refused and threw themselves at him, so he fled, throwing spears at them and killing one. This enraged them, and they threw their spears at him, intent on killing him, while he defended himself and threw his at them. In the end, he killed six of the sons and lightly wounded the seventh. When their father saw this, he called out, "Slave! Open the door for him!" which the slave did, and he left without a wound on him, and they never found out who he was because he was wearing a veil. His daughter was the ruin of his house and caused the death of his sons. Many an incident of this type has led to blood being spilled with impunity because the girl involved won't tell anyone the killer's name or who he is. Indeed, the most she'll do, if asked who did it, is say, "I don't know." Not a house with a female in it is spared such things, unless she's hideous or has some defect that makes people shun her.

Sultan ʿAbd al-Raḥmān tried to prevent the practice but couldn't. 3.1.108
He even put large numbers of eunuchs in the marketplace to stop the women from talking to the men and mixing with them, but they came up with some remarkable tricks to get around this. For example, if a man passed a girl who took his fancy, he'd say "*Yā bunayyah māluh rāsik shēn mitl dīk al-suktāyah*"[374]—*māluh* means "why?" and *shēn* in their parlance is the opposite of "beautiful"—and she'd say to him, "*Wēnu al-suktāyah al-shēn al-mitl rāsī*"[375]—*wēnu* meaning "where is it?"

Then he'd say "*Dīka*"—meaning "that one"—and point it out to her with his finger. Thus, she'd know where it was, and in the evening she'd go there and spend the night with him and the eunuch guards would have been of no use.

3.1.109 He also worked hard to put a stop to the drinking of alcohol, but failed. People came up with some astounding tricks. They went so far as to go to the houses of the brewers, buy alcohol from them, and pretend to any who might see them that they were buying bread. They'd say in their language, "*Tugúra baing sá*," meaning *Bread-you-at-is*, i.e., "Do you have any bread?" If the brewers feared they were spies, they'd send them away by saying, "*Á keeba*," meaning, "We do not," and if they knew they were unknown to the police,[376] they'd admit them to the house and give them what they wanted. While this was going on, the sultan gave orders that the breath of the high officers of state who attended his court (who were the persons most addicted to alcohol) be smelled, so they'd chew the branches of a tree called *shaʿlūb* to get rid of the smell; they'd drink their fill and then chew some of it, and the alcohol couldn't be smelled on their breath at all. These ways have become integral to their natures and part of their blood and flesh, and they are now accepted practice, even though they're forbidden in Islam.

3.1.110 One of their customs is that when a poor man marries and his better-off relatives refuse to help him with the expenses on the banquet day, he takes himself off to the livestock pasture in search of animals belonging to his closest relative and hamstrings as many as he needs, be it an ox or oxen, or a camel if the relative has any. If the relative has none of these, the man will slaughter sheep of the number required. If the animals' owner is aware of what he wants to do and forbids him before he's hamstrung any, he may fight him till he beats him. If the other still refuses to help him and summons him before the judge, the latter will oblige the first to pay the value of the beasts, in installments if he's not well off.

3.1.111 Another custom is that when a boy is circumcised, the other boys in the village, as well as any others who are related to him or know him, gather, starting from the third day after his circumcision and continuing until the seventh, and they take throwing sticks, go out into their village and the nearby villages, and kill any chicken they see or, if they can, catch it alive and take it, till they've collected a large number. No one dares stand in their way, and if any does, they beat him. They're young, so no law can be applied to them.

Another of their customs is to circumcise their daughters, though they have different ways of doing this. Some don't think it necessary at all, these being the non-Arabic-speaking Fur. Others—the great among them—perform a light circumcision, in the same way as the Egyptians. Yet others perform a circumcision so extreme that the place knits together and they have to insert a metal pipe to let the urine escape. When these marry off their daughter, the man can only deflower her after they have slit the place for him with a razor, there being women whose job it is to do this, and it's the same when she gives birth. This affects most of the daughters of the poor, who are always obsessed with men. They do it out of fear that they'll be deflowered out of wedlock, despite which they still get pregnant sometimes even in this state. They hold huge celebrations when girls are circumcised, and put on huge feasts. It's a custom of theirs for the circumcised girl's male relatives to stand outside the place where she's being circumcised, while the women are inside. If she cries out at the moment of circumcision and screams, they abuse her and leave, but if she endures, each of her male relatives gives her a gift, depending on how much he can afford and how closely related he is. Some give her a cow and others several cows, some a slave, and others a ewe or several ewes, so that she ends up a wealthy woman. Her father and mother give her more than all the rest, if they are rich. 3.1.112

It is their custom to demand high bride-prices for their daughters. A good-looking but poor girl may marry for twenty cows plus a slave girl and a male slave. The father and mother will take all of that and seal the contract with a heifer. This is why they celebrate the birth of a girl more than that of a boy, and say, "A girl 3.1.113

fills the homestead with good fortune, a boy reduces it to ruins." It's also their custom for a girl to remain at her father's house for one or two years after the consummation of the marriage, and she can only be made to leave and go to her husband's house with great effort. During this period, her father supports her, and anything that her husband brings is as a gift. Another custom is that if a man becomes engaged to a girl with whose father or mother he has previously been on friendly terms, and the girl too has been on friendly terms with his father and mother, that friendship comes to an end the moment they become engaged, and all behave like strangers to one another. From then on, if the man sees the father or mother of the girl to whom he is engaged, he turns around and goes another way, and they do the same. Likewise, the girl flees whenever she sees his father or mother. If the man enters her house during this period, he sends his greetings to her mother via the girl or her sister or a slave girl, or whoever is in the house, and her mother sends him her greetings by the same means, and they never meet. They go on like this till he consummates the marriage. Then, on the seventh day after the consummation, he goes out and kisses his father- and mother-in-law's heads and meets with them, along with the girl. Another custom of theirs is that the husband and the wife each regard the other spouse's relatives as their own. Thus, the man treats his father-in-law with respect and addresses him with the words "My dear father," while he addresses his wife's mother with the words "My dear mother" and her sister as "My dear sister," and she does the same.

CHAPTER 2

In two sections

Section 1: Marriage Practices among the Fur

Given that He who is unique in His essence, attributes, and acts—having not been disjoined from any and none having been disjoined from Him—needs neither spouse or offspring, the only one that has need of these last is that pitiful being, newly made, who has no support but God and likewise no aid, He, glory and power be to Him, being the Living, the Everlasting, whom «neither slumber nor sleep may overtake,»[377] Single, Solitary, Unique, Eternal, who has taken neither wife nor son,[378] «and who has no partner in His kingdom»[379] «and no like,»[380] who created Ādam, the father of humankind, from dust and created Ḥawwā', his spouse, from the shortest rib of his left side, as was just. 3.2.1

And given that God's intention in creating him was that he should be «a vicegerent on earth»[381] and fill it with his issue throughout its length and breadth, He instilled in them human lust, that propagation might proceed, as the Sublime Will has decreed it must. When Ḥawwā' was created, Ādam was enjoying a light sleep,[382] and when he awoke, he found her before him, limbs neatly disposed, and saw that she was pleasing. He asked, "Who are you, dearest beloved?" and she said, "I am Ḥawwā'. God has created me for your sake, Ādam, having decreed this from most ancient time." "Come to me," 3.2.2

he said. "No, you come to me," said she. So Adam got up and went to her, which is how it came about that men go to their wives.

3.2.3 And when he sat with her and touched her body with his hands and was seized by human lust and wanted to have intercourse with her as animal nature requires, he heard a voice say to him, "Gently, Ādam! Ḥawwā' can only be yours in religion through payment of a dowry and the making of a marriage contract." Then God, glorious and mighty, pronounced them in His eternal uncreated language man and wife, saying, "My power be praised! In My majesty lies dread of Me and all Creation are My slaves. I take you, O angels and habitants of the heavens, as My witnesses that I hereby give the marvel of My creation, Ḥawwā', to Ādam, My vicegerent, with, as dowry, that he glorify Me and celebrate My oneness,"[383] and this has been the practice of His children ever since.

3.2.4 However, given that climes and languages have diversified, tribes and conventional practices multiplied, each people's practice has come to differ from others', though the contract and the dower are the same. It is, for example, a practice of the Fur to raise their young people, females and males, together. Thus, when young, they watch over their flocks with no barrier between them, day in and day out. A boy and a girl may become friends from then on, and a bond of affection be tied that never wears, despite the passing of the years. When he loves her and she loves him, he becomes dependent on her and jealous of her and doesn't like to see anyone else talking to her. At that point, he sends his father or mother or a relative to ask for her hand. If they agree on terms and things go according to plan, people gather for the wedding, the witnesses come for the betrothal, and they set out many conditions and ask for ample assets, all of which go to the father and mother, or the maternal or paternal uncle. They conclude the contract for her on the basis of a small part of that copious wealth; we have given a brief account of this earlier to which you may refer.[384]

3.2.5 Following the conclusion of the contract, they set the matter aside, as though it were quite forgotten, for a long while. Then they meet and consult among themselves and agree when to hold the wedding. If the bride and groom belong to great houses and hold high rank, their relatives start preparing the slaughter animals and the drink many days before the wedding. Then they send messengers to their friends in the villages and say, "The wedding is on such and such a customary day." By this time, they will have assembled sufficient millet beer, the red wine they call *umm bulbul,*[385] the cattle, and the sheep; and the people arrive on the set day, troop after troop. Certain women bring with them small and large drums, each having three, two small and one large, of the same shape as the *darabukkah*, which she puts under her left arm. One, the largest, is on top, while the two smaller ones are next to it, underneath. Then she beats on the three of them with her hand, the whole set being known to them as the *dallúka*. Every time a group arrives, the women go out with the drums and beat them, singing their praises with songs such as the following:

Hay bānī! Hay banān!
Wa-banīna ḥiss al-banān!
O shakers of the lances,
Death spare you its advances!
Blinded be the eye of the envious!
O shakers of the spear,
Ruin come not near!
Dust in the eye of the envious!

Whenever she sings, she says before anything else the words

Hay bānī! Hay banān!
Wa-banīna ḥiss al-banān!

though in fact they mean nothing. Once I arrived at a wedding and a woman blocked my path and sang:

The sharif comes from the mosque,
Book in one hand,

Sword in the other.
Before, he brought
The Birqid as slaves.[386]

I used to know a lot of the words these women sing by heart, but I've forgotten them now.

3.2.6 Then the hosts come forward and receive the guests as they arrive. Each group includes men and women, and to each group the hosts assign a place and bring food and drink in accordance with their station. Some are brought different kinds of flour-and-butter paste and the beer that in Egypt is called *būzah*,[387] as well as boiled meat and grilled meats. Others are brought rounds of layered flaky pastry and the red wine known to them as *umm bulbul*. If a group of men of religion arrives, they bring them different kinds of flour-and-butter paste and *sūbiyā*,[388] known to them as *dééng saaya*. Then everyone naps where they are till the air cools and the shadows lengthen.

3.2.7 The girls now separate themselves from the women and the boys from the men, wearing the most beautiful finery they can obtain, and the girls[389] arrange themselves in rows, with a row of boys facing each row of girls. The women who carry drums also advance, beating their drums and singing their songs, and a row of girls moves forward at a leisurely pace, shaking their shoulders and crouching close to the ground, till they reach the row of boys. Each girl now moves in on a boy till her face is right in front of his and moves her head backward and forward in his direction till her braids (which on such occasions are anointed with perfume and the various kinds of scent they're familiar with) are striking him on the face, exciting the boy and causing him to brandish his spear over her head. Then she turns around and goes back. But the boy follows her all the way to her original place, where he now stands while she retreats till she reaches the place where he was standing before. The onlooker will now observe that the girls' row has taken up position where the boys' was, and vice versa. If there are any boys who haven't joined the row, and a girl wants one of them to meet her and get to know her, she leaves the row and goes to him, dancing, and throwing her head back, she brings it suddenly forward again so that her hair falls over his nose, at which he gets excited and cries out and brandishes his spear and follows her; if he does not, he is regarded with disapproval and must put on a feast for the girl who went up to him. Once each row has taken up position where the other was, the girls and the boys come forward, dancing, each group facing the other and each girl facing a boy, till the two rows meet in the middle, and each girl moves her head back and forth in the direction of the chest and face of the boy facing her, while the boy brandishes his spear over her head and lets out cries of joy, this cry being known to them as the *raqraqah*. All the boys and girls are intoxicated from what they've drunk, and they keep this up till night comes, when each group goes back to its assigned place and is brought food and drink.

Do not imagine for a moment, however, that this, which is called the *dallúka*,[390] is the only kind of dance they know. There is a dance called the *jêl*, another called the *lanngi*, and another called the *sangadiri*, and there is the dance of the male and female slaves, called *tawse*, and the dance of the Fur, called *tindinga*. There is also another dance, called the *bindalah*. At weddings, each type of person dances one type of dance. Thus, the beautiful daughters of the great dance to the *dallúka* with their like among the boys, the daughters of the middling class and their like among the boys dance the *jêl*, and lesser people dance the *lanngi*. 3.2.8

In the *jêl*, the women face the men, shake their shoulders, and stamp the ground with their right feet, and the men do the same, but in each circle there are women who sing, and the people dance to their singing. In the *lanngi*, some of the women sing, while the girls and boys stamp the ground, and each dances with his or her feet, right and left. The boys, for their part, make the sound known as *karīr*.[391] 3.2.9

In the *sangadiri*, the boys and girls assemble, and each boy takes a girl who is in front of him. She bends over and he takes hold of her 3.2.10

waist, so that together they form a sort of circular chain, meaning that the female puts her hands on the hips of the male in front of her and the male puts his hands on the hips of the female in front of him and all of them are bending over so that together they form a closed circle and they move very slowly, stamping their feet so that the ringing of the girls' anklets can be heard. The girls who sing stand outside the circle.

3.2.11 The *bindalah* is a slave dance. It consists of a male slave bringing the nuts—resembling coconuts—that they call *dalayb*, making holes in them (the nuts being round, like cannonballs), stringing three or four of them on a lace, and tying this to his leg like an anklet, on the right foot; each male slave does the same and a female slave stands behind each and they make a kind of circle. They also have a special sound they make. A slave advances toward another in the middle of the circle and competes with him at this sport, which is based on bodily strength and suppleness, as though they were performing acrobatics. After they've competed for a while, one of them will strike the other with the leg to which the nuts are tied and not stop till he makes him fall or fails in the attempt, the skilled performer being the one who topples his opponent with a single kick. The rest dance a dance in which there is no bending of the body, and all respond antiphonally to the female singers, who are outside the circle.

3.2.12 The *tawse* consists of a male slave beating on a large drum, with the women and the men around him in a circle, each man putting his hands on the hips of a woman and each woman putting her hands on the hips of a man, but standing straight up and not bending over. Then they move ahead slowly, the women striking their feet together so that their anklets ring. They all proceed in a circle in time to the drumbeats and also form a circle, with the female singers on the outside. The *tindinga* is a sport of the Birqid and the Fur and is most like the *tawse*, the only difference being that in the *tawse* they move slowly, while in the *tindinga* the movements are violent. In truth, though, these descriptions don't get to the heart of the matter, because seeing something is quite different from hearing about it: sometimes an observer sees things words cannot convey.

Each of these dances has its own song. The words sung by the women for the *jêl* go: 3.2.13

Yūbānī hay yūbānīn
The night is passing, my gold piece
My head is spinning
The night is passing, my gold piece
My head is spinning[392]

The words *yūbānī hay yūbānīn* mean nothing, but one of the women sings out: "The night is passing, my gold piece," and the others respond, "My head is spinning." They also sing:

The night passes
Darfur is loveless
My head yearns[393]

They also sing:

O little branch so tender
You've made me surrender
O little branch of sandal—
Over our little house you grow and dangle.[394]

For the *lanngi*, the women sing, among other things: 3.2.14

Boys,
Get rich!
Join Daldang, son of Binayyah![395]
The pounding of hooves sounds in Karyū.
Join Daldang, son of Binayyah![396]

For the *tindinga*, the women sing, among other things: 3.2.15

Báási Tahir dogólá
Bála bá díéng ába

Kitab musab láng álpen piá,
Tárímádó kábí raaye ela.
Tarang mado sagal dió jábí.[397]

It would take a very long time to list all the songs that go with each kind of dance.

3.2.16 After they've eaten and drunk, they process with the bride to the music of the *dallúka* drums, taking her on a tour of the village and ending at the place prepared for her deflowering. Then, a long while after dinner, the young men assemble and take the groom and accompany him in procession, singing and making the *raqraqah*,[398] till they come to the place in question, where they sit down outside. By this time, all the young women will have assembled with the bride, and the young men will have assembled where the groom is, and the groom will have appointed his dearest brother as "vizier" (for at that moment he's like a sultan), and the bride will have appointed a woman as her vizier, whom they call the méëram. Once the men have sat down with their groom, they call for the méëram, but she refuses to come out to see them till about two hours have passed, at which time the vizier presents himself to her and greets her politely, requesting her to bring the bride. She asks them, "Who are you, where have you come from, and who is the bride you seek?" The vizier replies, "We are guests come from faraway lands, and we seek the queen, so that she may entertain her guests." She says, "The queen is busy with a matter of great importance, but here am I, as her representative, to offer you hospitality, entertainment, and whatever you need." The vizier responds, "We know that you are a capable person and well up to the task, but we have something to say to her that we can reveal to no other." She then says, "If that is the case, then what is there for the queen, and what for me, for it is her custom not to come out from behind what conceals her or go to those who ask for her unless there is a reward," to which he answers, "Our wealth and our lives and whatever she may ask." They continue in this way, bandying words with one another, until they agree and that's the end of things. While this is going on, the bride is close by, behind a curtain, but she says nothing, and the groom too is silent, the argument being between the other two.

When they reach agreement, the curtain is lifted, the bride comes out, and the vizier says, "The queen is for the king, but what is there for us?" so the mééram calls out for the girls who are with the bride, and they come, and she tells them, "Girls, I want you to entertain the queen's guests tonight," and they reply to her, "With all love and honor!" The mééram knows each girl and her boyfriend, so she says, "You, so-and-so, be with so-and-so, and you, so-and-so, be with so-and-so," and so on till only the girls who have no boyfriends and the boys who have no girlfriends are left. Each boy then takes his girlfriend and spends the night with her—right where they are, if there's enough room. This is done as follows: the bride and the groom, the mééram and the vizier, and each couple spend the night together in one or two rows, depending on how much room there is. If there isn't enough room for all of them, those for whom there's room remain, along with the bride and groom, and the rest go, each boy taking his girlfriend to her house or to the house of one of her friends. He doesn't take her to his house because she wouldn't agree, since it's their custom that when a young man loves a girl and her mother finds out about it, the mother must never meet with him nor he with her. If she sees him on the path and can find no way to avoid him, she kneels on the ground and drapes her wrap over her head and face until he has passed, and he does likewise, meaning that if he sees her and recognizes her, he turns on his heel and flees, if he can. If he cannot, he turns his face to a wall or a tree till she has passed. If there is someone else with him, he sends her his greetings via that person, and she does the same after he's passed. If there is nobody with him and she has somebody with her, she sends him her greetings via that person. All this, in their view, is a matter of modesty and respect.[399] 3.2.17

For them, all the members of the wife's family are taboo. Her mother is like his mother, or to be treated with even greater respect; 3.2.18

her father is like his, or more so; and her brothers like his. The same holds true for her. If she sees his mother or father, she flees and takes another path and sends her greetings, or he sends her his, and must not come face to face with either of them, and she treats his father like her own, and so on, just as we have described when referring to the man. This is why she goes somewhere else with her boyfriend and won't agree to go to his house with him. In fact, if there are too many people and too few places, she still will not go with him to his house. Instead they will go into the open countryside and spend the night there. In the case of her father's house, however, given that she has a place of her own prepared for that purpose there, anyone she likes can spend the night with her there without her father seeing her. If the man goes there with her and leaves at dawn while her parents are asleep, neither of them will see her.

3.2.19 But let us return to our original topic. They pass the night, and when morning comes, each girl gets up and goes to her parents' house and performs her toilet, by which I mean that she washes her face and limbs; indeed, she may perform the ritual ablution of her entire body. Then she perfumes herself, adorns her eyes with kohl, and rearranges her finery. It is the same with the bride, who enters her mother's house and performs her toilet. Likewise, the men go to their houses, if they are nearby. If these are far away, as in the case of those who come from another village, each goes to a friend's house and performs his toilet there, and it's the same with the women: if a woman is from another village, she goes to the house of a friend and performs her toilet there, for each of the young women who goes to the wedding has with her her kohl, her perfume, and everything she needs. She performs her toilet and the women sit together till almost midmorning. Then the mééram goes to where the wedding festivities were held while the groom isn't there (by which I mean when he too has gone to perform his toilet) and, along with some of her friends, sets it to rights, cleaning it, spreading out mats, and preparing the places where people will sit. Then the groom comes and finds it clean, so he sits there along with his vizier, and the young men come in droves and sit with him.

After this, it's up to the hosts. If they want to, they may pass the whole seven days in dancing and *dallúka,* or they may limit the celebrations to one day. If it's clear that they want to keep things short, the guests stay until lunchtime, and after eating each returns to his village and only the people of the village where the festivities were held remain. If the guests do not want to keep things short and know that the hosts want to extend their celebrations to seven days, they take up residence. This is made obvious by new animals being brought to be slaughtered, wine being pressed, and other preparations. 3.2.20

Note: The people invited to such feasts from each of the villages bring with them either two cows or two bulls, or one bull or one cow, or ewes as a contribution for the host, and if they have relatives living outside their village who are invited, these bring bulls and cows over and above those brought by the people of their own village, in order to be of assistance. 3.2.21

They spend the whole of the rest of the day playing, laughing, and relaxing, eating and drinking, and engaging in pleasant conversation till the late afternoon. Then the drums, those called *dallúka*s, are beaten, and they do as they did the day before till night comes, when food and drink are brought. When they're finished with those, they gather, men and women alike, in the place where the celebrations are held, and talk till around midnight. Then each boy takes his girlfriend and spends the night with her in the same place as the day before, and they go on in this way for the allotted time. If more animals have to be slaughtered, the number prepared being too small for those present, the bride's father, or her brother or a relative, goes out to the pastures and hocks whatever animals he finds before him—a bull or two, or a cow, or ewes—and, having hocked them, sends the butchers, who slaughter the hocked animals and bring the guests their meat, and so it continues. If word reaches the 3.2.22

owner of the cattle, he either asks for the price and is compensated, or does nothing until he himself or one of his relatives holds a wedding, when he hocks whatever he wants of the cattle belonging to the man who hocked his, tit for tat. This is why, when a wedding is to be held, animal owners order their minders to take them far out into the savannah, since they only hock animals grazing nearby. Throughout this period, the bride is treated like a queen and her girlfriends are with her, playing and enjoying themselves, and it's the same for the groom.

3.2.23 Another custom of theirs is that the groom doesn't deflower his bride till after the seven days have passed, even though they spend the night in one another's arms with nothing between them. The grooms do this out of respect for the bride and her parents, saying that the first night is out of respect for her father, the second for her mother, the third for her brother, if she has one, or for her sister, and so on, till the seven days are up. They think badly of a man who hurries and deflowers her before then, saying, "What a hurry he was in!" That he should deflower her before three nights have passed is unthinkable.

3.2.24 A remarkable thing. It is their custom that a woman mustn't eat in front of her husband or any other man, and if her husband enters while she's eating, she gets up and flees. They see this as the acme of modesty and denounce any woman who eats in front of her husband. When I was there and saw this, I asked them, "How can she be ashamed to eat with her husband when she is not ashamed to sleep with him or let him enter her embrace, penetrate her, and see her vagina and every other bit of her?" "There's no harm in any of that," they replied, "but for her to open her mouth and insert food into it in front of her husband is an abomination."

3.2.25 Another custom of theirs is that the man doesn't take his bride and consummate the marriage in his own house: he does so in her parents' house, and she doesn't leave it and live with him till she's borne two or three children. If he should ask her to move in with him before this, she refuses, and they sometimes even get divorced over the issue. Another custom is that she never allows his name to pass her lips. Instead she will always say, "He told me such and such." If she's asked who told her, she'll say, "him"—this till such time as they have children, when she'll say, "the father of . . . ," supplying the name of their child, whether a boy or a girl.

Another of their customs is that the man doesn't support the woman until a year has passed since the wedding. If he brings her anything before then, he does so as a gift. At the same time, though, he always eats better than the rest of the family: they may cook any disgusting kind of mediocre food for themselves, but for him they'll slaughter a chicken or a pigeon or prepare meat. Another custom is that, while the man is in his father-in-law's house, they prepare very good food for him once, twice, or even three times a day, in addition to the dinner that he takes at night. The first meal is called in the Fur language *juri jaráng*, the second *tarnga jíso*, and the third *subu jelló*, their hope being that this will strengthen him for intercourse. In their Arabic such a meal is called a *warrāniyyah*. Most well-off people eat again after their dinner, because a guest may have come to see them, which requires that they not eat their fill out of respect for him; or the dinner may not have been good, so they must have a *warrāniyyah*. Their term *juri jaráng* means "take off the shirt," *juri* meaning "shirt" and *jaráng* meaning "take off." *Tarnga jíso* means "grasp the leg," *tarnga* meaning "leg" and *jíso* meaning "grasp." *Subu jelló* means "the coming of dawn." 3.2.26

The word *warrāniyyah* is Arabic and is derived from *warā'*,[400] meaning "behind" (the opposite of "in front"), because they eat it "behind" dinner, i.e., after they've eaten dinner. This is why you will find that some people, if they have a particularly dear friend, and he's had dinner with them and is about to leave, will prevent him from doing so till all the rest of the company has left. Then they'll call their servant and ask him, "Is there anything to eat?" at which the servant will bring them the *warrāniyyah* and they'll eat together. This is done only with their best friends. The *warrāniyyah* also comes in useful for the unexpected guest who arrives in the middle of the night. 3.2.27

3.2.28 The above applies to weddings. If the celebration is a circumcision, they do everything we've mentioned in terms of preparing food, millet beer, *umm bulbul*, and *dééng saaya*, and invite people and dance to the *dallúka* drums, and make a procession with the boy who is to be circumcised, the barber coming and circumcising him while his father stands by. If the boy being circumcised cries, his relatives treat him with aversion and leave him. If he is patient while being circumcised and does not cry, his father says, "Be my witnesses, everyone here! I hereby give my son a cow" or a bull or a male or a female slave, depending on what he can afford. His mother makes the same declaration, and every one of his relatives who is present gives him something. If his family is rich, he will receive much property from them, and become well off, all according to his family's access to or lack of resources. On the third day of the circumcision ceremonies, the other boys of his age get together and take their throwing sticks and roam through the village knocking down chickens and killing them in large numbers. From the fourth to the seventh day, they go to the neighboring villages and kill every chicken they lay eyes on. Each day they go to a different village to kill chickens, and the owners of the chickens see nothing wrong in that. If it's a female circumcision, they do everything we have described, except that they don't kill chickens. They don't go to as much expense over the circumcision of a female as they do over that of a male. Anyone reading this account will know that we've gone to some length to describe these things simply so that the best benefit may be provided, the greatest gain derived.

3.2.29 Know too that the men of Darfur undertake no business without the participation of the women. Indeed, these take part with them in all their affairs, exception made for major battles. This is why no wedding or funeral takes place without them and why without them nothing would be considered by the people of Darfur to have been properly done. Thus you'll find women present on all great occasions. An example is their *dhikr* ceremonies, which are of two kinds: those performed by the Arabic-speaking inhabitants of the country, by which I mean those who do not speak one of the non-Arabic languages, and those performed by the non-Arabic-speaking Fur.

The first kind is in accordance with the practice of a particular Sufi shaykh or holy man. In either case, a woman will be present at the circle of remembrance to chant to the men, and the rest of the women will stand behind her, saying nothing but watching their husbands and relatives to see which of them is the best performer: a man may chant on his own while the women, like the rest of the men, listen. 3.2.30

For example, a disciple of Shaykh Dafʿ Allāh once attended the *dhikr* ceremony of the disciples of Shaykh Yaʿqūb. There was tension between the two shaykhs' disciples, and once the *dhikr* had warmed up one of the disciples of Shaykh Yaʿqūb decided to make fun of Shaykh Dafʿ Allāh's disciples by singing: 3.2.31

> He who has no shaykh to protect him, oho[401]
> Shouldn't let himself get caught twixt shield and arrow
> He who has no shaykh worthy of veneration
> Shouldn't enter Yaʿqūb's circle of recollection

Shaykh Dafʿ Allāh's disciple heard this and understood that the man was referring to him, so he sang:

> We enter and shall leave in good health
> Pure in deed and intention
> Dafʿ Allāh's above me at every revolution

An amusing anecdote. A woman once attended such a ceremony and chanted: 3.2.32

> I'll pour you a big pot of beer
> I'm single and live on the edge of town
> Sufis, is none of you a fornicator?

Those performing heard her, among them a young man who understood what she meant. He'd been saying, "God lives!"[402] but he changed and started chanting, "I'm a fornicator! I'm a fornicator!"

3.2.33 The non-Arabic-speaking Fur stand in two lines or a circle during the ceremony, with a girl behind each man, and the women sing while the men chant, their chanting consisting of the sound called *karīr*.[403] One of the women's songs goes:

Kurú kirrô yé-ii áálima'ng nima-ii
Sa láng koo jánná
Sa láng koo

The meaning: *kurú* means "tree"; *kirrô* means "green"; *áálima'ng nima-ii* means "the shade of the scholars of religion"; *sa láng koo jánná, sa láng koo* means "It's true we're going to Paradise. It's true we're going to Paradise." Thus, the meaning of the whole is "The green tree is the shade of the scholars of religion, and we'll enter Paradise for sure, we'll enter Paradise for sure." Another chant of theirs goes:

Jibraaîla Mikaaîla
Kullu sibā mulkā l-jannah[404]

which means "Gabriel! Michael! Every good deed gives one possession of Paradise." And another chant of theirs goes:

Lullá káwi lullá,
Shâr ramadaan Alla'ng dawa-ii
Kál pááreng beeng kíye

which means "Daughters of God, O daughters of God![405] The month of Ramadan is God's remedy,[406] so rejoice in it!"

3.2.34 The Fur have many such customs; to pursue them would be to diverge into verbosity, and so induce, among the intelligent, animosity; we have said enough. Given that we have mentioned marriage and associated matters, however, it behooves us to provide a brief account of the guardians of women, namely, those persons who in Egypt are called *ṭawāshiyah* ("eunuchs") and "aghas of the harem" or, in Turkish, *kızlar ağası* ("girls' aghas"), because they have custody of the harem.

Section 2: Eunuchs (Known in Egypt as *Ṭawāshiyah*)

Given that the Truth, glorious and mighty, is jealous both of the well-being of His mortal slaves and of the maintenance of His strictures, just as He is bent on vengeance against those who overstep His bounds by committing what He has declared to be offenses, and given that covetousness is one of His attributes and that He has, for these reasons, prohibited injustice to Himself and to other than Him, He has caused covetousness to be embedded in man's nature from times past and immemorial. The first man to feel covetousness was Qābīl, with regard to his sister, Aqlīmā, when Ādam gave the order that she should marry Hābīl and he should marry the latter's sister, Dhamīmā.[407] Jealousy then led to the consequences that followed for each, with Qābīl killing his brother, as found in the text of the Qur'an.[408] Indeed, covetousness and jealousy are to be found in animals other than humans: animals are jealous of their females and fights occur. This is especially so given that the female has a stronger libido and carnal appetite, and no amount of manliness or zeal can hold her back. 3.2.35

Some people, having arrived at the pinnacle of covetousness and climbed to its very peak, go so far as to consider all women slaves. Among them are those so given over to jealousy that they feel jealous of their brothers and their sons. Indeed, some men go to such extremes that they feel jealous of the day and the night, and some are so jealous that they cannot bear that even the eyes of narcissi should behold their women. As the poet says: 3.2.36

> Lower your lids, you eyes of narcissi—
>   you make me too shy to kiss my sweet friend.
> When the beloved sleeps, his cheeks[409] lose their color,
>   yet your eyes are steady, and their lids never descend.

Some go to such extremes that they feel jealous of their own contact with the beloved, of the beloved's contact with them, and even of time and place. As the poet says:[410]

With you I feel jealous of my eye and of myself
and also of you, of where you are, of Time.
If I tucked you inside my eyelids
from now till Judgment Day, it still would not suffice.

Similar are the poet's words:[411]

Should he to my destruction set his mind,
I'd say, "Torturer, I beg you, give me more
and do not grant me your embrace,
For if I'm jealous of you, then of myself how much the more?"

One poet went to such exaggerated lengths as to be jealous of his own heart, saying:

With him, of my own heart I'm jealous.
A love that accuses part of me—how suspicious!

3.2.37 Afflicted as they were by the persistent, crippling malady of jealousy, people pondered how to guard their harems and could come up with nothing better than to place them under the guardianship of a person whose organs of procreation have been cut off, a person of whom one can feel sure, in both the long and the short term. Those most in need of such things are kings and princes, for it is indisputable that each of them collects as many women as he can, and given that the kings of the Blacks are the most assiduous of men in collecting women and go to the greatest lengths in this, each one, you will find, has a large number and enormous throng of eunuchs. The sultan of Darfur, for example, has around a thousand or more, and they have their own master, who is one of them and to whom they are like soldiers to a king. It is he who organizes them as needed to act as guards within the sultan's house, keeping the surplus with him to use in time of need.

3.2.38 Eunuchs are treated with respect by the great, especially in the lands of the Fur, where they possess—and to what a degree!—authority, influence, power, standing, repute, and a station unlike any other. They even have two eminent positions that only eunuchs may occupy, one of which is that of the shaykh-father, the second that of the door.[412] I note that the door is not peculiar to Darfur; it exists also in Tunis, and in Constantinople too. The eunuchs in Darfur come originally from the town of Rūngā. They castrate them there and bring them to Darfur as gifts.[413] They are, however, very numerous, and some are castrated in Darfur.

When I was there, I saw a youth with a pretty face and attractive 3.2.39
appearance, aged about eighteen, who had been castrated in Darfur. He had been a servant of Sultan Muḥammad Faḍl and was the best loved of those who'd been raised as part of his household. His star was rising, and the women were fond of him because he satisfied their innocent needs.[414] His name was Sulaymān Tīr. His peers, who were envious of him, slandered him before the sultan, who became angry with him and wanted to kill him. One of his viziers, however, advised him to castrate the youth, saying, "If it must be so, cut off the thing with which he harms you but don't kill him," so the sultan had him castrated and he survived. I met with him, and he had an excellent position and splendid clothes, though the sultan was distant with him because of what he believed to be his immorality and what had been said about him. I heard from trusted sources that he'd made a woman pregnant and this had shown, so she had been questioned and had said, "From Sulaymān Tīr." This was what made the sultan furious, and led to his castration. When it turned out that he was innocent, he gave him the woman and her child. We have mentioned earlier that Shaykh-Father Muḥammad Kurrā was accused of the same offense as Sulaymān Tīr, so he castrated himself with his own hand to remove any doubt. Thereafter he enjoyed the good graces of the sultan, and things went with him as they did.

A joke: an example of their effrontery and arrogance is that some 3.2.40
Fur emirs had gathered to relax, take their ease, and enjoy themselves, among them a eunuch. They set to eating and drinking, the eunuch along with them as though he were one of them. It happened that one of the emirs had a silk kerchief with him, and he

showed it to the gathering and said, "Do you know what this kerchief is good for?" One of them replied that it was good for wiping off sweat, another that it was good for looking attractive and adorning oneself, another that it was good for attaching to the bosom of a beautiful female, and so it went, each saying what he thought, while the owner of the kerchief kept saying no. When they grew tired of the business, they told him, "You tell us what it's good for." He replied, "It's good for wiping yourself off after sex," and they all thought this was a good answer and said no more. All of a sudden, they found that the eunuch had stood up and drawn his sword, with the intention of killing the owner of the kerchief, to whom he said, "Are you hinting at my having been cut? I shall certainly kill you!" They leaped toward him and spoke to him gently but he refused to take back his words until they'd mollified him by giving him all their horses. He was a eunuch belonging to the Successor, son of Sultan Tayrāb, both of whom we have spoken of earlier.

3.2.41 Another example of their effrontery is that in the days of Sultan Tayrāb, Muḥammad Órré Dungo[415] held the office of shaykh-father, and it is customary for the shaykh-father to go to his lands and seat of government every year in the spring.[416] There he gathers all the people together on the same day and reviews the men and inspects the soldiers. One extremely hot day, Muḥammad Órré Dungo had everyone assemble in a wide space in front of his house and didn't emerge to see them until the hottest part of the day had passed. Then he came out in all his splendor, riding his horse, his slaves shading him from the heat of the sun with parasols and fanning him. The soldiers now also came out and the people formed rows, making a circle, while he sat there watching them. The heat was intense, but he ordered the people to go down on their knees, still holding their weapons and shields. The ground was so hot it was hard to kneel, and the sweat flowed and the suffering intensified, but he just stood there awhile without telling them what was expected of them. The people grew thirsty and the heat took a great toll on them, but they endured what God had ordained for them, to the point that some died of thirst. When he saw how thirsty and dismayed everyone was, he was pleased, laughed, and said in the Fur language, "*Na-tū, na-tū, na-tū*[417]—«a frowning day, inauspicious!»"[418] and repeated the phrase two or three times. The number of people gathered for this *galanga*, or review, was around twenty thousand and included a righteous man called Shaykh Ḥasan al-Kaw. He now stepped forward and cried out three times at the top of his voice, "Silence, you infidel!" and the man was seized with terror at the shaykh, and turned and fled. Then the shaykh raised his hands to the skies and said, "O God, have mercy on Your slaves!" and before he'd stopped speaking, clouds had reared up like mountains, and the rain fell and everyone scattered. It became a celebrated day. The shaykh was angry because Muḥammad Órré Dungo had likened himself to God and the presentation of the people to him for review to that of their presentation for Judgment, while he'd likened the extreme heat of the sun to that of the Day of Resurrection, which is why he used the word *na-tū* to introduce the Noble Verse (*na* means "this," *tū* means "day," and the rest is the text of the Noble Verse).

An amusing anecdote: it is reported that the Shaykh-Father Muḥammad Órré Dungo of whom we speak was of limited intellect. By way of example, when he assumed office, Sultan Tayrāb ordered him to study so that he could learn to read and write. He engaged a man of religion to teach him, and the man wrote out the letters of the alphabet for him and began giving him daily lessons. This went on for a few days until the day came when the shaykh-father asked for a copy of the Qur'an. One was brought and, leafing through it, he saw a freestanding letter *wāw* and recognized it and asked the man of religion, "*A mang waawi*?" meaning "Isn't that a *wāw*?" "It is," said the man. Órré Dungo said, "I've finished the Qur'an!" and he ordered that animals be slaughtered and drums beaten and he held a great banquet. This was considered an example of his silliness and lack of brains. 3.2.42

Let us return to our original topic. Given the large number of eunuchs in the sultan's house, the place has not escaped defilement, 3.2.43

since women are devils whom none can control, and especially since the excuse may be made for them that many of those in the sultan's house are young and at leisure, and eat and dress well. This gives greater rein to their appetites, and, being prisoners there, they spend their time thinking of how to bring men in by any means possible. Some of them make friends with one of the male servants at the door. Others have old women who bring them men using the following stratagem: the old woman watches the young men until she sees one who is beautiful and has no down in his armpits and she works on him gently and eventually takes him to her house. Now—it being well known that the young Blacks do not shave the hair on their heads but let it grow so long that their tresses are like a woman's—she takes these tresses and braids them like a woman's and dresses him in women's finery such as necklaces and amulets, with *madraʿah* beads at his wrists[419] and *manjūr* beads around his waist,[420] and she dresses him in a pinafore, an apron,[421] and a body wrap, so that any who sees him will have no doubt that he's a woman, and she introduces him into the sultan's house along with other women. Once he's in, she loses all fear and hands him over to the woman who commanded her to get him. After that, he stays as long as God wills. And as long as God continues to provide cover for him, he will leave as he came in; if discovered, however, he will be killed. A number of things may lead to his discovery. One of the girl's co-wives may learn of his presence and ask her for him. The girl may then refuse, being too miserly to give him up, or the youth may not agree to go to her. Anger will then drive the other woman to inform on him, leading to his discovery. Or the sultan may order a search: then all the eunuchs come, he searches the huts with them, and they kill anyone they find. Another is that the young man may grow tired of staying there so long and leave on his own, but the doormen come across him as he's leaving and kill him. If God provides cover for him, though, he will escape. Most of those who enter in the way I have described leave only at night, or in the middle of a large group of women.

Some old women find ways to get women out of the sultan's house by disguising them in the clothes of some squalid profession and then taking them out right under people's noses. If the doorman or a eunuch happens upon her, they're told, "She's just a poor woman who came in with us to beg for a handout." In other cases, the eunuchs connive with the old woman; this occurs when the eunuch in question realizes that an abyss may open into which he could fall and be killed if he gets involved. In such cases, he says nothing, despite himself, and the woman comes and goes and takes in whomever she pleases, fearing no ill. Something of this sort happened involving a concubine of Sultan Ṣābūn's and her cousin Turqunak Muḥammad; we will mention this when we tell the history of Sultan Ṣābūn of Wāddāy, the Almighty willing.[422] 3.2.44

The women of the Blacks are more lustful and libidinous than other women for several reasons. The first is the region's excessive heat. The second is that they mix so much with men. The third is the lack of surveillance over them and the fact that they don't keep to their houses. It follows that these women are never satisfied with one husband or lover, as alluded to by the poet when he says:[423] 3.2.45

> You whom just one lover cannot please,
>   nor even two thousand in a single year,
> I think you must be what's left of Mūsā's folk,
>   for they won't put up for long with the same old fare.[424]

The fourth is that their husbands don't limit themselves just to them: if a man has the means, he'll marry four freeborn women and take concubines as well, depending on his social condition. However, women are the female counterparts of men and the appetitive soul is the same for everyone where lust and physical nature are concerned, especially since there is no one more jealous than a woman. Thus, they come up with ways to meet with men other than their husbands, each using a different stratagem to achieve what she wants. If a man can't afford to take concubines, he'll set his sights on some woman other than his wife, and when his wife finds out, her jealousy will drive her to meet with other men. The fifth is habit, for they are accustomed to mix with their male peers from their earliest years, so they grow up that way, and habit, if it takes hold, becomes a deep-seated trait. It follows that when she marries, she cannot limit herself to a single husband, unless God has mercy on her. As this trait is embedded in them, they get up to what they get up to. Thus, only a few can be found who limit themselves to their husbands, and as time passes, so corruption among these people increases.

3.2.46 An amusing fact. It is a tried and true fact that if a house catches fire in Darfur and the fire takes hold and they can't put it out, they cry, "Is there a chaste woman here?" and an old woman who has never committed adultery comes, pulls out her breechclouts,[425] and waves them at the fire, which will then be extinguished, if the Almighty wills. This is one of those things they've learned from experience. When I was there, a fire broke out and took hold in the sultan's grandmother's house, and the sultan himself came along with the high officers of the state. They were unable to put it out, and the sultan's crier called out, "Is there a chaste woman here?" The cry was repeated throughout the town and not one woman could go to the fire, showing that there isn't a single chaste woman in the place these days, though I've heard that some such are to be found among their desert Bedouin. Rarely, though, is a chaste woman to be found among the Blacks, for such women—given that they have no brain to restrain them, no fear to hold them in check, and no religion to observe—do whatever they want. Indeed, women boast of how many lovers they have, saying, "If I were ugly, no one would have come to me, and if I were not so beautiful, men wouldn't have been my intimates and performed doughty deeds for my sake."

3.2.47 It is an amazing fact that, in the Arab lands, if a woman grows old and has a son who is well-respected and well-known, this prevents her from committing adultery and running after men, either because she's aware that no one wants her, if she's old, or because she fears for her son's standing and the respect with which he is viewed. Not so the women of the Blacks. Thus my dearest friend (I won't mention his name so that I can keep his friendship) told me that the maternal uncle of Sultan Muḥammad Faḍl, who was called Muḥammad Taytal, was married off by his sister, called Anbūsah, who was the sultan's mother and aged about thirty-five, to a woman of her household, and held a great celebration for him that everyone hurried to watch.

My friend told me that he had been an onlooker. He said, "I was standing there when the sultan's mother came, along with a herd of women as lovely as gazelles. She was walking in front, they behind. She was a slave woman of hideous appearance, deformed physique, and base origin, for there are none in Darfur of origin baser than the Bīqū, to whom she belonged. All the onlookers marveled at the doings of the Almighty, that He should give this woman who was ugly in both person and origin precedence over those better favored in physiognomy, origin, pride, and beauty. She went in to see her brother Muḥammad Taytal, who had just consummated his marriage, stayed with him awhile, and then came out again. No sooner did she do so than we heard the ringing of anklets and jewelry, smelled a waft of perfume, and realized she was leaving. We stood in a line, but no sooner had I set eyes on her than she grabbed me by the hand and pulled at me to make me go with her. I tried to hold back but it looked as though I was refusing, so the women behind her pushed me. I didn't want people to notice, so I walked with her, side by side, her grip on me never loosening. 3.2.48

"On the way she told me, 'I'm tired' (even though it wasn't more than a hundred paces from her brother's house to hers, and I'm told that before her relationship with the sultan she'd been one of the lowest of the slave girls, and with a lowly job too, as she used to bring water and firewood from the countryside—and now she was tired out after walking a hundred paces?). Anyway, I told her, 'It must be from everything you've had to put up with today!' Then we entered her house, the eunuchs who were standing at the door not daring to say anything, even though they could see me with her. 3.2.49

3.2.50 "When she reached her room, she went in, so I went in with her. She let go of my hand, so I sat down on some cushions that were there while she flopped onto her bed, twisting and turning right and left and flapping her *manjūr* beads with her hands. She told me, 'I have a headache,' so I said, 'I'm sorry to hear that.' 'Recite some verses from the Qur'an over it,' she said. 'Maybe that'll make it go away.' So I went over to her, though I knew it was a trick to get what she wanted and that only her pride in her status prevented her from telling me, 'Get over here!' even though all the women who'd been with her had gone, and only she and I were left, plus a female slave sitting outside the door whom she could call to if she needed anything. Having twisted and turned a lot, but finding no sign that I was attracted to her, she called on me to recite verses from the Qur'an over her temple.

3.2.51 "When I placed my hand on her temple and began reciting, she started trembling and thrashing about like an animal being slaughtered, and moaning. Then the smell of perfume wafting off her reached my nose and this stimulated me and the vigor of the male seized me and I set about mounting her—but then I was overcome by fear of her son, the sultan, because every time he found a man with his mother he killed him; he'd done so many times before, when he'd burst in on her unannounced. She, however, had positioned men to watch for him and inform her when he was coming, and if anyone was with her she'd work out a way of getting him out. I was afraid for myself too, because I'd heard she suffered from *al-ḥaṣar*, which doctors call 'leucorrhea,' meaning that anyone who had sex with her caught it—especially as I'd seen men who'd caught it from her.[426] Overcome by fear on both these counts, I cooled off a bit. She'd taken a look at my state straight away, and when she saw how limp I'd become, she thought I must be hungry, so she called a slave called Dhirāʿ al-Qādir[427] and told her, 'Bring some good food!' So the slave brought two vessels, one of them holding pigeons fried in clarified butter, the other a round of flaky pastry with molasses, and she said, 'Eat!' I refused, making the excuse that I wasn't hungry, but she swore I had to, so I took some of the food, which I liked, and I was in fact in need of food.

"While I was eating, I heard violent activity and confusion outside, and the servants rushed in saying that the sultan had come. 'Take him away,' she said, and they got me out through the other door. The slave women led me at a fast pace till they'd gotten me out of the house enclosure. It was only through the grace of the Almighty that instead of going in to see her through the door he usually used, the sultan went in through the one I just referred to, leaving a guard at the first and going around till he came to the door through which I'd exited, for no sooner had I gotten out and moved away from the door than I saw the heads of the horses that had arrived. I stopped at a distance to see what would happen. I heard him saying to the doormen, 'Who came out this way just now?' and them replying, 'No one.' Then one of the horsemen said, 'I saw someone moving away and I think he may have been here.' All the others repeated, 'We didn't see anyone.' All this was going on as I stood there listening, and I thanked God I'd gotten out before they arrived, because, if they'd gotten to the door before I did, I'd have been done for."[428] 3.2.52

When I heard this story from him, I was quite astounded and realized that eunuchs are of use only if women have nothing in mind, but if they do, a eunuch avails nothing. Observe, my friend, how these goings-on were the doings of this woman, even though she was the mother of a monarch. If it had been anyone else, there would have been no end of talk, so how much more in her case? By and large, women have nothing good in them, with the exception of those whose chastity God has preserved. May He bless the poet who said:[429] 3.2.53

> Among them are some worth eighty young she-camels;
> for others one newborn calf's too much to pay.
> Some become a young man's bride when he's still poor,
> but he finds his courtyard stuffed with wealth one day.
> Some become a young man's bride when he's living high
> but finds one morn that for donkey fodder he can no longer pay.

Among them are those whose honor God does not protect:
when her husband's away, she goes to his neighbors to play—
So let the Merciful show no mercy to an unfaithful woman
and burn in His fire any who would her spouse betray!

Women are at the root of every disaster that occurs. How many a king has been killed for them! How many a kingdom ruined! How much blood spilled! They are devils made for us, as says the poet:

Women are devils created for us—
God save us from those devils' ways!

3.2.54 A strange thing: a concomitant of the fact that they've made eunuchs to preserve their womenfolk from other men ought to be that the eunuchs deal honestly with their masters regarding them, but that's not how things are. We've seen eunuchs who keep a number of women for their pleasure, the first I observed doing so being the Muḥammad Kurrā of whom we've spoken earlier. Someone in whom I have every confidence told me that when the latter saw he was about to be defeated in the fighting with Sultan Muḥammad Faḍl, he had a woman of exceptional beauty with him, and he cut her throat the night before he was going to die so that no one else might enjoy her. There is no jealousy more extreme than that. In Darfur and Wāddāy, I saw many eunuchs, each of whom possessed many women, and I asked men of experience what they did with them, given that the eunuchs were just like the women, in the sense that their organs of procreation were missing. I was told that they ground their bodies against the women and that when they did so they would become so excited that they would bite the woman painfully on ejaculating. At the time, because of my ignorance of medical science, I believed this, but now I do not, because the function of the member is lost with the loss of the member itself, and cause goes with effect whether we're talking about what is or what is not.

3.2.55 I also asked men of experience how the castration was carried out. One of them told me that the subject is brought and bound tightly, then the testes are grasped and removed with a sharp razor and a small metal cylinder is inserted into the urinary canal so that it doesn't become blocked. Clarified butter will have been heated over the fire till it's boiling and the site of the incision is cauterized, transforming the cut into a burn instead of a metal-inflicted wound. Thereafter, it's treated with changes of cotton pads and bandages until the man either recovers or dies, though only a few recover. If it be said that this constitutes the torture of a rational being and a disruption of the procreation whose increase is commanded by religion and should therefore be forbidden, I would reply, "Indeed, more than one scholar has made it clear that this is so, above all Jalāl al-Dīn al-Suyūṭī, God have mercy on his soul. He states that it is forbidden in his work *The Prohibition on Using Eunuch Attendants at the Tomb of the Prophet and his Descendants*. However, the prohibition applies to the one who carries out the act, and eunuchs are castrated by a certain Magian people[430] who bring them into the lands of Islam for sale or in payment of tribute, and only a rare few are castrated by Muslims. As far as employing them after castration is concerned, there is no harm in it; on the contrary, it brings with it great divine reward, for if people did not employ them, they would suffer from two perspectives, the first the fact of castration itself and the loss of great pleasure and disruption of procreation that that entails, the second that they would find it hard to make a living."

If it be said, "Emirs are like kings, and any who imitate them will 3.2.56
gather many women into their homes, all of them young, and at the same time it is a known fact that jealousy is as much present in them as it is in men because the former are the latter's counterparts, so how can these women be friends with one another, especially when the husband loves one of them and avoids the others?" I would reply that enmity occurs among them in keeping with their circumstances. Each would like her husband's face to be hers alone and that he be intimate with none but her; however, given that they are at the mercy of their husbands, especially when these are kings, they conceal their hatred and display affection, and this is the way of

women—they conceal what is inside and display its opposite. What a woman is hiding will appear only when she is no longer afraid and has regained her capacity to judge wisely. Only then will she reveal what has been lurking in her breast.

3.2.57 If I were asked how the women of the Blacks rank in terms of beauty, I'd say, "They fall into different classes. It's an acknowledged fact that the beautiful and the ugly are to be found in every tribe, but there are tribes among whom beauty is more common, and others among whom misshapenness is more common. The tribe in the lands of the Fur least known for beauty is the Tomorókkóngá, because they are a savage mountain people, and live roughly. The Karakriit are the same. We have stated before that women of the Bartī and Mīdawb tribes are more beautiful than those of other tribes.[431] The Bīqū, Barqū, Mīmah, and Tunjūr tribes come next, and the most misshapen women are those of the non-Arabic-speaking Fur. Next come the Dājū, the Birqid, and the Masālīṭ. By the same token, in Dār Wādday, it is the two tribes of the Ab Sanūn and the Malanqā (or Mananqā) that have the most beautiful women, followed by the Kūkah, the Mīmah, and Kashmirah, while those with the ugliest are the Tāmā, and after them the Birqid, the Masālīṭ, and the Dājū. One cannot draw comparisons between the beauty of Blacks and of others because of the difference in color."

3.2.58 Note: generally speaking, the most beautiful inhabitants of the lands of the Blacks, be they of the east or the west, are the women of ʿAfnū, followed by Bāqirmah, Barnaw, and Sinnār; those of middling beauty are the Wādday, followed by the Fur; and the ugliest are the Tubū and the Katakū. In summary, beauty is to be found in every tribe but may be less in one or more in another—glory be to Him who allocates what He wishes to whom He wishes and other than Whom there is no lord or object of worship! Thus, not everything that is brown is musk, not everything that is red a ruby, not everything that is black civet, not everything that shines a diamond, and you might, if you wish, add that not everything black is charcoal, not everything red flesh, and not everything white lime, for as much beauty may be found in brown and black as in shining white.[432] Now methinks I hear a voice saying, "Can dark and light, or shade and a hot wind, be equal?"[433]—and yet there are people who fall passionately in love with the brown-skinned, as when the poet says:[434]

> The dusky-skinned have something, whose beauty, once gazed upon,
> will never let your eye love white or red again.

Someone once loved black so much that he went overboard and said: 3.2.59

> For her sake, I love blacks—
> for her I even love black dogs!

I myself was once so taken with women of this persuasion that I declaimed:

> They censure me for loving a black-skinned girl (*sawdā*),
> Unaware that nobility (*siyādah*) lies in glory (*sawād*),
> So I told them, "Let me be and be not censorious,
> For the blacks (*sūd*) have become rulers (*sādū*) through their wealth (*sawād*)
> And most whites, were it not that their eyebrows
> And their cheek moles are of the darkest black (*sawād*),
> Would be neither loved nor looked at—
> But good qualities were ever the preserve of the masses (*sawād*)."

In the first line *sawād* is used to mean "rule, lordship" (*sūdad*), in the second to mean "wealth," in the third in its true meaning, and in the fourth to mean "a large number of people."

Another poet has said: 3.2.60

> "You've fallen for a girl who's black!" said they, so I replied,
> "'Tis the color of galias,[435] of musk, and of aloeswood!

I'm the type to whom love of whites would seem no virtue
even if there wasn't a single black left in the world."

And Learned Shaykh ʿAbd al-Raḥmān al-Ṣaftī says:

My soul I'd give for a brown-skinned boy, one spot of whose color
would invest white skin with beauty's name[436]
While one white spot upon his face would
transform the cloak of cuteness into shame.
It's not from his wine[437] that I've become drunk—
it's his sidelocks that drive us men insane.
His charms so envy one another that each
to be the down on his cheeks lays claim.

3.2.61 I countered[438] this with a poem of my own, which goes in part:

The truth is white! Forget a certain tribe
of obstinates and swollen heads who claim it's not!

Al-Ṣaftī also says:[439]

"You've fallen for a girl who's brown!" said they, so I told them,
"'Tis the color of galias, of musk, and of nightshade!
I've not abandoned the whiteness of white-skinned girls in error—
white hairs and shrouds make me so afraid!"

3.2.62 Some people go to great lengths in their praise of white and dispraise of black, claiming that the discernment of any who oppose this point of view has been blinded to the words of the Almighty: «We have blotted out the sign of the night, and made the sign of the day to see.»[440] The fact is that «Each man has a direction to which he's turned»[441]

for one man's meat, in love, is by another spurned.[442]

CHAPTER 3

In two sections

Section 1: Sicknesses of the Blacks; Their Dishes; the Healthiness of Their Various Climes; Hunting; and Some Animals

Mortal man should be aware that God has made specific to each territory things to be found in no other and allotted to each tribe a peculiarity to be found in no other. Thus, if one leaves his country for another whose air differs from that of his own, afflictions will beset him: he will become sick when the change of air has its effect on him and may die, or if he does not die, his sickness may be prolonged and his body not become well until, at length, it accustoms itself to the air of the country in which he has come to reside. 3.3.1

This being the case, children who are born of a father and a mother who are both Fur, for example, live longer and are more strongly built than others. This explains why one may find a man with ten or more children, all of whom are strong and healthy. The same applies to the Bedouin of the deserts there: none of them ever dies without first having looked on large numbers of offspring. Conversely, if a Fur man marries a Bedouin woman, or a Bedouin man a Fur woman, you will find that his offspring are weak and thin and only a rare few of them survive. This is one of those things that indicates that each country and race has something special not to be 3.3.2

found in any other, for any child born of parents of one and the same type and one and the same country is better built and has better health; if the converse is the case, you will find that he is weak, of a bad color, and thin.

3.3.3 In Darfur and Wāddāy, I saw that people resorted to bloodletting to protect their children's health. Once the child had completed forty days from the time of birth, they'd take it and make incisions on both sides—by which I mean on the right and the left—of its belly, making it bleed copiously. When it had completed three months, they'd do the same again; if they didn't, the blood was liable to rise up against it and kill it.

3.3.4 The childhood disease most widespread there is that called *abū l-lisān* ("tongue disease").[443] It afflicts the child in its epiglottis, i.e., in its uvula. This acquires an excrescence like a sparrow's tongue at the base of the tongue, which they treat by excision, using an instrument that looks like this

and consists of a blade mounted on a wooden handle. It comes with a smooth piece of wood, and the doctor first inserts this piece of wood until it reaches the site of the excrescence, the patient being tightly secured. Then he inserts the blade till its curved end reaches the base of the excrescence on the other side, the excrescence thus being between the blade and the piece of wood, and compresses the two of them, resulting in the excision of the excrescence. Then he removes the blade and the piece of wood together, and a small piece of flesh may be observed on the piece of wood. The doctor will previously have prepared a little natron by grinding it finely between two stones. The man wets his finger and puts it into the powder, which sticks to it, and inserts the finger into the patient's mouth, having first inserted the piece of wood, if the child's teeth have grown in. However, he does not let the latter intrude all the way to the site of the pain but rather until it intrudes just beyond the patient's teeth. Then he rubs the site of the excision well with the powder on his finger and the patient is cured. If this "tongue disease" is left untreated, the child's body will become emaciated and it will cause terrible diarrhea, possibly leading to death.

This is followed by another disease, which they call *umm* 3.3.5
ṣuquʿ,[444] which also afflicts only children. It consists of a softening in the uvula and the appearance on it of a pustule. This leads to the patient not drinking milk or eating, and a paling of the complexion. They therefore call in the doctor, who comes and grinds natron as previously described, places the piece of wood, on its own, in the patient's mouth, inserts his finger, and raises the uvula, bursting the pustule, from which blood and pus discharge. Then he wets his finger with his saliva, dips it in the natron, and rubs the pustule with it, along with the uvula. This time, however, he does this for three days in a row, after which the patient recovers.

Severe diarrhea may occur, but in this case the child should 3.3.6
be examined; if it's more than two years old and they find that its backside protrudes too much, they scrape it with a pottery shard, producing much blood, and reduce the child's food, after which the patient recovers. If the child is very young, say seven or eight months or so, they cauterize it around the navel, making four brands, in the following fashion: I mean that the navel should be in the middle, the brands above and below it and to its right and left.

Children may be afflicted by the disease called *al-ghuzayyil*, 3.3.7
which is caused by an injury to the brain that leaves the child waving its hands and feet about in an abnormal manner. In Egypt and Tunis, people say it comes from the jinn. This disorder afflicts a child who is left alone somewhere. It kills many children in Egypt, Tunis, and the Arab countries. To treat it, the Egyptians have recourse to written amulets[445] because they believe that it's caused by jinn. Thus, they fetch someone well known for spells, incantations, and conjurations and he makes written amulets for the patient and performs his spells. This may or may not coincide with the patient's pain being cured. The people of the Lands of the Blacks treat the disease by cauterization of the forehead and by obtaining some millet-cane

pith, which they pass back and forth over a fire until it catches and forms a flame like that of a trimmed candle, with which they cauterize the patient, who recovers immediately. Another children's disease found there is *abū ṣuffayr*; it's an affliction that spoils the child's skin color and produces a distinctive yellow. It is what's called in medical books "yellow jaundice."

3.3.8 There are also nonspecific diseases that affect young and old alike. Among these are *wirdah*, which is a fever, from which almost everyone suffers at least once a year. It is at its peak there during the rainy season and at the beginning of the spring, which they call *darat* and which is the same as our autumn. This fever is of different kinds: there is time-specific fever, which comes every day at a certain hour; quotidian fever, which comes every second day; tertian fever, which comes every third day; and quartan fever, which comes every fourth day, this last being the strongest; tertian is a shade less strong.[446] There is also total fever, which leaves the sufferer only upon recovery or at death and which in Egypt is called *al-nōshah*; doctors now refer to it as "gastrointestinal inflammation."[447] All these types are known to the people of the Lands of the Blacks, without distinction, as *wirdah*. Among the nonspecific epidemic diseases is smallpox, which to them is as the plague is to Egypt, and which they fear since it is often very deadly. If anyone contracts it, they remove him from the village to somewhere in the countryside and build him a reed hut, called a *karbābah*, leaving someone who has already had the disease to tend to him. Each time another falls sick they take him there and so it continues, this being precisely the same as quarantine. Note: The people of these lands who most fear smallpox are the desert Bedouin, because once it enters a tribe it decimates it. Thus, they fear it more than anyone else.

3.3.9 A prominent man of the Birqid tribe, called ʿUthmān wad ʿAllaw, told me that he had once been sick with smallpox and suffered through it. Then God cured him. When the papules formed scabs, and before these had healed over, he was greatly bothered by the flies, so he used to veil his face. He told me, "One day, I was wearing my veil and standing at the door of my house when I saw a Bedouin coming along, walking as though terrified. When he saw me, he approached till he was close and saluted me. Then he said, 'Tell me the truth! Is there smallpox in this village of yours?' 'God preserve us from the evil of hiding the truth!' I said and I lifted the veil from my face. The moment he saw me he let out a great cry and fell to the ground. At his cry, his Bedouin brothers came and picked him up and took him away. I fled the moment his brothers arrived, so they wouldn't kill me. I heard afterward that he died three days later."

The people of the Lands of the Blacks claim, among other super- 3.3.10
stitions, that the smallpox is a creature of which nothing is ever seen but the tracks, which stick to the person and then kill him. I heard many of them say that they had seen its tracks; they connive with one another over this and believe one another. I asked them what its tracks looked like and they said, "Its tracks are round spots that follow one another, like this oooooo in single file. In any house where we see these tracks of a morning, we find its inhabitants have been stricken."

An Amazing Thing. When he came to Cairo in 1257 [1841–42],[448] 3.3.11
Judge al-Dalīl, chief judge of the kingdom of Wādday, told me that the disease called *al-hayḍah*—known as "the yellow air" to the Egyptians—[449]which came to Egypt from the Hejaz in the year 1247 [1831–32], spread to their country and devastated it, killing large numbers of people, "though we'd never thought it could spread so far—so glory to Him who effects what He desires; nothing can stand in the way of His wisdom!"

Another nonspecific disease that occurs frequently among them 3.3.12
is the Frankish disease,[450] which they call *al-jiqqayl*, whose prevalence is due to the prevalence of depravity and for which the only cure they have is cauterization. They do this by fetching an iron instrument that they call a *ḥashshāshah*.[451] The instrument is elongated and flat, about two inches wide and five or six inches long. They heat this in the fire till it turns red. It has something in the form of a cylinder mounted in the middle, crossways. When the

instrument has reddened, they take it out of the fire and pour a little water over the cylinder and insert into it a length of wood by which they can lift it, and with it they cauterize the place where the disease has appeared. No exceptions are made. When the disease is observed on anyone, they cauterize him—assuming he is married—using force if necessary. With this treatment God cures him very quickly.

3.3.13 This disease is more common in Kordofan than in Darfur and more common in Darfur than in Wādday, so much so that one only rarely hears of someone becoming sick with it in Wādday. The reason it's so frequent in Kordofan is that those who contract it there believe that the more people they infect, the better they'll get. They have no idea that even if they infect a hundred thousand, it will in no way alleviate their own condition. You find that anyone who has it, man or woman, will infect many more, which is why it's common among them. It is less common in Darfur, though it is widespread there, because, while they have people who are not ashamed to let everyone know that they are sick and therefore infect others (though these are few), they also have people who are ashamed to do so and therefore stay at home until they get better (these are numerous). In Wādday, however, everyone who contracts the disease keeps to his house until he recovers, so it is of rare occurrence.

3.3.14 Another such disease is *al-ḥaṣar*, which is leucorrhea.[452] Similar is *al-habūb*, which is wind trapped in the lower part of a woman's or a man's belly (though more often found in women).[453] Both, they claim, are infectious.[454] Another disease widespread among them is leprosy, which eats away the fleshy part of the nose and the ends of the digits. Vitiligo is also widespread, though less so. Another disease is *abū l-ṣufūf*,[455] which is pleurisy, which they treat by scarification of the ribs; they cut four or five rows, each row consisting of four or five cuts, as here, rubbing the place after scarification with natron powder; a large quantity of blood comes out of the openings and the afflicted person gets better. Another is guinea

worm (*al-farandīt*), which is widespread among them; in Egypt it is called *al-fartīt*. It consists of a swelling that occurs in the leg or the hand or some other place. Pus forms in it so they slice it open and a long white thread like a sinew but softer emerges from the place where it has been sliced. It would seem to be an animal because it goes in and out. The treatment is to slice open the swellings and warm them with leaves of Sodom apple daubed with clarified butter heated over the fire.

Diseases of the limbs from which they suffer include *al-sūtiyyah*, 3.3.15
which is a disease that affects the knee and consists of a swelling like *al-farandīt* but does not produce a thread. Much pus is formed inside the swelling and it only gets better if three rows of deep incisions are made at the affected place, each row consisting of three or four incisions from which copious pus will then emerge; following daubing with clarified butter and warming, the patient will recover. Another is *al-duqrī*,[456] which is a disease that affects the leg along its length. It consists of a swelling like that of *al-sūtiyyah* except that the former extends along the shin while the latter is limited to the knee. It is treated the same way as *al-sūtiyyah*, except that the incisions are made in two rows at the back of the leg and two at the front. Other diseases that affect children are measles and *al-burjuk*, which is scarlet fever. Other nonspecific diseases are pain in (by which I mean enlargement of) the spleen, and dropsy in all its forms. Most epidemic diseases occur among them except for the plague and tuberculosis, which are not present (tuberculosis may occur, but is rare).

Surgery is well advanced among them because of the frequency 3.3.16
of conflicts and wars. They sew up wounds; if someone's guts come out they can even put them back in place and sew over them so that the man recovers. They also know how to treat head wounds of all types. There are people, called *shallangīn*s, who are able to operate with great skill on eye cataracts, though I was unable to find out how the operation is performed or what instruments they use for it. I knew one such celebrated individual, a man called Hajj Nūr.

They do not, however, employ amputation, scission, or excision, and scrotal hernias are rare. That is all I know about the topic.

3.3.17 Their doctors are their old men; one rarely finds a young man among them. People flock to those who are masters of the craft of medicine, even traveling for days, and they respect them utterly. The treatments they use most often are scarification and cauterization, and the only things they use for internal treatments are tamarind, honey, and clarified butter made from cows' milk.

3.3.18 An Amazing Thing. My teacher, Faqīh Madanī al-Fūtāwī, may clouds of mercy hover above him, informed me that he was afflicted with gout—pain in the joints, called in medical books "the disease of kings"—and that a Bedouin man prescribed standing in clarified cow butter. "So," he said, "I ordered a large quantity of clarified cow butter brought and it was heated over the fire till it was completely melted. Then it was taken off the fire and left till it had cooled enough for a person to be able to stand it and they hung me a rope from the ceiling of the house with its two ends in my hands and emptied the butter into a large wooden bowl. I washed my feet, stepped into the butter, and took hold of the rope, which made it possible for me to stand for all that time. Suddenly I felt as though the butter were running through my body like a poison, ascending first to my legs, then my knees, and then my thighs, after which it flowed into the upper half of my body. I could feel it climbing through my body little by little till it reached my neck, and then I started to feel dizzy and fainted, and would have fallen but the servants caught me and wrapped me in my clothes and laid me down on my bed, though I was unaware of all that. I slept on through the rest of the day and that night too, and in the morning woke up feeling as lively as if I had been released from shackles. I could see that a great quantity of foul-smelling sweat had come out of me, and that was how God cured me." So many people told me that the desert dwellers do this that it was as though the information had achieved the status of common wisdom. Because they practice magic so much, they use written charms a lot and they have people who are well known for that, the most famous being Fallātā.

They manage childbirth as follows. When a woman is taken by birthing pangs, old women come and tie a rope for her from the roof of the house, which she grasps, standing, and leans on every time the pain becomes intense. She also keeps her feet wide apart until the newborn falls, whereupon one of the women attending her catches it and cuts its umbilical cord. The women then lay the mother on her bed. When the baby is one week old, they prepare a meal to celebrate, each according to his means, the women gathering with the new mother, the men with the father. They will have slaughtered a ewe, and the women and men eat the meat and name the baby; then they disperse. During that week, in the mornings, they feed the mother *madīdah*, which is what Egyptians call *ḥarīrah*, the people of the Maghreb *ḥasūw*, and Franks *crème*. At noon, they give her chicken to eat, if they are well-off; if they are poor, *madīdah* again. This is composed of millet flour and *tabaldī* or *hijlīj* flour. If made with *hijlīj*, it is somewhat bitter and if with *tabaldī* it's sour. Once the newborn is two or three months old, the mother starts carrying it on her back, tying it there with her wrap; this way of carrying the child is called *qūqū*. She puts the child there and goes about her business, be it farming or bringing water or fuel, till it is grown. 3.3.19

Another of their customs is that the women suckle their children for two years or less, as elsewhere in the Islamic world. And they do not give their daughters away in marriage until they have attained puberty and learned the value of a man. I lived seven years among them and never saw a bride marry before she had grown to maturity, and if she were betrothed before that, the man would only consummate the marriage after she had done so, as it is their custom that the man should marry and then leave the girl alone for a period. Some of them only consummate their marriage after two years, others after three; if one of them is in a hurry, he will consummate it after a 3.3.20

year. In any case, they are given possession of their brides only after the latter have reached maturity. The preceding applies to virgins; if the woman has been married before, the man consummates the marriage the day of the wedding, or the following day.

3.3.21 They memorize the Qur'an very late in life because they read it only at night, in the schools, since by day a boy is out in the countryside with his flocks or cattle; he takes his tablet when he returns in the evening and goes to the school. Each boy also has to bring firewood one day a week. They light a fire and sit around it, making use of its light. By this light they memorize and copy out the Qur'an, but they memorize it poorly, which is why only a few of them know it well by heart. The study of the sciences also occurs at an advanced age since there are few scholars. Most of what they study is religious law and theology. The rational sciences[457] are very rarely taught, though that's more than one can say for grammar, which they hardly study at all. Of the sciences of rhetoric relating to motifs, metaphors, and figures of speech, and of logic and prosody, they know nothing but the names. Anyone who knows that much will have traveled to another country, such as Egypt, and come by their knowledge there. On returning to his country, he becomes the scholar of his locality. They pay the greatest attention to the spirit world and to magic, calling the science of magic the science of *ṭibb* and the one who practices it a *ṭabbābī*.[458] This science is found mostly among the Fullān. We may describe later what Faqīh Mālik did with the sons of the sultans and how he bewitched them so that they returned to the sultan's capital after first fleeing from it,[459] and the doings of Faqīh Tamurrū.[460]

3.3.22 Note: Darfur, though a single territory and realm, varies in terms of its air. The healthiest part of it is the Dunes, which is why one finds that the desert Bedouin there are strong and bold, their land being free of rottenness and impure air. It has, however, little water; as we have mentioned earlier, some of these Bedouin live two or more days from any water.[461] The next healthiest is the country of the Zaghāwah, known as Dār al-Rīḥ, which is why one finds that the

Zaghāwah and the Bidayāt who live there are extremely strong and sound of limb. The worst part of Darfur in terms of air is the High Plain, because of the copiousness of its waters, especially in the mountains of Jabal Marrah. The strongest part is the sultan's capital, followed by Kūbayh and Kabkābiyyah. Silā, Fanqarū, Bīngah, and Shālā are the places with the foulest air because of their high humidity and continuous rainfall, which lets up for only two or three months a year.

Despite all the sicknesses I've described as being found in the lands of the Fur, they all love their homeland and feel at ease there. 3.3.23 If one of them is transported to another country, he weeps for it and wishes he could return. This is an instinct that has been created in humans and with which the heart has been imprinted from time immemorial. Because of this the Chosen One, may God bless him and give him peace, longed for Mecca like a lover; had not God commanded him to live in Medina, he would, for sure, have stayed there. However, given that the diseases of the Land of the Blacks are not epidemic and fatal in nature, their lifespans are longer than others'. This is why you find so many old people among them, even some who have passed one hundred and twenty. Seventy-, eighty-, and ninety-year-olds are almost too numerous to count, too many to render in account, and this despite the conflicts, wars, and trials with which they have been afflicted. There are no two tribes among them who in bloodshed have not been involved and between whom no feud is ongoing, unresolved, including feuds between the Bartī and the Zayādiyyah, the Banū ʿUmrān and the Mīmah, the Fallāta and the Masālīṭ, the Brown Misīriyyah and the Rizayqāt, the Majānīn and the Banū Jarrār, the Zaghāwah and the Maḥāmīd—feuds too many to number. And this is not to mention the conflicts between their petty kings that erupt out of rage, or the killings that occur when they're in their cups or during quarrels over maidens with "swelling breasts, like of age";[462] absent these, they'd be as numerous as Yājūj and Mājūj and their race, and fill to overflowing every meadow, every open space.

3.3.24 Were you to say, "If things are as you describe, how is it that old women are few, even though they don't fight one another or go to war, and if what's been said regarding the small number of men is true, elderly women should have a significant presence, while in fact they are similar in number to men, or fewer?" I would reply, "Given how much they mourn for the men who've been killed for their sake, and given the harm and suffering they put up with when these die, they are vulnerable to terrible, fatal diseases resulting from their psychological reactions. That said, there are still more of them than of elderly men. I was in a town that was relatively poorly developed and held relatively few inhabitants, namely, Abū l-Judūl, and I saw many elderly men and women there, and every time I entered a village I would see even more, even though they live in conditions that are extremely debased—so much so that were someone from our country to suffer them even once, he'd lose all vigor, for most of what they eat is either bitter or rotten, though they believe it to be the best food anyone could wish for."

3.3.25 Once, after I'd had just arrived in their country and before I'd become used to their ways, they made *waykah*[463] at home and invited me to eat some, but I refused. When my father heard, he said, "If you aren't ready to eat that kind of food with your bread, why did you come here?" and he didn't know what to do. He'd go to great lengths to please me, and would make me rice puddings. When I went to the sultan's seat and stayed at the house of Faqīh Mālik al-Fūtāwī, dinner was brought. I thought the dish accompanying the bread was bitter and asked, "What's this?" and was told, "It's *waykah* made from *hijlīj*." I refused to taste it so they brought me another dish, but it smelled rotten to me so I asked, "Why is this rotten?" and they told me, "It's *dawdarī waykah*," which they find very good. Again, I refused to taste it. Faqīh Mālik was told of this so he sent me fresh milk with honey and I ate some. When he came to his reception room to pass the evening with his friends, he asked me, "Why wouldn't you eat either the *hijlīj* or the *dawdarī waykah*?" I said, "One was bitter and the other rotten," and he said,

"This is the food that suits our country. Anyone who doesn't eat such things should worry about falling ill."

Dawdarī is *waykah* made from the bones of sheep, cattle, or any other animal. They take the knee and chest bones, strip them of the meat, put the bones in a vat, and leave them for a few days till they become putrescent. Then they take them out and grind them up in a mortar until the bones and meat have turned into a paste and make them into balls the size of large oranges. When they want to cook, they take a bit from a ball and dissolve it in water, removing any pieces of bone that may remain with a strainer. Next, they pour the same water into a cooking pot and put it on the fire and leave it till it has thickened. They now fetch a small pot into which they've put a little chopped onion and they fry this in a little clarified butter and add it to the large pot, along with a certain amount of salt, pepper, and *kumbā*, if available. It's a dish found only in the houses of the Fur emirs. 3.3.26

The *waykah* made with *hijlīj* may be made from either the leaves or the fruit. To make the kind that is made from leaves, they harvest the fresh young leaves and pound them. These are then put into a pot over the fire and stirred with a stick till well mixed with the water and fat already there. If made from the fruit, the method is to take the fruit and steep them in water. Then they crush them by hand until the flesh is all transferred to the water. They take that water and strain it into a pot. The poor add a little fat to it and eat it. The rich leave it over the fire till it thickens, then make a fried garnish like the one we described when speaking of *dawdarī*, adding pounded jerked meat, and pour the water onto it and leave it all on the fire till completely blended. It is then taken off the fire. This is one of their most splendid *waykahs*. It is the food of their rich. 3.3.27

The poor, as noted above, eat unhusked millet, and the food that goes with it is quite disgusting, consisting of either *kawal*[464] or small fresh *hijlīj* leaves, which they call *nyúlmá*, or sesame lees, or green *hijlīj* fruit, called *ʿanqallū*, or its mature fruit. For all of these they use *kumbā* ashes instead of salt, as real salt is scarce and expensive. 3.3.28

The best-off among the poor are those who have sheep or a cow they can use for fresh milk, whose butter they can take, and whose buttermilk they can use as an accompaniment to food. They see meat only once every few months, if a cow or bull is slaughtered in the village and they divide it up, in which case the poor man may buy a portion, depending on his means, paying in *mudd*s of millet, nothing else. It follows that most of their young men are keen hunters.

3.3.29 We've mentioned earlier too that every Saturday the ŏrnang beats his drum and all the young men go off with him on a hunt.[465] All of them return in the evening with at least something, as their forests are full of wild animals. The animal they hunt most is rabbit; after that gazelle, then fox, then wild cattle. If they come across a *taytal* that is sick or they happen upon one inadvertently, they kill it and divide up its meat. The *taytal* is a wild animal that looks like the domestic cow but is smaller in size, the largest being the size of a calf. It has two horns that incline slightly as they rise, either backward or forward, and that are two handspans or less in length. Though wild, it is somewhat sluggish; it runs away only when faced by a large number of people. If there are only one, two, or three men, it stands still and looks at them placidly. When they see one, the Fur customarily call out to it, "*Taytal*, you infidel!" and it trains its eyes on them as though quite unconcerned and only moves if they get very close. When this happens, it walks away slowly, and only trots off if it sees they're serious in their pursuit. The difference between the *taytal* and ordinary wild cattle is that the *taytal*, though a form of the latter, is smaller and its horns grow straight, like the horns of the gazelle, with a large space between them at the top, and it is yellow all over. The term "wild cattle" includes the black, yellow, and piebald forms, the color of the latter being mixed with a lot of white. Its horns are as thick and curved as those of the domestic cow and it is the same size as a cow too. This shows us that the *taytal* is a kind of cow, with differences as noted.[466]

3.3.30 Certain people devote themselves to hunting animals and have no other profession. Each kind of hunter equips himself appropriately.

The young men rely entirely on dogs and throwing sticks. The smiths use special equipment. The hunters we mentioned as having no other profession are smiths, and fall into two groups.[467]

One group devotes itself exclusively to the hunting of quadrupeds, such as gazelle, wild cattle, elephant, buffalo, hyena, lion, rhinoceros, and so on. These hunters band together in teams of five or six persons. They go to the track along which the elephant or whatever will pass on its way to water and dig in it a pit deeper than a man's height. In the middle of the pit they hammer a stake with a pointed end, sharp as a spear at the tip, and lay a latticework of thin sticks over it, and cover these with grass. Then they cover the grass with soil. The elephants, or lions or wild cattle or buffalos or rhinoceroses, come to drink and pass over this pit, so when their weight becomes too much for the sticks to bear, they break beneath their feet and one or two animals fall in. When the weight of the animal comes down on the stake in the middle, the spike enters its flesh and the animal is immobilized until the one who dug the pit comes and finishes it off, and takes its meat after removing its skin. They make the meat into jerky, which they call "shreds" because they shred it, meaning they cut it into strips. Some of it they also eat undried. 3.3.31

If the animal is an elephant, they remove its tusks and hide and make the meat into jerky. If it's a rhinoceros, they remove its horn and hide and make its meat into jerky, some of which they eat and some of which they sell. Each team has a group of people in the village who each week go and look for them, bringing them what they need by way of supplies and so on. These people have a camel, which they load with whatever jerky, hides, horns, and elephant tusks they find with the hunters. The hides they make into shields and whips; they sell the ivory, rhinoceros horns, and whips to the merchants and the shields to the soldiery. They are a people who recognize no law and are called Darmūdīs; others never contract marriages with them, and the Darmūdīs will marry only their own kind. 3.3.32

Others use traps, as follows. They go where the wild animals are, bringing a tether of strong leather that they make into a large loop. 3.3.33

When a wild animal passes over it and its foot enters the loop—which is circular and resembles a noose—and the animal raises its foot, it becomes caught in it. The loop is well secured with pegs, so the animal can neither break it nor pull it out, and it remains trapped like that till they come and kill it. Others climb trees beneath which wild animals nap, having with them one or two of the spears of the broad, sharp kind, as in the illustration: The hunter stays at the top of the tree until the animal arrives, naps, and settles down. He fixes his eye on one that is close to him and stabs it in the belly as it sleeps. This causes the rest of the animals to run away, but the one that has been stabbed stays put and the hunter descends to finish it off.

3.3.34 Some devote themselves exclusively to hunting birds, the best of those hunted there being the bustard. This is an enormous bird, larger than a turkey, in color white shading into yellow and green. It grows extremely fat during the hot season, and its meat is tender and delicate. It feeds on a certain kind of worm that is common there, as well as small insects. The hunter brings some of these worms and insects and will have on him some line that he's carefully made out of well-plaited sinew so fine the bird can scarcely see it. He goes to the places where these birds are hunted, and when he sees bustards in a particular place, ties an insect or a worm onto the line, ties the line to the bottom of a tree, goes toward the bustards, and drives them (bustards being so sluggish that they can hardly fly even when a person is close enough to catch them) in the direction of the insect or worm, till it sees it. As soon as it does so, the bird rushes toward it and swallows it. When the insect is in its craw and the bird wants to leave, the line prevents it from doing so. The hunter comes, cuts its throat, sets it beside him, and if there are more bustards there ties another insect to the line. There is another bird also to be found there called *abū ṭanṭarah*:[468] it is white, slightly larger than the bustard, and has a long conical sac on its neck that is wide at the bottom and narrow at the top. Like the bustard, it eats insects.

Another group hunts small birds with a net. These are the Darmūdīs who earn the least, because they have to cover the cost of grain, as sparrows, whydahs,[469] and the like alight only on grain. Such a hunter goes to the place where he wants to hunt, such as close to a river or pond, and sets up his net. The net is square and looks like this: 3.3.35

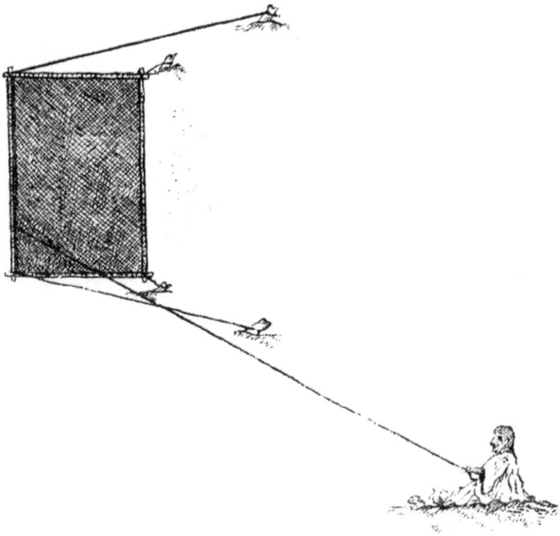

It has four pegs, two of which are tied directly to two of its corners while two are tied to two long ropes attached to its two other corners. The pegs are hammered into the ground, and close to one of its upper corners is a strong, very long rope. Then the net is set upright and grain scattered in front of it. The hunter takes the end of the long rope and stays there, at a distance. When the birds have come down in large numbers on the grain, he pulls the net down on them using the rope in his hand. The interstices of the net are very narrow so no birds can escape and nothing can get through. The owner of the net then goes and extracts the birds. If it contains anything of high value, such as a parakeet or a parrot or the like, he takes out its wing feathers and leaves it in his basket; if it doesn't, he cuts the birds' throats and scatters more grain. When I was there I had a net, and used to hunt with it at home. Often, I was able to satisfy my appetite with the birds I caught. There are others who are fond of hunting apes and monkeys in the mountains, but I don't know how they catch them.

3.3.36 Better than all the above is hunting using gunpowder, for anyone with a good musket can eat as much meat as he likes with no effort. Some of the wealthy buy a Darmūdī slave and use him just for hunting; if the slave is clever, his master will never go without meat. At the home of my teacher Faqīh Madanī, I saw a slave called Saʿīd, who was advanced in years. Faqīh Madanī told me Saʿīd was a hunter and fed me gazelle meat, mentioning that it was Saʿīd who had shot it, and that Saʿīd had to bring him meat two or three times a week. I started looking for a slave like him but couldn't find one.

3.3.37 One group devotes itself exclusively to hunting giraffe and ostrich, namely, the Bedouin of the savannah, such as the Maḥāmīd, the Zabadah, the ʿIrayqāt in Dār Wāddāy, the Majānīn, the Zayādiyyah, and the ʿIrayqāt and Banū Jarrār in Darfur. They all hunt on horseback. The best hunter is the one with the fastest horse—when one of them catches sight of his prey, he doesn't track its spoor but chases it till he comes alongside it. When the prey is within reach, he hocks it. Though ostriches run fast, there are those who can out-gallop them. As for giraffes, however, a horse can only barely outrun them, so it takes a horse that runs like the wind to actually catch up with one. The Bedouin of the savannah in Darfur and Wāddāy are blessed with every comfort they could wish for, except millet, sorghum, and clothing. Their requirements in terms of these, however, they buy with whatever clarified butter, cattle, wild-animal skins, cows, and camels they do not need for themselves. They can even afford to import into Dār Wāddāy and Darfur scabbards, waterskins, leather butter flagons, ropes made from leather strips (which they call *wajaj*), whips, and other things besides.

3.3.38 Their clarified butter is from their own cattle, and their honey from trees—the bees nest there and they harvest it. Hunting is widely practiced, which is why you'll find that ostrich feathers have no value for them, and the same goes for rhinoceros horn. When I was in Dār Wāddāy, a merchant came from Fezzan looking for ostrich feathers and asked Sharif Aḥmad al-Fāsī, who was vizier after my father, to write him a letter of recommendation to Shaykh Shūshū, shaykh of the Maḥāmīd, and order the Bedouin to hunt for him at a reasonable price. He brought with him fifty French dollars. The sharif wrote him a letter to that effect, and the merchant went to the Maḥāmīd with a Bedouin guide. He stayed there awhile and when he came back told us that when he reached the place where the tribe had settled and asked after the shaykh's tent, he was shown the way, received with the most lavish hospitality, and put up in the grandest style. When he showed Shaykh Shūshū the sharif's letter, the shaykh became yet more generous in his hospitality and treated him with extraordinary kindness and charity, allocating him a tent with its furnishings and everything he needed, and appointing a senior male and female servant to see to his needs.

The merchant had brought with him a gift for the shaykh, which he presented to him and which the latter accepted and requited with gifts of his own. Then the merchant handed the fifty dollars over to the shaykh, and the shaykh summoned the Bedouin and told them, "This man is a stranger who has claimed my hospitality and sought my protection, and he desires ostrich feathers. If any of you would like some of these dollars, let him go hunting tomorrow morning. For each *ẓalīm* ostrich he brings he will receive a half dollar, and for each *rabdā'* ostrich a quarter dollar."[470] The Bedouin leaped to obey his request and set off to hunt the next morning—in one day they brought around twenty *ẓalīms*. The man stayed with them for some twenty days, during which he collected about one hundred *ẓalīms*. The shaykh had loaded these onto his camels, and gave him a large stock of provisions. Among the items he provided was ostrich fat, of which the merchant brought a large quantity. He also arrived with large quantities of honey, *kenykenya* candy, *hijlīj* kernels, and yellow jujube fruits. He sold the *ẓalīms* in Wārah for 3.3.39

three dollars apiece and was left with only around ten skins. He made a large profit.

3.3.40 Giraffes have no value as a trade item, except for their skins, which they sell. They eat the meat fresh and jerked. The Bedouin also have more rice, sawa millet,[471] *kūrayb*, *hijlīj*, tamarind, honey, yellow jujube fruits, and *hijlīj* kernels[472] than anyone else. Milk is so abundant among them that it has no value: they take the clarified butter and throw away the curds. It's so plentiful that anyone who goes to their settlements, especially those of the Rizayqāt, the Brown Misīriyyah, and the Ḥabbāniyyah, will find the nearby streams and ponds awash with milk.

Section 2: Currency among the People of Darfur

3.3.41 It is acknowledged in theology that the Truth, may His names be exalted, has no need of place or particularity. He possesses absolute sufficiency and is in no need of any of His creation, while all creatures need His bounty, plead for His charity, and crowd together at the gates of His mercy. He has therefore bestowed on them the gaze of His benevolence, granting to each that which will support him and his family, while favoring some over others in terms of the livelihood they receive, making some kings, others rich men, and yet others paupers. He has created for them means to use in pursuit of their livelihoods and commanded them to strive and struggle lest they fall into poverty.

3.3.42 As a part of His vast favor, He has made buying and selling permitted to men, so that they can obtain what they hanker for and be relieved of misery. Thus, in civilized countries He has made the two forms of specie[473] sources of consolation by means of which men may obtain the things needed for their daily lives and necessary for them to accumulate wealth. Likewise, He has in His glory and exaltedness assigned to each realm a recognized mintage and gold and silver coins they recognize.

3.3.43 Given that the people of the Lands of the Blacks are so far from civilization and its might, and live in a darkness as savage as the blackest night, most of them, it must be said, cannot tell gold from brass or tin from lead. Even those whose lands contain gold as a mineral sell it as ore, believing that to sell it that way is more proper. This ignorance is particularly characteristic of Darfur—it has no metals other than those imported from other lands,[474] so that even the most splendid of its women's jewelry consists, as noted above,[475] of different kinds of stone. Predictably, then, these people do not have the benefit of silver and gold as currency for their use. Despite this, given that merchants have set foot in their country and that their cities have grown because of the presence therein of commercial establishments, they have come up with equivalents of minted currency with which to carry on commerce and to buy what they want. For this purpose, they are divided into different areas, and each area has adopted the currency it finds appropriate for daily use.[476]

The first area is the *fāshir*, the headquarters of the sultanate and seat of government. The people there have made rings of tin with which they buy whatever meat, chicken, perfumes, fuel, vegetables, and so on they need. In the language of the Fur these rings are called *tărne* and come in two forms, thick (called *tărne tonga nia*) and thin (called *tărne bayyâ*). They use these as currency in their small-scale transactions, as stated earlier.[477] For larger transactions, they use *takākī* (plural of *tukkiyyah*), which are pieces of cotton cloth ten cubits in length and one cubit in breadth. This cloth is of two types: *shīkah*, which is of a light, loose weave, and *katkāt*, which is of a heavy, compact weave. Four *takākī* of the former are equivalent to one French dollar, as are two and a half of the latter. For all other transactions, they barter. For major transactions, they price things in slaves. Thus, they may say, "This horse is for sale for two, or three, *sudāsī*s," the *sudāsī* being, in their parlance, a slave who, when measured from heel to earlobe, is six handspans tall; *sudāsiyyah* is used for females. A *sudāsī* is equivalent in value to thirty *takākī* of six blue, or eight white, lengths of camlet, or to six head of cattle, or to ten French dollars. People make their purchases using whichever of these currencies they possess. They know nothing of the sequin, the 3.3.44

piaster, the franc, the *khayriyyah*, or any other currency used by the people of the cities, with the exception of the French dollar, which they call "the cannon coin."[478]

3.3.45 The people of Kūbayh, Kabkābiyyah, and Sarf al-Dajāj use *ḥarish* as currency. These are beads that are neither thick nor thin, some of which are green, some blue. They gather these beads into strings of one hundred; we've already described them in the section on women's finery and adornment.[479] They use these as currency for their small-scale transactions in place of the *tǎrne* used in the *fāshir*. It is remarkable that in these three markets one can't buy even a sip of water with *tǎrne*—all exchange is in *ḥarish*, in quantities from five to a hundred beads, and in anything from one to ten to countless strings. Among them the *tukkiyyah* is worth eight strings, and everything else is the same as in the *fāshir*.

3.3.46 In Qirlī and its dependencies they use *pôlgo*, which is manufactured salt extracted from the ground in the form of dirt. They pour water on it, or so I imagine, so that the impurities and soil particles settle, then strain, filtering the water, which is small in quantity, and put the filtrate into finger-shaped molds. On cooling, this hardens and turns into finger-shaped pieces. I saw the places where they extract this salt and saw the filtering vessels, which resemble Frankish cooking pots. I have no idea who introduced this craft to them, and the people of the country don't know either. The most they are likely to come up with if any were to ask, "Who taught you this craft?" would be, "Our fathers used to do it, so we do it too; we don't know who first practiced it." I have used this salt as currency myself and bought it; it has a remarkably delicious taste, different from that of natural salt, but is cloudy and brownish.

3.3.47 There are three kinds of salt in Darfur—*zaghāwī*, which is a natural salt taken from Bīr al-Zaghāwī, *pôlgo*, which we have just described, and *mīdawbī*, which is also a natural salt but bloodred in color. *Mīdawbī* is extracted in pieces as large and round as millstones and so heavy that a camel can carry only two. It tastes delicious, more so than the two other kinds, and is more expensive. We have no idea how it comes to be red. To summarize: the most expensive kind of salt is the *mīdawbī*, the middling is the *pôlgo*, and the cheapest the *zaghāwī*. The people who fall within the market area of Qirlī and its dependencies use *pôlgo* as currency for small-scale transactions in the same way that in Kūbayh they use *ḥarish*, and in the sultan's capital *tǎrne*. Salt isn't sold among them by volume or weight, but by finger. A given item may be sold for one finger of *pôlgo*, two fingers of *pôlgo*, three fingers of *pôlgo*, and so on. All other transactions they conduct the way the others do.

In the Kusā market area, they use tobacco—which is called *tābā*, in their language as in the languages of the Franks[480]—as currency. This is a remarkable coincidence, and not something peculiar to the people of Darfur: all the Blacks call tobacco *tābā* (the people of the Fezzan and Libyan Tripoli call it *tabgh*). In 1232 [1816–17], I saw a poem by a member of the Bakrī family on the permissibility of using tobacco; I think it was written in the middle of the ninth century [late 14th/15th c. AD].[481] He says: 3.3.48

God, All-powerful, has caused to appear in this Egypt of ours
    a plant called *tabgh*, let no one this gainsay,
Written with *t* and two dots, an undoubled *b*,
    and *ghayn* (the *ghayn* being voweled with an *a*).

And from the same poem:

To any who claims, in his ignorance, that it's forbidden,
    to him "On what evidence and per what Qur'anic verse" say,
And "It intoxicates not and neither has God forbidden it
    so whence your claim that God says nay?"

And still from the same poem:

If you inhale its smoke, you'll find yourself cured,
    So forget not "In God's name!" before you puff away,
And say thereafter, "Praise is due to God alone,"
    for when you praise the Lord, more grace will come your way.

3.3.49 This *tābā* consists of pyramid-shaped cones made of tobacco leaves pounded while still green in a wooden mortar till they achieve a doughlike consistency. They make this into cones, which they dry in the sun. Once the cones have dried out, they take them to their market and use them as currency for small-scale transactions. This kind of tobacco has such a strong smell that one almost faints on smelling it. The cones come in two sizes, large and small; the large are the size of a large pear, the small the size of a small pear.

3.3.50 In Karyū, Rīl, and al-Shaʿīriyyah, they use skeins of spun cotton yarn as currency, each skein being ten cubits in length and containing precisely twenty strings. They use these skeins for small-scale transactions. For trivial transactions they use cotton harvested from the bush, i.e., still in the boll out of which it has burst; they use small amounts of this cotton, such as one, two, or three ounces, by rough estimation or guesswork, without weighing. Major transactions are as in the other markets.

3.3.51 The market area of Numlayh and its dependencies use onions as currency; they make all their trivial purchases with these, as well as with cotton and cotton skeins. For other purchases, they use *takākī*. They are unfamiliar with both *shawātir* and dollars as currency.

3.3.52 In Rās al-Fīl, they use hoes, which are pieces of iron hammered flat and with a cylindrical attachment, as in the picture: They insert a handle into the cylindrical end and use the hoe to dig around the plants; they cut the weeds that are among the plants, which is why one such hoe is called a "weeder."[482] They use these as a currrency for

their small-scale and trivial transactions ranging from one to two to twenty hoes.[483] For larger transactions they use *takākī* and *shawātir* as in the other markets.

3.3.53 The Tomorókkóngá use copper bracelets as currency. This is for their major transactions; for their small-scale transactions, they use *khaddūr* beads. Descriptions of their bracelets and of *khaddūr* beads appear earlier[484] in the section on women's finery, so there's no need to repeat them here.

The people of the desert use millet as currency for all their small-scale transactions, in quantities such as a handful, or enough to fill the cupped palms, or twice that amount, up to half a *mudd*. Their other, major, transactions are made with *takākī* and dollars, as in the rest of the markets. What they most commonly use as currency, though, is cattle. They say, "This horse costs ten head of cattle" or "twenty head of cattle." 3.3.54

Behold, dear observer, how diverse are the currencies used by the people of a single realm, and how varied their conditions: one finds that some people believe a certain thing to be an object of value, while others believe that same thing to be worthless! The monarch doesn't insist they use one currency in all markets; on the contrary, he has left each group to follow the system to which it has become accustomed. Glory to Him who effects what He desires! Let us now rein in the pen from its canter over the parade ground of currencies and commercial transaction, for what we have stated is enough by any consideration. 3.3.55

A Chapter on the Plants That Grow in Darfur; on Magic, the Making of Amulets, and Geomancy; and on Other Matters

4.1 Know that He who is without need of any when, where, or how and is devoid of any tyranny, injustice, or prejudice has divided things up, arranged them in order, and sent them down, each to its appointed place. He has put extreme cold in the lands of the north and the hottest possible heat in those of the south. He has also, however, out of His mercy for His mortal slaves, bestowed warmth on the people of the north through the agency of clothes and of homes where men may gather without feeling the cold, and has turned on the people of the south the gaze of succor and mitigation by causing rain to fall on them when the summer is at its height.

4.2 Given that the territory of the Fur is of this second type, and that in summer thirst becomes extreme, the downpours that extinguish the blazing fire of that heat are an act of kindness from the Mighty, the Forgiving—for they sow at the coming of the summer rains and call that season the "autumn." It is for this reason, or so I imagine, that they cultivate neither wheat nor barley nor fava beans nor lentils nor chickpeas, and grow no apricots, peaches, apples, pomegranates, olives, plums, pears, citrons, sweet lemons, oranges, almonds, hazelnuts, pistachios, walnuts, medlars, or the like.

4.3 Instead, they grow millet, which is a small yellow grain they use as food for themselves, their mounts, and their cattle. It is their primary means of subsistence. They also grow sorghum in its various forms, calling it *mārīq*. It consists of different types. There is a kind called *ʿazīr*, which is red sorghum; a kind called *abū shalawlaw*, which is white sorghum; and a kind called *abū abāṭ*, which in Egypt is called Syrian sorghum.[485] Wheat is grown only in Jabal Marrah, where there is abundant rain, and Kūbayh and Kabkābiyyah, where they water it from wells until it matures, as already mentioned.[486] The millet that they have is of two kinds, an ordinary kind and a kind called *dinbī*,[487] which is what is grown by the non-Arabic-speaking Fur in the mountains and elsewhere. It is a cereal like ordinary millet but whitish in color and with larger ears; it also ripens some twenty days before the latter. It is little found in the Darfur plain, where they are less familiar with it than they are with yellow millet. Of the different kinds of sorghum, they are familiar only with the white and don't eat much of that, despite their familiarity with it. The kind called *abū abāṭ* they grow in small quantities because they find it tasty; they eat it grilled and don't store it as grain. They dislike the kind called *ʿazīr*; only the poor eat it, or others when they have no choice. Rice grows wild there in ponds and watercourses without being sown; they gather as much of it as they can during their spring[488] and cook it with milk as a luxury dish. They have another kind of cereal too that is similar to rice but isn't rice, called *difrah*; it has a small grain, smaller than rice, slightly flattened and extremely white. They are more familiar with this than they are with rice.

They cultivate a great deal of sesame but, remarkably, don't use 4.4
it to make oil. They eat it as a grain and use it in their cooked dishes. Honey is also plentiful there, though they make no use of the wax; in fact, they take the honey and throw the wax away, though no one is in greater need of it, or of sesame oil, than they, since they use dry fuel to light the lamps in their houses. Similarly, despite the plentiful supply of fuel wood, they don't use it to make charcoal, which would be of use to them; in fact, they don't even know what it is.

They also grow black-eyed peas and watermelons alongside the 4.5
millet. The black-eyed peas are like those found in Egypt but larger,

growing to nearly the same size as fava beans in Egypt. The watermelons are of a smaller size, like those found in the melon patch at the end of the season, which, if one breaks them open, turn out to be unripe; the ones in Darfur, however, are ripe, despite their small size. They have three different uses for watermelon. First, they eat them as soon as they ripen, as we do our melons; they also drink the juice. Second, they take the melon, remove its rind using a knife, and cut it into four pieces, which they leave till dry. They store it, treated this way, in large quantities, and when they need it, pound it in a wooden mortar till it turns to flour, which they use to make a broth that they drink called *madīdah*, which is what the Franks call *crema*.[489] Sometimes they eat the dried watermelon unpounded and uncooked. Third, they gather large quantities of the seeds, which they store and pound as needed. They also pulverize the rind, remove the flesh, and cook the rind to be used as a condiment or, again, make *crema* from it.

4.6 In Kūbayh, Kabkābiyyah, and the valleys of the Fur mountains, they grow onions, garlic, pepper (which has a small grain), coriander, and cress, as mentioned earlier.[490] They also grow different varieties of squash and a type of cucumber. In Kūbayh and Kabkābiyyah, they also grow cucumber, long cucumber, eggplant, Jew's mallow, and okra; elsewhere they do not.[491] There is a seasonal watercourse between the village called al-Marbūṭah and the sultan's capital that is called Wādī l-Kūʿ. It is flooded during the autumn due to the copious rains, and only those who know how to swim can cross it, as it has a strong current. When the wadi floods, and the water overflows its banks and soaks into the ground, okra sprouts in large quantities and they rush there from nearby parts and gather it, dry it, set it aside, and use it as something to eat with their bread for the rest of the year. This wadi traverses Darfur from beginning to end breadthwise, and has its origin in Jabal Marrah. It has a belt of acacia trees on either bank, and when it overflows it covers approximately two miles in either direction, except in a few places where the sands constrain it. In some places it's as wide as the Khalīj in Cairo,[492] in others twice as wide. One traveling along its bank can go for fifteen days. I describe it as being between al-Marbūṭah and the *fāshir* simply because I passed it so often at that point; in fact, it runs a long way, as I've explained. They also grow a kind of bean whose pods grow below ground; it is not the same as the bean now called in Egypt the Sinnār bean, because the first has remarkable colors, including bright red, yellow, white, and brown, as mentioned above.[493]

As far as trees are concerned, they have none that are well-known, with the exception of the date palm, which is found in Kūbayh, Kabkābiyyah, Sarf al-Dajāj, and Numlayh, as mentioned in the course of the earlier discussion of Jabal Marrah.[494] At Numlayh there are some banana trees, and at Qirlī bitter lemons. All the rest of the trees in Darfur grow naturally in the countryside. The most useful of these is the *hijlīj* tree, of which there are two kinds, yellow and red, the names according with the colors of the fruit, which are the size of large unripe dates. The *hijlīj* is a tree that grows to a great size, like the sycamore-fig in Egypt. Its leaves are slightly rounded, and its fruit tastes sweet, with a hint of bitterness, and has a distinctive smell. The fruit also has an outer covering around it, a rind that is neither thick nor thin and which they peel off to better suck on the fruit, the latter consisting of a woody piece covered in a kind of coating that they either suck off or soak in water. When that is gone, the woody piece, which is to say the kernel, turns white. This is itself a covering for something like a pine nut in shape and in whiteness, which is a seed, albeit larger than most seeds. This, however, is bitter in taste, so they steep it in water for around three days, changing the water every day. This removes its bitterness. At this point, some salt it, others roast it, and yet others stew it with honey. Salted, it tastes like salted almonds. There is another kind of *hijlīj*, which is the red *hijlīj*, the flesh of whose ripe fruits they take, adding gum and then kneading the two together, producing something deliciously sweet and sour. In sum, they eat the *hijlīj* fruit prepared in a variety of ways. 4.7

4.8 The *hijlīj* has useful properties not to be found in any other of their trees. They throw none of it away; on the contrary, they use every part of it. The leaves they cook when fresh and juicy as a condiment for bread. If someone has a worm-infested wound, they chew some of these leaves till they turn into a kind of paste and spit this into the wound. This cleanses it of the worms and cleans out the rotten flesh, so that it starts to heal. The fruit of the *hijlīj* can be taken when green and pounded in a mortar till it turns into a paste and can be used like soap for washing clothes; it makes a foam like soap that removes the dirt and cleans clothes washed in it, though it does make them slightly yellow. If it is not the fruiting season, the roots of the tree are taken and pounded and used to wash clothes, for they act in the same way. The wood is used for lighting in the houses at night in place of oil lamps because it makes no smoke. From its wood, too, reading tablets are made, and from its ash *kumbā* is made, a liquid salt extracted from the aforementioned ash; it is used for cooking but is bitter. They use it when they have no ordinary salt, which is costly and hard to come by.

4.9 There is also the jujube,[495] which comes in two forms, "Arabic" and *karnū*, the second being larger than the first, having fleshier fruits, and differing from it in color, the fruits of the ordinary "Arabic" jujube being red when ripe, while those of the *karnū* are yellow. The former also has more useful properties than the latter, one of which is that a paste made from its fruit prevents defecation. Before it is pounded and kneaded, its outer skin is scraped off. Then they make it into disks, which they dry and eat. When its kernel is broken open, two seeds will be found inside, each in a pocket of its own. The Bedouin take this small seed and dry it in the sun. Then they stew it with honey, and it turns into something delicious called *kenykenya*, which they sell in Darfur and which is eaten as candy; also, if anyone with roundworm chews *karnū* leaves and swallows his saliva, it kills the worms and expels them dead.

4.10 There is also the *tabaldī*, which is a vast, mighty tree with a hollow trunk that grows in the deserts. When desert dwellers grow extremely thirsty in the dry season, they go to the *tabaldī* and find rainwater that has collected in its cavity. They drink and their thirst goes away. The tree has large oblong fruits like almond trees, and inside these are red seeds like lupine seeds in size and carob seeds in color. These contain a white flour with a sour taste that people eat by the handful. They taste bitter, and eating them on an empty stomach prevents defecation. They make a *crema* using the flour, which makes it delicious.

There is also the *dulab*, which the Egyptians call *al-jawz al-hindī.* 4.11
This tree isn't found throughout Darfur, however, only in the south. In Fur parlance it is called *dalayb*.[496] The trees are as tall as date palms, or taller, and produce a large nut, inside which is an extremely delicious juice, especially before it is fully ripe; it is almost as sweet and tasty as milk.[497]

Also among their trees is the *ḥummayḍ*, which is a huge thorny 4.12
tree that has a fruit like a large apple but with a pit. It is deliciously sour and is white in color, shading to yellow. Another is the doum palm, well-known in Upper Egypt and also called *muql.* Another is the *ʿandurāb*, a tree of medium height and girth that bears a fruit resembling black nightshade, though it is deep red and seedless. This fruit is very sweet and ripens at the start of the *darat*, which is to say, in their language, the spring, which is the beginning of autumn in our country.

Another is the *qiddīm*,[498] which is a tree very like the pomegran- 4.13
ate. It bears a small fruit that is divided into two halves and covered with a bright-red skin and is extremely sweet. The pit is large, and I can't think of another fruit we know that resembles it enough to compare it to.

Another is the *mukhkhayṭ*, which is a small tree that bears a fruit 4.14
like that of the jujube but bitter. It is taken and steeped in water for several days, which rids it of its bitterness. Then it's sprinkled with salt, stewed, and eaten. Some people dry it after the steeping and pound it until it turns into flour, from which they make a thick paste with clarified butter. This they do only during times of high prices and extreme hardship.

4.15 Another is the shea, which resembles the tree that produces the nuts called walnuts. It bears a fruit like the chestnut, though the chestnut has a flattened shape whereas this one looks like a hazelnut, though larger, about the size of a chestnut (the chestnut is what in Turkish lands is called *kestane* and in Tunis *qaṣṭal*). The fruit has a fatty flesh and is found only in the southern extremity of Darfur, i.e., toward the country of the Fartīt, where the people extract an oil from it. I've seen this and it seemed to me that it was most like sesame oil in appearance and olive oil in taste. They use it as a rub and also make it into a condiment to eat with their various dishes. Carob and sycamore-fig are also found, but are of poor quality and have no useful properties.

4.16 They grow cotton in both its local variety, which they call "Arabic," and its Indian variety, which they call *lawī*. They make the most complete use of it because they not only get their clothes from it but also use it as currency, as we have described in the chapter on such things.[499]

4.17 The number of trees whose fruit is not eaten is large, almost too large to count, but we shall mention the best known and most useful. One of the most useful is the Sodom apple, which is a low, many-branched tree whose trunk is coated with something white resembling grease. Its large leaves crumble when pressed between the fingers and emit a white, milk-like juice when torn. It has fruit like a ball that is filled with something like down or nap that's so light it flies about in the air. This tree has useful properties, one being that its juice, if placed on an animal's hide, removes the hair. They peel off its bark, and inside are found fibers as fine as silk; these are gathered and threads are spun from them that they use to sew waterskins. Ropes are also spun from the fibers, and are good for tying things and securing loads. The nap inside the fruit is used for stopping up holes in waterskins. If they steal a donkey or a horse, and want to change the color of part of its hair, they anoint with its juice the place they want to change; the hair disappears, and white hair grows back in its place. In such cases, there will be doubt as to who is its owner, though some owners are familiar with the ruse, having been subjected to it before. Its wood is as light as that of the *qafal* tree. I've seen them blackening gunpowder with the charcoal made from it. There's a specimen at the Abū Zaʿbal hospital, and many are to be found in Upper Egypt too.

There is also a tree called *ḥashāb*. It is thorny and gum arabic is extracted from it. I've seen it and gathered the gum from it while it was still soft and stretchy like mastic. It grows in arid, sandy places. There is also the sant tree, which is the tree that produces *qaraẓ* pods. It is huge and thorny. And there is the *ṭalḥ*, which belongs to the same species as the sant. *Ṭalḥ* grows taller than a man, its bark is red, and it has long thorns like needles. Its leaves are made up of smaller leaves. The umbrella thorn acacia is a tall tree that grows higher than a man but is smaller than the *ṭalḥ*, while the color of its bark is whitish green. It has white thorns and each leaf is made up of smaller leaves. Another such tree is the *kitir*. This is a thorny tree with many branches; its thorns are like hooks. It also produces a gum that is harvested, though *ḥashāb* gum is more expensive and of better quality. 4.18

Another tree is the *laʾūt*,[500] which is a small tree with small thorns and many branches that have a greenish tinge that never disappears even if the wood dries out. When its bark is peeled off, a distinctive, unpleasant odor may be smelled. Another is *qafal*, which is a tree that is neither large nor small but grows mostly in the mountains. Another is the *ḥarāz*. This is a thorny tree of enormous size whose trunk grows so large that two men cannot put their extended arms around it. It provides extensive shade; some are so large that a hundred or more may sit in its shade. 4.19

In general, the trees whose fruit is not eaten are useful for other purposes. They cut timber from them for their houses. The pods of the sant are used for tanning, and its long branches as pillars for their houses. They use the bark of the *laʾūt* to tie the ceiling beams of their houses together and use its branches to make ceilings and *ṣarīf*s, which serve the same function as enclosure walls around our 4.20

houses. From *kitir* and *ḥashāb* they take gum, and sometimes they cut off their thorns and make them into hedges for pens for their animals, because generally speaking every house has a *zarībah*, which is a kind of outer wall, and a *ṣarīf*, which is a kind of inner wall, with the houses in the middle, much like tents with dust-breaks erected around them.[501] The houses are made either of millet canes or of thin canes called *marhabayb*, the second being used only by the rich and the great men of the state. It is a cane with few knots, and is as thin as a reed, yellowish white, and sweet-smelling; the smell is strongest after rainfall.

4.21 The plants found in the Lands of the Blacks are so numerous that the different species are too many to count, and to their number no end or limit can be found. I am acquainted only with those that are well-known and widespread and whose fame has filled the globe, for at the time I was but a youth, ignorance my very robe. Despite this, and because I mixed so much with the Blacks and made so many journeys with them, I learned many by name, though I can't distinguish each and every one of them.

4.22 Among them are the *shāw*, a tree that occurs in large and small varieties, the small being more plentiful than the large. The small variety is taller than a man, and its bark is green compared to that of the large variety, because the bark of the large form is "dusty," by which I mean gray (which is a color close to white but not as bright). When it puts forth fruit these come as clusters of berries resembling small grapes, which the inhabitants of the Lands of the Blacks eat. Those that ripen are black, and those not quite ripe are red, while those that are unripe are green. They taste sweet, with a certain piquancy, and the leaves, if I remember correctly, are ovoid, or almost so, and green both above and below.

4.23 The *baṭṭūm* is a large tree, impressive to look at, grayish in color, with a thick trunk, hard wood, and small ovoid leaves with teeth around their edges. At the bottom, the bark of the trunk appears irregularly cracked. Its fruits resemble those of the *shāw*, as do its clusters, but the *baṭṭūm* has long tails to its berries, and its fruits, which are smaller than those of the *shāw*, cannot be eaten. Its trunk reaches more than twice a man's height and divides into many branches.

The ebony tree is a medium-sized tree with a dark-green bark. Ebony is its heartwood: when the bark is peeled off, a black wood is exposed, though the black is not very intense when the wood is green; the more it dries, though, the blacker it becomes. The best ebony is that taken from the roots. It is not found in Darfur but imported from Dār Fartīt. The jackalberry tree is the same, but the jackalberry has fruit like hazelnuts in size, sweet tasting, with a certain toughness, like gristle. The *jaʿjaʿ* is another medium-sized tree, with a reddish trunk and branches with few bifurcations.[502] It has long thorns and the stalks of its leaves are so short one might think they were stuck straight onto the branches; these leaves are round and deeply indented. The fruits resemble medlars and contain compartments, but are gristly and have a certain woodiness. To the best of my recollection each fruit contains four compartments with walls between them. 4.24

In the lands of the Fartīt (who are the Magians among the Blacks[503] and who live south of the borders of Darfur) grows *qanā*, from which they make the shafts of their spears; most of the shafts of the spears of the officers of state in Darfur are of this bamboo, which is very beautiful and is imported from Dār Fartīt. 4.25

Plants that have special properties include the *kilí* tree, which is of medium size, without thorns, and bears a fruit like a medlar but woody. The fruit is steeped in water, and given to one charged with a crime to drink.[504] The color of the fruit resembles that of sour, dried pomegranates. The *shaʿlūb* is a semiwoody tree with numerous soft, thin branches, which spread out and interweave with one another until the tree, when standing alone, ends up looking like a hill.[505] It has fruits like large green dates with neither pit nor kernel that contain a milky, somewhat viscous juice. The fruits taste sweet at the beginning and piquant at the end; it is green, the green never disappearing, even when they dry out. If someone 4.26

who's been drinking wine chews them, they get rid of the smell, as noted earlier.[506]

4.27 Another is the *daqarah*,[507] which is a grassy plant that grows in hard soils. Its leaves are delicate and somewhat rounded. When the leaves are pounded in a mortar and their juice squeezed for three days, morning and evening, into a diseased eye that is acutely inflamed and swollen, it will cure it. I was in the market at Numlayh once (not the time I went to see the mountain)[508] and I picked up some pepper with my hand and toyed with it for a moment. Then there was a gust of wind and my eyes got dust in them so I rubbed them with my hand, forgetting about the pepper. It hurt terribly and my eyes immediately became inflamed and swollen. I mounted and left but couldn't go on riding because of the terrible pain, so I entered a town and spent the night in the house of an old woman. I was unable to sleep and spent a horrible night, my eyelids inverting and emitting a viscous liquid. I feared I might go blind and had no idea what could save me.

4.28 In the morning, the old woman came and saw my eyes and felt sorry for me. "That's easily dealt with," she said, and she called a young daughter of hers, aged perhaps seven or eight, and told her, in the language of the Fur, "Go to the foot of the mountain and bring me some leaves of the plant called *daqarah*." The girl went off and was away awhile. Then she came back, bringing a large quantity of leaves, which the old woman took and some of which she pounded between two stones till they turned into something resembling dough. She ordered me to open my eyes and take her hand, and she squeezed some of the juice of this plant into my eyes. At first it felt cool to the eyes, but then it began to itch, though without pain, as though there were worms in my eyes. I wanted to rub them, but couldn't because I was being held down, so I had to suffer some discomfort until the itching died away and I fell asleep. I slept deeply for a long time, not waking till it was almost time for the afternoon prayer, and I felt a lightness in my eyes and the pain had gone. At night, she came and squeezed some more juice into my eyes, and I slept most comfortably. In the morning, she squeezed some more again, and my eyes cleared, as though they'd never been inflamed. I slaughtered a fat ram for a feast to celebrate my recovery and gave the old woman a fat young goat.

Most plants and trees fruit at the end of the "autumn," which is the summer in our country, because they call our summer autumn and our autumn *darat*, by which they mean spring in their parlance, though our spring they call summer.[509] The only thing they agree with us on is the winter—when it's winter in their country it's also winter in ours. During the true summer, it rains where they are, and they sow their crops; the first rainfall there coincides with the appearance of the Twins, this being what they call "the sprinkle."[510] In the Crab,[511] the clouds open, there's lots of rain, and the wadis fill. It is this, you may be interested to know, that causes the rising of the Blessed Nile. That the plentiful rains where the Blacks live are the cause of the rise of the Nile in Egypt is confirmed by, among other things, the great rise in prices that occurred in Egypt in 1253 [1837–38], when an *irdabb* of wheat was sold for 150 piasters or even more, the cause being the failure of the Nile flood to rise as normal. At the time, I had no firm information as to whether the same had occurred in the Lands of the Blacks or not, and my doubt remained unresolved until 1257 [1841–42],[512] when Judge al-Dalīl, chief judge of the kingdom of Wāddāy, arrived and told me that in the year in question there was so little rain that the earth failed to produce any plants, food prices rose, and the people ate carrion and dogs. This is a remarkable coincidence and the best evidence that the rise in the River Nile is due to the rains in that country—an instance of the divine wisdom comprehensible to God alone. 4.29

At the time of "the sprinkle," strong winds and violent storms often arise, most often in the late afternoon. When they blow, you see in the distance something like a cloud, which is sometimes red, while the horizon fills with dust in the direction of the storm. Most storms come before sunset, and rarely from the south. When they come from the east, they bring great quantities of sand with them 4.30

from the Dunes, over which they pass. Every storm is accompanied by rain, because before it passes there is thunder. After the sprinkle, the rains fall, with thunder so strong it can cast damaging thunderbolts. Once I saw a thunderbolt hit a *hijlīj* tree and break off a huge branch before piercing the ground like an arrow. Another hit a house, and even before it pierced the ground the whole place caught fire and a man was hurt when his arm was burned. They told me that a thunderbolt will not go near anyone with iron on him, which is the opposite of what the Franks believe.

4.31 In their summer season, which we call spring, dust devils become frequent, and mirages can be seen on the ground; I know no other country that has as many dust devils and mirages as the Land of the Blacks. Their best and most beneficial rain falls at night, while people are asleep; even if accompanied by thunder it does less damage than the thunder that comes during the day. Rainbows are so frequent there when the rain is falling that one may appear in four or five different places during a single hour. Some are like a bow and some a straight line, though these are few; most are curved.

4.32 The "sprinkle" lasts for about fifteen days, during which time they sow millet and various kinds of sorghum. The "autumn," or rainy season, at its longest lasts no more than sixty days, not counting the sprinkle; the average is sixty days including the sprinkle. There is no limit to how short it can be. Most often, it lasts forty-five or fifty days; less than that means drought and crop failure. Then there is nothing, unless heavy rains come during that period and thoroughly irrigate the soil, which tends to happen especially at the end of the season, when the sowing is coming to an end. If the rainy season goes on for a long time and the rains are plentiful, they call it "Twins' autumn."[513]

4.33 In Darfur and Dār Wādday, the names of the months are Arabic; the Roman,[514] Coptic, and Persian months are unknown. Educated persons use the same currently well-known names that were used by the ancient Arabs, such as Muharram, Safar, Rabiʿ, etc.[515] The common people, however, use other names, which, though they have Arabic meanings, are bastardized forms. They begin the calendar with Shawwal,[516] but use another name, calling it al-Faṭur; Dhu l-Qaʿdah they call al-Faṭrayn, Dhu l-Hijjah they call al-Ḍaḥiyyah, Muharram they call al-Ḍaḥiyyatayn, Safar they call al-Waḥīd, Rabiʿ al-Awwal they call al-Karāmah, Rabiʿ al-Thani they call al-Tawm, Jumada al-Awwal they call al-Tawmayn, and Jumada al-Thani they call Sāyiq al-Tīmān.[517] Only Rajab and Ramadan have been spared change. They say Rajab, but they call Shaʿban al-Quṣayyar, and Ramadan Ramaḍān.

To sum up, the special properties of the plants of Darfur are so remarkable that I'm afraid to list them all lest people call me a liar, and I won't be able to find anyone to bear out my claims. Most of these special properties are in the roots. There are plant masters with many students who spend most of their time traveling, climbing the heights of mountains, descending deep into the bottoms of wadis to dig about for plants, and teaching their students. People of this type are called *muʿrāqī*s, and in Darfur their skills are recognized. They are always stubbornly at odds with one another, each wanting his reputation to soar higher than his rivals'. They put all the roots into goat, sheep, or even cow horns. 4.34

These roots are of different kinds. Some are for love and acceptance; the roots used for these purposes are called *nārah*.[518] The man most famous for these in our day was named Bakurlūkū; he had his headquarters at Jadīd al-Sayl. Any man in love with a girl who rejected his advances because she didn't like him would go to Bakurlūkū and get *nārah* from him and massage his face and hands with it and then go to his beloved and rub his hand on her shoulder or any other part of her body. At this, her heart would become so full of love for him she'd be unable to leave him. Then he could do with her as he wished: if he asked for her hand in marriage and her parents refused, she'd run away with him to wherever he wanted, and he could marry her in spite of them. Also, anyone who had business before the king's court and was afraid that it might not be seen to, would go Bakurlūkū, obtain a piece of *nārah* from him, massage 4.35

some of it between his hands, and rub it on his face. He'd then discover that the king had taken a fancy to him and seen to his business, even if he had harbored ill will toward him. Bakurlūkū became so famous for these things that the women used to sing songs about him, saying:

> Bakurlūkū could make them give away
> Two girls for one *sadā*

meaning that if Bakurlūkū wanted to bring down the cost of dowries, he could have a man marry two girls for a single *sadā*, a *sadā* being ten cubits of straight yarn. Apropos of this, it happened that one day a man brought me some *nārah* that he claimed was very powerful and that he said he'd obtained from Bakurlūkū. He offered to sell it to me but I told him, "Fellow, only a man whom women hate has need of *nārah*, but I'm still in my youth as you can see, and blessed with wealth—if I wanted the king's daughter she wouldn't be beyond my reach, so how much less so other girls? The kind in need of it is afraid of the king's power, but I'm safe from that—I'm not from this country; I'm a descendant of the Prophet, and I've been granted protected status by the king. Offer it to someone else. Others need it more than I do, because I'm a love potion in and of myself!"

4.36 Other roots are used to cause harm. There's a kind used to kill one's enemies. To do this, obtain the deadly root and thrust it into the shadow of the head of the man whose death is desired. He will feel the effects immediately, his brain will become inflamed, and he'll lose consciousness. If an antidote isn't quickly administered, he will die. If the desire is to render a particular limb of his useless, the root is stuck into the shadow of the limb, whether hand or foot, whose disablement is desired. That limb will immediately feel pain, become inflamed, and swell up. Sometimes buboes like those of the plague will appear on it, and if it isn't treated quickly, the limb will swell, eventually losing sensation in the sinews, and all its functions will be disabled.

If one wants to make someone dizzy and nauseous, there are roots that are put on embers whose smoke is then captured, for example in the sleeve of a garment. This is then carefully folded and dispatched to the intended victim. The latter will then open the sleeve of the garment or the like close to his nose, the smell of the smoke of the root will fill his nose, and he will straightaway fall down, legs in the air. If not treated immediately, he will stay like that for days. 4.37

There are roots whose special property is to induce sleep. These are used by thieves, who place them in a horn and at night enter a place whose occupants are awake. They wave the horn containing the root at them three times and God blocks the occupants' ears, so that they become insensible to everything. The thief then enters and takes whatever he wants. Sometimes he will slaughter a ewe, flay it, grill some of its meat, eat it, and place a piece of its liver in the hand of each person in the place, then take what he wants and leave. After he's left the house, they revive and ask each other about the man they saw, each saying, "I saw him but I don't know what he did." When they search their place, they find that he's left nothing and has succeeded in getting away with what he's taken. At this, they bite their fingertips in grief, for he's escaped and there is nothing they can do about it. 4.38

To sum up, such things are well known in Darfur and not forbidden. I asked my teacher, Faqīh Madanī al-Fūtāwī, the brother of Faqīh Mālik of whom we spoke earlier, and he told me that the books of revelation sent down to Ādam, Shīth, Ibrāhīm, and other prophets were buried in the ground; God then made these plants grow where the books were buried, their seeds were scattered by the blowing of the winds over the land so that the plants became common and widespread, and by trial and error people learned to take advantage of their special properties. I say it's all a form of magic. 4.39

Another type is the kind that uses writings and charms to invoke the upper and lower angels. This kind of magic produces many 4.40

extraordinary things. Trusted sources in Darfur informed me that at the battle between the Successor and Sultan ʿAbd al-Raḥmān, the Successor had a number of men firing muskets, and the sultan's side put a spell on them so that the powder would spill out of the musket as though wet, making no sound, while the sultan's muskets, on the contrary, made lots of noise and did a great deal of damage.[519]

4.41 Similarly, when Sultan ʿAbd al-Raḥmān died and his son Sultan Muḥammad Faḍl assumed his place, the sons of the sultans, such as those of Sultan Tayrāb, Sultan Abū l-Qāsim, the Successor, and Sultan ʿUmar, refused to accept him and rebelled. They mounted their horses, rode out to the villages, and gathered a mighty army. Shaykh-Father Muḥammad Kurrā was afraid that harm might befall the country, so he summoned Faqīh Mālik al-Fūtāwī and told him of his fears regarding the havoc that might ensue. But Faqīh Mālik assured him that he would bring the sons to his feet in humiliation. Shaykh-Father Muḥammad Kurrā then dispatched an army under the command of Malik Muḥammad Daldan, nephew of Sultan Muḥammad Faḍl, and Faqīh Mālik accompanied it. He worked his magic when the sons of the sultans were about two days' march from the sultan's capital. That evening, after he'd cast his spell on them, they mounted their horses, fearing that Malik Muḥammad Daldan might attack them with his army and seeking to put distance between them. However, they lost their way and spent the night moving in the direction of the capital, with Malik Daldan in pursuit. When morning came and they found themselves close to the capital, they regretted they'd ever set off. Shaykh-Father Muḥammad Kurrā heard they were there and sent an army against them. When it arrived, the army of Malik Muḥammad Daldan closed in on them because he was right behind them. Finding themselves between the two armies, the people who'd rallied to the sons of the sultans lost their resolve, and the sons were left with a small band. Malik Muḥammad Daldan then arrested them and took them to Shaykh-Father Muḥammad Kurrā, who commanded they be sent to prison, thereby ridding himself of their evil doings. This was due to magic:

without it they would have run rampant, ravaging Darfur, and the damage would have been beyond repair.[520]

The magic specialists in Darfur are the Fullān. I met one of them, a man called Faqīh Tamurrū—spelled *a* after *T*, *u* after *m*, double *r*, and *ū* at the end—of whom remarkable things were said. People there so often stated these things and affirmed their truth that they turned into one of those things that can't be denied simply because the number of those reporting them is too great for them to be colluding in a lie. For example, a holy man of Darfur whom I trusted told me that once he went with the aforementioned Faqīh Tamurrū from Jadīd Karyū to the sultan's capital and then back again with him to Jadīd Karyū. "When we were on the road," he said, "we found the heat of the sun unbearable. Faqīh Tamurrū was riding a camel, and he took his cloak, unfolded and refolded it, held it between his hands, recited over it certain names, and then tossed it into the air. It spread out above his head like a patch of shade," and shaded him and his friend from the heat of the sun as though it were being held by a man at each end; it followed them like a sunshade wherever they went. This is one of the strangest and most remarkable things one could hope to hear. In another example, the two of them were proceeding on the same journey when it rained on them. Faqīh Tamurrū told a servant who was with them, "Get me a handful of soil." When the man handed him the handful of soil, he took it in his hand, recited a few words over it, and sprinkled the earth over his head—the clouds moved aside and the rain started falling to their right, while they proceeded in the dry, without a drop falling on them. I've been told that once the Masālīṭ fought with the Fullān and defeated them and were tracking them as they retreated, intending to exterminate them. The Fullān worked a little magic and bewitched the eyes of the Masālīṭ, with the result that they saw the tracks of those retreating back to front, as though they were the tracks of people coming toward them. 4.42

I was told by my teacher, Shaykh Madanī al-Fūtāwī, may clouds of mercy hover over him, that the king of Barnaw had a scribe of 4.43

great accomplishment, who was God-fearing and righteous in the extreme. The chief vizier went to him and said, "Our monarch commands you to write a letter to so-and-so containing the following." The scribe, however, refused, responding, "I write only when the sultan himself tells me to do so, or sends me some token to show that his messenger is telling the truth." The vizier went to the sultan and told him what the scribe had said, so the sultan summoned the man and said to him, "I hereby grant you permission to the effect that, whenever this vizier of mine tells you, 'Write such and such!' in my name, you may do so."

4.44 Now, the seal with which royal commands were sealed was in the keeping of the scribe in question, so he obeyed the sultan's command and started writing for the vizier whatever he wanted. Then one day the vizier came to him and said, "Our monarch commands you to write to Malik So-and-so that he should go to the tax collector so-and-so, kill him, impound his wealth, and send it, along with his head." The man wrote this but the sultan had no idea what was going on and was surprised to see the courtyard filled with treasures: slaves, cattle, camels, and flocks of sheep and goats, along with someone's head on the point of a spear. The sultan inquired and was told, "This is the head of so-and-so and these are his assets. He was killed at your command." The sultan denied this, summoned the scribe, and asked him, "Who ordered this man to be killed and his wealth impounded?" "You did," replied the scribe. "When?" he asked. The scribe said, "At such and such a time, so-and-so, your vizier, came to me and told me, 'Write to so-and-so, the *malik*, in such and such a place, that he should go to the tax collector so-and-so in such and such a place, cut off his head, send it on a spear, and send all his assets.'" "I never commanded you to do that," said the sultan, "so how could you, with all your intelligence and professionalism, write to him so without seeking my permission?" "God aid our master!" the man replied. "You summoned me on such and such a day and told me, 'Whenever this vizier of mine tells you, "Write to so-and-so" in my name, do so!' I have obeyed your command from that time on and gone ahead and written everything he ordered me to."

The sultan now grew angry and said, "I never ordered you to write whatever he asked on a matter as important as this! I commanded you to write what he asked in matters of no danger to the state. Do you imagine that things of this sort can happen without my permission?" And the scribe replied, "Our master made no exceptions when he commanded me to obey the vizier." The sultan grew angrier still and ordered that the scribe be seized, but no one could lay a hand on him, for every time someone stretched out a hand to seize him, it would go stiff, its owner unable to bend it, and it would be like a piece of wood. When the sultan saw this, he said to him, "Release these men!" but the scribe said, "I will release them only when the sultan releases me from his service." The sultan released the scribe from his service, and the scribe released the men in turn, and their hands relaxed and became as they had been. This demonstrates the truth of words of the Prophet, may God bless him and grant him peace, when he said, "All things fear the one who fears God, and he who has no fear of God, God will cause to fear all things." 4.45

Also to be numbered among such wonders is the story told by the people of Darfur to the effect that there are two tribes subject to the Fur, one called the Masālīṭ, the other the Tomorókkóngá,[521] who assume the shapes of animals. The best-known version of the story, though, is that the Masālīṭ take the shapes of hyenas, cats, and dogs, while the Tomorókkóngá take the form of lions only. Even more remarkably, they say that after three days a man of this tribe who dies will rise from his grave, go to another village, marry there, and live on for a time. The Darfurians commonly say that the sultan has a group of men from this tribe whom he sends on his personal business and that they have a *malik* who rules them. They even go so far as to say of this group that they can assume any shape and that if one of them finds himself in a tight spot and is afraid he'll be captured, he turns into wind. 4.46

4.47 I was there when the man in charge of this group, who was called ʿAlī Kartab, was still alive. He was old and feeble, a poor soldier in whom it was almost impossible to detect any sign of wealth. Then he died, and his son took his place. He was a well-built young man, hideous to look at but giving every sign of being well-off. He rode the best-bred horses and had servants and pomp. He and I became friends and I went to his house several times. His name was ʿAbd Allāh Kartab, and I happened once to find myself alone with him, so I asked him about what people said about his assuming different shapes, and that he could travel a ten-day journey in an instant. He distracted me with talk of other things and gave me no information, so I didn't pursue the matter on that occasion. Then, on another occasion, I asked him again and he smiled and said, "Goodness gracious, I never thought you'd believe such talk!" Then he distracted me with talk of other things, till I left his house. After this, he denied knowing me and took to walking past me without turning to look in my direction, so I too left him alone once I saw how he snubbed me. I can think of no reason for it except that I'd questioned him repeatedly about this business.

4.48 Once I traveled in a slaving party with a petty king named ʿAbd al-Karīm ibn Khamīs ʿArmān. His father had been one of the sultan's greatest viziers but the sultan had turned against him and held him in prison till he died. His son became a servant of the state and was eventually sent to raid the Fartīt. He owed me a debt, so I went with him to get it out of him.[522] We had penetrated three months deep into Fartīt country and were in a place where no pulses or vegetables were to be found. One day he invited me to eat with him, so I went into his house and found green onions and cucumbers, each as fresh as if they had been pulled that minute from their bed. I asked about them and where they'd come from and he said, "Darfur." I asked him who'd brought them to him and how they'd stayed fresh in spite of the distance, especially the cucumbers, which were as juicy as could be. He said, "They were brought in the shortest possible time. Look at the date on this letter." So I took the letter and looked at it and found it was from a friend of his in Darfur, and that the date was the morning of that very day. I was astounded and showed my amazement that such a thing could be, and when he saw how surprised I was he said, "Don't be surprised. There's a party of Tomorókkóngá with us and they have the ability to change their shapes and go to the farthest place in the shortest time." I said, "I'd like you to show me some of them," and he said, "And so I will."

When we'd assembled our caravan and reached Darfur, we spent the night on the outskirts of a Tomorókkóngá village whose name I've forgotten. In the morning, crowds of people came to salute the *malik*, with whom I was sitting. He welcomed them, provided them with hospitality, and gave their leaders handsome robes, which pleased them greatly. When we wanted to depart, their chief said, "We advise you, if you see any lions on your way, to do them no harm, as any lions you may see in this neighborhood are from our village." "In that case," said the *malik*, "we'd like to hear from some of your friends right now." "To hear is to obey," said the chief, and he picked out three individuals by name, who rose and went off into the open country. A short while after they'd disappeared from sight, we heard a mighty lion's roar that struck terror into our hearts and panicked the riding animals. "That," they said, "is the voice of so-and-so." Then that lion stopped, and another lion close to the first roared three times. "That," they said, "is so-and-so." That stopped, and after it a roar was heard that was so much mightier than the first two that our hearts almost leaped from our breasts on hearing it. "That," they said, "is the voice of so-and-so," and they named him and sang his praises. A little later the men came back, in their human form, and kissed the *malik*'s hand. He was delighted with them, offered them food, and gave them fine robes to wear, and we bade them goodbye and went on our way. At this point the king told me, "Those are the people who brought us the onions and cucumbers when we were on the far side of Dār Fartīt." 4.49

To these wonders may be added the pronouncements of geomancers when they perform their operations, for they speak of 4.50

events that have happened to a person of which no one but God Almighty knows anything and report things as though they were occurring before their very eyes. One of the things that has made me believe in what they say is that, when I wanted to leave Darfur and go to Dar Wāddāy, there was in the town where I was a man called Sālim. He had an in-law in another town called Isḥāq who was skilled at geomancy. I was depressed because my travel arrangements weren't going well, so Sālim asked me, "Would you like to go with me to see my in-law Isḥāq, and have him cast the sand for you and tell you what he sees?" I accompanied him to the in-law's town, which we entered late in the morning, only to find that he wasn't there but working his farm. We waited until he returned, when he welcomed us as honored guests and brought us an excellent lunch. Then Sālim told him, "The sharif has come to ask you to divine for him." "To hear is to obey," said the man, and he performed his divination and told me things for which I called him a liar but which, I swear, came to pass—as though he'd been reading from the Preserved Tablet: not one word he said turned out to be untrue. Among the things he told me was, "You will soon go to Dār Wāddāy with all your family except your stepmother, who will not go with you." I called him a liar and said, "How can she not go when she's the one who most needs to?" but God made his words turn out true, and she didn't go with us: she played a trick, staying with us up to the last night before our departure, then running away, leaving her daughter who was seven years old. When we woke, we looked for her but could find no trace of her, so we left without knowing what had happened to her. Likewise, he told me, "On the night of your arrival at your father's house, they will bring you a slave girl with the following characteristics," and it turned out as he'd said. Also, he told me, "You will not meet up with your father in Dār Wādday," and so it was; I only met up with him in Tunis. He also told me, "The walls of your father's house are red, as though plastered with *mughrah*," which is a type of stone, red in color and crumbly, that they crush until smooth and use to plaster houses; they make red ink from it too, mixing it with water and gum. And he told me, "Your son will ride a gray horse there," and it came to pass, and "the sultan will bestow slave women and other things on you," and it was as he said.

One of the most remarkable things that occurred when we were at his house was that some quarreling women came to him and asked him to divine in order for them to discover the whereabouts of some property that had gone missing, and so determine which of them had taken it. He performed his divination and said, "You've lost some red beads strung on a thread, and they're hidden in the entryway to so-and-so's house." Then one of the women got up and fetched the beads from the entryway of the house in question, as he had said, but he did not say which of them had taken them. He was extremely knowledgeable about geomancy. 4.51

My uncle, Sayyid Aḥmad Zarrūq, told me something similar, to wit that when my father, clouds of mercy and favor hover above him, accompanied Sultan Muḥammad Ṣābūn on his campaign against Jabal Tāmah, he lost a nine-year-old camel and sent out slaves and servants to search for it. They left, were gone a long time, and in the end returned emptyhanded, so my late father gave up on it. One of his companions was a man who knew how to divine using geomancy. One of those present said to him, "You're a geomancer. If you know, show us whether the camel will return or not." The man performed his divinations and said, "The camel is right here, nearby. Go look for it among your neighbors' camels." They found the camel kneeling in the midst of the herd, identified it, and brought it to him. This represents the acme of perfection in the science of geomancy. 4.52

Similarly, a sharif in Wāddāy told me that a group of religious scholars were gathered somewhere, one of whom had an expert knowledge of geomancy while another claimed the same but falsely. They were swapping tales of their experiences with that science, and the one who merely pretended to have that knowledge said, "I divined for Malik So-and-so and army commander so-and-so and gave them information about such and such." One of the company 4.53

asked him to divine for them, which he did, saying things that made no sense. Then the man who really knew turned to the shapes that had been formed and contemplated them. Eventually he said, "I have good news for you. Tomorrow you will receive sixty head of slaves from the sultan," and it was as he said.

4.54 As our talk has turned to geomancy, let me set out an epitome that will allow the observer to contemplate its nature, forms, and names, along with its patterns, be they auspicious, inauspicious, or neutral. Its patterns are sixteen in number, of which the first is "the Road," which looks like this:  This is excellent for one who intends to travel, even better for one who is asking about the arrival of one who is absent, and bad for one who is sick, in which case it indicates the road to the grave.

4.55 The second is "the Group," which looks like this:  This is an auspicious shape, except for a sick person, in which case it indicates people gathering at his funeral.

4.56 The third is "the Jawbone," which looks like this:  This pattern is auspicious in all cases.

4.57 The fourth is "the Upside Down," which looks like this:  This pattern is inauspicious in all cases except that of a pregnant woman, when it means she will give birth to a male.

4.58 The fifth is "the Gathering," which looks like this:  This pattern is auspicious for all activities, except the collection of money.

4.59 The sixth is "the Knot," which looks like this: 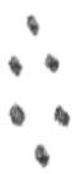 This is an inauspicious pattern unless the question posed concerns a pregnant woman.

4.60 The seventh is "the Incoming Threshold," which looks like this:  This is an auspicious pattern in all cases. If one is sad and has this as the first or second pattern in his series, his sadness will vanish; if one is waiting for someone to come, he will come quickly; and if one is in hard straits, his difficulties will disappear.

The eighth is "the Outgoing Threshold," which looks like this: 4.61

This is an inauspicious pattern indicating the death of one who is sick, postponement of the fulfillment of a need, disruption of one's affairs, or the divorce of a wife.

The ninth is "the Incoming Fist," which looks like this: 4.62

This is a mixed pattern that indicates collection of money and victory over one's enemy, but also death of a sick person and imprisonment of someone wanted by the authorities.

The tenth is "the Outgoing Fist," which looks like this: 4.63

This indicates the failure to return of what has previously left the hand, the disappearance of a runaway slave, and the flight of slaves, but it may also indicate release from imprisonment, travel, and removal from one place to another.

The eleventh is "Whiteness," which looks like this: 4.64

This is a good pattern in all cases except for a sick person, in which case it indicates a shroud.

The twelfth is "Redness," which looks like this: 4.65

This is a sign of the spilling of blood and, for a sick person, the grave, but it is auspicious for a pregnant woman as she will give birth to a male; it is also a sign of red garments, just as "whiteness" is a sign of white garments.

The thirteenth is "the Bed," which looks like this: 4.66

This is an auspicious pattern that points to joy and happiness, that a pregnant woman will give birth to a female, and that things will turn out in the best possible way.

The fourteenth is "Pure of Cheek," and looks like this: 4.67

This is an inauspicious pattern that is a sign of young men, unknown enemies, long imprisonment, and an invalid giving up the ghost.

The fifteenth is "Incoming Support," and looks like this: 4.68

This is an auspicious pattern that is a sign of support from God, victory, fulfillment of a need, and an end to suffering for the sick, the imprisoned, and the pregnant.

4.69 The sixteenth is “Outgoing Support,” and looks like this:  This pattern is a sign of benign matters, except where battling one’s enemy is concerned, when it is a sign of the defeat of armies and failure to achieve victory.

4.70 If someone wants to “cast the sand” in the manner described above, he fetches clean sand free of rocks and spreads it on the ground. Then, using his middle finger, he makes four rows of holes in the sand without counting the number of holes in each row and going from left to right, so that it looks like this:  Then he moves his finger along the row, going from each pair to the next, erasing every second hole until he gets to the end of the row. If the last hole is the second of a pair, he leaves it in place, and, likewise, if a single hole, he leaves it in place. Then he writes down first the total number of holes resulting from the application of this procedure to the first row, and below it the result for the second row. He continues doing this until all four rows have been so treated. From this procedure one or other of the sixteen preceding patterns will result. If he cannot find sand, he may cast the line using beans or chickpeas. He does this by taking a fistful without counting, dropping the beans or chickpeas, and moving through them two by two, leaving the last in place, whether it be a single bean or the second of a pair, as described above.[523]

4.71 As to the means of generating the different patterns and their interconnections, the names, letters, planets, and outcomes, and the outcomes of outcomes that are associated with each, these all depend on the books written on the science of geomancy, so we will not speak of them at greater length. We have provided this brief epitome so that any who peruses this travel narrative of ours may be well informed as to the nature of geomancy as a whole, and so that the work not be devoid of this useful information, though God knows best.

Colophon

This beautiful, elegant, weighty copy was printed as a lithograph at the deluxe printing house of Monsieur Kaeplin, in the dazzling city of Paris, using, through God's grace and boon, the hand and penmanship of Monsieur Perron. Production was completed—at his expense, under his supervision, and as a result of his zeal—at the end of the month of November of the year 1850 of the Christian era. Thanks are due to God at commencement and completion, and we beseech Him to grant us His most perfect benediction. 5.1

Amen.

Notes

1 Q Quraysh 106:2; the reference is to the two yearly trading caravans that set off from Mecca in the days before Islam, one in the winter, to Yemen; the other in the summer, which went first to Tābūk, then bifurcated, part going to Buṣrā (then a Ghassanid capital of Provincia Arabia, today a provincial center in southern Syria) and part to Gaza. The reference—like the others in this preamble—serves to introduce the theme of "journeying," signaling that the author viewed this as the work's dominant motif.

2 The Prophet Muḥammad is said to have traveled with trading caravans to Buṣrā as a youth, first with his uncle Abū Ṭālib, later on behalf of his first wife, Khadījah.

3 Q An'ām 6:11.

4 A *sayyid* is a "descendant of the Prophet Muḥammad." The placement of al-Tūnisī ("of Tunis") in the middle rather than at the end of the name allows the author to rhyme *al-mannān* ("most gracious") with *Sulaymān*.

5 The author begins his life story in the middle: the period to which he refers was that between his return to Tunis in 1813 after his sojourn in Darfur and Wadai and his subsequent move to Egypt and entry (probably in or shortly after 1823) into the service of its ruler, Muḥammad 'Alī (r. 1805–48; d. 1849). His account of his birth and early years is to be found in the Prolegomenon, Chapter 1 below.

6 Literally "the banner is knotted for . . . ," an idiom meaning that the subject is offered a position of leadership, or promoted.

7 Attributed to Imam Muḥammad ibn Idrīs al-Shāfiʿī (150–204/767–820).

8 A proverb: "appearances may be deceptive" (see al-Maydānī, *Majmaʿ al-amthāl*, 2:156).

9 Attributed to Imam Muḥammad ibn Idrīs al-Shāfiʿī.

10 Meaning, presumably, getting flogged.

11 I.e., Muḥammad ʿAlī, viceroy of Egypt. The verses are presumably the author's.

12 As a vassal of the Ottoman sultan, Muḥammad ʿAlī sent troops to the Hejaz in a campaign lasting from 1811 to 1818 and recovered Mecca and Medina from the forces of the first Saudi state.

13 Muḥammad ʿAlī's eldest son, Ibrāhīm Pasha, took Syria and Lebanon from the Ottomans and occupied them from 1831 to 1840.

14 Egyptian intervention in the Morea, intended to suppress Greek resistance to Ottoman rule, began in 1823 and ended in 1828.

15 Egypt's first modern medical school opened at Abū Zaʿbal, northeast of Cairo, in 1827 (Heyworth-Dunne, *History of Education*, 125).

16 On Nicolas Perron and his role in the creation of this text, see Introduction, pp. xxxiii–xxxiv.

17 A pedagogical poem by Muḥammad ibn al-Ḥasan ibn Durayd (222–312/838–933).

18 Earlier editors have identified the final chapter of the lithographic edition with this conclusion (al-Tūnisī, *Tashḥīdh*, 1965, 303, n. 1). However, that chapter does not bear this title and the abruptness with which the text ends may indicate that the author never in fact wrote a conclusion. In this edition, the final chapter is treated as such (as the Book Proper, chapter 4).

19 The line is from a longer poem by Abū l-Ṭayyib al-Mutanabbī (see *al-ʿArf al-ṭayyib fī sharḥ dīwān Abī l-Ṭayyib*, 96).

20 I.e., Muḥammad III ibn ʿAbd Allāh (r. 1171–1204/1757–90), of the Alawite dynasty.

21 Pilgrims often took, and still take, the opportunity to engage in trade offered by the presence of large numbers of people from all over the Islamic world.

22 Meaning the clamor of voices exclaiming, "We have obeyed your call, O God, we have obeyed your call" and the sacrifice of sheep, both activities to which pilgrims are bidden.

23 I.e., *hādhī* ("this") preceding *al-Kuthub* is a variant of *hādhihi.*

24 The Beloved is the Prophet Muḥammad; his two companions are the caliphs Abū Bakr al-Ṣiddīq (r. 11–13/632–34) and ʿUmar ibn al-Khaṭṭāb (r. 13–23/634–44), who are buried next to him.

25 Attributed, with variants, to Imam Muḥammad ibn Idrīs al-Shāfiʿī.

26 Attributed, with variants, to Imam Muḥammad ibn Idrīs al-Shāfiʿī.

27 Q Baqarah 2:261.

28 The verses are from al-Ḥarīrī's *Maqāmah on a Gold Piece* (*al-Maqāmah al-dīnāriyyah*), the third of his fifty *maqāmah*s (see al-Ḥarīrī, *Maqāmāt al-Ḥarīrī*, 19–25).

29 Al-Ḥarīrī puns on the similarity between the words *badr* (literally "full moon")—a conventional term for a beautiful girl or boy—and *badrah* ("a purse," i.e., ten thousand dirhams).

30 By other accounts, Ḥusayn Pasha was ʿAlī's uncle (al-Sharīf al-Hādī, *Tārīkh Tūnis*, 84).

31 ʿAlī invaded Tunis in 1735; according to other accounts, however, Ḥusayn was not killed in 1735, but fled to Qayrawān in central Tunisia and was finally defeated and decapitated in 1740 (al-Sharīf al-Hādī, *Tārīkh Tūnis*, 84).

32 The *qawwāṣ* (more correctly spelled *qawwās* and meaning "archer") was an armed escort who provided protection to and cleared the way on the street for important persons and Europeans, and was known to the latter as a "kavass."

33 I.e., Muḥammad ʿAlī; in fact, it was Khusraw Pasha, viceroy from 1802 to 1803, who failed to pay the Albanian irregular forces in Egypt their wages, thus triggering the series of events that led in 1805 to the assumption of power by their commander, Muḥammad ʿAlī. Khūrshīd Pasha (1804–5) was the viceroy who replaced Khusraw and stepped down in Muḥammad ʿAlī's favor.

34 Unidentified; according to Umar ("Travels," 54, n. 4), the title al-Amīr al-Kabīr ("the Great Prince") indicates that this person was the

head of the syndicate of descendants of the Prophet. By "our shaykh of shaykhs" the author probably means "the greatest teacher of our day."

35 "regency": Arabic *al-ʿamal*, which, in grammatical parlance, means the "regency" exercised by one word over the form of another (as when a preposition requires that the noun it governs be in the genitive case), but in nontechnical terms means "employment, work," with here the connotation of "work as a *ʿāmil*," i.e., a political agent. In contrast, the negative particle *mā* does not change the form of the word that follows it.

36 An error for Maḥmūd (ibn Bakkār) al-Jallūlī (Ibn Abī l-Ḍiyāf, *Itḥāf ahl al-zamān bi-akhbār mulūk Tūnis wa-ʿahd al-amān*, 3:23); al-Jallūlī's son Muḥammad features below.

37 This incident took place on Jumada al-Thani 16, 1206/February 10, 1792 (Ibn Abī l-Ḍiyāf, *Itḥāf*, 3:20).

38 On this idiom, see n. 6.

39 I.e., he became the cynosure of all eyes.

40 The battle took place on July 13, 1807 (see Ibn Abī l-Ḍiyāf, *Itḥāf*, 3:47, where the name of the site of the battle is given as Salāṭah).

41 The author confuses al-Ḥājj Abī l-Ḍiyāf (d. 1838), chief secretary to Yūsuf the Seal Bearer and the person intended here, with his son Aḥmad ibn Abī l-Ḍiyāf (1217/1802–3 to 1291/1874), who wrote a history of the Tunisian state entitled *Itḥāf ahl al-zamān bi-akhbār mulūk Tūnis wa-ʿahd al-amān* (*A Presentation of the History of the Kings of Tunis and the Covenant of Security to the People of the Age*); see Ibn Abī l-Ḍiyāf, *Itḥāf*, 3:96.

42 According to Ibn Abī l-Ḍiyāf, that year was not the date of the death of Ḥammūdah's father, ʿAlī Pasha II, but the one in which he designated his son as his heir (*Itḥāf*, 3:11). Ḥammūdah's actual rule began with his father's death in 1196/1782.

43 Following an invasion by the forces of the Ottoman provincial authorities of Algiers in 1756, Tunis had become a vassal of the latter. In 1807, Ḥammūdah Pasha rebuilt the walls of the citadel of al-Kāf (Le Kef), just east of the border with Algeria, which had been destroyed

by the Algerians, and reestablished the independence of Ḥusaynid Tunis (see al-Sharīf, *Tārīkh Tūnis*, 86, 90).

44 The mosque—Masjid Ṣāḥib al-Ṭābiʿ—was built between 1808 and 1814 and survives.

45 Chronograms are poems in which certain words may be read both as words and as dates, using the system known as *ḥisāb al-jummal* (see n. 47); they are a common feature of congratulatory poetry from the ninth/fifteenth century onward.

46 "Yūsuf, counselor of Him Who Is Most Content with God's Favors" (*Yūsufu khōjatu l-raḍiy*): a play on the seal bearer's name plus the title *Khōjah*, a Turkish-Persian loanword, meaning, in origin, "teacher," afforded persons of substance of foreign origin and used of Yūsuf below (§2.1.25); *al-raḍī* refers to Ḥammūdah Pasha, as does *al-bahī* in the following hemistich.

47 Under a system known as *ḥisāb al-jummal* (see *EI2*, art. "Ḥisāb al-d̲j̲ummal"), letters of the alphabet are assigned numerical values and the letters grouped for mnemonic purposes into clusters forming pseudo-words. In the western (i.e., Maghrebi) system, these mnemonics are *ayqash-bakar-jalas-damat-hanath-waṣakh-zaʿadh-ḥafaḍ-ṭaghaẓ*, where ا = 1, ي = 10, ق = 100, ش = 1,000 (for remaining *ayqash* values, see al-Tūnisī, *Tashḥīdh*, 1965, 26, n. 1). Here, بشربه ("on drinking of it") provides the following numerical values: ب = 2 + ش = 1,000 + ر = 200 + ب = 2 + ه = 5, i.e., 1209 (= AD 1794–95).

48 Both the structure and the building remain unidentified; the area in which the fountain was located was cleared in a series of demolitions that started in the 1920s and continued until the 1950s, creating the present-day square in front of the shrine.

49 Or, punningly, "His way is inclined to good works, [that] Maḥmūd."

50 This and the following chronograms use, in contrast to the preceding, the eastern version of *ḥisāb al-jummal* (see n. 47), whose mnemonics are *abjad-hawwaz-ḥuṭṭī-kalaman-saʿfaṣ-qarshat-thakhadh-ḍaẓagh*, where the first ten letters in the sequence equal one through ten, the next nine indicate the decades, the next nine the hundreds, and *gh* equals one thousand.

51 I.e., from Ibrāhīm (Abraham), who is described in the Qur'an as the friend (*khalīl*) of God (see, e.g., Q Nisā' 4:125). Ibrāhīm is represented in the sanctuary surrounding the Kaaba ("the Sacred House" and "the House of God") by a small open-sided building (*maqām*) in which is kept a stone on which the patriarch is said to have stood while he supervised its construction, along with his son Ismāʿīl (Ishmael) (Q Baqarah 2:127).

52 Presumably, this stood next to the tomb of Shaykh al-ʿAfīfī, which survives, close to the later mausoleums of the khedivial royal family in the area of the tomb of Qāyitbāy in Cairo's Lesser Cemetery.

53 Al-Suhā (Alcor, or Ursa Major 80), from a root denoting "inattention, failure to notice" is a dim star that forms a pair with a brighter star called al-Mi'zar (the Waist Wrapper). The ability to distinguish al-Suhā from al-Mi'zar was considered proof of excellent eyesight. Thus, the author means that al-Maḥrūqī's glory was so bright that it was visible even at a vast distance.

54 Yūsuf died on Safar 12, 1230/January 23, 1815 (Ibn Abī l-Ḍiyāf, *Itḥāf*, 3:110).

55 Meaning "he after whom none more noble will come" and a punning allusion to his office of seal bearer.

56 *Bandar* is a Persian loanword that the author feels the need to explain (possibly to Perron, the copyist, rather than to his potential Egyptian readers, since the word is used in Egypt).

57 Sinnār is referred to as an island because it was embraced by the Blue and White Niles, in the cotton-producing region of modern Sudan still known as al-Jazīrah ("the Island").

58 Al-Quṣayr is on the coast of the Red Sea. Travelers would have taken a boat up the Nile to Qūṣ or Qinā in Upper Egypt and from there crossed the Eastern Desert to the port. It would have been while crossing the former that the author's father and grandfather crossed paths, as described below.

59 Attributed to the panegyricist Abū l-Fatḥ Maḥmūd ibn al-Ḥusayn al-Ramlī (ca. 360/970–71), of Mosul and then Aleppo, known as Kushājim.

60 Browne mentions that "I have observed that the people of our caravan, in such places as afforded stones for the purpose, used to collect four or five large ones, thus raising small heaps at proper distances from each other. This affords them some satisfaction at their return; but in many places, where the sand is loose and deep, it becomes impracticable.... Three times, in the course of our journey, the caravan was quite at a loss for the road, though some of the members of it had made ten or twelve journies to and from Dar-Fûr" (*Travels in Africa*, 248).

61 North Africans were famed for their curative talismans.

62 The Islamic day starts at sunset of the day before (according to Western reckoning) and is divided into two twelve-hour periods. "The third hour" of a Friday therefore refers to either the third hour after the sunset on the preceding Thursday, or to the third hour, i.e., sometime in the morning, of the Friday itself, which is probably what is meant here, as the author does not specify otherwise. The Friday closest to the fifteenth day of Dhū l-Qaʿdah (the eleventh month of the Islamic year) fell on the seventeenth of that month and was equivalent to July 30, 1790.

63 See n. 34.

64 Students resident at al-Azhar lived in halls or hostels (*riwāq*, pl. *arwiqah*) organized on sectarian and/or regional lines. There was no hall exclusively for Maghrebi *sayyid*s, so the author may not be using the term literally here.

65 The third surah of the Qur'an.

66 I.e., al-Ṭāhir was passing through Cairo on his way from Tunis to the Hejaz.

67 In 1212 H, the pilgrimage month (Dhū l-Hijjah, the last of the Islamic year) started on May 17, 1798.

68 France's three-year occupation of Egypt, led by Napoleon Bonaparte, began in July 1798.

69 A combined Ottoman-British force retook Egypt from the French in 1216/1801 and Ottoman rule through viceroys sent from Istanbul was

restored. Egyptians frequently referred to the viceroy as "the vizier" or minister, since many viceroys held that rank in the Ottoman hierarchy.

70 I.e., to Paradise.

71 The first and third lines of a poem by Kamāl al-Dīn Abū l-Ḥasan ʿAlī ibn Muḥammad ibn Nabīh (560/1164–65 to 619/1222–23).

72 Abū Tammām Ḥabīb ibn Aws al-Ṭāʾī (ca. 189–232/805–45) (cf. al-Ṣūlī, *The Life and Times of Abū Tammām*, 306/7).

73 The caravanserai was located in the Ṣanādīqiyyah quarter in the heart of Cairo and served as the main distribution point for all goods from Sudan (Walz, "Wakalat al-Gallaba: The Market for African Goods in Cairo" 263–86; Abū l-ʿAmāyim, *Āthār al-Qāhirah al-islāmiyyah fī l-ʿaṣr al-ʿUthmānī*, 3/2:237).

74 Al-Fusṭāṭ, the first capital of Islamic Egypt, close to today's Miṣr al-ʿAtīqah (Old Cairo), was the location of the customs office and all boats coming from the south had to stop there to be assessed and taxed, while all travelers for Upper Egypt embarked there.

75 I.e., our ship.

76 Q Hūd 11:40. The reference is to Noah's ark.

77 I.e., the antagonism between the black races (the "sons of Ḥām (Ham)") and the Semites (the "sons of Sām (Shem)").

78 See n. 2.

79 These verses appear, with differences, in the collected works of Muḥammad ibn Idrīs al-Shāfiʿī, where they are described as being of dubious attribution (al-Shāfiʿī, *Shiʿr*, 265).

80 These lines and those immediately following are from al-Ṭughrāʾī's *The Non-Arabs' Poem in Lām* (*Lāmiyyat al-ʿAjam*) (lines 33, 34, and (for the following) 3), written in conscious imitation of al-Shanfarā's celebrated *The Arabs' Poem in Lām* (*Lāmiyyat al-ʿArab*) and famous for its arcane vocabulary.

81 I.e., if the nobility bestowed by place were sufficient to ensure the satisfaction of aspirations, the sun would never leave the domain of Aries—the ram, a noble creature—said domain being the first month after the vernal equinox (March 21–April 20).

82 The words echo the well-known saying "I have no she-camel in the affair and no he-camel," i.e., "I have no stake in the matter."

83 The verses occur with many variants and are attributed to Imam Muḥammad ibn Idrīs al-Shāfiʿī.

84 Perhaps the "Azharī shaikh" and "Shaikh Muṣṭafā" mentioned by Heyworth-Dunne as being attached to the veterinary school at Abū Zaʿbal (Heyworth-Dunne, *History of Education*, 133–34).

85 The poem contains a series of clues to words meaning "ship." In all cases, in this and the poems that follow, it is the consonantal skeleton of the word that matters; the unwritten short vowels between the consonants are not counted and may be changed to fit the author's needs.

86 The literal meaning of *kassāb* is "acquirer," allowing the author to pun on Muṣṭafā Kassāb's name.

87 The author means *fulk* ("ship"); however, the same consonants, revoweled as *falik*, yield "one with large buttocks," while *falaka thadyuhā* means "her beasts rounded out," which explains the references to the heart being tormented. There is an additional clue in the fact that *qalb* ("heart") also means "inversion (of the order of the root consonants of a word)," while *k-l-f*, root consonants of *kalifa* ("is enamored"), if read backward, yield *f-l-k*, root consonants of *fulk* ("ship").

88 *Fulk* occurs twenty-five times in the Qur'an, the first occurrence being Q Baqarah 2:164. It is this that those such as the addressee "constantly recite," etc.

89 I.e., *jāriyah*, which means both "ship" and "girl" (or "slave girl").

90 The radicals are *j-r-y*, from which *jārin*, meaning "runner," may be derived; *muhadhdhib* is the active participle of *hadhdhaba* meaning "(of a man and other things) to move fast (*asraʿa*)" (al-Fīrūzābādī, *Qāmūs*, s.v. *h-dh-b*).

91 I.e., *markib*, which, when spelt without short vowels, appears identical to *murakkab*, the last word in the line, thus forming a visual pun.

92 I.e., is one meaning represented by several different words.

93 I.e., this poem, or the letter that contained it.

94 The characteristics that follow may be applied to either a ship or a girl (see n. 89).

95 I.e., the girl, in her clothes, struts, etc., while the ship, when it raises its sails, moves fast.

96 I.e., the ship, when its sails are lowered, does not move, while the girl, when stripped of her clothes, is paralyzed by embarrassment.

97 I.e., the ship carries large, heavy goods that no human could lift, while, when the girl becomes pregnant, she bears something no man can: the wonder of a fetus.

98 I.e., the ship moves forward on its hull while the girl, in her efforts to make her way in this world (*fī saʿyihā*), progresses by lying on her back.

99 In terms of the ship, the reference may be to the oars of a galleon being arranged so as to allow them to wallop the water; in terms of a girl, the meaning may be that she opens her legs wide (on either side of her body) to allow herself to be "walloped."

100 In the first hemistich, which refers to the ship, *hawā* does duty for *hawāʾ* ("wind"), while in the second, which refers to the girl, it is to be taken in the sense of "love."

101 Cf. Q Hūd 11:37–38.

102 Cf. Q Hūd 11:41.

103 If the consonants of *baḥr* are reversed, the resulting word may be realized as either *ruḥb* or *raḥab*, both meaning "an open-armed welcome."

104 Again, *baḥr* ("sea"), spelled backward, can yield *raḥuba* "to be spacious or roomy."

105 I.e., if you remove the first letter of بحر (*baḥr*, meaning "sea") you are left with حر (*ḥarr*, meaning "heat").

106 I.e., if its letters are read out of order, the words *ḥabr*, meaning "an eminent scholar," *ḥibr*, meaning "ink," and *ḥarb*, meaning "war," may be formed.

107 I.e., بحر (*baḥr*) becomes بر (*barr*), meaning "dry land."

108 I.e., its wick.

109 The first two letters of *miṣbāḥ*, namely, *m* and *ṣ*, may be read on their own as *maṣṣ*, meaning "sucking," associated in Arabic poetry with saliva.

110 The remaining letters are *bāḥ*, which may be read as *bāḥa*, meaning "to divulge a secret."

111 If you remove the first consonant of *miṣbāḥ*, the remaining letters read *ṣabāḥ*, meaning "morning."

112 Q Nūr 24:35 *Allāhu nūru l-samāwāti wa-l-arḍi mathalu nūrihi ka-mishkātin fīhā miṣbāhun al-miṣbāhu fī zujājatin* . . . («God is the light of the heavens and the earth; the likeness of His Light is as a niche wherein is a lamp (the lamp in a glass . . .)» (Arberry, *The Koran Interpreted*, 356–57).

113 I.e., stars.

114 E.g., Q Baqarah 2:19 and frequently elsewhere.

115 If the first and last letters of *mudām* are dropped, one is left with *dā*, equal for these purposes to *dā'*, meaning "disease."

116 If the last letter of *mudām* is dropped, one is left with *mudā*, which is the plural of *mudyah*, meaning "knife."

117 Or, punningly, and referring to *mudām* rather than *mudyah*: "It entails the *ḥadd* penalty [meaning that the drinking of wine is an offence the penalty for which is specified in the Qur'an]—such is [the] incisiveness of the law."

118 If the first letter of *mudām* is dropped, one is left with *dām(a)*, meaning "to last."

119 Meaning that these members of the former Mamluk military elite had turned into defectors and freebooters taking advantage of the chaos that reigned in Egypt, and especially Upper Egypt, between the departure of the French in 1801 and the seizure of power by Muḥammad ʿAlī in 1805.

120 Manfalūṭ was safer than al-Minyā, not being controlled by rebellious Mamluks.

121 The author's memory apparently betrayed him: Abīrīs (today called Bārīs) is farther from al-Khārijah than Būlāq.

122 Browne writes, "This is a wretchedly poor place, the houses being only small square pieces of ground inclosed with a wall of clay, or unburned bricks, and generally without a roof. It furnishes good

water, and the people live by the sale of their dates" (Browne, *Travels in Africa*, 186).

123 According to ancient Arabian legend, Luqmān the Long-lived, a pre-Islamic figure to whom wise sayings are attributed, was granted as a reward for his piety a life as long as that of seven named vultures (the vulture being a popular symbol of longevity among the Arabs). The last vulture was named Lubad; when Lubad died, so did Luqmān.

124 *Shabb* means "alum"; the French translation glosses the name as ʿAyn al-Shabb, or "the Alum Spring" (El-Tounsy, *Voyage au Darfour*, 30, n. 1).

125 Browne reports further of Salīmah that "the jelabs [traders] related many fables concerning it; as that it had of old been inhabited by a princess who, like the Amazons, drew the bow, and wielded the battle-axe, with her own hand; that she was attended by a large number of followers, who spread terror all over Nubia, &c.; and that her name was Selimé" (*Travels in Africa*, 187).

126 According to Browne, the natron mined in the vicinity was exported to Egypt, where it was mostly used in the manufacture of snuff and fetched a high price (*Travels in Africa*, 186–87).

127 On this seal, see O'Fahey and Abu Salim, *Land in Darfur*, 28–29.

128 "loved scholarship and . . . hated ignorance": i.e., promoted Islam and combated paganism.

129 See Prolegomenon, Chapter 3.

130 Bīr al-Zaghāwī . . . Bīr al-Malḥah: al-Zaghāwī's Well . . . Salt Flat Well.

131 Most of the remaining fifty-six would have been loaded with trade goods.

132 Horses from Dongola, on the Nile in Nubia, were prized because of their large size compared to the native Darfurian breed; armored, they were used there as heavy cavalry (see O'Fahey, *Darfur Sultanate*, 196–98).

133 "Sweini is the general resort of the merchants trading to Egypt, both in going and returning, and thence derives its chief importance" (Browne, *Travels in Africa*, 237).

134 The delay may have been due to the fact that, at al-Suwaynah, "all strangers, as well as merchants of the country, coming with the caravan, are obliged to wait, till the pleasure of the monarch in disposing of them be known" (Browne, *Travels in Africa*, 189).

135 Jadīd al-Sayl (literally "the new place by the seasonal watercourse"): the term *jadīd* ("new (place)"), as here and in Jadīd Karyū, occurs frequently in western Sudan, reflecting the impermanence of human settlement.

136 Aḥmad Zarrūq was probably the son of the author's grandfather Sulaymān by the Ethiopian woman whom he married in Sinnār.

137 I.e., the Prophet Muḥammad, ʿAdnān being his ancestor in the twentieth degree.

138 Slaves were measured in handspans from their heels to their earlobes (see §3.3.44); a *sudāsī* ("sixer") measured six spans. A slave taller than seven spans was considered to be an adult and fetched a lower price (El-Tounsy, *Voyage au Darfour*, 39, n. 1). Thus the slaves mentioned here would have been young boys, as confirmed by Browne, who speaks of "a male slave, *sedasé*, about twelve to fourteen years of age" (*Travels in Africa*, 308).

139 Cf. Q Naml 27:17 «And there were gathered unto Solomon his armies of the jinn and humankind, and of the birds, and they were set in battle order.»

140 "Nature's tongue" (*lisān al-ḥāl*) is the faculty by which nonhuman and even inanimate actors are supposed to express themselves. Sulaymān (Solomon) is supposed to have been able to understand the speech of animals.

141 Meaning his "honorary uncle," his father's friend Sayyid Aḥmad Badawī.

142 Q Ḥujurāt 49:6.

143 Meaning here Darfurian Arabic.

144 Browne describes Kabkābiyyah as "the key to the Western roads [i.e., the western trade routes], as Sweini [al-Suwaynah] of the Northern" (*Travels in Africa*, 238).

145 Cf. §3.1.10 and following sections.

146 "the Sultanic Portals" (*al-aʿtāb al-sulṭāniyyah*): the name, while appropriate enough to a palace whose doorways had ceremonial importance (see §3.1.77), also evokes "the Sublime Porte" (*al-Bāb al-ʿĀlī*), as the palace of the Ottoman sultan in Istanbul was commonly known. Another Ottoman honorific appropriated by the sultans of Darfur was "Khāqān" (see §3.1.17).

147 Thus the author first met Shaykh-Father Muḥammad Kurrā in 1803, i.e., during the period between 1800 and 1804 when, as regent of Sultan Muḥammad Faḍl (whom he had been instrumental in installing), he was at the height of his powers and exercised nearly complete ascendancy over the sultanate. During this time, according to Nachtigal, he was honored as though he were the sultan and "the people fell back at a distance from his path, and squatted on one side, brushing the ground with the palms of their hands" (*Sahara and Sudan*, 299; see also O'Fahey, *Darfur Sultanate*, 61).

148 On this person, a close associate of Sultan ʿAbd al-Raḥmān, who raised him to high status and gave him great wealth, and on the prominent family of holy men, the Awlād ʿAlī, to which he belonged, see O'Fahey, *Darfur Sultanate*, 63 and, especially, O'Fahey, "The Awlad ʿAli."

149 Though the author describes Mālik al-Fūtāwī as his father's agent, from the latter's perspective he would have been his father's sponsor at court.

150 It may seem strange that the author identifies Mālik al-Fūtāwī as being of Arab descent almost in the same breath with which he states that he belonged to the Fullān (Fallātā), who are largely non-Arabic-speaking tribes originating in the western Sahel; however, the Fullān do indeed claim descent from ʿUqbah ibn Nāfiʿ (d. 63/683), conqueror of North Africa and a member of the Prophet's tribe of Quraysh.

151 Various sources attribute various origins to Muḥammad Kurrā (see O'Fahey, *Darfur Sultanate*, 66, n. 7).

152 See §§2.2.48–64 and §§2.3.1–39.

153 According to O'Fahey, the word is of uncertain origin and applied originally to the area in front of the sultan's compound where he gave

audience (*Darfur Sultanate*, 308). O'Fahey describes the *fāshir* as "an enormous complex of buildings and courtyards housing the sultan, his family and *harim*, stores of food, weapons and trade goods and a host of palace officials and their retinues; at a reasonable guess its personnel cannot have numbered much under three to four thousand" ("Slavery and the Slave Trade in Dar Fur," 88).

154 Nachtigal describes the cashmere shawl as "the principal ornament of the inhabitants of Darfur" (*Sahara and Sudan*, 248).

155 I.e., descendant of the Prophet Muḥammad; see n. 137.

156 I.e., descendants of the Prophet Muḥammad.

157 Perron spells the name "Homaydah" (El-Tounsy, *Voyage au Darfour*, 48), though Ḥumaydah is usually a male name, Ḥamīdah a female name.

158 The not very learned Faqīh Mālik presumably was mixing up the Qur'anic verse that refers to *kawāʿiba atrābā* (Q Naba' 78:33), or "young maidens of equal age," with that which refers to *yatīman dhā matrabah* (Q Balad 90:16), or "a needy person in distress." Thus what he meant to convey was that he had given the author a pretty young girl (*kawāʿib* may also be translated as "buxom maidens") of the sort mentioned in the Qur'an. Ironically, the author himself makes a mistake when he states that the singular of *kawāʿib* is *kāʿibah*—the correct form is *kāʿib*—and is wrong again when he says that *matrabah* occurs, like *kawāʿib*, in the Qur'an's descriptions of houris—the verse cited here is its sole occurrence. However, *atrāb* ("of equal age"), from the same root, does occur in the Qur'an in this context, at Q Ṣād 38:52 and Q Wāqiʿah 56:37, in addition to the verses cited above. For another example of Faqīh Mālik's flawed literary Arabic, see §2.3.34.

159 I.e., an assignment of land (*iqṭāʿ*) granted by the sultan to a favored person in return for political loyalty and a specified portion of the revenue. "Grants of land or privilege were used to accommodate newcomers, pre-eminently the *fuqara* and merchants" (O'Fahey, *Darfur Sultanate*, 137), to both of which categories the author's father belonged.

160 The inhabitants of Qirlī, close to Jabal Marrah, probably spoke Fur.

161 I.e., a little over 40 liters; thus, his father would harvest some 560 liters of cotton a day in this season.

162 Many such land grants are translated and reviewed in O'Fahey and Abu Salim, *Land in Darfur*.

163 Malik Khamīs ʿArmān: the name is given as Malik Khamīs ʿIrfān in Perron's Arabic text (al-Tūnisī, *Tashḥīdh*, 1850, 65) but appears in his French translation as "Armân" (El-Tounsy, *Voyage au Darfour*, 51) and again as ʿArmān at §4.48. O'Fahey has described how a fief from the sultan was assigned and demarcated by court officials such as, presumably, the person mentioned here (see "Awlad ʿAli," 158–59).

164 "staple grains" (*ʿaysh*): in Darfur, the term *ʿaysh* covers any grains used to make bread (mostly sorghum, millet, and maize) (cf. Qāsim, *Qāmūs*).

165 Thus Muḥammad may have spent no more than a scant two months with the father he had traveled so far to see, as indicated by the facts that, three days after he had been reunited with him at Ḥillat Jūltū (§2.2.28), he was dispatched by his father to Tandaltī on Shaʿban 1, 1218 to present himself to the authorities there (§2.2.30); father and son then spent the following month of Ramadan together, after which his father first traveled himself to Tandaltī (§2.2.33), then "in the shortest possible time" (§2.2.34) left for Tunis.

166 If this is true, Muḥammad Kurrā would have been proposing, as O'Fahey points out, "a dynastic change for the first and only time in the sultanate's history" (*Darfur Sultanate*, 61). With respect to affording Muḥammad Kurrā's brother the exclusively royal title "Báási," either the author is mistaken or its use by Muḥammad Kurrā was an indication of his aspirations for just such dynastic change.

167 According to O'Fahey, matters came to a head when Muḥammad Kurrā, presumptuously and no doubt provocatively, invited the sultan to eat with him, in violation of the taboo against the sultan's eating in public (*Darfur Sultanate*, 61).

168 In Sudanese Arabic, *rahad* means a depression that fills with water during the rainy season.

169 For a different account of this battle and of Muḥammad Kurrā's relations with Sultan Muḥammad Faḍl in general, see Nachtigal, *Sahara and Sudan*, 298–301.

170 Eunuchs of high rank, such as Muḥammad Kurrā, sometimes married, in order to appear to conform to social norms. The epithet Shīlfūt means in Arabic "take-and-go" and was a tribute to his boldness (El-Tounsy, *Voyage au Darfour*, 55 [54, n. 1]).

171 'Umar, known as 'Umar Lēl (or Lēle) ('Umar the Donkey, because of his stubbornness), was Aḥmad Bukur's grandson rather than his son, and succeeded his father, Muḥammad Dawrā (r. ca. 1720–30), whom the author does not mention. 'Umar Lēl was succeeded by his uncle (rather than, as given here, his brother) Abū l-Qāsim (r. ca. 1739–52), and Abū l-Qāsim was succeeded by Muḥammad Tayrāb (r. ca. 1752–53 to 1785–86) (for a genealogical table of the Keira dynasty, see O'Fahey, *Darfur Sultanate*, 40). Aḥmad Bukur is said, in fact, to have had over a hundred sons, of whom those named here were only, presumably, the most prominent; other sultans had even more (O'Fahey, *Darfur Sultanate*, 90). O'Fahey states that this great mass of "sons of the sultans" formed a distinct group within the state and as such "were provided with estates and revenues, as were their sisters, but rarely with commands or administrative responsibilities" (O'Fahey, *Darfur Sultanate*, 9).

172 In the French translation, "sultan Mohammed-Djaoudeh" (El-Tounsy, *Voyage au Darfour*, 56).

173 The equation of Dār Barqū with Dār Wāddāy is problematic: Nachtigal indicates that Borku, as he spells it, was in present-day northern Chad and not part of Wadai, being in the territory of the Ennedi, to the north. Volume II of his *Sahara and Sudan* is subtitled "Kawar, Bornu, Kanem, Borku and Ennedi."

174 According to Browne, whose sources seem to have been less sympathetic than the author's to the dominant narrative concerning Darfur's rulers, Sultan Tayrāb acquired his name because of his "habit of rolling in the dust when a child" (*Travels in Africa*, 277).

175 I.e., "seed grain."

176 I.e., Sultan Muḥammad Tayrāb.

177 I.e., before the amulet that had been tied in her hair as a child had been removed, which happens at puberty. The amulet would consist of a piece of paper bearing names of God or Qur'anic verses and be concealed in a small leather pouch.

178 I.e., a boy of the best of the line of Hāshim ibn ʿAbd Manāf, eponym of the clan of the tribe of Quraysh to which the Prophet Muḥammad belonged.

179 I.e., the Prophet Muḥammad, who is buried in Medina.

180 The anecdote is anachronistic: Abū Bakr al-Ṣiddīq died in 13/634, while Muḥammad ibn al-Qāsim was born *ca.* 72/695.

181 The sense of the maxim seems to be that women are dangerous, whether a man falls in love with one of them or she sets her sights on him.

182 The passage is not entirely clear; the words "as they would say" have been added in the translation and the likely sense of *durā l-ʿiyāl* is "children of the place," meaning here "children of the palace." The *soom,* located within the *fāṣhir*'s public area, was, according to Nachtigal, "the assembly place where the people come together for conversation or for a common meal" (*Sahara and Sudan,* 335); according to O'Fahey, it also functioned as a school where the palace pages or cadets were taught (*Darfur Sultanate,* 310).

183 On the office of counselor (*amīn*), see §3.1.56.

184 According to Nachtigal, the departure of the Fur tribe known as the Musabbaʿāt ("the Massabat") from their ancestral home in Jabal Marrah was the result of a succession struggle (*Sahara and Sudan,* 355); O'Fahey describes them as "in origin Keira adventurers who had been cast out or fled the sultanate" (*Darfur Sultanate,* 53). Eventually, the Musabbaʿāt became "a tribal designation for a group of communities stretching from Darfur to Kassala in the eastern Sudan" (*Darfur Sultanate,* 53–54).

185 According to Perron, the Shāyijiyyah lived "between Darfur and Kordofan but closer to the former" (El-Tounsy, *Voyage au Darfour,* 67, n. 1), but the name is not found in other sources. It seems likely

that Perron misconstrued the name "al-Shāyiqiyyah," with *q*, which the author no doubt pronounced in the Sudanese fashion as *g*, and interpreted the latter as the letter *jīm*, pronounced as *g* in Egypt (where Perron lived). This is especially likely given that the progression in this list from Dongola to the Rizayqāt Arabs is otherwise from east to west. The Shāyiqiyyah are a tribe who live on the Nile in northern Sudan.

186 "Hashim . . . attempted . . . to create a state in central and eastern Kordofan that would rival or possibly supplant Darfur and Sinnar" (O'Fahey, *Darfur Sultanate*, 54).

187 See §2.2.38.

188 See §2.2.40.

189 I.e., all the sons of Sultan Aḥmad Bukur who were still in line of succession and their offspring.

190 Following Muḥammad Tayrāb's successful invasion of Kordofan in 1785, Darfurian rule continued there until 1821, when it fell to Egyptian forces.

191 On Sultan Muḥammad Tayrāb's strategy of strengthening the ties between his eldest son and the children of his viziers, presumably in the hope of forming a loyal, cohesive elite around his designated successor, see §2.2.40.

192 This is the penultimate line of the "suspended ode" (*muʿallaqah*) of Zuhayr ibn Abī Salmā (d. AD 609).

193 Al-Mutanabbī, *al-ʿArf al-ṭayyib*, 522.

194 According to Perron, who presumably had it from the author, the reference is to a well-known fable: a sheep was waiting to be slaughtered but the knife had been lost in the sand; the would-be butcher had abandoned the idea of killing the sheep when the latter, pawing at the sand, uncovered the knife; it was then slaughtered.

195 Abū l-Fatḥ al-Bastī (ca. 400/1010); the second hemistich of the Arabic forms a visual pun: *arā qadamī arāqa damī*.

196 See n. 137.

197 According to O'Fahey, the title means "powerful mother" (*Darfur Sultanate*, 116) and the holder was responsible for the production of food for the royal household (personal communication).

198 Muḥammad Kurrā's patron (see §2.2.44).

199 Umar ("Travels," 145, n. 1) identifies this person with Nachtigal's "Hasseb el-Agaran," the son of the sultan's uncle, Sultan Hārūt/Khārūt of the Zaghāwah of Kobe (*Sahara and Sudan*, 287). O'Fahey refers to him as "a military leader" (*Darfur Sultanate*, 56–57).

200 Perron renders this name "Djoutâ," i.e., Jūtā.

201 For the author to refer to Muḥammad Dukkumī, son of ʿAlī wad Jāmiʿ, at this point as a counselor is anachronistic, though he was eventually to become one (see §2.3.6 below).

202 I.e., to the grandsons of Sultan Aḥmad Bukur, all of whose fathers were referred to as "sultans," even though they might never have ruled as such.

203 O'Fahey outlines the dynamic underlying the conflicts among the "sons of the sultans," which lasted for approximately the first sixty years of the eighteenth century, by describing how "an old order of powerful Fur chiefs, strongly based on local loyalties, serving a sultan who was but *primus inter pares*, gave way to new institutions, a supra-tribal bureaucracy, maintained by grants of land and tax-rights, slave troops and increasing Islamisation, all centred on the sultan" (*Darfur Sultanate*, 45). In O'Fahey's analysis, ʿAbd al-Raḥmān (the Orphan), who "was poor, lived in obscurity, and had no children," appealed to the elite since "he would be in a weaker position to establish new lineages to compete with the old" (*Darfur Sultanate*, 56). O'Fahey also points out that "the civil war that followed was in effect between two generations, that of Ahmad Bukr and that of Tayrab" (*Darfur Sultanate*, 58).

204 See §2.2.38 and n. 171.

205 A less flattering portrait of Sultan ʿAbd al-Raḥmān is painted by Browne, who may have been influenced by his generally dyspeptic attitude to Darfur, just as the author may have been influenced by his situation as a client of ʿAbd al-Raḥmān's son and successor. Browne, who calls the sultan "the Usurper," writes that "after the victory [by which he gained the throne] . . . judging it right to maintain for a time the shew of moderation and self-denial, he employed that

dissimulation for which his countrymen are famous, in persuading them that his affections were fixed on the blessings of futurity, and that he was indifferent to the splendor of empire. . . . At length, finding his claim unquestioned, and his authority firmly established, the veil of sanctity, now no longer necessary, was thrown aside, and ambition and avarice appeared without disguise" (Browne, *Travels in Africa*, 279). Nachtigal's judgment is more balanced than either the author's or Browne's. He writes: "He had indeed his faults, and if his principles were just, he was also resentful and vindictive; he never forgave acts of hostility, and repaid them in his own time (*Sahara and Sudan*, 293) . . . [He] died after a prosperous reign of fourteen years . . . one of the best of Darfur's rulers, who had combined prudence and good sense with energy" (*Sahara and Sudan*, 296).

206 Perron spells the name "Djiddau" (El-Tounsy, *Voyage au Darfour*, 87).

207 The onlookers presumably meant that the moon was the last of the month (cf. "Orphan Friday," the last Friday of Ramadan).

208 On the importance of having a good excuse for not eating food offered by the sultan, see §3.1.43.

209 O'Fahey gives the name as "Umm Buza" (Darfur Sultanate, 51, 119).

210 Q Shuʿarāʾ 26:227.

211 I.e., carry out no orders but his.

212 According to Nachtigal, the name of this person was Ḥājj Mufliḥ (*Sahara and Sudan*, 290).

213 The war between ʿAbd al-Raḥmān and Isḥāq over the succession was to last for three years.

214 A set phrase that also occurs in the Qur'an (Q Āl ʿImrān 3:155, 166); other occurrences have been left unnoted.

215 "God is greater" (*Allāhu akbar*): i.e., God is greater than all else.

216 The master of the tax collectors (*malik al-jabbāyīn*) was responsible for "the collection and storage of the revenues . . . throughout the state. . . . He was one of the greatest of the state officials and controlled an extensive hierarchy of subordinates" (O'Fahey, *Darfur Sultanate*, 203). Nachtigal states that "The taxes which these people had to pay consisted chiefly of tribute in the form of corn and cattle,

property tax customs dues and the so-called *diwan*," the latter being a levy imposed every four years "according to the occupations of the tribes and the yield of the regions" (*Sahara and Sudan*, 358–59). For a comprehensive review of the tax system in Darfur, see O'Fahey, *Darfur Sultanate*, 202–12.

217 I.e., they will be guiltless if they rise up against you.

218 "until such time as God delivers his verdict": meaning, with perhaps deliberate ambiguity, either "until God decides between us in battle" or "until the Day of Judgment."

219 Q Aḥzāb 33:37.

220 The Arabic term *abnā' al-ʿArab* (literally "Sons of the Arabs") was commonly used in Egypt at the time (e.g., in the 1848 census) to distinguish Arabic-speaking from Turkish-speaking Egyptians.

221 A "trickle" of guns was imported to Darfur each year, but these appear to have been used, as is implied here, mainly for hunting (O'Fahey, *Darfur Sultanate*, 200, n. 22).

222 In an appendix to his French translation of this work, Nicholas Perron mentions, as an extreme illustration of the absolute inviolability of the person of the sultan and all his family, that Zabādī, after receiving the reward he had been promised, was executed (El-Tounsy, *Voyage au Darfour*, 376–77).

223 Q Aḥzāb 33:38.

224 The ancestral tombs of the Keira sultans were located at Ṭurrah in Jabal Marrah, where on important occasions sacrifices were made and prayers offered for their souls.

225 See, e.g., al-Mutanabbī, *al-ʿArf al-ṭayyib*, 308–9, with differences. The fourth (or, in some editions, the third) line of the poem is missing. It runs: *wa-arāka d-dahru mā tuḥāwilu fī l-ʿidā / ḥattā kaʾanna l-ṣurūfa anṣārū* ("And Fate will show you what you seek in your enemies / as though even its twists were allies").

226 "Rīl is the key of the South and East roads" (Browne, *Travels in Africa*, 239).

227 According to O'Fahey, the establishment of the sultan's seat at Tandaltī, which lies east of Jabal Marrah, consolidated the reorientation of the

sultanate to the east and to Nilotic Sudan. Tandaltī was strategically placed, close to the main west-east route through Jabal Marrah and provided with water by the *rahad*, or seasonal lake. It was also only a day's journey to the southeast from the trade entrepôt of Kubayh and close enough to the rain-fed area of the mountains to be supplied with agricultural products (*Darfur Sultanate*, 64–65).

228 Browne makes it clear that the alcohol in question was millet beer (*marīsah*) (*Travels in Africa*, 224–25)—which al-Tūnisī gives the more literary name of *mizr*—and dates the edict to March 1795 (*Travels in Africa*, 291). Millet beer is a lightly fermented beverage widely drunk in sub-Saharan Africa and regarded by some as an important component of the diet in protein-poor environments.

229 One supposes that the sound must be something like *krrrrruuuu*.

230 Here and in the rest of the passage, the Bedouin plays on the literal meaning of Sultan ʿAbd al-Raḥmān's epithet, al-Rashīd. The epithet was not merely a sign of his subjects' adulation but a title awarded the sultan by his Ottoman counterpart in thanks for a gift of ivory and ostrich feathers (O'Fahey, *Darfur Sultanate*, 69). Browne claims that, before receipt of the gifts, the Ottoman sultan had been unaware of Darfur's existence (Browne, *Travels in Africa*, 215).

231 I.e., he may start to think of establishing a dynasty of his own.

232 On becoming shaykh-father, Muḥammad Kurrā would have automatically taken charge of the territories pertaining to that office, i.e., Dār Dālī, the lands to the east of Jabal Marrah.

233 The point of the following passage may be to demonstrate ʿUmar al-Tūnisī's right to be numbered among the scholars who paid allegiance to the sultan and who were supported by him.

234 The rational sciences include mathematics, astronomy, logic, philosophy, and medicine. The transmitted sciences are those concerned with matters of faith, in particular, the Qur'an, the Hadith, and law.

235 ʿUmar al-Tūnisī's works have not survived.

236 Umar believes that Musāʿid, a son of Sharif Surūr, head of the Dhawī Zayd dynasty that then ruled Mecca, had probably fled to Darfur to escape family conflicts ("Travels," 182, n. 4).

237 The administration of justice lay largely in the hands of the sultan and the local authorities, in concert with the *fuqarā'*, who together ruled in most cases according to Fur customary law, though the influence of Islamic law increased with time. This system "was only partly modified by the appointment of some of the latter [i.e., the *fuqarā'*] as *qāḍīs* [judges]" (*Darfur Sultanate*, 217), most of whom were attached to the entourages of the same authorities. A few judges, such as ʿIzz al-Dīn al-Jāmiʿ (here called al-Jāmiʿī), did, however, hold fairly independent positions (same reference).

238 O'Fahey identifies this person with Aḥmad Aghā, an associate of Murād Bayk (the Mamluk leader who in collusion with the British tried to return Egypt to Mamluk rule following Napoleon's departure), sent by the latter to spy on Darfur ("The Affair of Ahmad Agha," 202–3).

239 I.e., the servants were prevented from entering the courtyard that contained the sultan's living quarters; see the Plan of the Sultan's Seat (§3.1.91).

240 See §2.2.57.

241 The kind of bowl referred to, the *jafnah*, is defined as holding enough to satisfy ten men (see Lane, *Lexicon*, s.v. *j-f-n*).

242 Literally the Mother of Ḥabīb, the term that would have been used habitually to refer to her.

243 No doubt to the caves there where princes were imprisoned; see §3.1.16, §3.1.24.

244 The "secret of the letter" (*sirr al-ḥarf*), also called "the science of letters" (*ʿilm al-ḥurūf*), deals, in its cosmological aspect, with the relationship between divine speech and the manifest world, and, as an occult practice, with the making of talismans such as "magic squares" formed of letters (*awfāq*, sg. *wafq*).

245 The name is written so in the lithograph, but should perhaps be Jidd al-ʿIyāl ("the Grandfather of the Little Children").

246 The quotation is a paraphrase of one in the *Memorandum on the Conditions of the Dead and Matters Pertaining to the Hereafter* (*al-Tadhkirah fī aḥwāl al-mawtā wa-umūr al-ākhirah*) of Muḥammad

ibn Aḥmad ibn Abī Bakr ibn Farḥ al-Anṣārī al-Qurṭubī (d. 671/1273), a leading Andalusian Mālikī scholar (*al-Tadhkirah*, 513–14). In this passage, al-Qurṭubī reports a hadith, on the authority of Muslim on the authority of Anas, that runs, in one version, "Hell will continue to have people thrown into it and will say, 'Are there more?' until the Lord of Might puts his *qadam* [in other versions, *rijl*] into it, when it will draw back upon itself and say, 'Enough! Enough!'" Since both *qadam* and *rijl* might be understood in their common sense of "foot," al-Qurṭubī points out that both also have the sense given here and must be so understood, since God does not possess limbs (same reference, 513).

247 The story demonstrates the Faqīh's stupidity because, when al-Sanūsī addresses him (in mixed Darfurian and literary Arabic, as signaled in the Arabic text by the voweling *Fir* rather than the correct form *Firra*), he takes his son's words *Fir! Binā rajulun* to be a rereading of the phrase *fa-marra binā rijlun* and accepts it as correct, whereas the son is in fact trying to draw his attention to the arrival of Jidd al-ʿAyyāl, whose appearance at the head of a host of men and animals must have scared the youth. Al-Sanūsī must have been at least eighteen years of age, the age of majority, and hence of validity as a witness, according to the Mālikī rite. Perron understands the anecdote, which he relegates to an appendix (see El-Tounsy, *Darfour*, 119 and 425), slightly differently.

248 This second invasion of Kordofan took place in about 1206/1791–92 (O'Fahey, *Darfur Sultanate*, 66). The appointment of Muḥammad Kurrā as governor of Kordofan would have followed naturally from his position as governor of eastern Darfur.

249 Nachtigal says that Muḥammad Kurrā "made himself and the extreme east of the country more independent than Abd er-Rahman could allow . . . the *abu shaykh* undertook military expeditions in all directions on his own initiative . . . while he restricted himself to sending tribute to Abd er-Rahman, but no longer obeyed his orders" (*Sahara and Sudan*, 294–95).

250 On the enmity between Counselor Muḥammad (Dukkumī) and Muḥammad Kurrā, see §2.2.62.

251 O'Fahey comments that "There was no precise or automatic rule of succession" (*Darfur Sultanate*, 59). Sultan ʿAbd al-Raḥmān is said to have had four sons. One of these, Muḥammad Abū l-Madyan (of whose existence al-Tūnisī may have been unaware), eventually escaped from Darfur only to return in 1843 as an Egyptian-backed pretender; his campaign to unseat Muḥammad Faḍl failed (Nachtigal, *Sahara and Sudan*, 303, n. 1).

252 Perron gives the latter's name as Muḥammad Bukhārī.

253 Nachtigal estimates that Muḥammad Faḍl was eleven or twelve at the time (*Sahara and Sudan*, 298).

254 I.e., at the doors to the sultan's house.

255 According to Nachtigal, Muḥammad Kurrā had previously approached each of the royal princes in secret and "and promised the government to each of the most eligible, persuading the others to agree to whatever he, Kurra, would propose. Accordingly, to the question which he put to them publicly, they were unanimous in answering, 'We are all content, *abu shaykh*, with whatever you will do'" (*Sahara and Sudan*, 298–99).

256 Against this account, Nachtigal states that Malik Ibrāhīm was the only one of those summoned to oppose the shaykh-father's selection, telling him that "he saw blood in the features of the royal boy . . . and of blood Darfur had . . . had enough" (*Sahara and Sudan*, 299). Malik Ibrāhīm also warned that the shaykh-father that he "should take heed of what he was doing, for at some time he would himself be the man who had most to fear from the young prince" (same reference).

257 I.e., Muḥammad Faḍl's cousins, sons of the other sons of Sultan Aḥmad Bukur.

258 See §2.2.36.

259 See §3.1.16, §3.1.24.

260 See §2.2.37.

261 The term "kings" as used here is ambiguous, referring on some occasions to the sultans of Darfur and on others to its "petty kings," i.e., the tribal and clan chieftains (see further, Note on the Text, pp. xliii–xliv).

262 A form of Wāddāy (Wadai); see §3.1.2 below.

263 According to Nachtigal's editors, the term had acquired by his day "a curiously wide currency in the Middle East, where it was popularly applied to . . . the western, and sometimes also the central, Sudan" (*Sahara and Sudan*, 4:233, n. 1); by Sudan, the editors mean here the Sudanic belt of countries (see Introduction, p. xxxiv), not the modern state of that name. Umar attributes this broader use to the fact that its inhabitants were the first West Africans to make the pilgrimage to Mecca (*Travels*, 209, n. 1). For more on the term, see al-Naqar, "Takrur."

264 I.e., the easternmost.

265 A Tunjūr state existed in Darfur and Wadai in the sixteenth century; however, the relationship of the Tunjūr state to the Keira state that superseded it lies, as O'Fahey puts it, "tantalisingly beyond our ken" (O'Fahey, *Darfur Sultanate*, 25; see also more generally 24–33).

266 On the identification of the Fullān as Arabs, see §2.2.29 and vol. 1, n. 150.

267 The trajectory outlined here, which can be followed on the author's map of Darfur (§3.1.12, images), runs north-northwest to south-southeast, rather than simply north to south, which explains why it ends at "the eastern limits of the Fur." A major inaccuracy in the map is that it places Rīl northwest of Jadīd Rās al-Fīl, whereas in reality it lies southwest of it.

268 Arabic *al-Ṣaʿīd*, a term also used in Egypt, where it applies to the Nile Valley from Cairo south to Nubia (i.e., Upper Egypt).

269 The title ába dima'ng appears to predate the Keira dynasty and to be associated with the Konyunga, "the most powerful of the Fur clans after the Keira . . . according to one tradition the *takanawi*s were chamberlains to the [Keira] sultans at Turra" (O'Fahey, *Darfur Sultanate*, 118).

270 Perhaps meaning that the *dārawiyyah* are so called because they trace their origin to some *dār* (tribal territory) elsewhere.

271 Perron writes: "The shaykh had no idea of what a map was. He simply placed the localities relative to one another and not in such a way as to show the distances as one would measure them on a geographical scale. The shaykh's long stay in Darfur, as well as his intelligence, allow us to accept his information as accurate and preferable to that derived from the accounts of European travelers. None of the latter was able, as he was, to roam through the country in all directions or explore it as thoroughly" (El-Tounsy, *Voyage au Darfour*, 135, n. 2). Despite this, the map contains some major errors. To name but one, Dār Ába Umá appears in the map to the west of Jabal Marrah whereas in fact it lay to its southeast, around today's Kas (personal communication from R. S. O'Fahey).

272 The episode is recounted not in this book but in the author's account of his time in Wadai (see El-Tounsy, *Voyage au Ouadây*, chapter eight).

273 For the author's systematic presentation of the hierarchy of office-holders of the Darfurian state, see below §§3.1.50 ff., and for O'Fahey's critique of this, see n. 53.

274 Given in other sources as *abbo uumo*, which is said to mean "Lord of the Fontanelle" in Fur—despite the author's later characterization of this official as being, in military terms, "the sultan's spine"—see O'Fahey, *Darfur Sultanate*, 177–78.

275 On the association of certain titles with parts of the sultan's body, see §§3.1.50 ff. below.

276 All these places were at some time *fāshir*s, or royal compounds.

277 O'Fahey writes: "Both within and on the margins of the provinces a number of tribes, or more accurately tribal territories, preserved their identity and a degree of administrative autonomy" (*Darfur Sultanate*, 181).

278 "the Dunes" (*al-qawz*): an area of stabilized dunes with poor, light, but cultivable soil in the open wooded country that stretches from

the Jabal Marrah range eastward into Kordofan (see O'Fahey, *Darfur Sultanate*, 4).

279 "saint" (*walī Allāh*): literally "a ward of God," meaning a person who enjoys God's special favor and to whom He often grants the power to perform miracles; in the literature on Sufism, the term is sometimes rendered "friend of God."

280 According to informants, *tómbol* is the generic word for "drum" in Fur.

281 I.e., Europeans.

282 It is not obvious what the author means by this. The same sentence (*wa-ammā lughatuhum fa-hiya lughatun fī-hā ḥamās*) was listed, along with other faux pas, by Aḥmad Fāris al-Shidyāq as an example of the pernicious influence of Nicholas Perron on the text (al-Shidyāq, *Leg*, 4:443). Grammar, however, cannot be the issue, as the sentence is grammatically correct. Perhaps al-Shidyāq thought that this was an unsophisticated or absurd way to describe a language.

283 *kéla* means "we come"; "come!" is *béla.*

284 The author's memory may have betrayed him: according to informants, *murtá'ng* means "horse" while *yáa* means "mother of" but is not used of animals.

285 In fact, the Turkish for "he came" is *gitti*, with a hard *g*; perhaps the author assumes that because in Darfurian (and generally in Sudanese) Arabic the soft *g* replaces the hard *g* of Egyptian Arabic, the two phonemes are equivalent.

286 The French translator transcribes these as *saba, temâny, tiçâh*, presumably to represent how the Fur pronounced them.

287 Thus eleven is *wayye na tog*, and twenty *wayyenga aw* (*wayyenga* being the plural of *wayye*).

288 Cf. Q Rūm 30:23; 30:22.

289 Cf. Q Mā'idah 5:48.

290 I.e., the sultan may not be questioned as to the wisdom of his commands but a simple plea by one person on behalf of another may be entertained.

291 See §2.3.5.

292 "Grandmothers" (*ḥabbūbāt*): the word, if taken to be Arabic (plausible given its form), might be interpreted as "the Beloveds." However, Nachtigal asserts that the word (which he spells differently) means "grandmother" and implies that it derives from the Fur title *abo* and refers to "widows or aged relations of the royal house, whose land was exempt from all taxes and dues" (Nachtigal, *Sahara and Sudan*, 4:326, also n. 2). Nachtigal's glossary describes the complex usage of the word in Darfur and Wadai (*Sahara and Sudan*, 4:408).

293 Though the author uses the word *kurbāj*, which usually means a leather whip, to describe these, they must be the same as the "royal throwing irons . . . carried before the king on public processions" described by Nachtigal, which likewise were struck against one another and flourished (*Sahara and Sudan*, 4:337). O'Fahey describes "throwing knives" (*sambal*) as being "the wartime version of the common wooden hunting-stick (*safarog* or *dorma*) [for which see §2.3.8] . . . shaped like a large question mark, with sharpened edges and wings to ensure straight flight . . . carried three or four at a time in a holster and . . . a formidable weapon, [though requiring] great skill to be effective" (*Darfur Sultanate*, 194).

294 The liquid may have been wheat soaked in water and boiled (Arabic: *balīlah*) (see O'Fahey, *Darfur Sultanate*, 93, n. 26).

295 Literally "the House of Copper" (*dār al-nuḥās*).

296 Copper kettledrums were "the paramount symbol of autonomous authority throughout Darfur and beyond" (O'Fahey, *Darfur Sultanate*, 183). The sacred drums of the Keira dynasty numbered seven, some of which were regarded as male, others as female. The smallest but most sacred was that called the Victorious (al-Manṣūrah), mentioned in what follows; others were the White and the Liar. The drums served "as a rallying point in time of war and the ultimate symbol of legitimacy" (O'Fahey, *Darfur Sultanate*, 183).

297 The Arabic translation is more or less word by word; the meaning is "So-and-so's hands are [i.e., So-and-so is] outside and humbly greet[s] you": *falān* in Perron's transliteration is equal to *fulān* (Arabic: "so-and-so").

298 The Fur does not include “even their followers and their servants.”

299 See §2.2.44.

300 See §3.1.67 and §§3.1.71–75.

301 *dónga dáíng sīdī*: “(They give you) the hands, my lord.” This is how the phrase is understood by modern informants; Perron may have misunderstood, since the speaker is the sultan and not the petitioner; cf. n. 37.

302 According to Nachtigal, if the sultan responded directly to a greeting, he did so “without opening his mouth with a faint drawling ‘hm’, or at most replied with a scarcely audible low *afia*, good health” (*Sahara and Sudan*, 4:327).

303 The festival probably took place in February or March (O’Fahey, *Darfur Sultanate*, 94, n. 29).

304 According to other sources, what follows constituted a separate feast, called the kundanga (meaning “human liver,” on the significance of which see below), held three days after the drum festival, and the flesh eaten was that of a specially slaughtered wether rather than that of the bulls used to make skins for the drums. “If the ‘covering of the drums’ was a public affirmation of royal power in its eminent symbol, the drums, the kundanga feast was a direct and fearsome affirmation by the Keira clan of loyalty to the ruler, a kind of trial by ordeal” (O’Fahey, *Darfur Sultanate*, 95–96).

305 O’Fahey notes that evidence for human sacrifice at the drum festival is “contradictory and inconclusive,” with some sources claiming that it was abolished by Sultan Sulaymān Solongdungo, the dynasty’s founding father, others that it survived as late as Sultan Muḥammad al-Ḥusayn (r. 1838–73) (*Darfur Sultanate*, 96 and 96, n. 37).

306 “Mantle!” (*burnus*): the French translator understands this to mean “Protector [of the nations]!” (El-Tounsy, *Voyage au Darfour*, 168). The sultans of Bornu wore richly decorated burnooses (Nachtigal, *Sahara and Sudan*, 3:119), which suggests that the mantle was a symbol of authority elsewhere in Sudanic Africa.

307 "Breaker and scatterer of the unlevied mountains" (*firtāk al-jibāl bi-lā dīwān*): The meaning is uncertain. The word *firtāk* may be related to *fartaq* "to cut something up into tiny pieces and scatter them" (Qāsim, *Qāmūs*, art. *fartaq*). By "unlevied mountains" presumably are meant mountains whose tribes did not pay the four-yearly tribute referred to by Nachtigal (*Sahara and Sudan*, 4:359), i.e., tribes living beyond the reach of any authority.

308 See §3.1.38.

309 Also *dilí*, according to informants. The tree is said to be important, particularly in places where rainfall is scarce, as it holds a huge quantity of water in the roots; it has not been identified.

310 Nachtigal also describes "the great drum festival," adding details not mentioned by the author, including many relating to its pagan origins (*Sahara and Sudan*, 4:338–40); for a description of this and other royal rituals that incorporates all available accounts, see O'Fahey, *Darfur Sultanate*, 92–99.

311 This "first sowing" started three days in advance of the great drum festival.

312 In the original, this section is titled "On the Offices Held by the Kings of the Fur and Their Garments and the Functioning of the Sultan's Court and So On"; however, the present section in fact deals only with offices, while the descriptions of the functioning of the sultan's court and the garments of the kings of the Fur are allocated their own sections (§§3.1.77–92 and §§3.1.93–96, respectively). The title has therefore been amended here and the sections on the court and on clothing have been given their own headings.

313 Many of the holders of the various titles listed in what follows held their offices by virtue of descent: "The Fur had come down from the mountains under a line of warrior sultans. In the course of their expansion, the lineage chiefs, ritual experts and war leaders . . . had grown into a class of hereditary title-holders" (O'Fahey, *Darfur Sultanate*, 47).

314 Elsewhere (§3.1.14) the Sultan's Face; as the author is the only source for these associations of officials with parts of the sultan's body, it is not possible to say which is correct.

315 According to Fur informants, the author is mistaken: ába poor-ii is simply an honoric title that might be given to anyone in power; "Father of the Fur" is poora'ng ába.

316 Nachtigal describes the kaamíne as "the king's shadow" (*Sahara and Sudan*, 4:326–27). He adds: "Despite his lofty title, in actual importance the *kamene* stood third in the royal household, definitely inferior to the [shaykh-father], and facetious people there called him 'the cow's vagina' . . . corresponding rather to our 'neither fish nor fowl'" (*Sahara and Sudan*, 4:328). O'Fahey characterizes *kaamíne* as a ritual title from the remote past (*Darfur Sultanate*, 113).

317 On this office, see also §3.1.9 and following paragraphs.

318 Apparently from Fur *dunggú*. The *dinqār* was made of wood (see §3.1.39); no Fur chief could possess a copper drum, for that was the exclusive prerogative of the Keira sultans, though the sultan might grant that right to a non-Fur vassal (see O'Fahey, *Darfur Sultanate*, 184).

319 On this office, see also §3.1.9 and §§3.1.11–12.

320 See, e.g., §2.2.29.

321 See also §2.2.43. Nachtigal describes the counselors as the king's confidential advisors (*Sahara and Sudan*, 4:330, 403).

322 See also §2.2.43 and Glossary.

323 "the chief of": missing in the Arabic. The French translation has "Après le soum-in-dogolah viennent les chefs kôrkoa" (El-Tounsy, *Voyage au Darfour*, 174).

324 Presumably the full title was "master of the órré bayyâ," in parallel with the "master of the órré dee" mentioned below.

325 The sultan received a regular flow of slaves as tribute (and to ensure protection from raids) from the non-Muslim Fartīt tribes, as he did from war and from raiding by his subjects, one tenth of those captured being paid to him as a tax (see further O'Fahey, *Darfur Sultanate*, 208–12).

326 According to Perron, the word originally meant "a bracelet worn above the elbow" (El-Tounsy, *Voyage au Darfour*, 176, n. 1); it probably derives from Arabic *dumlaj* "upper arm."

327 See §3.1.15.

328 Nachtigal states that "The taxes which these people had to pay consisted chiefly of tribute in the form of corn and cattle, property tax, customs dues and the so-called *diwan*," the latter being a levy imposed every four years "according to the occupations of the tribes and the yield of the regions" (*Sahara and Sudan*, 4:358–59).

329 These words, though printed in the original as prose, form a hemistich in *basīṭ* meter.

330 Browne gives the following description of what appears to be a *mooge* at a royal ceremony: "A kind of hired encomiast stood on the monarch's left hand, crying out, *à plein gorge*, during the whole ceremony, 'See the bufalloe . . . the offspring of the buffaloe, a bull of bulls, the elephant of superior strength, the powerful Sultan Abd-el-rachmân-el-rachîd! May God prolong thy life!—O Master—May God assist thee, and render thee victorious!'" (*Travels in Africa*, 213–14).

331 §3.1.59.

332 §3.1.38.

333 In standard Arabic, *khādim* means "male servant"; in Darfur, however, it means "female slave or concubine" (O'Fahey, "Slavery," 84).

334 Meaning that she had given birth to her daughter, and her daughter had given birth to the sultan. See also §2.3.4.

335 See n. 52.

336 See §2.2.30.

337 O'Fahey points out that the sultan's residence "was the Fur household writ large; the male and female entrance, the layout of the huts, the *diwan*s or places of audience, the messes . . . where men ate communally—all were features common to royal palace and prosperous households alike" (*Darfur Sultanate*, 101).

338 "Thin canes" (see Glossary). When the author speaks, here and elsewhere (e.g., §3.1.86), of "construction," he apparently has in mind specifically the roofing material used. Both Browne (*Travels in*

Africa, 286) and Nachtigal (*Sahara and Sudan*, 4:260) state that the walls were made of clay, covered in the case of the homes of the better off by white, red, or black plaster (Browne, same reference), while modern sources specify that *marhabayb* is a roofing material (see, e.g., Tully, *Culture and Context*, 93–94).

339 According to Perron, on the author's authority, the *liqdābah* or *rākūbah* was an open-sided structure; if walled, e.g., with canes, it was called a *karabābah* (El-Tounsy, *Voyage au Darfour*, 186, n. 1).

340 Qāsim, *Qāmūs* (sg. *mutraq*): "light stick from a recently cut branch."

341 See §3.1.41, images.

342 Perron elaborates: "When the audience is during the day, the sultan sometimes remains mounted throughout, which is to say for perhaps one or two hours. He has for this purpose horses trained to remain perfectly still and accustomed to doing so" (El-Tounsy, *Voyage au Darfour*, 190).

343 See §3.1.40.

344 The author apparently intended to deal with construction in Wadai in greater detail later (see El-Tounsy, *Voyage au Darfour*, 192, n. 1) but the passage has not been identified in the *Voyage au Ouadây*.

345 The *Voyage au Ouadây* states that the sultan "sits for this purpose [i.e., that of holding public audience] in a room that looks out over the public square of the *fāshir*" (El-Tounsy, *Voyage au Ouadây*, 365).

346 Arabic: *ʿaqadah*. See El-Tounsy, *Voyage au Darfour*, 192, and *Voyage au Ouadây*, 365.

347 See El-Tounsy, *Voyage au Ouadây*, 366.

348 Meaning that they make their roofs with millet stalks, see §3.1.78.

349 Thus, the homestead as a whole is surrounded by an outer fence of thorny branches (*zarībah*); inside are the houses, or huts (*buyūt*), which are roofed with millet stalks and each of which is surrounded by an inner fence that serves as a dust-break (*ṣarīf*). A later reference (§4.20) indicates that subsidiary *zarībah*s for animals, here meaning circular pens fenced with branches, might be located within the larger enclosed space.

350 The significance of this addition is unclear, given that the author has already used the term *bayt* (pl. *buyūt*) to designate houses in general. It has no equivalent in the French translation.

351 According to Nachtigal, the royal dwelling "was enclosed only by a straw fence, with a thick, high, broad thorn hedge inside. This formed an oval with the longer axis running from northeast to southwest, and it took at least a quarter of an hour to go round it" (*Sahara and Sudan*, 4:261).

352 From "of the inner fence" to "millers" is absent from the Arabic and has been supplied from the French translation (El-Tounsy, *Voyage au Darfour*, 200–1). That an equivalent passage was part of the original is evidenced by the abruptness with which the sentence stops in the lithographed edition and the absence there of the expected description of the sultan's quarters. In addition, the occurrence of the phrase "as I have said" indicates that this passage in the French is not simply an elaboration of Perron's.

353 See n. 52.

354 Umar states (*Travels*, 306, n. 1) that this consisted of a copy of the Qur'an, which presumably was kept in a gilt holder or had gilt covers.

355 Lane describes the early nineteenth-century Egyptian *milā'ah* (*milāyeh* in his transcription) as "a kind of blue and white plaid" which the men "throw . . . over the shoulders, or wrap . . . about the body" (Lane, *Manners and Customs*, 32, n. 5).

356 "a couple of inches" (*qīrāṭān*): the term *qīrāṭ* (from which English "carat") is not commonly applied to cloth. Its basic sense is "one twenty-fourth part," so what is meant here may be two twenty-fourths of a pik (Arabic: *dhirāʿ*, otherwise "cubit"), a measurement of length used in the eastern Mediterranean that varied from country to country. In 1885, the Egyptian pik was equal to 26.37 inches (Baedecker, *Egypt*, 28).

357 Perron describes the *durrāʿah* as "a piece of white cloth that the Negresses place over their breasts, passing it under the armpits, tying it almost like a belt, and throwing the loose end over their left

shoulder. The same piece of cloth also serves them as a cover for the body, at least to the knees" (El-Tounsy, *Voyage au Darfour*, 258, n. 1).

358 *ʿaqīq* in fact means "agate."

359 *dam-l-raʿāf* ("blood from the nose"): this voweling, specified in the lithograph edition (al-Tūnisī, *Tashḥīdh* 1850, 192), rather than the standard *dam al-ruʿāf*, may be intended to represent the Fur pronunciation, which is given in the French translation as "dengueraf" (El-Tounsy, *Voyage au Darfour*, 208, n. 3).

360 *Erythrina abyssinica*, sometimes called "lucky bean tree."

361 The author may have added this qualifier in the belief that his Egyptian readers would be more familiar with the common (fava) bean (*fūl*), which is green when fresh, brown when cooked.

362 Writing in 1937, A. J. Arkell states that such waist beads "are quite out of fashion and the younger generation will have nothing to do with them, occasionally referring to them with contempt as the jewellery of slaves" (Arkell, "Hebron Beads," 300); by that time, all such beads had come to be known in Darfur as *manjūr* (see below) (same reference, 302).

363 Meaning "tranquil noontime sleep," implying, according to Umar, that the women who wear them "could afford to sleep most of the day without doing any housework" (*Travels*, 315, n. 1).

364 Perhaps meaning "squared off" or "chipped, nicked" (Dozy, *Supplément*); however, Arkell believes the word may have an Indian origin ("Hebron Beads," 300, n. 1). Today in Egypt, the *manjūr* is a broad leather belt to which goat's hooves have been attached that is worn by one of the musicians involved in the exorcism ceremony known as the *zār*; by shaking his waist, he produces a sound like that of maracas.

365 Perhaps meaning "crude, rough to the touch" (Qāsim, *Qāmūs*; Dozy, *Supplément*).

366 On the history of Hebron, or al-Khalīl, as a beadmaking center, see Francis, "Beadmaking in Islam."

367 From the Arabic root *kh-d-r*, related to concealment. Nachtigal writes, referring to Wadai, that they are "used as women's ornaments, worn under their clothing around the waist" (*Sahara and Sudan*, 4:201).

368 See §3.1.100.

369 Browne lists "brass wire" among the goods regularly imported to Darfur from Egypt (*Travels in Africa*, 303).

370 Specifically, *Artemisia arborescens*.

371 From the civet cat (Qāsim, *Qāmūs*); civet, as an ingredient in perfumes, is in fact taken from the perineal gland, rather than the skin, of the animal..

372 Perhaps the same as *dāyūk*, a name applying to "*Solanum spp.*" (Vogt, *Murshid*, 278).

373 The French translation explains that by "brother" the man means lover and that the lover does this "as a way of consoling himself" (El-Tounsy, *Voyage au Darfour*, 212).

374 The words are colloquial (hence the author's explanation) and mean "Girl, why is your head as ugly as that hut?"

375 "Where's that hut that's as ugly as my head?"

376 The text says, "If they knew they were strangers." Perron's translation understands this to mean the above (El-Tounsy, *Voyage au Darfour*, 215).

377 Q Baqarah 2:255.

378 Cf. Q Jinn 72:3 but also Isrāʾ 17:111.

379 Q Isrāʾ 17:111.

380 Q Ikhlāṣ 112:4.

381 Q Ṣād 38:26.

382 Perron states, presumably on the authority of the author, that Muslims believe that Adam was allowed to sleep only lightly so that he would be aware of the extraction of Eve from his rib cage, be conscious that she was flesh of his flesh, and therefore love her more (El-Tounsy, *Voyage au Darfour*, 222, n. 1).

383 The wording mimics that used at marriage ceremonies.

384 See §3.1.113.

385 Literally "Mother Nightingale." Perron says that it is made of sprouted barley and is a fizzy wine "like champagne and very intoxicating" (El-Tounsy, *Voyage au Darfour*, 426–27).

386 The Birqid were a people living in southeastern Darfur. They rebelled under Sultan Muḥammad Tayrāb and were brought more firmly

under Darfurian rule (O'Fahey, *Darfur Sultanate*, 51–52). It may be that the singer sought to flatter the author by associating him with this (by then long past) incident.

387 Barley beer (also sometimes *būẓah*).

388 A viscous cold drink of slightly fermented rice, sugar, and water that is not considered alcoholic.

389 Despite having originally made it clear that the dancers are *young* men and women (*shubbān, shābbāt*), the author proceeds, in the Arabic, to refer to them frequently throughout the rest of the section as "men" (*rijāl*) and "women" (*nisā'*). In the translation, the dancers are referred to as "boys" and "girls" throughout, for clarity.

390 Presumably because of its association with the drums of the same name; see §3.2.5.

391 Described as "a sound in the chest like the sound made by one who is being throttled or is making a great effort" (Qāsim, *Qāmūs*).

392 According to Perron, the author glossed the verse as follows: "The night passes and leaves. O my love, my treasure, you who are as dear to me as a gold piece, come, for my head is spinning with sleep; come sleep with me" (my translation). The *mutqāl* referred to in the Arabic is explained by Perron, on the same authority, as meaning "a piece of gold, or a weight used mainly to weigh gold" (El-Tounsy, *Voyage au Darfour*, 429).

393 According to Perron, the author glossed the verse as follows: "By Darfur is meant the world. For the Darfurians, Darfur is the universe . . . [*jafah*] means 'without happiness, without love' . . . [*nawā*] means 'wanting' (to sleep), meaning 'My head has need of sleep; come with me'" (my translation) (El-Tounsy, *Voyage au Darfour*, 429).

394 According to Perron, the author glossed the verse as follows: "O you whom I love, you lean toward us like a flexible branch, love sweeps us away and you make us sigh for you. You love me, you prefer me to the other girls of the village and by so doing excite their jealousy of me and attract their vengeance because they believe that you must have disparaged them to me. O you whose love reminds me of the scent

of sandalwood, you grow like its sweet-smelling branches and you lean over our dwelling places to cast your shade over them (meaning, to stay with us forever). With you, happiness will also always be here" (my translation) (El-Tounsy, *Voyage au Darfour*, 429–30). The unusual spellings *furayaʿ/furayʿā* in the Arabic may point to a Fur word that the author did not understand, perhaps *periya*, "a kind of spice cut from the twig of a tree" (informants).

395 I.e., Muḥammad *Daldan* wad Binayyah (see Glossary).

396 According to Perron, the author glossed the verse as follows: "Young Darfurians, go with brave Daldang to seek rich booty and become wealthy. Run, catch up with him! His horsemen are still at Karyū!" (my translation). Perron notes that Daldang, son of Binayyah, a princess, raided the Fartīt during the reign of Sultan Muḥammad Faḍl and returned with vast booty in the form of slaves, occasioning the composition of these lines (El-Tounsy, *Voyage au Darfour*, 430). He also notes that the "riches" are to be used by the young men to pay dowries (El-Tounsy, *Voyage au Darfour*, 233). O'Fahey regards Daldan as a typical *fāris*, or professional warrior imbued with a chivalric ethos fighting for booty, a figure common in eastern Sudanic Africa during this period (*Darfur Sultanate*, 121).

397 The translation of this song, which is entirely in Fur, goes (from Perron's French), "Children of Báási Ṭāhir, You and your father, You swore on the Qur'an, But in Kūbayh you've set, Treachery's foot by breaching its walls" (my translation) (El-Tounsy, *Voyage au Darfour*, 233–34, 431). Perron points out that the song is hardly appropriate for a wedding and is sung simply to allow people to dance.

398 See §3.2.7.

399 "The Fur compare their chiefs, their parents and their wives' parents to the sun [for] 'You cannot look them in the face'" (O'Fahey, *Darfur Sultanate*, 176). The author has already touched on this custom above (§3.1.113).

400 The expected form would be *warāniyyah*, but both *Tashḥīdh* 1850 and 1965 write it as given above. The word does not occur in Qāsim's dictionary of Sudanese Arabic.

401 "to protect him, oho" (*farajābā*): according to Perron, on the authority of the author, the word *farājābā* ("to protect him") in the Arabic text consists of *farāj*, meaning "as protection," plus the meaningless syllables -*ābā*, added to fill out the line and provide the rhyme (El-Tounsy, *Voyage au Darfour*, 434).

402 *Allāh ḥayy*, a chant used in *dhikr*.

403 See §3.2.9.

404 The first line uses the Fur forms for the names Gabriel and Michael but the second line appears to be Arabic.

405 This translation follows Perron's, which reads, "Filles de dieu, ô filles de dieu!" (El-Tounsy, *Voyage au Darfour*, 249); presumably the women singers are referring to themselves.

406 According to Perron, on the author's authority, the fasting month of Ramadan is described as God's remedy because during it "God cures souls of their faults, or corrects the defects in men" (El-Tounsy, *Voyage au Darfour*, 437).

407 According to legend, Qābīl and Hābīl (Cain and Abel) each had twin sisters, Aqlīmā and Labūdā (thus elsewhere for the second, though the name given here is Dhamīmā), each destined to be the bride of the other. Qābīl, wanting to marry his own twin, agreed to let the matter be settled by God but, when God's judgment went against him, he murdered Hābīl and married his twin (*EI2*, G. Vajda, art. *Hābīl wa-Ḳābīl*).

408 Q Mā'idah 5:27–32.

409 "his cheeks": Arabic poetic convention addresses the beloved using masculine grammatical forms, regardless of the actual gender of the addressee.

410 Attributed by Yāqūt al-Ḥamawī to Ḥafṣah bint al-Ḥājj al-Rakūniyyah (ca. 530–89/1135–91), a poet and princess of Granada, and by others to another aristocratic Andalusian poet, Walladah bint al-Mustakfī (d. ca. 484/1091), daughter of the Umayyad caliph al-Mustakfī bi-llāh.

411 By the Egyptian poet Yaḥyā ibn 'Īsā ibn Maṭrūḥ (592–649/1196–1251), also known as Jamāl al-Dīn.

412 I.e., the orondolong, or "doorposts," who controlled access to the sultan.

413 Rūngā was in Dār Rungā, a territory south of Darfur inhabited by Fartīt, or pagan, enslaveable, people, from whom the slaves to be made into eunuchs would have come. "Gifts" probably means here "gifts for the sultan," i.e., tribute (see §3.1.60).

414 "their innocent needs" (*awṭārihinna ghayri l-khanāʾ*), *khanāʾ* being perhaps from *khanī*, meaning "foul-mouthed."

415 According to Perron, the name means in Fur "black young man" (El-Tounsy, *Voyage au Darfour*, 254).

416 I.e., the hot rainy season that occurs toward the end of the year (see §3.3.8 below).

417 According to informants, the phrase is more correctly *in attô*; however, the author apparently heard it as given (see below). The meaning is "This is the Day, this is the Day, this is the Day" (El-Tounsy, *Voyage au Darfour*, 438).

418 Q Insān 76:10, the reference being to the Day of Judgment.

419 See §3.1.103.

420 See §3.1.102.

421 "pinafore . . . apron": see §3.1.97.

422 The author tells the story of Sultan Muḥammad Ṣābūn's attack on Tāmah, in which his father was involved and on one occasion even saved the day, in his second work (El-Tounsy, *Voyage au Ouadây*, 187–210).

423 Abū Nuwās (ca. 140–98/757–813).

424 Cf. Q Baqarah 2:61 «And when you said, "Moses, we will not endure one sort of food."»

425 See §3.1.97.

426 Since leucorrhea is an exclusively female condition, the author may be confusing it with a sexually transmitted disease such as gonorrhea, which also produces a discharge in males. Elsewhere *al-ḥaṣar* is defined as "retention of the urine" (Qāsim, *Qāmūs*).

427 Literally "The Arm of the All-Capable."

428 The author commented to Perron: "The affair caused great public scandal. I knew several Fur who, more unfortunate than my friend, had cause to repent of having satisfied the desires of women who seduced them" (El-Tounsy, *Voyage au Darfour*, 263, n. 1).

429 The first line is attributed to Fayṣal ibn Muḥammad al-Jumaylī (875–965/1470–1557); the rest are attributed to Imam ʿAlī ibn Abī Ṭālib (d. 40/660).

430 I.e., by pagans. It is stated above (§3.2.38) that most eunuchs in Darfur were castrated by the Rūngā, a non-Muslim tribe living southwest of Darfur within the sphere of influence of Wadai. The term "Magian," i.e., Zoroastrian, believed to have its origins in the situation of Zoroastrians as non-Muslims living in contact with Muslims in Iraq (formerly) and Iran, was also applied to non-Zoroastrians (e.g., the Vikings, see *EI2*, art. *al-Mādjūs*) by premodern Arab writers; the same terminology was used by the Fur, who referred to pagans as *majusinga* (O'Fahey, *Darfur Sultanate*, 167).

431 See §3.1.14.

432 The Arabic reads *al-abyaḍ al-shāhiq*, literally "braying (like a donkey) white" or "breath-inhaling white"; perhaps a slip of the pen for *abyaḍ sāṭiʿ* "radiant white."

433 Cf. Q Fāṭir 35:19–21 «Not equal are the blind man and the seeing man, and the shadows and the light, and the shade and the torrid heat» (Arberry, *Koran*, 446).

434 Attributed to Qays ibn al-Muwallaḥ, known as Majnūn Laylā (first/seventh century).

435 I.e., of different kinds of galia moschata, "a perfume composed of musk, ambergris, camphor and oil of ben" (Lane, *Lexicon*).

436 I.e., even a little of the beloved's color, in the form of a beauty mark, would be enough to make a white person beautiful.

437 I.e., his saliva.

438 "Counter-poems" (*muʿāraḍah*), with which a poet attempts to contradict, or outdo, an older poem while retaining the original rhyme and meter, are an established genre (see *EAL* 1/82).

439 Al-Ṣaftī's is also a counter-poem, "outdoing" the one that opens "You've fallen for a girl who's black!" above.

440 Q Isrāʾ 17:12.

441 Q Baqarah 2:148.

442 The quotation forms a hemistich (meter: *ṭawīl*) that appears in the work of many poets and seems to be proverbial, though it is sometimes attributed, incorrectly, to Bashshār ibn Burd.

443 Literally "the father of the tongue" or "that of the tongue." Tonsillitis may be meant.

444 The literal sense is unknown; elsewhere *umm ṣuquʿ* is defined as "a swelling in the sinuses" (Qāsim, *Qāmūs*).

445 I.e., verses of the Qur'an written on slips of paper, which are then attached to relevant parts of the patient's body.

446 Quotidian, tertian, and quartan fevers are symptoms of infection by different strains of malaria; it is not clear what "time-specific fever" refers to.

447 I.e., typhoid fever.

448 The date of his visit is given in the French translation as October 1841 (El-Tounsy, *Voyage au Darfour*, 341).

449 I.e., cholera.

450 "the Frankish disease": a sexually-transmitted disease; probably syphilis or gonorrhea.

451 A kind of hoe (see §3.3.52).

452 See §3.2.51 and n. 166.

453 The same word is applied to the intense dust storms carried on weather fronts that affect Sudan, where they were first described, as well as other parts of the world, and that are known in English as "haboobs."

454 Perron believed that the malady in question was "hysteria": "Hysteria, as is well known, sometimes manifests itself in men but is frequent in women. I find it hard to believe that the lubricious habits of the inhabitants of Darfur and other regions of Sudan, the frequency of sexual intercourse, the ardor of their temperaments, and the hot

climate are not sufficient causes to engender hysteria among men there much more frequently than among the men of our countries. This would explain their belief that this malady is contagious" (El-Tounsy, *Voyage au Darfour*, 285, n. 1).

455 "Causing rows."

456 Unidentified.

457 See §2.3.23.

458 Elsewhere, *ṭibb* means "medicine" (as a science and a profession); a practitioner of medicine is called a *ṭabīb*.

459 See §4.41.

460 See §4.42.

461 The author does not, in fact, refer to this elsewhere.

462 Cf. Q Naba' 78:33.

463 This dish, a stew made from rehydrated ingredients, is typically made from okra (see, e.g., Qāsim, *Qāmūs*); however, as the following shows, it may be made from a variety of ingredients.

464 Either of two bushes (*Cassia absus* and *Cassia tora*, see Vogt, *Murshid*, 294). The method of preparation is described as follows: "It is chopped, stalk and leaves, then gathered, wrapped, and placed in tightly sealed earthenware pots until it ferments and becomes as soft as dough. Impurities are then removed and it is turned into small disks and left to dry. When used, it is crumbled like a condiment or spice" (Qāsim, *Qāmūs*).

465 There is no such earlier reference.

466 On the basis of the descriptions that follow, "wild cattle" may mean any of various species of hartebeest (still found in the extreme southwest of Sudan), while by *taytal* may be meant the Bubal hartebeest, once present in North Africa but now extinct.

467 On the face of it, the text contradicts itself (people cannot have no occupation other than hunting and at the same time be smiths), and the passage is absent from the French translation; the solution may lie in the fact that smiths formed an outcaste group in Darfur as elsewhere in the Sudanic lands; below (§3.3.32), the author gives them the alternate name of Darāmidah and says they are outlaws and marry

only among themselves. Thus, the hunters in question may have belonged to this group by birth but lived exclusively from hunting.

468 Perron hazards that this may be the marabou stork (*Ardea argola*) (El-Tounsy, *Voyage au Darfour*, 307, n. 1).

469 "whydahs" (*abū mūsā*): the identification is tentative and based on Cave and MacDonald's naming of the paradise whydah "abu mus" [*sic*] (Cave and MacDonald, *Birds of the Sudan*, 414).

470 Ordinarily, *ẓalīm* means "male ostrich" while *rabdāʾ*, a feminine adjective, means "of a grayish color." Perron explains, however, on the author's authority, that in the usage of Darfur *ẓalīm* means (of an ostrich) "having four large and four small pure-white plumes" while *rabdāʾ* means "having eight gray plumes" (El-Tounsy, *Voyage au Darfour*, 459).

471 *dafra* (*Echinochloa colona/frumentacea*) (voweled in the lithograph as *difrah*) is a cultivated grass (see Vogt, *Murshid*, 279; also https://en.wikipedia.org/wiki/Echinochloa_colona accessed 1 January 2016).

472 "*hijlīj* kernels": Perron transcribes the word as *serneh* and describes them as "kernels of the *hijlīj* fruit from which the bitterness has been removed by maceration in cold water" (El-Tounsy, *Voyage au Darfour*, 459). The fruit and leaves of the same tree were also eaten (see, e.g., §3.3.19, §3.3.25, §4.7).

473 I.e., gold and silver coin.

474 On the contrary, copper ore, mined at Ḥufrat al-Nuḥās in the far southwest of the sultanate, was one of Darfur's most lucrative exports (O'Fahey, *Darfur Sultanate*, 80), while Browne refers to "copper, white, in small quantity" as a regular export (*Travels in Africa*, 304).

475 See §2.2.26.

476 These were the catchment areas of the markets of various towns, as is made clear further on (§3.3.47).

477 No earlier reference has been found. According to Browne, the size, and therefore value, of these rings varied greatly: "These rings are made of so many sizes, that I have known sometimes twelve, sometimes one hundred and forty of them, pass for a given quantity and quality of cotton cloth" (*Travels in Africa*, 290).

478 The Spanish (rather than the French) dollar bore the image of two pillars, which were interpreted in Arab countries as cannons (see Lane, *Manners and Customs*, 573).

479 See §3.1.102.

480 E.g., (approximately) French *tabac*.

481 Various members of the Bakrī family, which claims descent from the first caliph, Abū Bakr al-Ṣiddīq, were prominent in Egypt as scholars, poets, and religious leaders from the sixteenth century through the seventeenth and later, and tobacco first appeared in Egypt in 1606 (Zack, *Egyptian Arabic*, 70). The author is, therefore, mistaken in attributing the poem to the ninth century AH/late fourteenth to late fifteenth centuries AD.

482 The word *ḥashshāshah* ("hoe") is an instrumental noun derived from the word *ḥashīsh* ("weeds, grass").

483 By 1830, these hoes had been reduced, as a part of their conversion into a true currency of purely conventional value, to two or three inches in length, and an observer failed to recognize them for what they were (see O'Fahey, *Darfur Sultanate*, 243).

484 For copper bracelets see §3.1.103 and for the red-and-white cylindrical beads called *khaddūr* see §3.1.102.

485 I.e., Indian corn, maize (*Zea mays*).

486 See §3.1.22.

487 I.e., "dimbi," a red-seeded cultivar of pearl millet (*Pennisetum glaucum* L., also known as "bulrush millet"); by "ordinary millet" the author probably means other, white-seeded, pearl millet cultivars (see Ali and Idris, "Germination," 1).

488 I.e., the hot rainy season that occurs in autumn (see §3.3.8).

489 See also §3.3.19.

490 See §2.2.27 and §3.1.20.

491 The last statement is contradicted by what follows, not to mention that okra is a staple of the diet in Darfur and Sudan generally. Perron corrects the author by translating as follows: "One rarely finds these vegetables elsewhere, though an exception must always be made for okra."

492 Perron states that this canal—al-Khalīj al-Miṣrī ("the Cairo Canal") in full—which ran southwest to northeast through the center of Cairo, was about twenty feet wide (El-Tounsy, *Voyage au Darfour*, 327, n. 2); it dated probably to pharaonic times, was re-dug on several occasions, and was filled in in 1897.

493 See §3.1.101. By "a kind of bean whose pods grow below ground" the author may mean either the peanut (*Arachis hypogaea*), introduced into western Africa from South America in the sixteenth century and known in Egypt today as "Sudanese beans" (*fūl sūdānī*) or the indigenous Bambara groundnut (*Vigna subterranea*); the same applies to "the Sinnār bean."

494 See §3.1.20.

495 The nabk (Arabic: *nabq*), or Christ's-thorn jujube (*Ziziphus spina-christi*).

496 The tree denoted in Fur by the word *dalayb* (see below) is the deleb palm or toddy palm (*Borassus aethiopum*), whereas the fruit denoted by *al-jawz al-hindī* (literally "Indian walnut") is the coconut, whose seeds resemble those of the deleb palm. The term *dulab* does not occur in Arabic dictionaries; the author may have confused Fur *dalayb* with Arabic *dulb*, which, however, refers to the plane or sycamore.

497 According to Nachtigal, the people of Darfur also ate the seeds of the deleb palm (Nachitgal, *Sahara and Sudan*, 4:238).

498 *qiddīm*: perhaps a local pronunciation of or an error for *qiḍḍīm* (*Grewia tenax*) (Bakri and El Gunaid, "Plants Use," 63).

499 See §3.3.49.

500 Probably a local pronunciation of or an error for *laʿūt* (*Acacia nubica*) (Bakri and El Gunaid, "Plants Use," 63).

501 See §3.1.86.

502 Umar defines *jaʿjaʿ* as *Fadogia glaberrima*, a member of a genus of flowering plants found widely in tropical Africa (*Travels*, 451).

503 See §3.2.56 and n. 172.

504 See §3.1.46.

505 I.e., the tree comes to look like a solid object, not like an ordinary tree with branches sticking out.

506 See §3.1.109.

507 Umar identifies it as a species of *Adenium* (dogbane) (*Travels*, 453. n. 3).

508 See §3.1.18, and what follows.

509 I.e., what is called "autumn" (*al-kharīf*), the rainy season, occurs in Darfur during what in Egypt is the summer, while the hot season (*al-darat*) that follows this "autumn" in Darfur is called the spring (*al-rabīʿ*) because it is when the plants grow, and what is called spring in Egypt, they call summer (*al-ṣayf*) in Darfur. Depending on latitude, the rainy season in Darfur starts between September and October and ends between November and December.

510 The Twins (al-Jawzāʾ) are the stars Castor and Pollux of the constellation Gemini, which appears in Darfur in late June; thus the "sprinkle" (*al-rushāsh*) is what are sometimes called "the little rains" that occur during the dry season.

511 I.e., the constellation of Cancer.

512 See §3.3.11 and n. 191.

513 Perhaps because the constellation of the Gemini is associated with the onset of the rains (see §4.29), and therefore with abundance of rain in general.

514 By the Roman (*rūmī*) calendar the author probably means the Julian calendar.

515 These old Arabic names are also the names of the Islamic calendar, hence still in use.

516 The Islamic year starts with the month of Muharram; Shawwal is the tenth month.

517 The meanings of the Darfurian names for the months of the Islamic year are (following the author's explanations to Perron): al-Faṭur (Shawwal) = "Breaking of the Fast" (because this is the month following the fasting month of Ramadan); al-Faṭrayn (Dhu l-Qaʿdah) = "Double Breaking of the Fast" (because this is the second month after Ramadan); al-Ḍaḥiyyah (Dhu l-Hijjah) = "the Sacrifice" (because the Great Feast,

when animals are sacrificed, falls on the tenth day); al-Ḍaḥiyyatayn (Muharram) = "Double Sacrifice" (because this is the month after al-Ḍaḥiyyah); al-Waḥīd (Safar) = "the Lonely" (because it comes between two months that have their own, significant, names, meaning that it is a kind of orphan month); al-Karāmah (Rabiʿ al-Awwal) = "the Miracle" (because this is the month in which God first revealed the Qur'an to the Prophet Muḥammad); al-Tawm (Rabiʿ al-Thani) = "the Twin" (i.e., the month that is the twin of the month that follows); al-Tawmayn (Jumada al-Awwal) = "Double Twin" (see the preceding); Sāyiq (Sā'iq) al-Tīmān (Jumada al-Thani) = "the Driver of the Twins" (because it follows immediately after the Twins); al-Quṣayyar (Shaʿban) = "the Short" (because, as it precedes Ramadan, it always seems too short) (El-Tounsy, *Voyage au Darfour*, 468–69).

518 The word *nārah* is not to be found in the dictionaries but is presumably from *nār* "fire."

519 See §2.3.13.

520 According to Browne, the sons of the sultans (whom he refers to as the rightful heirs of Muḥammad Tayrāb), following their defeat, "are now [in 1794] wandering about, scraping a miserable subsistence from the parsimonious alms of their usurping uncle" (Browne, *Travels in Africa*, 278).

521 The Tomorókkóngá are generally regarded as a subgroup of the Fur.

522 I.e., the author expected to recover his debt in the form of slaves captured during the raid.

523 The text in this passage is so laconic that it has been necessary, while following the Arabic as closely as possible, to draw on the French translation, which expands on it (El-Tounsy, *Voyage au Darfour*, 365–66) in the following instances: "erasing every second hole"; "and moving through them"; "as described above." Perron describes even his own translation of the text as "much too abridged" and follows it with a further explanation, some one thousand words in length, that he was given by the author orally (El-Tounsy, *Voyage au Darfour*, 366, n.1).

GLOSSARY

Names of persons are alphabetized by the first element of the name. Names are given in the form in which they appear in the text, which generally reflect al-Tūnisī's spelling. Other spellings found in the literature (especially O'Fahey, Nachtigal, and Browne) are given in parentheses, e.g., "Fartīt (elsewhere Fertit)." The ascription "Fur" in parentheses after an item indicates that the word is used in the Fur language, but not necessarily that it is ultimately of Fur origin (many terms used in Fur are also used by other ethnic groups). The names of beads, other accessories, and perfumes are ever changing. Items (such as certain plants and diseases) that it has proven impossible to identify satisfactorily are omitted here and dealt with in the notes.

Ab Sanūn a people, also called Kodoi, related to the royal family of Wadai.

ába dima'ng (Fur) see Dār Ába Dima'ng.

ába poor-ii (Fur) according to the author, a title of the kaamíne.

ába umá (elsewhere abbo uumo*; Fur)* commander of the rearguard of the army and hereditary ruler of Dār Umá (Dar Uumo), one of the four primary provinces of Darfur, southeast of Jabal Marrah.

abbo (Fur) a title of respect.

ʿAbd al-Raḥmān al-Rashīd sultan of Darfur (r. 1202/1787 to 1218/1803–4).

Abīrīs (= Bārīs) an outlying oasis west of the al-Khārijah group, fifty-four miles from the town of al-Khārijah.

abū abāṭ Indian corn, maize (*Zea mays*).

Abū ʿAbd Allāh Muḥammad al-Wirghī (d. 1190/1776) Tunisian chancellery secretary and poet.

Abū l-Judūl an estate or group of villages near Tandaltī (El-Fasher) granted to the author's father as a fief and where the author lived during his stay in Darfur.

Abū Muḥammad Ḥammūdah Pasha Ḥammūdah Pasha ibn ʿAlī II (r. 1196–1229/1782–1814), ruler of Tunis.

Abū l-Qāsim sixth historical sultan of the Keira dynasty (r. ca. 1739–52); preceded by ʿUmar Lēl and succeeded by Muḥammad Tayrāb.

Abū l-Ṭayyib al-Mutanabbī see al-Mutanabbī.

abū ṣaffayr (so voweled in the original) jaundice.

abū l-ṣufūf pleurisy.

Abū Zaʿbal a locality north of Cairo, where the first modern Egyptian medical school was opened on February 28, 1827, attached to a military hospital; the school was transferred to Qaṣr al-ʿAynī in Cairo in 1837.

Ādam Adam, father of humankind; also a male given name.

Adiqiz (Agadez) formerly a city-state, now a region of central Niger.

ʿAdnān putative ancestor of the Northern Arabs, i.e., those who speak Arabic as it is commonly known, versus the Southern Arabs, who speak the now largely extinct South Arabian languages.

ʿAfnū Hausaland.

Aḥmad Bukur (or Bukr) (r. ca. 1700–20) third of the historical Keira sultans, associated with the second phase of Islamization of the Darfur state.

Aḥmad ibn Sulaymān a teacher in Tunis and the maternal uncle of the author's father.

Aḥmad Zarrūq an uncle of the author's; presumably a son, born in Sennar, of his grandfather Sulaymān.

al-Alfī Muḥammad Bayk al-Alfī (d. 1226/1811), a Mamluk army commander who, shortly before the events described by the author, had played a role in the failed attempt to restore Mamluk control over Egypt; his sobriquet, from *alf* ("one thousand"), means "purchased for a thousand dinars."

ʿAlī, Imam ʿAlī ibn Abī Ṭālib, cousin and son-in-law of the Prophet Muḥammad and fourth caliph (r. 35–40/656–61), famed for his wise sayings.

ʿAlī al-Darwīsh ʿAlī ibn Ḥasan ibn Ibrāhīm al-Ankūrī al-Miṣrī (1211–70/1797–1853), Egyptian poet, laureate to the viceroy ʿAbbās I.

ʿAlī al-Ghurāb ʿAlī ibn al-Ghurāb al-Ṣafaqisī (d. 1183/1769), poet from Sfax, known for eulogies of the rulers of Tunis and bawdy verse.

ʿAlī Pasha I ʿAlī I ibn Muḥammad (r. 1148–70/1735–56), second Ḥusaynid ruler of Tunis.

ʿAlī wad Jāmiʿ a grandee at the court of Sultan ʿAbd al-Raḥmān and patron of Shaykh-Father Muḥammad Kurrā.

Anbūsah (elsewhere *Umm Būsa*) a slave woman belonging to Sultan ʿAbd al-Raḥmān and mother of his successor, Sultan Muḥammad Faḍl.

ʿandurāb a tree: either *Cordia monoica*, "snot-berry tree," or *Cordia sinensis*, "gray-leaved cordia."

ʿanqallū green fruit of the Jericho balm tree (*hijlīj*).

the Anṣār literally "the helpers"; i.e., the men (of the peoples of Aws and Khazraj) of Medina who supported the Prophet Muḥammad, as distinguished from the Muhājirūn or "emigrants," i.e., his Meccan followers who moved with him to Medina.

ʿaqīq round agate beads.

ʿArafah al-Dusūqī al-Mālikī Muḥammad ibn Aḥmad ibn ʿArafah al-Dusūqī (d. 1230/1815), a prominent Mālikī jurisprudent and scholar of his day.

al-Azhar the premier mosque and teaching institution of premodern Cairo, built 361/972.

báási (Fur; approx. "royal") a title originally given the brother of the sultan and later extended to apply to all his male relatives.

Bāb al-Muʿallā Mecca's most ancient cemetery.

Banī ʿAdī a town in Upper Egypt near the west bank of the Nile in the governorate of Banī Suwayf and the terminus of the so-called Forty Days Road (*Darb al-Arbiʿīn*) between Egypt and Darfur.

the Banū Ḥalbah cattle-herding nomads living south of Jabal Marrah.

the Banū Jarrār cattle-herding nomads belonging to the Fazārah group.

the Banū ʿUmrān cattle-herding nomads belonging to the Fazārah group.

al-Bāqirmah (Bagirmi) formerly, a state southeast of Lake Chad in what is now Chad.

Baradiyyah in the Wadai sultanate, a goblet drum.

the Barajūb probably, the swamps of Baḥr al-Ghazāl and Baḥr al-Jabal, south of Darfur.

the Barqū a people, originally from Wadai, with many communities in Darfur (cf. Dār Barqū, a name for Wadai).

the Bartī (Berti) a people living in eastern Darfur, formerly speakers of a now-extinct Nubian language.

al-Basūs, War of a pre-Islamic intertribal conflict fought toward the end of the fifth century AD that lasted forty years and was blamed on an old woman called al-Basūs whose camel had been killed by a member of a rival tribe.

baṭṭūm a tree: probably terebinth (*Pistacia terebinthus*).

Bawwā a wadi in northern Darfur, perhaps the same as the "Wadi Howa" on modern maps.

the Bidāyāt a non-Arabic-speaking people found in northwestern Darfur.

bindilah a kind of dance.

Bingah a Fartīt people living on the southern fringes of the sultanate.

the Bīqū (Beigo) a Dājū-speaking people of originally servile status living in southern Darfur.

Bīr al-Malḥah ("Salt Flat Well") alternative name of Bīr al-Zaghāwī.

Bīr al-Zaghāwī ("al-Zaghāwī's Well") a well on the road from Asyut to Darfur south of Laqiyyah, also called Bīr al-Malḥah.

the Birqid a people living east of Jabal Marrah and south of Tandaltī (El-Fasher) who spoke a Nubian language.

Bornu (Barnaw) from 1380 to 1893, an empire that at its height incorporated parts of what are now Nigeria, Chad, Cameroon, and Niger; in the author's day, the state immediately west of Wāddāy (Wadai).

al-Bukhārī, Muḥammad ibn Ismāʿīl (194–256/810–70) author of an authoritative collection of some eight thousand sound prophetic hadiths.

Būlāq (1) the name of two localities in Cairo, one (Būlāq Abū l-ʿIlā) being the city's port, on the east bank of the Nile; the other (Būlāq al-Dakrūr) a settlement on its west bank, in Giza; (2) a village on the caravan route from Asyut to Darfur, seventeen miles west of al-Khārijah.

al-burjuk scarlet fever.

būzah in Egypt, barley beer; elsewhere usually spelled *būẓah*.

the Caravanserai of the Jallābah (Wikālat al-Jallābah) a *wikālah* was a combined warehouse and hostel for merchants; the *jallābah* were traveling merchants drawn largely from Upper Egypt and northern Nilotic Sudan who traded between the Sudanic countries and Egypt. The greater part of their trade from Darfur was in slaves, but ivory, ostrich feathers, wild-animal parts, camels, and other merchandise were also taken to Egypt, while beads, tin, cloth, swords, coffee, paper, and more were taken from Egypt to Darfur.

counselor (Arabic: amīn, pl. umanāʾ) a confidential advisor to the sultan of Darfur.

the Dājū a people living in southern Darfur whose ancestors are said to have ruled the first Darfurian state and who were superseded in the sixteenth century by the Tunjūr.

al-Dalīl, Judge chief judge of Wadai, who passed through Cairo in October 1841 on his way to Mecca and there met with both the author and Nicolas Perron.

dallūkah set of three goblet drums.

dam-l-raʿāf (= *dam al-ruʿāf*, literally "nosebleed blood") a kind of coral bead.

damsuga (Fur) personal spirit guardian purchased from the jinn.

Dār literally "house" and, when followed by the name of a group or individual, "land of, territory of"; hence Dār Fartīt ("the Land of the Fartīt"), Dār Bagirmi ("the Land of the Bagirmi"), Dār Wāddāy ("Wadai"), Dār al-Tikináwi (Darfur's northern province, governed by the Tikináwi).

Dār Ába Dima'ng (Dar Aba Dima; Fur) literally "The Land of the Lord of Dima'ng"; an autonomous area southwest of Jabal Marrah ruled by a line of hereditary chiefs.

Dār Bandalah a Fartīt people, non-Muslims living on the southern fringes of the sultanate.

Dār Mallā (Mali) formerly (tenth to fifteenth centuries AD), a western Sudanic empire between the Upper Senegal and Upper Niger rivers.

Dār Qimir (Dar Qimr) a sultanate subject to Darfur, north of Dār Masālīṭ and south of Dār Zaghāwah, ruled by a dynasty allegedly originating from the Jaʿaliyyīn ethnic group in the Nilotic Sudan.

Dār al-Rīḥ literally the Land of the Wind; an alternative name for Dār al-Tikináwi, the sultanate's northern province.

Dār Rūngā the territory of a Fartīt (non-Muslim) people living on the southwestern fringes of the sultanate.

Dār Silā (Dar Sula) a Dājū-speaking kingdom lying between Darfur and Wadai and paying tribute to both.

Dār Ṣulayḥ (also Dār Ṣāliḥ) an alternative name for (Dār al-) Wādday (Wadai), either because its inhabitants claimed descent from one Ṣāliḥ (of which Ṣulayḥ is the diminutive) ibn ʿAbd Allāh ibn ʿAbbās, or because its second founder, Sultan Jawdah (r. ca. 1747–75), bore the epithet al-Ṣāliḥ, meaning "the Righteous."

Dār Tāmā, Dār Tāmah an area between Darfur and Wadai in the west, never comfortably part of Darfur or of Wadai; it takes its name from the Tāmā (Tāmah) people of Jabal Tāmā.

Dār Tunbuktū (Timbuktu) a state on the Niger River, today in Niger.

darat a period of extreme heat lasting about forty days from the end of the rainy season (see *kharīf*), during which the sorghum ripens.

Darfur a formerly independent sultanate located between al-Wādday (Wadai, now eastern Chad) on the west and Kordofan on the east; since 1916, part of Sudan. The name is a contraction of Dār al-Fūr, the Land of the Fur.

darmūdī member of an outcast group of hunters and smiths.

dawdarī kind of *waykah* (q.v.) made from bonemeal.

dééng saaya (Fur) a slightly fermented drink of rice, sugar, and water (= Arabic *sūbiyā*).

dhikr Sufi ceremony that, through rhythmic movement and sound, allows the participant to achieve mystical unity with God; the specifically Fur form of the *dhikr* described by the author differs, however, from this norm.

difrah a grain; probably sawa millet.

dimlij (pl. damālij) literally "bracelet"; subchief under the authority of a *shartāy*.

dinbī "dimbi," a cultivar of pearl (bulrush) millet.

dinjāyah a mud-brick storehouse within the *fāshir* (q.v.) of the sultan of Darfur.

dinqār a large wooden drum of state.

Dongola a town on the Nile in Sudanese Nubia.

dullong (Fur) a kind of small clay pot.

al-duqrī osteomyelitis.

durdur a circular wall of mud forming the foundation of the walls of the houses of members of the elite.

durrāʿah a length of cloth wound around the upper half of a woman's body.

durzūyah a wooden pillar used to support the roof of a *tukultī* (q.v.).

emir army commander.

The Epitome (al-Mukhtaṣar) an authoritative handbook of Islamic law according to the Mālikī school of jurisprudence by Khalīl ibn Isḥāq al-Jundī (d. 776/1374).

Fallātā, Fallātah (from Kanuri, "people"; Fellata) name of a nomadic people found from Mauritania to eastern Sudan, who call themselves Fulbe (sg. Pullo); also called here Fullān (sg. Fullānī), from the Hausa.

the Fanqarū (Fongoro) a people living in southern Dār Ába Dima'ng.

faqīh (1) (used of non-Darfurians; plural *fuqahā'*) a man trained in Islamic legal science, a jurisprudent (2) (used of Darfurians; plural, anomalously, *fuqarā'*) a holy man, i.e., a man, not necessarily learned, from a family, usually of non-Darfurian origin, credited with religious charisma (*barakah*) and supernatural powers who often acted as a village schoolmaster.

the Farāwujayh (Feroge) a Fartīt (non-Muslim) people living south of Baḥr al-ʿArab.

fardah apron-like garment worn by women.

Fartīt non-Muslim peoples living on the southern margins of Darfur; they were regarded as enslaveable by the raiders from the north; despite this, it was recognized that in some way the Fartīt were related to the Fur.

fāshir the compound forming the seat of the sultan's government, in former times itinerant but from 1791 located permanently at Tandaltī (now known as El-Fasher, capital of the federal state of North Darfur); the term, which is used from Lake Chad to the Nile, is of unknown origin and seems to have referred in the first instance to the open space before the encampment of a king or chief.

the Fazārah a generic term for the cattle-owning, Arabic-speaking nomads of southern Darfur.

feathers (Arabic: rīsh) (1) "the feathers": the sultan's ceremonial fan; (2) a kind of bead.

Fezzan Libya's southwestern province.

Fullān (Fulan, Fulani, Fulbe) an alternative name for the Fallātā (q.v.).

fuqarā' see *faqīh.*

Fur the largest ethnic group in Darfur, forming about one third of the population and speaking a Nilo-Saharan language. Sultans from the Fur ruled Darfur from the mid-seventeenth century until 1916.

al-Fusṭāṭ site of the first capital of Egypt under Muslim rule, just south of Cairo.

The Glittering Ladder *The Glittering Ladder on Logic* (*al-Sullam al-murawnaq fī l-manṭiq*) by 'Abd al-Raḥmān ibn Muḥammad al-Akhḍarī (918–83/1512–75), a well-known didactic poem on logic.

the Ḥabbāniyyah (Habbania) an Arab-speaking, cattle-herding, semi-nomadic people of southern Darfur.

al-habūb wind trapped in the lower belly.

Hadith the corpus of reports (hadiths) of the words or actions of the Prophet Muḥammad.

the Hafsids the dynasty that ruled Tunisia and eastern Algeria from 627/1229 to 982/1574.

al-Ḥājj title of Muslims who have made the pilgrimage to Mecca.

al-Ḥajjāj al-Ḥajjāj ibn Yūsuf (ca. 41/661 to 95/714), governor of Iraq, who brutally crushed several revolts against Umayyad rule.

Ḥalfāwīn a historic district of Tunis (Halfaouine).

Ḥalq al-Wād the fortified port of Tunis (La Goulette).

Ḥammūdah Pasha see Abū Muḥammad Ḥammūdah Pasha.

ḥarāz a tree: apple-ring acacia (*Faidherbia* (or *Acacia*) *albida*).

al-Ḥarīrī al-Qāsim ibn ʿAlī al-Ḥarīrī (446–516/1054–1122), Iraqi prose writer, poet, and civil servant, author of fifty immensely popular *maqāmāt* (compositions in a highly polished style), which he arranged in a work of the same name.

ḥarish a kind of bead worn by poor women and used in certain localities as currency.

Ḥasan wad ʿAwūḍah chief imam of Kūbayh under Sultan ʿAbd al-Raḥmān.

al-ḥaṣar leukorrhea.

ḥashāb a tree: gum acacia (*Senegalia* (or *Acacia*) *senegal*); elsewhere spelled *hashāb*.

ḥashshāshah a kind of iron hoe.

al-hayḍah cholera.

Ḥawwāʾ the first woman, the Qurʾanic equivalent of Eve; also a given name.

the High Plain (al-Ṣaʿīd) the name given in Darfur to the area from Rīl south to the farthest limits of the country.

hijlīj a tree: Jericho balm (*Balanites aegyptiaca*).

Ḥillat Jūltū village in the district of Abū l-Judūl.

ḥummayḍ a tree: marula (*Sclerocarya birrea*).

al-Ḥusayn, Shrine of mosque in Cairo containing a tomb said to hold the head of al-Ḥusayn, grandson of the Prophet Muḥammad.

Ḥusayn ʿAmmārī al-Azharī Bedouin shaykh from Kordofan, known as the introducer of tobacco to Darfur.

Ḥusayn Pasha al-Ḥusayn I ibn ʿAlī al-Turkī (r. 1117–48/1705–35), founder of Tunis's Ḥusaynid dynasty.

Ibn Ājurrūm's Text (al-Ājurrūmiyyah) widely used brief compendium of Arabic grammar, formally entitled *al-Muqadimmah al-Ājurrūmiyyah*, by Abū ʿAbd Allāh Muḥammad ibn Dāʾūd al-Sanhājī (672–723/1273–1323), known as Ibn Ājurrūm.

Ibn Ḥajar Aḥmad ibn Muḥammad ibn ʿAlī ibn Hajar al-Haythamī al-Makkī al-Ansārī (909/1503–4 to 973/1565–66), an influential Shāfiʿī jurist.

Ibrāhīm the builder of the Kaaba, identified with biblical Abraham; also a male given name.

Ibrāhīm al-Riyāḥī Ibrāhīm ibn ʿAbd al-Qādir ibn Aḥmad al-Riyāḥī al-Tūnisī (1180–1266/1766–1850), Mālikī jurist, chief mufti of Tunis, and poet.

Ibrāhīm wad Ramād powerful Fur clan chief and Master of the Drums during the reign of Sultan ʿAbd al-Raḥmān; his name, "son of Ashes," alluded to his illegitimacy.

the Illumined City Medina.

Imruʾ al-Qays (sixth century AD) celebrated pre-Islamic Arabian poet.

the ʿIrayqāt (Ireigat) an Arabic-speaking, camel-herding people forming part of the Northern Ruzayqāt.

irdabb a dry measure equal to 198 liters.

iyā kurī (Fur: "mother" + "power") title of the sultan's premier wife.

ʿIzz al-Dīn al-Jāmiʿī (elsewhere, al-Jāmiʿ) a judge during the reign of Sultan ʿAbd al-Raḥmān and later chief judge of Darfur and its territories; member of the Jamāwiʿah family of holy men whose ancestor came from the east and was invited to settle in Darfur by Sultan Sulaymān Solóng.

Jabal Marrah mountain range in western Darfur; homeland of the Fur and cradle of the Keira dynasty of Darfur sultans (see O'Fahey, *Darfur Sultanate*, 3, 33–36). The author refers to a specific peak within the range as "the true Marrah" and on his map of Darfur draws a Little Jabal Marrah (presumably the same) about halfway between the north and south ends of the range but slightly to the west. It has not proven possible to identify this peak.

Jabal Tāmah see Dār Tāmah.

(Jadīd) Karyū a village south of Tandaltī, on the estate of Faqīh Mālik al-Fūtāwī.

(Jadīd) Rās al-Fīl a village in southeast Darfur, northeast of Rīl; formerly a *fāshir* (q.v.).

Jadīd al-Sayl a village near Tandaltī (El-Fasher).

jallābah (sg. jallāb) traveling merchants trading between Egypt and Sudan.

Jarkū perhaps modern Jarkul, near Mellit.

jêl (Fur) kind of dance.

al-jiqqayl a sexually-transmitted disease; probably syphilis or gonorrhea.

jūghān or jūkhān a tree: jackalberry (*Diospyros mespiliformis*).

kaamíne (kamni, kamene; Fur) the "shadow sultan," an ancient ritual title of enormous prestige but little power.

kaʿb al-ṭīb literally "the best of perfumes": a perfume made from a certain root.

the Kabābīsh an Arabic-speaking group of camel nomads living between Kordofan and Sennar.

kabartū in the Wadai sultanate, officers of the law, executioners, and musicians of a low caste.

Kabkābiyyah (Fur; literally "they threw down their shields") a town ninety-two miles west of Tandaltī (El-Fasher), named in reference to the defeat of invading Wadaian forces by those of Darfur under Sultan Aḥmad Bukur.

al-Kāf a city in northwest Tunisia (Le Kef).

Kalīlah and Dimnah (Kalīlah wa-Dimnah) a book of animal fables translated by ʿAbd Allāh ibn al-Muqaffaʿ (second/eighth century) from the Persian and ultimately of Indian origin.

kalkaf a fine cotton cloth.

kamkūlak in the Wadai sultanate, a counselor attending the sultan at audience; or one of four with this title, one of whom was in charge of the administration of the sultan's palace while the other three assisted with the administration of the sultan's estates; said to mean "sweeper of the sultan's house" (same reference).

kanfūs (pl. kanāfīs) women's breechclouts.

Karakriit one of the three great sections of the Fur; the Karakriit live in and to the east of Jabal Marrah.

karbābah reed hut.

karnū a variety of jujube.

kāshif literally "uncoverer, inspector"; in contemporary Egypt, governor of a minor province, as a rule drawn from the Turkish-speaking military elite.

the Kashmirah a people living in Wadai.

Katakū (Kotoko) formerly a kingdom covering parts of modern Cameroon, Nigeria, and southwest Chad.

katkāt a kind of heavy *tukkiyyah* (q.v.) of a compact weave.

kawal either of two bushes (*Cassia absus* and *Cassia tora*) and the condiment made from their fermented leaves and stalks.

kenykenya (Fur) a kind of candy made from dried jujube seeds.

Khabīr literally "expert"; title of the leader of a desert caravan; also a given name.

khaddūr kind of bead worn by poor women and used as currency for small purchases; Nachtigal describes the beads as large and made of clay.

Khalīl [ibn Isḥāq al-Jundī] (Khalīl al-Mālikī) (d. ca. 1365), author of *The Epitome* (q.v.).

kharīf the rainy season in Darfur, which starts between September and October and ends between November and December depending on latitude.

Khāqān a title of the sultans of Darfur, as also of the Ottoman sultan.

al-Khārijah (Kharjah) a group of oases in Egypt west of Asyut.

khayriyyah an Egyptian gold coin of the value of nine piasters (see Lane, *Manners*, 573).

Khūrshīd Pasha Aḥmad Khūrshīd Pasha, Ottoman governor of Egypt from 1804 until ousted by Muḥammad ʿAlī in 1805.

kilí a tree (unidentified) producing a drink used to determine the innocence or guilt of accused persons.

kīm horn bracelets worn by women.

Kīrī a village; according to informants it is close to Qirlī at the foot of Jabal Marrah.

kitir a tree: blackthorn (*Senegalia mellifera*).

kóór kwa (Fur) literally "spearmen"; slaves with spears who stood behind the sultan as part of his bodyguard when he held audience and surrounded him when he rode out; among them were young boys who sang and made music with whistles and maracas. They were also used as messengers and for other services.

Kordofan the region from Darfur's eastern border almost to the Nile; unlike Darfur, and Sennar to its east, Kordofan never underwent a process of state formation. Today, as part of Sudan, the area is divided into the federal states of North and South Kordofan.

Kūbayh (Kobbei, Kobbé) a town, now abandoned, thirty-five miles northwest of Tandaltī (El-Fasher). Kūbayh formed the southern terminus of the trade route between Asyut in Egypt and Darfur (the "Forty Days Road"), was inhabited almost exclusively by traders, and constituted the commercial capital of Darfur; in its heyday in the eighteenth and first half of the nineteenth centuries, it may have been the largest town in the sultanate, with six to eight thousand inhabitants.

the Kūkah a people of southwestern Wadai.

kumbā (or kanbū: both occur in the text; from Fur kômbo*)* as defined by the author, a liquid extracted from the ash of the *hijlīj* tree (Jericho balm, *Balanites aegyptiaca*) and used as a salt substitute.

Kunjáara (Kunjaara, Kunyjaara) one of the three great sections of the Fur people and that to which the Keira dynasty belonged; the Kunjáara live in and to the east of Jabal Marrah.

kūrāyāt literally "grooms"; four high officials in charge of the sultan's horses and servants. The word, though presumably Fur, was not recognized by informants.

kūrayb either of two grasses that are used for fodder and as famine foods: Egyptian crowfoot grass (*Dactyloctenium aegyptium*) and dropseed grass (*Sporobolus festivus*).

kurnug a kind of house resembling a *tukultī* but whose roof is raised on four rather than two wooden pillars (see §3.1.86, images).

Kusā a region of central Darfur.

laddāy a woman's headpiece of silver wire and beads.

lanngi (Fur) a dance.

Laqiyyah (Leghea, Laguyeh, Lagia) an uninhabited oasis on the route from Asyut to Darfur, south of Salīmah and close to the northern marches of Dār Zaghāwah.

lawī a variety of the cotton known as "Indian."

liqdābah (apparently from Fur libdenga*)* a roofed, open-sided structure within the sultan's compound used as an audience hall, mess, etc.

Little Jabal Marrah (Jubayl Marrah) the author's name for the peak, probably that usually referred to on modern maps as the Deriba Caldera, that lends its name to the entire Jabal Marrah mountain range and plateau.

Lubad According to ancient Arabian legend, Luqmān the Long-lived, a pre-Islamic figure to whom wise sayings are attributed, was granted, as a reward for his piety, a life as long as that of seven named vultures (the vulture being a popular symbol of longevity among the Arabs). The last vulture was named Lubad; when Lubad died, so did Luqmān.

madīdah a broth made from pounded desiccated watermelon.

madraʿah a bead bracelet worn by women.

Magian literally "Zoroastrian"; applied in Darfur to the pagan peoples on its southern borders.

the Maḥāmīd cattle-herding nomads of the Fazārah group.

the Majānīn Arabic-speaking camel-herding nomads living in eastern Darfur and western Kordofan.

Makk a title, equivalent to "king," used by rulers in the Nile Valley, such as the Makk of Sennar; also used by the chief of the Birgid of Darfur.

the Malanqā (also Mananqah) a subgroup of the Ab Sanūn (q.v.).

malik a title used of (1) a king; (2) a tribal chief or person related to the royal family to whom some of the accoutrements of Sudanic royalty (such as the possession of copper war drums) pertained; (3) an official in charge of a significant place or specialized group. See further Note on the Text, pp. xliii–xliv.

Mālik al-Fūtāwī Mālik ibn ʿAlī ibn Yūsuf al-Fūtāwī (d. ca. 1820), a prominent member of the Awlād ʿAlī family of holy men and an influential vizier at the court of Sultan ʿAbd al-Raḥmān; sponsor of the author's father.

Mālikī follower of the school of jurisprudence established by Mālik ibn Anas (179/795); most African Muslims, apart from those of Egypt, are *Mālikī*s and the designation often appears in names, e.g., Shaykh ʿArafah al-Dusūqī al-Mālikī.

the Mananqah see Malanqā.

Mandarah a kingdom (ca. 1500–1893) and people in what is today northwest Cameroon.

Manfalūṭ a city in Upper Egypt on the west bank of the Nile north of Asyut.

manjūr a bead worn by women of the middle class.

manṣūṣ (literally "squashed") round, flattened amber beads.

maqāmah a short independent narration written in ornamental rhymed prose with verse insertions, a common plot-scheme, and two constant protagonists: the narrator and the hero.

al-Maqs (Macs, Maghs, Mughess) the southernmost oasis of the Khārijah complex, uninhabited in the author's day.

al-Marbūṭah a village on the banks of Wādī l-Kū' not far from Tandaltī (El-Fasher).

marhabayb a species of thin cane (*Cymbopogon nervatus* and/or *proximus*) with which houses are roofed; elsewhere sometimes spelled *marḥabayb*.

mārīq a generic name for sorghum.

Marrah see Jabal Marrah, Little Jabal Marrah.

the Masālīṭ (Maṣālīṭ, Mesalit) a large people with its own language living to the west of Jabal Marrah.

al-Mazrūb a well marking the northern entry into Darfur for those coming from Asyut in Egypt.

mééram (Fur) a title given to the daughter of the sultan of Darfur or to younger marriageable women of the royal family in general, as opposed to the *habbūbāt*, and to the representative of the bride and her friends at a wedding.

The Memorandum (al-Tadhkirah) see al-Qurṭubī.

the Mīdawb (Meidob) a people living on Jabal Mīdawb in far northeastern Darfur who speak a language of the Nubian group.

mīdawbī a kind of naturally occurring salt.

the Mīmah a people centered on the town of Wada'ah east of Wādī Ku' in eastern Darfur.

al-Minyah a city in Upper Egypt on the west bank of the Nile.

mishāhrah a bead worn by women.

the Misīriyyah (Misiriyah, Messiria) the Brown Misīriyyah (al-Misīriyyah al-Ḥumr) are camel nomads living in northern Kordofan, the Black Misīriyyah (al-Misīriyyah al-Zurq) are cattle nomads living in southern Kordofan; both peoples have offshoots in Darfur.

mooge (singular and plural; Fur—pronounced as two syllables) jester cum eulogist cum crier who shouted the praises of his master (for example, the sultan) on public occasions, was licensed to speak audaciously, and sometimes acted as public executioner.

the Mother of the Book the Qur'an.

mudd measure of volume used for grain; Perron states, on the author's authority, that the Sudanese *mudd* was equal to the Egyptian *malwah*, i.e., 4.125 liters.

Mughulṭāy al-Turkī Mughulṭāy ibn Qalīj ʿAbdullāhi al-Bakjarī al-Miṣrī (689–762/1290–1361), Egyptian historian and Hadith scholar of Turkic origin, also known for his book on martyrs for love, *al-Wāḍiḥ al-mubīn fīman ustushhida min al-muḥibbīn* (*The Clear Exposition Concerning Those Who Gave Their Lives for Love*).

mughrah a stone from which a red pigment is obtained.

al-Muhallabī, the vizier al-Ḥasan ibn Muḥammad al-Muhallabī (291–352/903–63), administrator and general for the Buyid princes of Baghdad, and a litterateur.

Muḥammad ʿAlī (r. 1805–48) ruler of Egypt under the nominal suzerainty of the Ottoman state.

Muḥammad Daldan (Fur: Daldang) wad Binayyah (d. 1804?) Keira warlord and slave trader, styled "King" because he was a grandson of Sultan Muḥammad Tayrāb.

Muḥammad Faḍl (elsewhere usually al-Faḍl) ninth sultan of Darfur of the Keira dynasty (r. ca. 1730–39), preceded by his father, ʿAbd al-Raḥmān, and succeeded by his son, Muḥammad al-Ḥusayn.

Muḥammad al-Ḥasanī Muḥammad III ibn ʿAbd Allāh (r. 1171–1204/1757–90), ʿAlawid ruler of Morocco.

Muḥammad ibn al-Qāsim ʿImād al-Dīn Muḥammad ibn al-Qāsim al-Thaqafī (ca. 695–715), a Muslim general best known for the conquest, at an extremely young age, of Sindh and Multan.

Muḥammad al-Jallūlī Ḥusaynid governor of Sfax in Tunisia in the late eighteenth or early nineteenth century.

Muḥammad Kurrā (d. 1804) in Fur "Muḥammad the Tall"; a palace servant in the days of Sultan Muḥammad Tayrāb who rose to become, despite temporary setbacks, shaykh-father under sultans ʿAbd al-Raḥmān and Muḥammad Faḍl and, for a time, master of Kordofan. His rivalry with Muḥammad Faḍl led to his death. The author was a protégé of Muḥammad Kurrā's associate Mālik al-Fūtāwī and met Muḥammad Kurrā shortly before the shaykh-father's death.

Muḥammad al-Maḥrūqī likely the leading merchant of that name (d. 1232/1816–17) appointed by Muḥammad ʿAlī to advise his son Ṭūsūn when the latter was given responsibility for the campaign (1811–16) against the Āl Saʿūd rulers of the Hejaz.

Muḥammad al-Muknī nineteenth-century governor of Fezzan (southern Libya).

Muḥammad Órré Dungo a eunuch belonging to Sultan Muḥammad Tayrāb and a shaykh-father.

Muḥammad Shihāb al-Dīn al-Miṣrī Muḥammad ibn Ismāʿīl ibn ʿUmar (1210–74/1795–1857), known as Shihāb al-Dīn al-Miṣrī, a scholar and poet who became coeditor of the official *Egyptian Gazette* (*al-Waqāʾiʿ al-Miṣriyyah*), was associated with the royal family, and wrote much occasional verse.

Muḥammad Tayrāb (r. ca. 1752–53 to 1785) third son of Aḥmad Bukur to become sultan of Darfur; invaded Kordofan toward the end of his reign and incorporated it into the sultanate, thus creating the largest premodern state within what is now the Sudan.

mukhkhayṭ a tree: *Boscia senegalensis*.

Murād Bayk Murād Bayk al-Qazdaghlī, a Mamluk who ruled Egypt in partnership with Ibrāhīm Bayk from 1784 until the French invasion in 1798.

muʿrāqī literally "rooter"; one skilled in the gathering and use of medicinal plants.

al-Musabbaʿ brother of Sultan Sulaymān Solóng (q.v.); left Darfur for western Kordofan, parts of which his descendants thereafter ruled.

al-Musabbaʿāwī, Hāshim (fl. 1770–1800) a descendant of al-Musabbaʿ who, during the reign in Darfur of Sultan Muḥammad Tayrāb, attempted to create from his base in Kordofan a state that would rival or supplant that of Darfur.

Musāʿid (ibn Surūr) a member of the family of the Dhawū Zayd dynasty of rulers of Mecca resident in Darfur during the author's time there.

al-Mutanabbī Aḥmad ibn al-Ḥusayn Abū l-Ṭayyib al-Mutanabbī (ca. 303–54/915–65), a renowned poet of the Abbasid era.

nārah a love potion.

Nufah (Nupe) a state, founded in the mid-fifteenth century, in what is now north-central Nigeria.

Numlayh a village in Jabal Marrah, in the area inhabited by the Karakriit, a clan of the Fur (not to be confused with Nimule, a town in South Sudan).

Nūr al-Anṣārī a holy man living in Kubayh and married to the daughter of Sultan ʿAbd al-Raḥmān.

nyúlmá (Fur) sesame lees.

The One-Thousand-Line Poem (al-Alfiyyah) a popular textbook of grammar in the form of a poem of some thousand lines, by Muḥammad ibn Mālik (ca. 600–72/1203–74).

ŏrnang (Fur) the representative of the men at a wedding and organizer of hunting parties for the young men of a village; the ŏrnang may be evidence of a residual age-grade system, comparable to that of the Maasai or the Zulu, in which he acted as a war leader.

orondolong (Fur) literally "the door posts"; the highest officer of state, also known as "the sultan's face" (or "the sultan's head"). In peace, he acted as majordomo of the sultan's compound and the main intermediary between sultan and subjects; in war, he marched at the head of the sultan's army. He also governed four tribal territories.

órré bayyâ (Fur) literally "the narrow door," but generally referred to as "the women's door": the southern entrance to the sultan's compound or *fāshir*; also, in the author's usage, the superintendent of the *warrābāyah*, who supervised the eunuchs of the harem and acted as jailer and executioner.

órré dee (Fur) "the men's door": the northern entrance to the sultan's compound or *fāshir*.

órré'ng ába (Fur) a title listed by the author as that of a member of the state hierarchy who governed two tribal territories, without further explanation of the title's meaning or its holder's role.

pǎw (Fur) artificial coral.

Perron, Nicolas (1798–1876) the translator from Arabic into French of *The Land of the Blacks* (*Voyage au Darfour*) and other works.

The Poem on Words Ending in –ā and ā' (al-Maqṣūrah) a pedagogical poem by Mūhammad ibn al-Ḥasan ibn Durayd (223–321/838–933).

pôlgo (Fur) kind of manufactured salt, sold in finger-shaped pieces.

poora'ng ába (Forrang Aba; Fur) literally "Father of the Fur"; the guardian of Fur law and custom, a ritual title dating from the Fur state's remote past.

Preserved Tablet the urtext of the Qur'an, preserved in Heaven.

the Protected City an epithet of Cairo.

qafal a tree: perhaps in this context frankincense (*Boswellia papyrifera*) or African myrrh (*Commiphora africana*); identification is tentative as the word was applied to a number of trees used in perfumes, medicines, and incense.

qanā savannah bamboo (*Oxytenanthera abyssinica*).

qaraẓ the pods of the sant acacia (*Acacia nilotica*), used for fodder.

Qimir see Dār Qimir.

Qirlī (Gurly, Gerli, Gerle) a settlement, now disappeared, that the author places between the northern end of Jabal Marrah and Kabkābiyyah on the west, site of a *fāshir* of Sultan Muḥammad Tayrāb.

The Qualities *The Prophetic Qualities* (*al-Khaṣā'iṣ al-nabawiyyah*), a work on the qualities of the Prophet Muḥammad by Egyptian historian and Hadith scholar Mughulṭāy al-Turkī.

qudānī an indigo-dyed cloth.

quffah in Egypt, a large basket.

qūqū the practice of carrying a baby by tying it to its mother's back.

al-Qurṭubī Muḥammad ibn Aḥmad ibn Abī Bakr al-Anṣārī al-Qurṭubī (d. 671/1273), author of a renowned commentary on the Qur'an and other works, including his *Memorandum on the Conditions of the Dead and Matters of the Hereafter* (*al-Tadhkirah fī Aḥwāl al-Mawtā wa-Umūr al-Ākhirah*); originally from Cordoba, Spain, he relocated to Egypt.

al-Quṣayr a port on Egypt's Red Sea coast, the point of embarkation for pilgrims going to the Hejaz.

Quss Quss ibn Sāʿidah (sixth century AD), a pre-Islamic Arabian Christian renowned for the eloquence of his preaching.

rabdāʾ (of an ostrich) having four small, pure-white plumes.

Rajab seventh month of the Islamic calendar; it has the epithet "the Separate" because, under the pre-Islamic system according to which no fighting was allowed during certain months, it was the only such month that was neither preceded nor followed by another sacred month.

Rās al-Fīl see Jadīd Rās al-Fīl.

al-Raṭlī Pond one of thirteen ponds or lakes that existed in Cairo until the nineteenth century.

rééka (Fur) a kind of large basket.

The Reliable Compendium (*al-Jāmiʿ al-ṣaḥīḥ*; *al-Ṣaḥīḥ*), a collection of some eight thousand sound hadiths, by Muḥammad ibn Ismāʿīl al-Bukhārī (194–256/810–70).

Rīfā a son of Sultan Aḥmad Bukur who was passed over for the succession in favor of ʿAbd al-Raḥmān.

Rīl town in southeast Darfur (Dār Birqid); formerly a *fāshir*.

Rīz a son of Sultan Aḥmad Bukur who was passed over for the succession in favor of ʿAbd al-Raḥmān.

Rizayqāt (Rizayqat, Rizeigat) a group of nomadic Arabic-speaking peoples with northern (camel-herding) and southern (cattle-herding) sections, the former living in the north and west, the latter in the south and southeast of Darfur.

rubʿ a measure of volume used for grain, equivalent to 8.25 liters.

Rūngā a town in Dār Rungā (q.v.).

ruqād al-fāqah (literally "restful sleep") a kind of large bead worn by the women of the rich.

Ṣābūn, Muḥammad sultan of Wadai (r. ca. 1805–16).

the Sacred House the Kaaba at Mecca.

al-Ṣaftī probably Aḥmad al-Sāʾīm al-Saftī, shaykh (rector) of the mosque-university of al-Azhar in Cairo from 1838 to 1847.

Salīmah (Selima) an uninhabited oasis on the route from Asyut to Darfur, between al-Shabb and Laqiyyah.

sangadiri (Fur) a dance.

ṣanṭ sant acacia (*Vachellia* (or *Acacia*) *nilotica*).

Sarf al-Dajāj town northwest of Jabal Marrah and west of Kabkābiyyah; according to Perron, *sarf* (Fur) means "brook"; thus the name means "Chickens' Brook."

ṣarīf internal fence within a homestead acting as a dust-break for the huts.

sayāl umbrella thorn tree (*Vachellia/Acacia tortilis*).

sayyid male claiming descent from the Prophet Muḥammad; also the title of such a man, used interchangeably in this work with "Sharif."

sequin gold coin minted in Venice.

al-Shabb (Sheb) literally "alum"; a small oasis north of Salīmah on the road from Asyut to Darfur.

al-Shāfiʿī, Muḥammad ibn Idrīs (150–204/767–820) a leading jurist from whose teachings emerged one of the four canonical schools of legal interpretation, and a much-quoted poet.

al-Shaʿīriyyah a village near Tandaltī (today's El-Fasher).

Shālā a Fartīt people living on the southern fringes of the sultanate.

shallāngīn (Arabization of Fur *sagala kin*) traditional eye doctors specializing in the removal of cataracts.

shaʿlūb a vine (*Leptodenia arborea*).

sharāmīṭ literally "shreds": jerked meat.

sharif a male claiming descent from the Prophet Muḥammad; also, the title of such a man, used interchangeably in this work with "Sayyid."

shartāy (pl. sharātī) head of a *shartāyah*, one of the districts into which the provinces of the sultanate of Darfur were divided. The *shartāy* was the representative of the ruler and his village was the center for the collection of taxes, the administration of justice, and the levying of troops.

shāshiyyah in Tunisia, a rigid red felt cap similar to that called a tarboosh in Egypt.

shāw a tree: arak (*Salvadora persica*).

shawtar (pl. shawātir) a kind of camlet (a fine woolen fabric, originally of camel hair), sometimes dyed blue, and used in some areas as currency.

shaykh-father (Arabic: al-ab al-shaykh; Fur: abbo shaykh (daali)) chief eunuch and traditionally governor of the eastern region (Dār Dālī); the holder, though not necessarily himself a slave, was head of the slave hierarchy. Arabic *ab* "father" assimilates Fur *abbo*, a title of respect.

shīkah a kind of raw calico (*tukkiyyah*) of light, loose weave.

Shīth Seth, third son of Ādam and Ḥawwāʾ (Adam and Eve) and one of the first prophets.

shūsh small red seeds used to make amulets and as hair decorations for women.

shuwūr a bead bracelet worn by women (synonym of *madraʿah*).

Silā see Dār Silā.

Sinnār (Sennar) a town in the area between the Blue and White Niles now known as al-Jazīrah; home of the Funj sultanate, which lasted from 1504 until its conquest by Egyptian forces under Muḥammad ʿAli's son Ibrāhīm in 1821.

Ṣirāṭ a promontory on the coast of Tunisia between Sejnane and Tabarka (Cap Serrat).

Sodom apple a tree (*Calotropis procera*; Arabic: *ʿushar*).

soom'íng dogólá (Fur) the pages' house (literally "the children's house"). The author describes these pages or cadets as agents who oversaw the sultan's business. The *soom,* located within the *fāshir*'s public area, was also the assembly place where the people came together for conversation or for a common meal; it also functioned as a school where the palace pages or cadets were taught.

soomiit (Fur) a kind of bead.

sūbiyā in Egypt, a cold, thick nonalcoholic drink of slightly fermented rice, sugar, and water.

sudāsī (fem., sudāsiyyah) literally a "sixer": a slave measuring six handspans from heel to earlobe.

suktāyah a kind of house (see §3.1.86, images).

Sulaymān al-Azharī father of the author's teacher Aḥmad ibn Sulaymān, and the maternal grandfather of the author's father.

Sulaymān ibn ʿAbd al-Malik ibn Marwān sixth caliph of the Umayyad dynasty (r. 96–99/715–17).

Sulaymān Solóng (r. ca. 1660–80) founding father of the Keira dynasty in its historical manifestation. This sultan, generally known as Sulaymān Solongdungo (meaning "the Arab" and/or "of reddish complexion"), who ruled from ca. 1660 to 1680, though regarded as the first historically documented sultan of the Keira dynasty, is said, in Fur tradition, to have been preceded by at least three earlier sultans. With his two immediate successors, Mūsā and Aḥmad Bukur, he was responsible for the transformation of their Fur tribal kingdom into a multiethnic empire and played a major role in the Islamization of the Darfurian state.

Sulaymān al-Tūnisī the author's paternal grandfather

suspended ode (muʿallaqah) one of the seven renowned poems by seven renowned poets that (according to legend) hung in the Kaaba in the days before Islam.

al-sūtiyyah inflammation of the knee joint.

al-Suwaynah (Sweini) the first village in Darfur reached by caravans coming from Asyut.

al-Suyūṭī, Jalāl al-Dīn a prolific Egyptian polymath (d. 911/1505).

tābā tobacco.

ṭabābī a practitioner of the science of magic (*ṭibb*).

tabaldī a tree: the baobab (*Adansonia digitate*).

Tabaldiyyah a place northeast of Nyala where Sultan ʿAbd al-Raḥmān inflicted a defeat on his rival Isḥāq.

Ṭāhir a son of Sultan Aḥmad Bukur to whom Muḥammad Kurrā allegedly pledged allegiance when the latter revolted against Sultan Muḥammad Faḍl.

al-Ṭāʾif a city in the Hejaz ninety miles northeast of Mecca.

takākī see *tukkiyyah*.

al-Takrūr a name used in northern Africa to designate West Africans in general; now pronounced Dakrūr.

Tāldawā a hill northeast of Nyala.

ṭalḥ a tree: red acacia (*Vachellia* (or *Acacia*) *seyal*).

Tāmā, Tāmah see Dār Tāmā, Dār Tāmah.

Tamurrū al-Fullānī a holy man known for his skill as a magician.

Tandaltī a town east of Jabal Marrah where Sultan ʿAbd al-Raḥmān established his *fāshir*, or royal compound, in 1206/1791–92. Subsequent sultans maintained the tradition; El-Fasher is now the name of the capital of North Darfur State.

Tărne (Tarni; Fur) a village southwest of Tandaltī (today's El-Fasher).

tărne (Fur) a ring of tin used as currency.

tawse (Fur) a dance, performed by slaves.

Ṭaybah a name for Medina, site of the tomb of the Prophet Muḥammad.

thawb a large wrap worn by women.

ṭibb magic.

*tikináwi (*takanawi*; in the author's spelling* takaniyāwī*; Fur)* title of the hereditary governor of Dār Zaghāwah in the sultanate's northern region (also known as Dār al-Tikináwi); the tikináwi had a position of command in the army and was known as "the Sultan's Left Arm."

tindinga (Fur) a dance.

togjêl (Fur) a kind of goblet drum.

Tomorókkóngá (Tamuurkwa; Fur) one of the three great sections of the Fur people; the Tomorókkóngá live to the west of Jabal Marrah.

the Tubū (Toubou, Tebou) an ethnic group speaking a Nilo-Saharan language that inhabits parts of today's Chad (where they are concentrated in the Tebesti region), Libya, Niger, and Nigeria.

al-Ṭughrāʾī Muʾayyid al-Dīn Abū Ismaʿīl al-Ḥusayn ibn ʿAlī al-Ṭughrāʾī (453/1061 to 514/1120–21), Arab poet and administrator under the Saljuq sultans of Mosul and Baghdad.

al-Tuhāmī Abū l-Hasan ʿAlī al-Tuhāmī (d. 416/1025); poet and scholar of Yemeni origin.

tukkiyyah (pl. takākī) raw or unbleached calico; bolts of the latter ten cubits in length and one in breadth were used by poor women to make their robes and also, especially in the area around the sultan's capital, as currency.

tukultī a kind of house with a roof raised on two wooden pillars (see §3.1.86, images).

al-Tūnisī, ʿUmar ibn Sulaymān see ʿUmar ibn Sulaymān al-Tūnisī.

al-Tūnisī, Sulaymān see Sulaymān al-Tūnisī.

Tunjūr a people living in central Darfur who in the sixteenth century superseded the Dājū as its rulers and as rulers in Wadai; in the mid-seventeenth century, they were themselves succeeded in Darfur by Fur sultans of the Keira dynasty.

Turqunak in the Wadai sultanate, one of sixteen freeborn men, four of whom acted as overseers of persons of the royal blood and four as captains of the sultan's bodyguard, while eight assisted the *kamkūlak*s (q.v.) in the provinces.

Turūj a generic and pejorative term applied by Darfurians to enslaveable tribes living south of Kordofan.

al-Ṭuwayshah a town close to Umm Kidādah on Darfur's border, and its surrounding district.

ʿUmar ibn Sulaymān al-Tūnisī the author's father.

ʿUmar Lēl (or Lēle) (r. ca. 1730–39), fifth historical sultan of the Keira dynasty, preceded by his father Muḥammad Dawra and succeeded by his uncle Abū l-Qāsim.

umm bulbul literally "Mother Nightingale"; a kind of barley wine.

the Victorious (al-Manṣūrah) smallest and most sacred of the royal kettle-drums of the Darfur sultans.

vizier a general title (rather than an office) of high officials in the courts of Tunis, Darfur, and elsewhere.

al-Wāddāy (Waddāy, Wadadāy) Wadai, formerly a sultanate immediately to the west of Darfur, also called Dār Ṣulayḥ or Dār Ṣalīh; today part of Chad.

Wādī l-Kūʿ a seasonal watercourse running south from Jabal Sī (north of Jabal Marrah), on whose banks at Tandaltī Sultan ʿAbd al-Raḥmān built his *fāshir*.

Wārah the capital of the sultanate of Wadai.

warrāniyyah a meal eaten in addition to regular meals.

waykah a dish made from rehydrated ingredients, most commonly okra.

Yājūj and Mājūj monstrous peoples who, according to the Qur'an and the Torah (where they are called Gog and Magog), will invade the world on the last days before the Day of Judgment; they are said by some to number 400,000, by others to be nine times as numerous as humans.

Yūsuf Pasha Yūsuf Pasha al-Karamanlī (1795–1832), hereditary governor of Libyan Tripoli.

Yūsuf the Seal Bearer (Muhurdār) Yūsuf Ṣāḥib al-Ṭābiʿ (ca. 1765–1815); a slave, possibly Moldovan, bought at around age thirteen in Istanbul by Bakkār al-Jallūlī, an army commander and rich merchant of Sfax. Yūsuf was raised in the Jallūlī household and presented to Ḥammūdah Pasha, ruler of Tunis, when he was eighteen; he rose to be the latter's principal minister and the country's most powerful figure, with control over much of the economy. He was assassinated not long after his sponsor, Ḥammūdah Pasha, died.

al-Zaghāwah peoples speaking a language of the Nilo-Saharan family and living on the northern marches of Darfur and in Wadai.

al-Zaghāwī (or, Bīr al-Zaghāwī) a well on the road from Asyut to Darfur south of Laqiyyah, also called Bīr al-Malḥah.

zaghāwī a kind of naturally occurring salt.

zakat a property tax disbursed by the state in the form of alms for specified categories of persons.

ẓalīm (of an ostrich) having four large and four small pure-white plumes.

zarībah a fence of thorny branches surrounding a homestead.

al-Zarqāʾ a spring in Medina.

the Zayādiyyah Arabic-speaking camel-herding nomads of the Fazārah group living in the northeast of Darfur.

ẓufr literally "fingernail"; *Unguis odoratus*: fragments of the operculum, or plug, of certain kinds of mollusks, which when broken up resembles blackish fingernails and which is used in perfumes.

Bibliography

Abū l-ʿAmāyim, Muḥammad. *Āthār al-Qāhirah al-islāmiyyah fī l-ʿaṣr al-ʿUthmānī*. 3 vols. Istanbul: Markaz al-Abḥāth li-l-Tārīkh wa-l-Funūn wa-l-Thaqāfah al-Islāmiyyah bi-Istānbūl (IRCICA), 2003–15.

Ali, Siddig A. M. and Abdellatif Y. Idris. "Germination and Seedling Growth of Pearl Millet (Pennisetum glaucum L.) Cultivars under Salinity Conditions." *International Journal of Plant Science and Ecology* 1, no. 1 (2015): 1–5.

Al-Naqar, Umar. "Takrur, the History of a Name." *The Journal of African History* 10, no. 3 (1969): 365–74.

Arberry, Arthur J. *The Koran Interpreted*. Oxford World's Classics. Oxford: Oxford University Press, 1982.

Arkell, A. J. "Hebron Beads in Darfur." *Sudan Notes and Records* 20, no. 2 (1937): 300–5.

Artin, Yacoub Pacha, ed. *Lettres du Dr Perron du Caire et d'Alexandrie à M. Jules Mohl, à Paris, 1838–1854*. Cairo: F. Diemer, 1911.

Baedecker, K., ed. *Egypt. Handbook for Travellers. Part First: Lower Egypt with the Fayûm and the Peninsula of Sinai*. Second edition, revised and augmented. Leipzig: Karl Baedecker; London: Dulau and Co., 1885.

Bakri, M. Ahmed and F. Hassan El Gunaid. "The Plants Use for Traditional Treatment in East Darfour State, Sudan." *University of Bakht Alruda Scientific Journal*, no. 8 (September 2013): 56–66.

Browne, W. G. *Travels in Africa, Egypt, and Syria, from the Year 1792 to 1798*. London: T. Cadell Junior and W. Davies, 1799 [Ecco Eighteenth Century Collections Online Print Editions].

Cave, Francis O. and James D. MacDonald. *Birds of the Sudan, Their Identification and Distribution.* Edinburgh and London: Oliver and Boyd, 1955.

Clot Bey [Antoine Barthélemy Clot]. *Kunūz al-ṣiḥḥah wa-yawāqīt al-minḥah*, translated by Muḥammad al-Shāfiʿī, edited by Muḥammad ʿUmar al-Tūnisī and Nicolas Perron. Cairo: Būlāq, 1844.

De Waal, Alex, ed. *War in Darfur and the Search for Peace.* Cambridge, MA: Harvard University Press, 2007.

Dozy, R. *Supplément aux Dictionnaires Arabes.* 2 vols. Leyden: E. J. Brill, 1881 (offset: Beirut: Librairie du Liban, 1968).

EAL = Meisami, Julie Scott and Paul Starkey, eds. *Encyclopedia of Arabic Literature.* 2 vols. London and New York: Routledge, 1998.

EI2 = P. Bearman, Th. Bianquis, C. E. Bosworth, E. von Donzol, and W. P. Heinrichs, eds. *Encyclopaedia of Islam.* 2nd ed. Leiden: E. J. Brill, 1960–2009.

El-Tounsy, Mohammed Ebn-Omar. *Voyage au Darfour*, translated from the Arabic by Dr. Perron. Paris: Benjamin Duprat, 1845.

———. *Voyage au Ouaday*, translated from the Arabic by Dr. Perron. Paris: Benjamin Duprat, 1851.

Fabre, Antoine François Hippolyte, ed. *Dictionnaire des dictionnaires de médecine français et étrangers ou traité complet de médecine et de chirurgie pratiques, par une société de médecins.* 8 vols. Paris: Germer Baillière, 1840–41.

Fahmy, Khaled. "Translating Bichat and Lavoisier into Arabic," unpublished paper presented at the Middle East, South Asian, and African Studies Colloquium, Columbia University, February 9, 2015.

Al-Fīrūzābādī, Muḥammad ibn Yaʿqūb. *Al-Qāmūs al-muḥīṭ wa-l-qābūs al-wasīṭ fī al-lughah.* 2nd ed. 4 vols. Cairo: al-Maktabah al-Ḥusayniyyah al-Miṣriyyah, 1344/1925–26.

Flint, Julie and Alex de Waal. *Darfur: A Short History of a Long War.* London: Zed Books, 2005.

Francis, Peter, Jr. "Beadmaking in Islam: The African Trade and the Rise of Hebron." *BEADS: Journal of the Society of Bead Researchers* 2 (1990): 15–28.

Gray, Richard. *A History of the Southern Sudan, 1839–1889*. London: Oxford University Press, 1961.

Heyworth-Dunne, J. *An Introduction to the History of Education in Modern Egypt*. London: Luzac and Co., [1939].

Hill, Richard. *A Biographical Dictionary of the Sudan*. 2nd ed. London: Frank Cass, 1967.

Holy, Ladislav. *Neighbors and Kinsmen: A Study of the Berti of Darfur*. London: Christopher Hurst, 1974.

Hunwick, John O. and R. S. O'Fahey, eds. *Arabic Literature of Africa*. Vol. 1, *The Writings of Eastern Sudanic Africa to c. 1900*. Compiled by R. S. O'Fahey. Leiden: E. J. Brill, 1994.

Hunwick, John O. "Leo Africanus's Description of the Middle Niger, Hausaland and Bornu." In *Timbuktu and the Songhay Empire: Al-Sa'di's Tarikh al-Sudan Down to 1613 and Other Contemporary Documents*, edited and translated by John O. Hunwick, 272–91. Leiden: Brill, 1999.

Ibn Abī l-Ḍiyāf, Aḥmad. *Itḥāf ahl al-zamān bi-akhbār mulūk Tūnis wa-ʿahd al-amān*. 9 vols. Tunis: al-Dār al-ʿArabiyyah li-l-Kitāb, 1999.

Lane, Edward William. *An Account of the Manners and Customs of the Modern Egyptians: The Definitive 1860 Edition*. Introduction by Jason Thompson. Cairo: The American University in Cairo Press, 2003.

Lane, Edward William. *An Arabic-English Lexicon*. 8 vols. London: Williams and Norgate, 1863–93.

Lentin, Jérôme. "Middle Arabic." In *Encyclopedia of Arabic Language and Linguistics*. General editor Kees Versteegh. Vol. 3, 215–24. Leiden–Boston: Brill, 2008.

McGregor, A. J. *Darfur (Sudan) in the Age of Stone Architecture c. AD 1000–1750: Problems in Historical Reconstruction*. Cambridge: Archaeopress, 2001.

Al-Maydānī, Aḥmad ibn Muḥammad. *Majmaʿ al-amthāl*. 2 vols. Cairo: al-Maṭbaʿah al-Khayriyyah, 1310 AH.

Messaoudi, Alain. "Perron, Nicolas." In *Dictionnaire des orientalistes de langue française*, 2nd ed. Edited by François Pouillon, 750–51. Paris: IISMM-Karthala, 2008.

Al-Mutanabbī, Abū l-Ṭayyib. *Al-ʿArf al-ṭayyib fī sharḥ dīwān Abī l-Ṭayyib*. Edited by Nāṣīf al-Yāzijī, revised by ʿUmar Fārūq al-Ṭabbāʿ. Beirut: Dār al-Arqam ibn Abī l-Arqam, n.d.

Nachtigal, Gustav. *Sahara and Sudan*. Vol. 3, *The Chad Basin and Bagirmi*. Translated from the original German, with an introduction and notes by Allan G. B. Fisher and Humphrey J. Fisher. London, C. Hurst, 1987. Vol. 4, *Wadai and Darfur*. Translated from the original German, with an introduction and notes by Allan G. B. Fisher and Humphrey J. Fisher with Rex S. O'Fahey. London, C. Hurst, 1971.

O'Fahey, R. S. and M. I. Abu Salim. *Land in Dar Fur*. Cambridge: Cambridge University Press, 1983.

O'Fahey, R. S. "Egypt, Saint-Simon and Muḥammad ʿAlī." In *The Exploration of Africa in the Eighteenth and Nineteenth Centuries*, 17–36. Edinburgh: Centre of African Studies, University of Edinburgh, 1972.

———. "Two Early Dar Fur Charters." *Sudan Texts Bulletin 1* (1979): 13–17.

———. "Slavery and the Slave Trade in Dar Fur." *Journal of African History* 14 (1973): 29–43.

———. "The Awlad ʿAli: A Fulany Holy Family in Dar Fur." In *Gedenkschrift Gustav Nachtigal, 1874–1974*, edited by Herbert Genslmayr, 147–66. Bremen: Übersee-Museum, 1977.

———. "The Archives of Shoba." *Sudanic Africa: A Journal of Historical Sources* 1 (1990): 71–83 (part one); 2 (1991): 79–112 (part two).

———. "A Prince and His Neighbours." *Sudanic Africa: A Journal of Historical Sources* 3 (1992): 57–93.

———. "Endowment, Privilege and Estate on the Central and Eastern Sudan." *Islamic Law and Society* 4 (1997): 258–67.

———. "The Conquest of Darfur, 1873–82." *Sudan Notes and Records,* New Series 1 (1998): 47–67.

———. *The Darfur Sultanate: A History*. New York: Columbia University Press, 2008.

———. *Darfur and the British*. London: Christopher Hurst, 2017.

———. "The Affair of Ahmad Agha." *Sudan Notes and Records* 53 (1972): 202–3.

Perron, Nicolas. *Al-Jawāhir al-saniyyah fī l-aʿmāl al-kīmāwiyyah*. Edited and translated by Muḥammad al-Tūnisī, Muḥammad al-Harrāwī, Darwīsh Zaydān, and Husayn Ghānim. 3 vols. Cairo: Būlāq, 1260/1844.

Qāsim, ʿAwn al-Sharīf. *Qāmūs al-lahjah al-ʿāmmiyyah fī l-Sūdān*. 2nd ed. Cairo: al-Maktab al-Miṣrī al-Ḥadīth, 1985.

Al-Qurṭubī, Muḥammad ibn Aḥmad ibn Abī Bakr Faraj al-Anṣārī. *Al-Tadhkirah fī aḥwāl al-mawtā wa-umūr al-ākhirah*. Edited by Aḥmad Ḥijāzī al-Saqqā. Cairo: Maktabat al-Kullīyāt al-Azhariyyah, [1980].

Al-Shāfiʿī, Muḥammad ibn Idrīs. *Shiʿr al-Shāfiʿī*. Edited by Mujāhid Muṣṭafā Bahjat. Mosul: University of Mosul, 1986.

Al-Sharīf, Muḥammad al-Hādī. *Tārīkh Tūnis*. 3rd ed. Tunis: Dār CERES li-l-Nashr (Centre d'Études et de Recherches Économiques et Sociales), 1993.

Al-Shayyāl, Jamāl. "Duktūr Birrūn (Dr. Perron) wa-l-shaykhān Muḥammad ʿAyyād al-Ṭanṭāwī wa-Muḥammad ʿUmar al-Tūnisī." *Majallat Kulliyyat al-Ādāb, Jāmiʿat Fārūq al-Awwal* 2 (1944): 179–221.

Al-Shidyāq, Aḥmad Fāris. *Leg over Leg*. Edited and translated by Humphrey Davies. 4 vols. Library of Arabic Literature. New York: New York University Press, 2013–14.

Al-Ṣūlī, Abū Bakr Muḥammad ibn Yaḥyā. *The Life and Times of Abū Tammām*. Edited and translated by Beatrice Gruendler. Library of Arabic Literature. New York: New York University Press, 2015.

Al-Ṭanṭāwī, Muḥammad ʿAyyād. *Aḥsan al-nukhab fī maʿrifat lisān al-ʿArab*; *Traité de la langue arabe vulgaire*. Leipzig: Wilhem Vogel, 1848.

Theobald, A. B. *ʿAli Dinar: Last Sultan of Darfur, 1898–1916*. London: Longmans, 1965.

Tully, Dennis. *Culture and Context in Sudan: The Process of Market Incorporation in Dar Masalit*. New York: SUNY Press, 1988.

Al-Tūnisī, Muḥammad ibn al-Sayyid ʿUmar ibn Sulaymān. *Tashḥīdh al-adhhān fī sīrat bilād al-ʿArab wa-l-Sūdān*. Paris: Benjamin Duprat, 1850.

———. *Tashḥīdh al-adhhān fī sīrat bilād al-ʿArab wa-l-Sūdān*. Edited and annotated by Khalīl Maḥmūd ʿAsākir and Muṣṭafā Muḥammad Musʿad. Cairo: al-Dār al-Miṣriyyah li-l-Taʾlīf wa-l-Tarjamah, 1965.

Umar, H. S. "Al-Tunisi: Travels in Darfur. Translation, Collation and Annotation of *Tashhidh al-Adhhan bi Sirat Bilad al-Arab wa-l-Sudan*" (master's thesis, Bayero University, Kano, 1976).

Vogt, Kees. *Murshid ḥaqlī li-l-taʿarruf ʿalā l-ashjār wa-l-shujayrāt al-shāʾiʿah fī l-manāṭiq al-jāffah fī l-Sūdān wa-subul ikthārihā wa-fawāʾidihā*. Translated by Kamāl Ḥasan Bādī. London: SOS International, n.d.

Walz, Terence. "Wakalat al-Gallaba: The Market for African Goods in Cairo." *Annales Islamologiques* 13 (1977): 263–86.

———. *Trade between Egypt and Bilad as-Sudan*. Cairo: Institut Français d'Archéologie Orientale du Caire, 1978.

Zack, Liesbeth. *Egyptian Arabic in the Seventeenth Century: A Study and Edition of Yūsuf al-Maghribī's Dafʿ al-iṣr ʿan kalām ahl Miṣr*. Utrecht: Landelijke Onderzockschool Taalwetenschup, 2009.

List of Images

Index

Ab Sanūn, §3.2.57
ába ăw mang, §3.1.52
ába dima'ng, xvi, §3.1.9, §3.1.14, §§3.1.53–54, §3.1.92, 284n269. *See also* Dār Ába Dima'ng
ába poor-ii, §3.1.51, 290n315
ába umá, §3.1.14. *See also* Dār Ába Umá
abbo uumang, xvi
'Abd Allāh Juthā, §§2.2.59–60, 277n200
'Abd Allāh Kartab, §4.47
'Abd al-Ḥamīd, xxiv
'Abd al-Karīm (son of Ḥasan wad 'Awūḍah), §2.3.22
'Abd al-Karīm ibn Khamīs 'Armān, §4.48
'Abd al-Raḥmān al-Rashīd ("the Orphan") (sultan of Darfur), xv, xix–xx, §2.2.15, §§2.2.24–25, §2.2.33, §2.2.34, §2.2.38, §§2.2.57–59, §2.2.61, §2.2.64, §§2.3.1–33, §2.3.35, §3.1.38, §3.1.73, §3.1.85, §3.1.108, §§4.40–41, 271n148, 277n203, 277n205, 278n213, 280n230, 282n249, 283n251
'Abdullāhi (caliph), xxii
Abīrīs, xxxix, §2.2.11, 268n121
abū abāṭ. *See* sorghum
Abū 'Abd Allāh Muḥammad al-Wirghī, verses by, §2.1.20
Abū Bakr al-Ṣiddīq (caliph), §2.1.4, §2.2.41, 260n24, 275n180, 304n481
Abū l-Fatḥ al-Bastī, verses by, §2.2.53
Abū l-Fatḥ Maḥmūd ibn al-Ḥusayn al-Ramlī. *See* Kushājim
Abū l-Hasan 'Alī al-Tuhāmī. *See* al-Tuhāmī
Abū l-Judūl, §§2.2.27–28, §2.2.30, §2.2.34, §2.3.21, §3.1.15, §3.3.24
Abū Muḥammad Ḥammūdah Pasha, §§2.1.14–15, §2.1.17, §2.1.19, §§2.1.20–21, 261n42, 261n43, 262n46
Abū l-Qāsim (sultan of Darfur), xv, §§2.2.38–40, §4.41, 274n171
abū shalawlaw. *See* sorghum
abū ṣuffayr. *See* jaundice
abū l-ṣufūf. *See* pleurisy
Abū l-Ṭayyib al-Mutanabbī. *See* al-Mutanabbī
Abū Tammām Ḥabīb ibn Aws al-Ṭā'ī, verses by, §2.1.33
abū ṭanṭarah (bird), §3.3.34, 303n468
Abū Za'bal, xxvii, xxxi, §1.6, §2.2.4, §4.19, 259n15, 266n84
Abyssinia, §2.1.26
acacia, §4.6, §4.18, 305n500

Darfur, Darfurians (cont)
§§4.39–42, §4.46, §§4.48–50, 258n5, 269n127, 269n132, 271n146, 271n147, 271n148, 271n150, 271n153, 272n154, 272n159, 273n162, 273n164, 273n166, 273n167, 274n171, 274n174, 275n182, 275n184, 275n185, 276n186, 276n190, 276n197, 277n199, 277n203, 277n205, 277n205, 278n209, 278n216, 279n221, 279n227, 280n230, 280n236, 281n237, 281n238, 282n247, 282n248, 283n251, 283n256, 284n261, 284n265, 284n267, 285n271, 285n273, 286n285, 287n292, 287n296, 291n333, 294n362, 295n369, 295n386, 296n393, 297n396, 299n413, 300n430, 301n454, 302n467, 303n470, 303n474, 304n491, 305n497, 306n509, 306n509, 306n510, 306n517
Darmūdī, §3.3.32, §§3.3.35–36
date palm. *See* palm
dawdarī, §§3.3.26–27. *See also waykah*
dāyūq (tree), §3.1.104
dééng saaya, §3.2.6, §3.2.28
Dhamīmā, §3.2.35, 226n147
dhikr, §§3.2.29–33, 298n402
al-Dibbah, §§2.2.33–34
dimlij (pl. *damālij*), §2.2.34, §3.1.63, 291n326
dinbī, §4.3. *See also* millet
dinjāyah, §3.1.91
dinqār (drum), §3.1.39, §3.1.53, §3.1.80, 289n58
disease, §2.1.6, §2.1.9, §2.2.9, §§3.3.4–5, §§3.3.7–8, §§3.3.11–15, §3.3.18, §§3.3.23–24, §4.27, 268n115, 299n426. *See also* cholera; dropsy; *al-duqrī*; *al-ghuzayyil*; gonorrhea; guinea worm; *al-habūb*; jaundice; *al-jiqqayl*; leucorrhea; leprosy; measles; plague; pleurisy; scarlet fever; smallpox; *al-sūtiyyah*; syphilis; tuberculosis; *umm ṣuquʿ*; vitiligo; *wirdah*
dollar, xxx, §2.3.32, §§3.3.38–39, §3.3.44, §3.3.51, §3.3.54, 304n478
Dongola, xxxix, §2.2.18, §2.2.48, 269n132, 275n185
doum palm (*muql*). *See* palm
dropsy, §3.3.15
drum, xvi, §2.2.14, §2.2.30, §2.2.37, §2.2.52, §2.2.54, §2.3.5, §2.3.39, §3.1.22, §3.1.34, §§3.1.38–39, §3.1.42, §§3.1.45–46, §3.1.53, §3.1.69, §3.1.70, §3.1.83, §3.1.90, §3.1.92, §3.1.95, §3.2.5, §3.2.7, §3.2.12, §3.2.16, §3.2.22, §3.2.28, §3.2.42, §3.3.29, 286n280, 287n296, 288n304, 288n305, 289n310, 289n311, 290n318, 296n390. *See also baradiyyah; dallúka; darabukkah; dinqār*; kettledrums; *naqāqīr; togjêl; tómbol*; the Victorious
Drum House (House of Copper), §3.1.38, §3.1.45, §3.1.90, §3.1.92, 287n295
Dukkumī. *See* Muḥammad Dukkumī
dulab. See palm
dullong, §3.1.86
the Dunes, §3.1.16, §3.3.22, §4.30, 285n278
al-duqrī (disease), §3.3.15
durdur, §3.1.86

al-fartīt. *See* guinea worm
al-Fāshir, xviii, xix–xx, xxii–xxiv, xlvin23. *See also* El-Fasher
fāshir, xvi, xliii, §2.2.30, §3.1.14, §3.1.77, §3.1.87, §§3.3.44–45, §4.6, 271n153, 285n276, 292n345
fava beans, §3.1.65, §4.2, §4.5, 294n361. *See also* bean
Fazārah, §3.1.5. *See also* Maḥāmīd; Majānīn
feathers, §3.1.40, §3.1.72, §3.1.100, §3.3.35, §§3.3.38–39
the feathers (the sultan's fan), §3.1.40, §3.1.94
Fez, §2.1.22
Fezzan, xxxix, §2.1.9, §3.3.38, §3.3.48
franc, §3.1.76, §3.3.44
France, xii, xxiii–xxiv, xxvii–xxviii, xxx–xxxiv, xlixn45, ln46, ln47, lin55, §1.6, §2.1.33, §2.3.24, 264n68, 264n69, 268n119
the Frankish disease. *See al-jiqqayl*
Franks, §3.1.28, §3.3.12, §3.3.19, §3.3.46, §3.3.48, §4.5, §4.30. *See also* Europe
French, xxxiii–xxxvi, xli, xlviin26, xlviiin39, liin56, liin57, §3.3.38, §3.3.44, 269n124, 273n163, 274n172, 279n222, 286n286, 288n306, 290n323, 293n350, 293n352, 294n359, 295n373, 297n397, 301n448, 302n467, 304n478, 304n480, 307n523
Friend of God. *See* Ibrāhīm (Abraham)
fruit, §4.17, §4.20, §4.29. *See also ʿanqallū*; banana trees; *baṭṭūm*; *dāyūq*; *hijlīj*; *ḥummayḍ*; jackalberry; jujube; *kilí*; *mukhkhayṭ*; pomegranate; *qiddīm*; *shaʿlūb*; *shāw*; shea; Sodom apple; *tabaldī*; tamarind; watermelon
Fullān. *See* Fallātā
fuqarāʾ. *See faqīh*
Fur, x–xi, xiii–xvii, xx, xxiv, xxxiv, xlii–xliii, xlvn1, xlvin10, xlvin11, §2.2.27, §2.2.29, §2.2.39, §2.2.43, §2.3.5, §2.3.18, §2.3.28, §§3.1.3–4, §3.1.7, §3.1.9, §§3.1.1–12, §3.1.19, §3.1.29, §3.1.31, §3.1.33, §3.1.35, §3.1.37, §§3.1.41–42, §3.1.47, §3.1.51, §3.1.53, §3.1.59, §§3.1.67–68, §§3.1.70–73, §3.1.76, §3.1.78, §3.1.80, §3.1.82, §3.1.83, §§3.1.84–88, §3.1.97, §§3.1.104–5, §3.1.112, §3.2.4, §3.2.8, §3.2.12, §3.2.26, §3.2.29, §§3.2.33–34, §3.2.38, §§3.2.40–41, §§3.2.57–58, §3.3.2, §3.3.23, §3.3.26, §3.3.29, §3.3.44, §§4.2–3, §4.6, §4.11, §4.28, §4.46, 271n153, 272n160, 275n184, 277n203, 281n237, 284n267, 284n269, 265n14, 286n280, 286n286, 287n292, 288n298, 289n312, 289n313, 290n315, 290n318, 291n337, 294n359, 296n394, 297n397, 297n399, 298n404, 299n415, 300n428, 300n430, 307n523, 307n521
al-Fusṭāṭ, xxxix, §2.1.35, §2.2.1, 265n74
al-Fūtāwī. *See* Madanī al-Fūtāwī; Mālik al-Fūtāwī

galanga, §3.2.41
garlic, §3.1.19, §4.6
Gemini (The Twins; al-Jawzāʾ), §4.29, 306n513. *See also* Twins' autumn

al-Zaghāwī's Well. *See* Bīr al-Zaghāwī
zakat, §3.1.65. *See also* taxation
ẓalīm, §2.3.39, 302n461. *See also* *ostrich*
Zamzam (*iiya baasi* to Muḥammad al-Ḥusayn), xvi
Zamzam Sendi Suttera (*iiya baasi* to Abū l-Qāsim), xvi
zarībah, §§3.1.86–87, §4.20, 292n349
Zawānah Kāshif, §§2.3.24–28, 281n238
Zayādiyyah, §3.3.24, §3.3.37
zinc, §3.1.103
Zoroastrian. *See* Magian
ẓufr, §3.1.104
Zuhrah (wife of ʻUmar al-Tūnisī), §2.2.34

About the NYU Abu Dhabi Institute

The Library of Arabic Literature is supported by a grant from the NYU Abu Dhabi Institute, a major hub of intellectual and creative activity and advanced research. The Institute hosts academic conferences, workshops, lectures, film series, performances, and other public programs directed both to audiences within the UAE and to the worldwide academic and research community. It is a center of the scholarly community for Abu Dhabi, bringing together faculty and researchers from institutions of higher learning throughout the region.

NYU Abu Dhabi, through the NYU Abu Dhabi Institute, is a world-class center of cutting-edge research, scholarship, and cultural activity. The Institute creates singular opportunities for leading researchers from across the arts, humanities, social sciences, sciences, engineering, and the professions to carry out creative scholarship and conduct research on issues of major disciplinary, multidisciplinary, and global significance.

About the Translator

Humphrey Davies is an award-winning translator of some twenty-five works of modern Arabic literature, among them Alaa Al-Aswany's *The Yacoubian Building*, five novels by Elias Khoury, including *Gate of the Sun*, and Aḥmad Fāris al-Shidyāq's *Leg over Leg*. He has also made a critical edition, translation, and lexicon of the Ottoman-period *Brains Confounded by the Ode of Abū Shādūf Expounded* by Yūsuf al-Shirbīnī, as well as an edition and translation of al-Sanhūrī's *Risible Rhymes* from the same era, and a translation of the thirteenth-century *Book of Charlatans* by Jamāl al-Dīn ʿAbd al-Raḥīm al-Jawbarī. In addition, he has compiled with Madiha Doss an anthology in Arabic entitled *Al-ʿāmmiyyah al-miṣriyyah al-maktūbah: mukhtārāt min 1400 ilā 2009* (*Egyptian Colloquial Writing: selections from 1400 to 2009*) and co-authored, with Lesley Lababidi, *A Field Guide to the Street Names of Central Cairo*. He read Arabic at the University of Cambridge, received his Ph.D. from the University of California at Berkeley, and previous to undertaking his first translation in 2003, worked for social development and research organizations in Egypt, Tunisia, Palestine, and Sudan. He is affiliated with the American University in Cairo.

The Library of Arabic Literature

For more details on individual titles, visit www.libraryofarabicliterature.org

Classical Arabic Literature: A Library of Arabic Literature Anthology
Selected and translated by Geert Jan van Gelder (2012)

A Treasury of Virtues: Sayings, Sermons, and Teachings of ʿAlī, by al-Qāḍī al-Quḍāʿī, with the *One Hundred Proverbs* attributed to al-Jāḥiẓ
Edited and translated by Tahera Qutbuddin (2013)

The Epistle on Legal Theory, by al-Shāfiʿī
Edited and translated by Joseph E. Lowry (2013)

Leg over Leg, by Aḥmad Fāris al-Shidyāq
Edited and translated by Humphrey Davies (4 volumes; 2013–14)

Virtues of the Imām Aḥmad ibn Ḥanbal, by Ibn al-Jawzī
Edited and translated by Michael Cooperson (2 volumes; 2013–15)

The Epistle of Forgiveness, by Abū l-ʿAlāʾ al-Maʿarrī
Edited and translated by Geert Jan van Gelder and Gregor Schoeler (2 volumes; 2013–14)

The Principles of Sufism, by ʿĀʾishah al-Bāʿūniyyah
Edited and translated by Th. Emil Homerin (2014)

The Expeditions: An Early Biography of Muḥammad, by Maʿmar ibn Rāshid
Edited and translated by Sean W. Anthony (2014)

Two Arabic Travel Books

Accounts of China and India, by Abū Zayd al-Sīrāfī

Edited and translated by Tim Mackintosh-Smith (2014)

Mission to the Volga, by Aḥmad ibn Faḍlān

Edited and translated by James Montgomery (2014)

Disagreements of the Jurists: A Manual of Islamic Legal Theory, by al-Qāḍī al-Nuʿmān

Edited and translated by Devin J. Stewart (2015)

Consorts of the Caliphs: Women and the Court of Baghdad, by Ibn al-Sāʿī

Edited by Shawkat M. Toorawa and translated by the Editors of the Library of Arabic Literature (2015)

What ʿĪsā ibn Hishām Told Us, by Muḥammad al-Muwayliḥī

Edited and translated by Roger Allen (2 volumes; 2015)

The Life and Times of Abū Tammām, by Abū Bakr Muḥammad ibn Yaḥyā al-Ṣūlī

Edited and translated by Beatrice Gruendler (2015)

The Sword of Ambition: Bureaucratic Rivalry in Medieval Egypt, by ʿUthmān ibn Ibrāhīm al-Nābulusī

Edited and translated by Luke Yarbrough (2016)

Brains Confounded by the Ode of Abū Shādūf Expounded, by Yūsuf al-Shirbīnī

Edited and translated by Humphrey Davies (2 volumes; 2016)

Light in the Heavens: Sayings of the Prophet Muḥammad, by al-Qāḍī al-Quḍāʿī

Edited and translated by Tahera Qutbuddin (2016)

Risible Rhymes, by Muḥammad ibn Maḥfūẓ al-Sanhūrī

Edited and translated by Humphrey Davies (2016)

A Hundred and One Nights

Edited and translated by Bruce Fudge (2016)

The Excellence of the Arabs, by Ibn Qutaybah
Edited by James E. Montgomery and Peter Webb
Translated by Sarah Bowen Savant and Peter Webb (2017)

Scents and Flavors: A Syrian Cookbook
Edited and translated by Charles Perry (2017)

Arabian Satire: Poetry from 18th-Century Najd, by Ḥmēdān al-Shwēʿir
Edited and translated by Marcel Kurpershoek (2017)

In Darfur: An Account of the Sultanate and Its People, by Muḥammad ibn ʿUmar al-Tūnisī
Edited and translated by Humphrey Davies (2 volumes; 2018)

War Songs, by ʿAntarah ibn Shaddād
Edited by James E. Montgomery
Translated by James E. Montgomery with Richard Sieburth (2018)

Arabian Romantic: Poems on Bedouin Life and Love, by ʿAbdallah ibn Sbayyil
Edited and translated by Marcel Kurpershoek (2018)

Dīwān ʿAntarah ibn Shaddād: A Literary-Historical Study, by James E. Montgomery (2018)

Stories of Piety and Prayer: Deliverance Follows Adversity, by al-Muḥassin ibn ʿAlī al-Tanūkhī
Edited and translated by Julia Bray (2019)

Tajrīd sayf al-himmah li-stikhrāj mā fī dhimmat al-dhimmah: A Scholarly Edition of ʿUthmān ibn Ibrāhīm al-Nābulusī's Text, by Luke Yarbrough (2019)

The Philosopher Responds: An Intellectual Correspondence from the Tenth Century, by Abū Ḥayyān al-Tawḥīdī and Abū ʿAlī Miskawayh
Edited by Bilal Orfali and Maurice A. Pomerantz
Translated by Sophia Vasalou and James E. Montgomery (2 volumes; 2019)

The Discourses: Reflections on History, Sufism, Theology, and Literature—Volume One, by al-Ḥasan al-Yūsī
Edited and translated by Justin Stearns (2020)

Impostures, by al-Ḥarīrī
Translated by Michael Cooperson (2020)

Maqāmāt Abī Zayd al-Sarūjī, by al-Ḥarīrī
Edited by Michael Cooperson (2020)

The Yoga Sutras of Patañjali, by Abū Rayḥān al-Bīrūnī
Edited and translated by Mario Kozah (2020)

The Book of Charlatans, by Jamāl al-Dīn ʿAbd al-Raḥīm al-Jawbarī
Edited by Manuela Dengler
Translated by Humphrey Davies (2020)

English-only Paperbacks

Leg over Leg, by Aḥmad Fāris al-Shidyāq (2 volumes; 2015)

The Expeditions: An Early Biography of Muḥammad, by Maʿmar ibn Rāshid (2015)

The Epistle on Legal Theory: A Translation of al-Shāfiʿī's Risālah, by al-Shāfiʿī (2015)

The Epistle of Forgiveness, by Abū l-ʿAlāʾ al-Maʿarrī (2016)

The Principles of Sufism, by ʿĀʾishah al-Bāʿūniyyah (2016)

A Treasury of Virtues: Sayings, Sermons, and Teachings of ʿAlī, by al-Qāḍī al-Quḍāʿī with the *One Hundred Proverbs* attributed to al-Jāḥiẓ (2016)

The Life of Ibn Ḥanbal, by Ibn al-Jawzī (2016)

Mission to the Volga, by Ibn Faḍlān (2017)

Accounts of China and India, by Abū Zayd al-Sīrāfī (2017)

Consorts of the Caliphs: Women and the Court of Baghdad, by Ibn al-Sāʿī (2017)

A Hundred and One Nights (2017)

Disagreements of the Jurists: A Manual of Islamic Legal Theory, by al-Qāḍī al-Nuʿmān (2017)

What ʿĪsā ibn Hishām Told Us, by Muḥammad al-Muwayliḥī (2018)

War Songs, by ʿAntarah ibn Shaddād (2018)

The Life and Times of Abū Tammām, by Abū Bakr Muḥammad ibn Yaḥyā al-Ṣūlī (2018)

The Sword of Ambition, by ʿUthmān ibn Ibrāhīm al-Nābulusī (2019)

Brains Confounded by the Ode of Abū Shādūf Expounded: Volume One, by Yūsuf al-Shirbīnī (2019)

Brains Confounded by the Ode of Abū Shādūf Expounded: Volume Two, by Yūsuf al-Shirbīnī and *Risible Rhymes*, by Muḥammad ibn Maḥfūẓ al-Sanhūrī (2019)

The Excellence of the Arabs, by Ibn Qutaybah (2019)

Light in the Heavens: Sayings of the Prophet Muḥammad, by al-Qāḍī al-Quḍāʿī (2019)

Scents and Flavors: A Syrian Cookbook (2020)

Arabian Satire: Poetry from 18th-Century Najd, by Ḥmēdān al-Shwēʿir (2020)

In Darfur: An Account of the Sultanate and Its People, by Muḥammad al-Tūnisī (2020)

Arabian Romantic: Poems on Bedouin Life and Love, by Ibn Sbayyil (2020)

Lightning Source UK Ltd.
Milton Keynes UK
UKHW012240240720
367105UK00008B/18

9 781479 804443

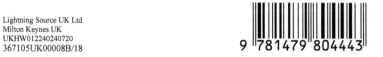